FACES IN THE CROWD

FACES IN THE CROWD

THE JEWS OF CANADA

FRANKLIN BIALYSTOK

UNIVERSITY OF TORONTO PRESS
Toronto Buffalo London

Toronto Buffalo London
utorontopress.com
Printed in the U.S.A.

ISBN 978-1-4426-0826-9 (cloth)
ISBN 978-1-4426-0441-4 (paper)
ISBN 978-1-4426-0444-5 (EPUB)
ISBN 978-1-4426-0443-8 (PDF)

Library and Archives Canada Cataloguing in Publication

Title: Faces in the crowd : the Jews of Canada / Franklin Bialystok.
Other titles: Jews of Canada
Names: Bialystok, Franklin, author.
Description: Includes bibliographical references and index.
Identifiers: Canadiana (print) 20220130604 | Canadiana (ebook) 20220130671 | ISBN 9781442604414 (paper) | ISBN 9781442608269 (cloth) | ISBN 9781442604445 (EPUB) | ISBN 9781442604438 (PDF)
Subjects: LCSH: Jews – Canada – History.
Classification: LCC FC106.J5 B49 2022 | DDC 971.004/924 – dc23

We welcome comments and suggestions regarding any aspect of our publications – please feel free to contact us at news@utorontopress.com or visit us at utorontopress.com.

Every effort has been made to contact copyright holders; in the event of an error or omission, please notify the publisher.

We wish to acknowledge the land on which the University of Toronto Press operates. This land is the traditional territory of the Wendat, the Anishnaabeg, the Haudenosaunee, the Métis, and the Mississaugas of the Credit First Nation.

University of Toronto Press acknowledges the financial support of the Government of Canada and the Ontario Arts Council, an agency of the Government of Ontario, for its publishing activities.

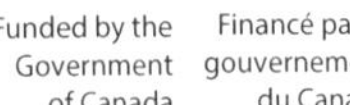

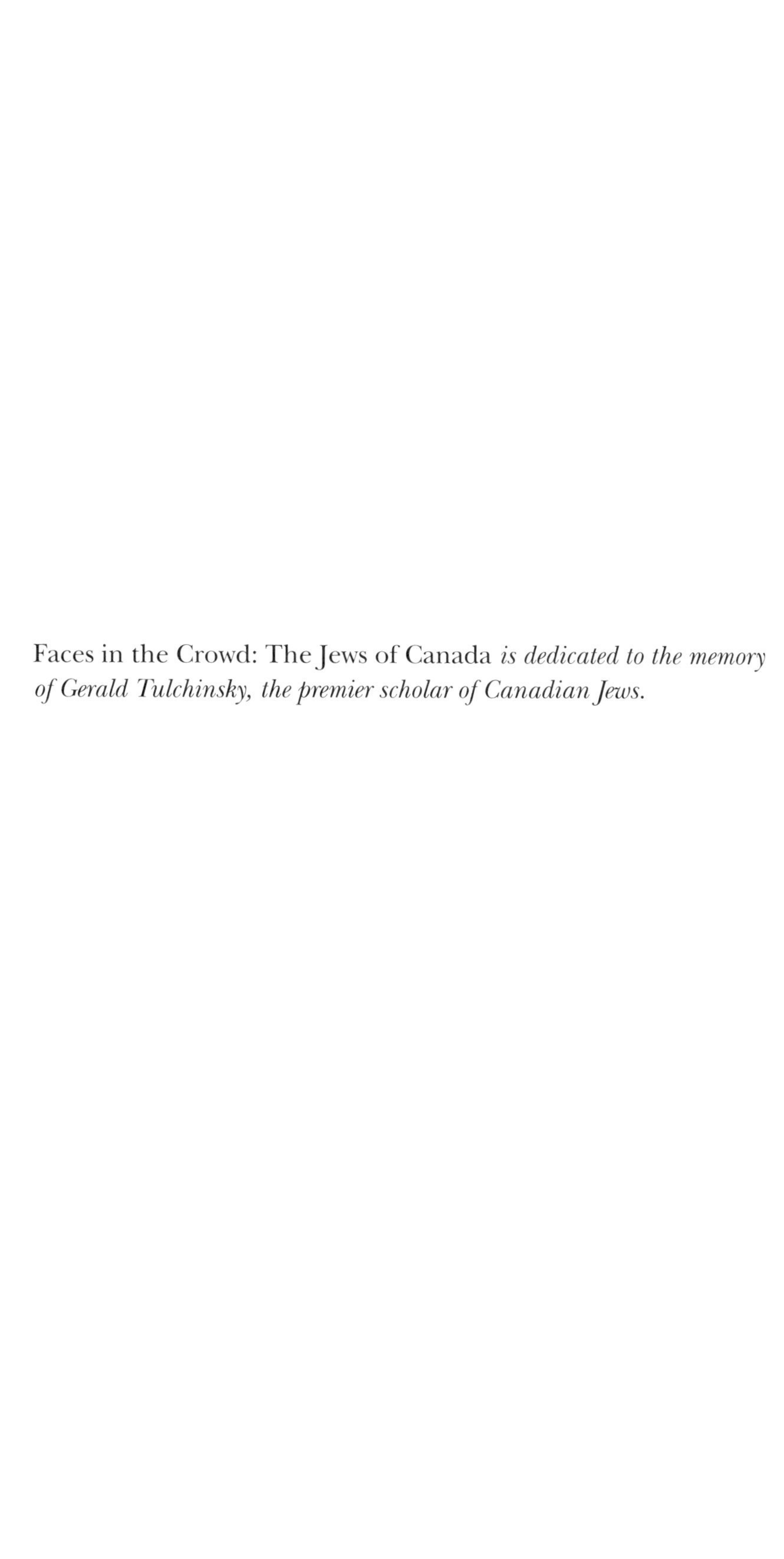

Faces in the Crowd: The Jews of Canada *is dedicated to the memory of Gerald Tulchinsky, the premier scholar of Canadian Jews.*

Contents

Preface

The Hart Memorial Trophy is awarded annually to the "player judged most valuable to his team" in the National Hockey League. It was donated by Cecil Hart, the coach of the Montreal Canadians in 1923, in honour of his father, Dr. David Hart. The Hart family descended from Aaron Hart (1724–1800), who was among the first English settlers in British North America. Hart was born either in Bavaria or in London to where his parents had immigrated. He has been described as an officer of the British Army that defeated the French forces in Montreal in 1760, terminating their colony of New France and founding British North America. More likely Hart was a provisioner to the British. The British commander became the administrator of Trois-Rivieres in 1762, and Hart's patron. Hart bought land from French seigneurs in the Thirteen Colonies, became involved with the fur trade that dominated the colony's economy, and in establishing retail trade along the St. Lawrence River. In 1768 he went to London to marry Dorothy Judah, cementing a commercial connection with her family. Further, he was associated with other Jewish merchants who had arrived from the Thirteen Colonies to Quebec in the wake of the British victory. At his death he was reputed to be the wealthiest person in the colony. Hart was survived by his four daughters and four sons. During the nineteenth century, while there was some measure of assimilation, the trophy is evidence that a portion of the family line remained intact. Historian Denis Vaugeois concludes that some immigrants kept their past secret while others simply didn't know their origins.

Ezekiel Hart

Source: Alex Dworkin Canadian Jewish Archives

Hart and his Montreal compatriots were exceptional among immigrants to British North America as they were English speakers and self-employed with commercial connections abroad. Nevertheless, a century after the arrival of this small group of entrepreneurs, there were scarcely one thousand Jews in British North America. Of those who followed, few had the advantages of the Harts and their cronies.

There are three interrelated phases with respect to the immigrant experience. The first is settlement which requires understanding the environment from which emigration occurred and the reasons for the choice of a new home (so-called push and pull factors) as well as where settlement was established. The second is adaptation to the physical environment of the adopted country, to its laws, language(s), customs, bigotry, establishing ethno-cultural/religious institutions, and establishing a livelihood. Third is heterogeneity of the immigrant community that is not necessarily uniform. Within the context of the community's experience historical experience, there is a measure of internal diversity that may disrupt, prolong, or accentuate adaptation.

The interplay of settlement, adaptation and diversity is uneven among immigrant communities and more so among individuals. The story of the Jews of Canada is unique on three fronts. First, until the arrival of immigrants from South and East Asia in the late nineteenth century, Jews were the only religious minority. Second, due to their expulsion from Israel by the Roman Empire in 70 CE, they were the only immigrant community in Canada that did not arrive from a homeland. Third, living in a Diaspora necessitated ongoing adaptation to the whims and vicissitudes of the dominant society, in which ostracization, expulsion, or devastation were ever present threats. Adaptation was an acquired trait as it was a central component of survival.

In the main, Jewish adaptation over two millennia has been a by-product of *being* Jewish. The constant in this process has been its portable scroll, the *Torah*, compiled in the first millennium CE, a compendium of Jewish history, faith, laws, (individual and communal), and responsibilities, written in Hebrew by scribes on parchment, which was installed in places of worship (synagogues) as Jews moved, by force or choice, to a new location. Being Jewish requires literacy which was rare among non-Jews until the nineteenth century. Adaptation has been an essential, but fluid requiring the adoption of native language (s), cultures, and abiding by their laws. One product of this historical experience has been internal diversity, most notably socio-economic stratification.

The history of the Jews of Canada is integrated with Jewish history, Canadian history, and international developments. These themes are interwoven in this account.

Structure

Faces in the Crowd: The Jews of Canada is divided into four parts, encompassing an introduction, twelve chapters, and an epilogue.

Part A, *Foundations 1760–1900,* is a summary of the initial periods of settlement and adaptation across Canada in two chapters. Chapter 1, "Creating a Community: The Jews of Quebec" examines the background and factors for the migration and settlement of the generation of Aaron Hart and its progeny, the formation of communal structures and networks, and the evolution of the Montreal Jewish community. Chapter 2, "The Jews of the Atlantic, Pacific, Ontario, and the Prairies" deals with the origins of Jewish settlement in these regions.

Part B, *Building A Community 1900–1945,* details Jewish settlement and adaptation primarily in the major urban centres in five chapters. Chapter 3, "The Great Migration," links the situation of the Jews of eastern and central Europe in the nineteenth century to the "push factors" that led them to a more welcoming environment, the "pull factors." Chapter 4, "Yiddish Canada," explores the Jewish immigrant neighbourhoods of Montreal, Toronto, and Winnipeg, where the traditional Yiddish world was transposed and adapted. Chapter 5, "Organizations," traces the origins and development of national and urban-based organizations, synagogues, charities, benevolent societies, and local federations that supported the immigrants. Chapter 6, "The Socio-Political Landscape: Workers, Liberals, Reformers, Radicals, Rogues," discusses political and social activists who sought to improve the difficult lives of immigrant workers in general and Jews in particular through collective action, and a minority who adapted outside the bounds of mainstream society. Chapter 7, "'The Line Must Be Drawn Somewhere': Shades of Antisemitism in Canada, 1760–1945," links the roots of modern European antisemitism to its gestation on Canadian soil. It also examines how Jews drew attention to the discriminatory government's immigration policies that ultimately refused to admit European Jews just as the spectre of fascism was ensnaring Europe.

Part C, *The Community Matures 1945–2000*, discusses in four chapters the developments in Canada, the Jewish world, and internationally, that contributed to the transition by Jews from recognizing themselves as immigrants to identifying as Canadians. Chapter 8, "'Into the Mainstream': From Immigrants to Canadians," begins with the contribution of the Jewish community to Canada's role at home and abroad during World War II and proceeds with its transition into the economic mainstream due to internal geographic and socio-economic mobility. Chapter 9, "Confronting History, 1945–1985," discusses how the community responded to international developments that affected the Jewish world: from the arrival and impact of Holocaust survivors to the creation of Israel, from Israel's subsequent wars with its Arab neighbours to the resurgence of antisemitism on the world stage and the dire circumstances for Jews in the Soviet Union and in Arab countries. These developments solidified the community and culminated in the appropriation of Holocaust memory as a marker of ethnic identity. Chapter 10, "Consensus and Continuity, 1985–2000," discusses the structure of the organized Jewish community and its apprehension regarding its preservation. Chapter 11, "The Jewish Diaspora Settles on Bathurst Street," depicts how emigration from the Jewish world and internal migration led to Toronto's ascension as the predominant centre of the community and a locus for Jews worldwide.

Part D, *Canada's Jews since 2000*, consists of Chapter 12, "The Ascent of Diversity in the New Millennium," and an Epilogue, "Hallelujah." The former analyzes the question of Jewish identity in an increasingly complex and fast-paced world and asks whether Canada has provided "no better home" for its Jewish population. The latter discusses the life and artistic output of Leonard Cohen as it relates to the Canadian Jewish experience.

Acknowledgments

To the Association for Canadian Jewish Studies and my fellow scholars: Pierre Anctil, Sharon Abron Drache, Paula Draper, Monda Halpern, Jack Lipinsky, David Koffman, Hernan Tesler-Mabé, Rebecca Margolis, Dow Marmur, Richard Menkis, Norman Ravvin, Chantal Ringuet, Leonard Rudner, Ira Robinson, Charles Shahar, Harold Troper, and Morton Weinfeld, for their scholarship and advice. To chief archivists Janice Rosen at the Alex Dworkin Canadian-Jewish Archives/Archives juives canadiennes and Donna Bernardo-Ceriz at the Blankenstein Family Heritage Centre, UJA Federation of Greater Toronto, for their invaluable assistance and direction. To Drs. Ellen (OC), Sandra, and Lauren Bialystok, for their forbearance, criticism, and patience. To the centres for Canadian Studies and Jewish Studies at the University of Toronto for the opportunity to engage students in this story, who, in turn, brought new issues and perspectives to the fore. I am indebted to the University of Toronto Press, and particularly to Natalie Fingerhut for providing the opportunity, guidance, and support in this endeavour. Finally, to the scientists, doctors, and nurses, and to donor family "x," for the miracle of organ transplantation that gave me a second life.

PART A

Foundations, 1760–1900

CHAPTER ONE

Creating a Community: The Jews of Quebec

NEW FRANCE

Although the first Jews to arrive in Canada came to Nova Scotia, their stay was short-lived. The first established community was in the colony of Quebec, centred in Montreal. This chapter explores the first century of Jewish life there, from the creation of British North America in 1760 to approximately 1867, when Canada became a nation. Although it took most of that time for a sizeable number of Jews to make their home there, we find that from the outset, the contribution of Jews to the commerce, politics, and society of Quebec far outstripped their meagre numbers. Here we can investigate their motivation for immigration, the process of adaptation and, by the end of the period under discussion, conclude that it was a diverse community in terms of socio-economic levels, origins, and religious expression.

The story of Canada's Jews begins in New France, the colony established during the reign of Louis XIV in the late seventeenth century. The initial pattern of settlement was along the banks of the St. Lawrence River, from the confluence with the Ottawa River downstream towards the Gaspe region. The capital, Quebec, was established at the point at which the St. Lawrence widened on its way to the Atlantic Ocean. Upstream, a port was established in Montreal. Midway was an entrepot, Trois Rivieres. The fledgling colony drew few settlers in the initial decades. By the reign of Louis XV, after 1715, the population grew rapidly due to an extremely high birth rate and a surprisingly low death rate. Stretched out in farms punctuated by villages, the colony was essentially agricultural, largely self-sufficient, but still dependent upon the mother country for manufactured goods. The socio-economic structure was semi-feudal, as the farms were leased to landlords, who in turn rented, in perpetuity, small plots to tenants who provided the labour. In turn, in the vast hinterland to the north, south, and west of the St. Lawrence, French explorers traded goods with Indigenous peoples, receiving furs in turn. Beaver hats had become fashionable in France, so that a flourishing trans-Atlantic trading network was created. The colonial staple, fur, was exchanged for the needs of the colony, which was administered by a governor, while its business was conducted by an intendant. A bishop oversaw religious and educational matters. By the early eighteenth century, a small middle class of professionals and entrepreneurs had emerged.

Officially, there were no Jews in New France. Having had been expelled from France in 1394, some were permitted to re-enter in the early seventeenth century. For the most part, they were the descendants of Spanish and Portuguese Jews (*Sephardim*) who themselves had been expelled from those countries a century earlier. But a proclamation in 1685 decreed that non-Catholics, i.e., Jews and Protestants, were prohibited from settling in the colonies. Thus, we find no record of Jewish life in New France. Nevertheless, it is possible that *conversos*, that is Sephardim who had converted, settled there. In 1738, a young man, Jacques La Farge sailed from La Rochelle. Upon examination it was revealed that La Farge was in fact a woman, and further, a Jew, named Esther Brandeau. Rather than being deported immediately, Church officials unsuccessfully attempted to persuade her to convert to Catholicism. She was returned to France at government expense. Perhaps other Jews arrived, but they would have been converts.

Unofficially, there was a small but relatively significant Jewish contribution to the colony. It was led by the Gradis family, of Portuguese descent, which had created a shipping corporation in Bordeaux. Its patriarch, David (d. 1751), became a French citizen in 1731. His son Abraham (d. 1780) expanded the family holdings. He first attempted to supply the colony with provisions in 1744, but some ships were destroyed in storms and the remaining ones returned to France. In 1748, during a war with Britain, his fleet successfully reached the colony. Gradis, who never set foot in North America, built warehouses in Quebec under a contract with the civil administration. This was fortuitous, for in 1756, the Seven Years War between France and Britain erupted in the colonies. As New France was a low priority, its defence relied more on private contractors than on the French forces. As such, Gradis was appointed a marine agent, responsible for recruiting troops and providing the essential materials for the sustenance and defence of the colony. He was linked to General Montcalm, the leader of the French force. Underequipped and with little aid from France, the French were fighting a losing battle in Canada. While Gradis chartered other ships, bringing his flotilla to fourteen, the French cause was doomed. In 1759, in the unsuccessful defence of Quebec, Montcalm was killed, and a year later Montreal was taken by the British, marking the conquest of New France. While the contribution of the Gradis family to the colony was notable, it should be kept in perspective. This was but one corporation of French traders and provisioners to the colony. Jewish enterprises from the Thirteen Colonies aided Montcalm's adversary, General Wolfe. Most notable was Alexander Schomberg, who participated in the capture of Louisbourg and Quebec, and directed the attack at Montmorency Falls.

THE FOUNDING FAMILIES

About two thousand Jews lived under British rule in the Thirteen Colonies in the mid-eighteenth century. They were acculturated, having emigrated from Britain and Germany. With the conquest of New France, a few enterprising individuals came to what was now called British North America. In 1760, Aaron Hart, his brother-in-law Samuel Judah, and Isaac Levy, who were provisioners to the British, came from the Thirteen Colonies, while Samuel Jacobs arrived from Halifax and received one of the first land patents. In 1764, a census showed that 18 or more Jewish adult males and 133 Protestants had settled in Quebec. In contrast, there were approximately sixty thousand residents of French descent. This tiny Jewish cohort, the first non-Christians in the colony, was indispensable to the British administration, active in trade, land development, and governance.

With their newly acquired territory, the British were eager to take control of the fur trade in and beyond the Great Lakes. Looking for entrepreneurs, they gave "passports" to prospective traders. One of the initial recipients was Ezekiel Solomons (1735–1805?), who moved from Albany to Montreal in 1760. He was arguably the first English-speaking person who reached the Upper Great Lakes. Born in Germany, Solomons capitalized on the French withdrawal from the fur trade. His trading base was in Fort Michilimackinac in Michigan, opposite present-day Sault Ste. Marie, and the northern point of the trade network that stretched from the western Great Lakes to the Mississippi and Ohio valleys. Soon after, Solomons joined forces with other Jewish fur traders – Gershon Levy, Chapman Abraham, Benjamin Lyon, and Levy Solomons. By 1763 their enterprise accounted for 40 per cent of all trade on the Great Lakes, greatly swelling the links in the chain of trade to forts at Detroit and Niagara and reaching Montreal and Quebec. Unfortunately, their endeavour was ill fated due to an uprising by Indigenous people still loyal to the French. Ezekiel Solomons remained undeterred and, returning to Michilimackinac, undertook new ventures that, by the 1770s, made him the dominant trader in northwestern Ontario.

Aaron Hart was the preeminent Jewish settler in the early decades of British North America. He was born in 1724 in London to Bavarian immigrants, moved to Jamaica in 1756, and then briefly to New York, where he provisioned the British forces in Quebec. He settled in Trois Rivieres in 1760, where he purchased seigneuries, engaged in the fur, weapons, and rum trades, opened a general store, and was reputed to be, at his death in 1800, the wealthiest man in British North America. As there were almost no young Jewish women in the colony, Hart had returned to London to marry his cousin Dorothea. They had eleven children, some of whom became almost as prominent as their father, as we will learn later in the chapter. Hart was a noted philanthropist, sharing his wealth with Catholic and Jewish institutions. He aided the British in the governance of the colony, acting as postmaster in Trois Rivieres, one of only four such posts in the colony, from 1763 to 1780. Although entwined with the British administration, Hart urged that a more representative assembly be established. He was one of about twenty-five Jews (virtually the entire Jewish male population in New France) that signed a petition in 1784 for constitutional reform. To a degree, their efforts resulted in the Constitutional Act of 1791 that divided the colony into Lower and Upper Canada with an elected assembly in each.

Lazarus David (1734–76), of German descent, was born in London and came to Montreal in 1760. He soon mirrored the success of Aaron Hart as a fur trader, merchant, landowner, and influential in the British administration. He married Phoebe Samuels and their four sons made major contributions to the economy of Lower and Upper Canada. David David (1764–1824), the eldest, was the first prominent Jew born in the colony. With his brothers, Moses and Samuel, together with their brothers-in-law, Myer Michaels and Andrew Hays, they established a trade in furs and other goods from Michilimackinac to Quebec. At the height of their business, they sold their enterprise to the North-West Company. Lazarus David was also founder of the Committee of Trade, a director of the Bank of Montreal, and a major investor in the port of Montreal and the Lachine Canal. At his death, his estate was valued at 70,000 pounds. One of Lazarus's grandsons, Aaron Hart David, was the first Jewish physician in British North America.

Samuel Jacobs came from Halifax to Quebec in 1760 where he was among the few people to receive a land grant. Continuing the career he had established in Halifax as a merchant and provisioner to the British, his influence grew when he and his partners were given permission to build a distillery. Moving to St. Denis, near Montreal in 1765, Jacobs remained an important cog in the commerce of the colony until his death in 1786. Unlike Aaron Hart, but much like Ezekiel Solomons, who had married Louise Debois in an Anglican church in 1769, Samuel Jacobs married a Catholic woman, Marie-Joseph Audette. Their son, John Levy Jacobs, was baptized. When their baptized son died in 1785, his burial in the Jewish cemetery was delayed until it was grudgingly permitted by the elders.

Marriage, central in the maintenance of religious and cultural continuity since their origins in the Middle East c. 1000 BCE, was complicated in these early decades of Jewish life in Quebec. As the first immigrants were single men, generally young but financially established, marriage to Jewish women had to be arranged in England or the Thirteen Colonies. Clearly this was not an easy situation; those like Jacobs and Solomons, who remained religiously observant, chose non-Jewish spouses. Other early Jewish settlers, perhaps less devout, who chose this option, left no Jewish lineage. Women historically had the responsibility of making a Jewish home and passing on the legacy of culture to their offspring, so that intermarriage naturally was an impediment to the continuity of Jewish life.

We know little about the first Jewish women, who either arrived via arranged marriages, or were born in Quebec in the early decades. The most prominent were Dorothea Judah Hart (b. 1749), Rebecca Franks Solomons (married 1775), Elizabeth Judith Myers, who came from Virginia to marry Moses Myers of Montreal, and Rachel Solomons. Frances David Michaels donated to the building of the first synagogue in 1778. By the turn of the century, there were a small number of marriageable women who had been born in the colony. Finally, we only have anecdotal information that other Jewish men may have come to British North America in these first decades but were not recorded because they lived nomadic lives in the wilderness. Following the custom of the French, legend has it that some cohabited with Indigenous women. The eminent novelist Mordecai Richler satirizes this practice in his sardonic novel *Solomon Gursky Was Here*.

Looking at the contribution of these early Jews to the British administration, we have remarked on Aaron Hart's position as postmaster. His brother-in-law, Uriah Judah, was the chief court clerk. Eleazar Levy was the first Jewish notary in North America, being appointed in 1766. John Franks was the first commissioner of chimneys in Montreal, being appointed in 1768, three years after a fire destroyed much of the city. John Lewis held the same position in Trois Rivieres. Jacob Kuhn was made a bailiff in Montreal in 1777. Franks, like Aaron Hart, Ezekiel Solomons, and Samuel Jacobs, remained confidants of the British long after having been provisioners to their troops.

The process of adaptation for immigrants essentially revolves around two questions. What traditions will be maintained? What traditions will be modified or abandoned? For Jews, who for two thousand years did not have a homeland and continually lived under foreign regimes, sometimes tolerated, rarely welcomed, often persecuted, and sometimes murdered, adaptation was, of necessity, ingrained, fluid, and inventive, where situations demanded a mindset and strategies for dealing with the dominant power that were unique among other immigrant groups. What remained constant throughout Jewish history was the creation of community institutions – a cemetery, a house of worship and education, a ritual bathhouse, the ritual slaughter of livestock. For the Jews of Quebec, this was no easy matter in these first decades because of the miniscule community. Nevertheless, cemeteries were designated in Quebec and Montreal. Ritual slaughter was more of a challenge that could not be met consistently. But when it came to prayer, the challenge was less daunting. The only requirement in Judaism for a congregation is ten adult men, constituting what in Hebrew is called a *minyan*, which can meet anywhere.

In 1766, the Jews of Montreal met when they could, without a rabbi, cantor, or synagogue. Twelve years later, a delegation led by David Franks and Ezekiel Solomons undertook subscriptions to build a synagogue in lower Montreal on St. James Street. The land was owned by fourteen-year-old David David who had inherited it on his father's death. It was named *Shearith Israel* (Remnant of Israel), after its namesake in New York, where some Montrealers had ventured for the Holy Days. Jacob Raphael Cohen from London was hired to be the rabbi, cantor, teacher, and ritual slaughterer. The Spanish and Portuguese Synagogue in New York donated a Torah, and this name also came to be identified with *Shearith Israel* in Montreal. Although the congregation was of *Ashkenazic* (western European) background, the design of the synagogue and the ritual followed Sephardic (literally, Spanish, but more generally understood as Jews from the Mediterranean littoral) traditions. The reason was that the congregants had come from the Thirteen Colonies and England, where Sephardic Jews were the first ones to put down roots and had built the first synagogues. Rabbi Cohen's tenure was short lived as a dispute arose regarding his pay. With his departure, the congregants took on the functions of religious leadership. Although the synagogue was in Montreal, its members lived throughout the colony. Notably legend has it that Solomons and other traders made the long trek from Michilimackinac and other posts annually for the Holy Days. For eighty years, it was the only place of Jewish worship and study in British North America.

One factor for the building of the synagogue was the American Revolution, which broke out in 1775. Numerous Americans in their support of Britain did not side with the rebels. Under threat, some of these loyalists moved north. Among them were a small number of Jews whose arrival augmented the need for a place of worship and study. While most of the initial immigrants supported the British, a small number sided with the revolution. The most notable pro-American Jew was Levy Solomons, the synagogue's first president, who was ousted in 1779 for his actions in aiding the Americans when they invaded Quebec.

The founding families in Quebec are unique in the annals of Canadian immigration. They did not have to undergo the most difficult challenges of adaptation to a new life, culture, and language, nor did they arrive penurious and without support. Further, they are the first recorded settlers who were not of the "founding European peoples of Canada," and the first immigrants who were not Christian. Moreover, the initial eighteen Jews recorded in the 1764 census and the small number that followed between 1764 and 1791 were either already commercially established in the Thirteen Colonies or England, or had the means and fortitude to embark on commercial ventures, no matter how risky, as in the case of the fur traders. Their language was English, their culture was British, their commerce was with the British, French, and Indigenous peoples. Indeed, the Reverend Gershon Mendes Seixas, a rabbi in New York, wrote in 1783 that "a Jew is a Protestant." By this he meant that "when a law referred simply to Protestants, it meant all non-Catholics" (and) "when it meant all Christian Protestants," it excluded Jews. Rather than being outsiders, these families were associated with the English political, military, and business elites in Quebec. For the founding families, the issue of settlement and adaptation had few complications in comparison with the travails of subsequent immigrants.

THE STRUGGLE FOR EMANCIPATION

With the passage of the Quebec Act in 1774, the British administration mollified the vast French-Canadian populace by ensuring that they had religious freedom, and that the civil law code would be based on the one in force during the French regime. Meanwhile the small group of British settlers struggled with the stultifying control of the colonial administration and had little voice in determining economic policy. Their displeasure was shared by the Jewish businessmen who joined their cause. In 1784 a petition to the governor for political reform included the signatures of some twenty-five Jews. With loyalist settlements along the banks of the upper St. Lawrence River and lakes Ontario and Erie, the colonial office passed the Constitutional Act in 1791. It created two colonies out of "old Quebec" – Upper Canada

(Ontario) and Lower Canada (Quebec). Upper Canada was headed by a lieutenant governor, and Lower Canada by the governor of the colony. The key result, in response to the clamour for change, was the creation of a legislative assembly elected by eligible males that was subservient to the governor and the executive council. Even so, the governor had the right to veto bills passed by the assembly, thereby preventing royal assent. In theory, this reform should have satisfied the British settlers and should have given assurance to the French that they had a voice via the assembly. Further, it should have maintained the full civil rights that the Jews had enjoyed since 1760. In fact, it led to a struggle for political self-representation that lasted more than half a century and created a climate in which Jews were denied the same constitutional rights as Christians.

While Jews had been appointed to posts of responsibility in "old Quebec" without difficulty, under the Constitutional Act, unwittingly, they lost that autonomy. Even though English speakers were eligible to become members, French Canadians considered the assembly their forum in so far as it controlled the taxation of major economic projects, such as canals. Consequently, they viewed non-Catholics as opponents who would side with the executive council.

Ezekiel Hart, born in Trois Rivieres in 1770 to Aaron and Dorthea Hart, following his father's footsteps, was elected in 1807. Yet, when Hart went to take the oath of office, he put his hand on his head, in Jewish deference to God, rather than on his heart, and held the Jewish Bible (Old Testament) rather than the Christian one (New Testament). Judge Louis Foucher, the electoral officer, refused to allow the oath to stand. Hart's appeal to the assembly was dismissed. The affair dominated the political and social discourse of the province. The newspaper, *Le Canadien*, printed letters, including this antisemitic screed: "By what right can a Jew be entrusted with the care of the interests of an entire people when he thinks only of himself and of his sect?[1] In contrast, the *Quebec Mercury* opined that Hart would not be viewed "as less capable of serving his country, because he differs in religious ceremony."[2] Hart was again elected in 1809, and when he swore the oath, he did so as required. Nevertheless, the assembly would not allow him to take seat, because, it felt that, as a Jew, he would not honour the oath. The governor, James Craig, in mollifying the French, upheld the assembly's decision.

The Hart affair revealed the cleavages in the province. It raised questions of eligibility and discrimination and may be considered the first instance of antisemitism in Canada. Hart's rejection, however, pointed more to the ethnic struggle of the French majority against British control than anti-Jewish enmity. By denying Hart a seat, it increased the French representation in the competition for dominance in the assembly.

Although Jews had achieved emancipation only in the United States and France after their respective revolutions, their relegation to second-class citizens in Upper and Lower Canada stymied the growth of the community. The situation became more complicated when non-Anglicans, considered to be dissenters, were denied representation. Samuel Hart, Ezekiel's son, a convert to Christianity, successfully petitioned to remove the barriers in 1832; it was the first time that Jews who were British subjects achieved civil and religious freedom.

"A GOLDEN AGE"

From 1831 to 1871, the population of Quebec doubled, from an estimated 550,000 to 1.2 million. While impressive, it was far outstripped by the growth of Ontario, where most immigrants chose to settle. The largest growth took place between the late 1840s and early 1850s due to the arrival of Irish Catholics in the wake of devastating Potato Famine. While Quebec was still overwhelmingly rural, Montreal was by far the pre-eminent city in British North America. Even so, in 1840, with a population of forty thousand, the commercial heart of the city was only five blocks deep. This core was dominated by the English. The colony remained ethnically divided, with the vast majority of French living in the rural hinterland. Quebec was gripped in the age of steam and trade, making transportation on the Great Lakes faster and safer. The advent of steam required the construction of canals, which led to trans-Atlantic travel by mid-century, and telegraph cables in the colony and across the Atlantic. Rail quickly became the dominant means of transportation and trade in the Canadas. The Grand Trunk Railroad united the Canadas, though it did not achieve the company's aspirations to terminate in Halifax. The initial trading staple, furs, was replaced by wheat and timber that was exported to Britain, Europe, and the United States via the Reciprocity Treaty of 1854.

Considering these rapid economic and social developments, political change was in the air. The Act of Union of 1840 created the Canadas, West (Ontario) and East (Quebec), in an uneasy alliance. Unable to form stable political coalitions, forced to find revenues to bankroll the transportation schemes, and with the American Civil War threatening to spill over into Canada, political visionaries in the colony looked for a more stable and independent constitutional arrangement. With similar requirements in Nova Scotia and New Brunswick, and with Britain's receding commitment to British North America, the four colonies united to form Canada in 1867.

In a letter from Benjamin Hart to Isaac Valentine on October 14, 1833, quoted by Montreal journalist Joe King,[3] we find a list of "ladies and gentlement's [*sic*] seats in the new Spanish and Portuguese Synagogue (*Shearith Israel*)." There are fifty-six names. Considering that in 1841 there were an estimated 154 Jews in the British North America, the list of names formed a tight, interrelated circle. Of further interest, all but approximately six people on the list came from seven families: Hays, Solomons, Joseph, David, Hart, Benjamin. Many were intermarried. One can speculate that there were some who had not been registered. Regardless, their impact on Quebec's development to 1871 was far out of proportion to their miniscule numbers. Historian Irving Abella opines that this was "a Golden Age" for the community.[4]

Aside from the Hart clan, two families (Hays and Joseph) were particularly influential in the mid-nineteenth century. Andrew Hays, of Dutch descent, came from England to Quebec in the early years after the conquest of New France and was an initial member of *Shearith Israel* in 1778. His son, Moses Judah was born in 1789. From 1831 until his death in 1861, he was one of the most important entrepreneurs in Quebec. He built the first municipal water system and was the owner of the Montreal waterworks in 1845, invested in the steam and sail ships, and accumulated real estate. A director of the Bank of Montreal, the owner of the prestigious Hays Hotel that briefly housed the parliament of the Canadas after the fire of 1849, he may be best known for his civic contributions and philanthropy. In 1831, Hays and Benjamin Hart were the first Jewish magistrates in British North America, and from 1845 until his death he was Montreal's police chief. He was also a founder and contributor to benevolent societies.

Henry Joseph was born in England in 1771. At the urging of his uncle, Aaron Hart, he came to Quebec in 1790, joining his older brother Judah in the town of Berthier, where they became the major merchants, and with their brother-in-law, Jacob Franks, invested in the freight traffic on the inland waterways. Eventually they established the largest chain of trading posts on the St. Lawrence. Henry married Rachel Solomons, the daughter of Levy, in 1803. They had thirteen children who all married Jews, which was uncommon. He died during the cholera epidemic in 1832. After Henry's death, his son Abraham (1815–86) moved to Quebec City where he established a wholesale grocery business. Abraham was involved in numerous exploits – as a major during the Rebellion of 1837, the president of the Quebec Board of Trade, the director of the Bank Nationale, a candidate for mayor of Quebec, and the vice-consul for Belgium. His brother Jacob Henry (1814–1907) moved to Montreal in 1830. He was an organizer of the first telegraph line in Canada, invested in the first railroads, and was a banker and president of the Montreal Elevator Company. Jacob's philanthropy made a major mark in the civic institutions and learned societies in Montreal.

A third brother, Jesse (1817–1904), was perhaps the most prominent of the Joseph children. Trained as lawyer, he was a diplomat, the founder of the Montreal Gas Company, and the director of the Montreal Street Railway. Jesse was a real estate mogul and operated the Royal Theatre, the leading playhouse in Canada. These exploits made him reputedly the richest man in Montreal in the 1850s. At his death, at 86, he was the president of the Spanish and Portuguese Synagogue. Given this impressive scenario, one should not overstate the impact of these families on Quebec's economy. As the Industrial Revolution roared through the province during the mid–Victorian era, it was the Anglo elite that dominated resource extraction and secondary manufacturing.

Although the role of the Joseph brothers and other notable Jewish entrepreneurs was a key ingredient in the economic development of Quebec, the most notable Jew in Quebec, indeed in all of Canada in the nineteenth century, was an immigrant rabbi, Abraham de Sola (1825–82), of the Spanish and Portuguese Synagogue. He was British, of Sephardic descent, and appointed rabbi of the synagogue in 1847.

The synagogue had lapsed in the late eighteenth and early nineteenth centuries but was rejuvenated when it re-opened in a new location in 1838. De Sola came from a lineage of eminent clergy. His grandfather was chief Sephardic rabbi of Britain. Despite his age, de Sola immediately made his mark within the Jewish community and within the wider Anglo leadership in the city. As a preacher, scholar, and teacher, he set the stage of the observance of Judaism and the learning of Jewish history that came to be a hallmark of Jewish life in the city. He wrote four books and numerous articles on these topics. De Sola was a founder of the Hebrew Philanthropic Society and the Benevolent Society. Within the wider society, de Sola received a law degree from McGill University, and became a professor of Hebrew and Oriental languages a year after his arrival. His prominence in intellectual circles led to his position as president of the Natural History Society. De Sola had strong connections to the Sephardic institutions in Britain and the United States, to the degree that he was asked by President Grant to open the Congress of 1872 with a prayer. Thoroughly anglicized, he did not learn French and had little connection with French intellectuals. His congregation was strictly Orthodox and steeped in Sephardic ritual. Following his demise, his son Meldola succeeded him, holding the post until his death in 1918.

While the upper echelon of Jewish society in Montreal was dominated by a handful of wealthy, observant, inter-connected, and anglicized families, there were at least two other layers on the socio-economic scale. The growth of the community, from fewer than one hundred in 1833 to approximately five hundred in 1861, was largely due to immigration. This "second wave," unlike the founding settlers, had its origins in Germany and Poland. They came without the advantages of their forebears – little or no knowledge of English language and custom, no economic or social connections to Jews elsewhere, and raised in the Ashkenazic tradition. Some, like Moses Ollendorf and Abraham Hoffnung, arrived with a background in commerce and some funds. They opened businesses centred on jewellery, tobacco, dry goods, and clothing. Henry Davis and Gottschalk Ascher came via London and Glasgow. By the 1870s, a few, like Davis, had entered the elite level of the prominent families, but most had modest enterprises that were subject to the risks associated with entrepreneurship. On a lower level were the bulk of the immigrants, who arrived without these advantages and experiences.

Although still numbering in the low hundreds, they constituted the Jewish working class – pedlars, small merchants, artisans – and their arrival as penurious immigrants necessitated support from the elite. As Judaism requires the community to provide for the less fortunate, the Hebrew Philanthropic Society was formed in 1848 and became the Young Men's Benevolent Society in 1863. It is noteworthy that one of its founders was Jacques Bloch, a French Jew.

One significant outcome of this group of immigrants was their desire to create their own congregation, as they felt disassociated in terms of ritual and social standing from the Spanish and Portuguese Synagogue. In 1846, recent arrivals from Russia, Poland, Germany, and England received a charter to incorporate a new congregation. They called it *Shaar Hashomayim* (the Gate of Heaven) Synagogue. It took more than a decade for them to raise the funds to buy the land and erect the premises, so that the synagogue did not open until 1859. It came to be known as the German and Polish Congregation, the first Ashkenazi synagogue in eastern Canada.

A central theme in Jewish history is the relations between Jews and non-Jews in the Jewish Diaspora. Jews have always been a minority, and, aside from periods during the biblical era, have never lived in an independent homeland. This is a complicated issue, as there have been rare periods of extremely good relations, difficult relations marked by restrictions and ostracism, which had been more of the norm, to outright persecution and murder. The only indication of antisemitism at the time was during the Hart affair. In general, the Anglo attitude toward Jews was benign: Nevertheless, traditional antisemitic myths were still in vogue. Historian Gerald Tulchinsky remarks that while antisemitism was marginal, "non-Jews did business with Jews despite the existence – possibly even the prevalence – of attitudes that held Jews in contempt, fear, or mistrust. They were, after all, considered to be an alien cultural element...."[5]

By Confederation, the elements of a Jewish community in Montreal were evident. It constituted the descendants of some of the first non-Christian, non-Anglo, and non-French settlers to British North America. They were established, anglicized, generally wealthy, and influential Canadians, who contributed to Canadian society at a rate far outstripping its small numbers for a century. They were joined by more recent immigrants, many from the Continent, who had different mother tongues, were the product of different cultures, and had to adapt to the new home in more challenging circumstances than did the founding families. Some entered the middle class, but most were of far more modest means. Montreal Jewry spanned the socio-economic spectrum, associated with French and Anglo Canadians, prayed in different synagogues, and established a diverse albeit tiny collective comprising approximately five hundred people, out of a total population of 107,000 in the city by 1871. The seeds planted by the first families in 1759 sprouted across the Dominion within a century.

General store, Saskatchewan

Source: Alex Dworkin, Canadian Jewish Archives

CHAPTER TWO

The Jews of the Atlantic, Pacific, Ontario, and the Prairies

In 1892 Jacob Mayer arrived with his family to Saint John, New Brunswick, from his native Russia, via Providence, Rhode Island. Around the same time, Benjamin Wonsul came to London, Ontario from Poland, with his wife and two children. Two more children, Jack and David, were born in London. But the Wonsul's stay in London was short lived; they moved to Youngstown, Ohio, where they changed their name to Warner. Meanwhile, one of the Mayer children, Louis B., left Saint John as a youth and eventually arrived in California in 1916. Jack and David Wonsul, now Warner, also came to California a year later than Mayer. In short time, Mayer and the Warners had established two of the premier film companies in the world – MGM (Metro Goldwin Mayer) and Warner Brothers. While it strains credulity to embrace Mayer and the Warners as Canadians, their heritage as Canadian children links us to the foundations of Jewish settlement aside from Montreal in the second half of the nineteenth century.

From a trickle at mid-century to 2,441 in 1881, by the turn of the twentieth century the number of Jewish immigrants outside of Quebec reached 16,401, during the "Great Migration." Jewish settlement was almost entirely urban. By 1901, 70 per cent lived in Montreal, Toronto, and Winnipeg, and another 15 per cent in the next ten most populous cities. While many Jewish migrants in the period between the British conquest and Confederation came from the United States, Britain, and Germany, and some were anglicized, the majority were Yiddish speakers from central and eastern Europe, penurious and less adaptable to rapid integration to Canadian society.

This chapter deals with the foundations of Jewish life outside of Quebec. Each region had unique patterns of settlement. In the Atlantic region there was a tiny core of Jews who settled mostly in Halifax and Saint John. Victoria rapidly emerged as the second largest settlement after Montreal by Confederation, with a nucleus coming to Vancouver by 1900. The bulk of Jewish immigrants came to Ontario, consistent with the pattern of settlement for all immigrants. There were perhaps fifty Jews there by the middle of the nineteenth century and approximately five thousand fifty years later. Our discussion differentiates between Toronto, which housed 20 per cent of the national total, from the rest of the province. Whereas most of that settlement took place in the growing industrial and commercial centres of Ottawa, Hamilton, Windsor, and London, one could, in addition, find Jewish life in numerous smaller towns. The Prairies were the last region to welcome immigrants. By 1900, Winnipeg housed the country's third largest Jewish community and farm colonies were being established on the Prairies.

Jewish settlement in this period could be found across the Dominion, but, aside from Montreal, it was almost invisible in the rapidly growing Canadian landscape. Jews represented only 0.3 per cent of the total population at the turn of the twentieth century.

ATLANTIC CANADA

The early settlement of Jews on the Atlantic coast is a curious mix of a presence in the 1700s followed by about a century without evidence of Jewish life. A trickle of European Jews were drawn to Newfoundland and Isle Royale (Cape Breton during the French regime) as merchants because the region's resources were attractive to the European powers. In 1713, France ceded Newfoundland and Acadia (Nova Scotia and New Brunswick) to England, while retaining Isle Royale, the port of which, Louisbourg, rivalled Quebec City by the 1740s as a centre of the triangular trade in the Atlantic. The Rodrigues family, Portuguese conversos, settled in Louisbourg, where one street was name *rue des Juifs.* Supposedly six French Jews settled in Prince Edward Island in 1732, but this is undocumented. Britain had obtained Prince Edward Island

and Cape Breton from the French due to the Treaty of Paris in 1763. A rabbi, Isaac Carrigal, is said to have visited Cape Breton in 1773, and the Richard brothers, presumably Jewish, came to Glace Bay a decade later.

Not open to dispute is that in 1749, Halifax was established by the British as a counterweight to Louisbourg, and some thirty Jews from Newport, Rhode Island arrived two years later as merchants servicing a growing population involved in fishing, defence, and trade. Most notable were Isaac Levy, who came from Germany via the American colonies, and Israel Abrahams. Levy mined coal in Cape Breton and Abrahams produced textiles, glass, and soap. The nascent settlement in Nova Scotia grew with the arrival of the Loyalists from the Thirteen Colonies, who fled the American Revolution because of their allegiance to Britain. Among them were Jacob Louzada, Abram Florentine, Isaac de Costa, and Samuel Hart. Hart, from New York, was elected to the legislature in 1791 as a "true Christian," after converting to Christianity. At this point the track of Jewish life grows cold. There were few Jewish merchants remaining in Halifax by 1820, and the first Jewish settler to New Brunswick did not arrive until 1856. The first documented Jew in Newfoundland was Simon Solomon who arrived in 1792 from England, but he converted two years later.

The saga regained momentum in the mid-nineteenth century. To this point, the colonies had been isolated from the major economic and demographic growth of the Canadas. 1840 British North America was both diverse and fractured in terms of ethnicity, language, and religion. Over the next several decades, the isolation of the Atlantic region was reduced by the creation of small railroads in New Brunswick and Nova Scotia, and the opening of the Intercolonial Railroad from Quebec to Halifax in 1876. These occurred within the context of further transportation and communication developments, namely the introduction of steamships and the telegraph. Without the inclusion of the Atlantic colonies into Confederation, this economic growth and the attendant immigration would not have been possible.

It is within this context that we can explore the foundation of Jewish life in the region. In Nova Scotia, there were two pockets of settlement that raised the Jewish population from 19 in 1881 to 449 in 1901, reaching 2,161 twenty years later – a figure which has remained relatively constant to the present. In Halifax, a community was re-established with the arrival of about one hundred immigrants from eastern Europe. In 1904 the Starr Street Synagogue (renamed the Baron de Hirsch Hebrew Benevolent Society) was the centre of Jewish life until the devastating Halifax explosion in 1917, while the mining industry attracted a significant Jewish presence in Cape Breton. A synagogue was established in Glace Bay in 1902 and a Ladies' Aid Society several years later. Its high point was in the 1920s, when about 110 families were resident supporting a Hebrew school and a Yiddish theatre. In Sydney, Russian immigrants worked in the Whitney Pier Section as peddlers and merchants, establishing a synagogue in 1913. Its Jewish population and evolution mirrored that of Glace Bay. In both towns, the Jewish presence was central to commercial life of the island until the middle of the twentieth century.

New Brunswick in the second half of the nineteenth century did not benefit from the developments in trade, transportation, and immigration to the degree that Nova Scotia did. An exception was the port of Saint John, which was the fifth largest city in Canada in 1871. Here, and, to a much lesser extent, in Moncton, we find the stirring of Jewish life. While there is anecdotal evidence of intermarried Jewish peddlers in New Brunswick already in the eighteenth century, the first Jew recorded was Joseph Samuel, who, in 1856, opened a general store in Chatham. His son Solomon and his cousin Morden Levy opened another outpost in Richibucto.

Saint John, however, was the maritime magnet for Jews looking for an opportunity to participate in the commerce at the busy port. Solomon and Alice Hart arrived in 1858 and were joined by brother-in-law Nathan Green, a tobacconist. Brothers Abraham and Israel Isaacs came from England in 1878 and married into the Hart family. The clan was the nexus of a community that grew with arrivals from eastern Europe, so that by 1896 there were about thirty families accounted for. Their patriarchs included Jacob Jacobson, the first Yiddish speaker, and the abovementioned Jacob Mayer. This vibrant group established the first Jewish cemetery in the Maritimes in 1880, which served the region until 1930; a Hebrew Benevolent Society to aid the newcomers; and in 1898 the synagogue *Achavath Achim* (Brotherly Love) for $10,000 with donations from American Jews and Christians. The first women's organization, the Daughters of Israel, began in 1899, and it came to play a major role in family assistance and pre-school education in the city. The *Deutscher Shul* (German Synagogue) started in 1903. With the immigration influx the community became the major centre of Jewish life east of Montreal, numbering 848 residents in 1921. A further 173 lived elsewhere in the province, mainly in Moncton and Fredericton.

Saint John provides an excellent snapshot of a small, flourishing Jewish community at the turn of the twentieth century. The first arrivals were of Anglo and Germanic origin, who quickly adapted to Canadian life because of their familiarity with English and because they had capital to invest. The second group of arrivals, from eastern Europe, was often transient, finding the means to survive difficult. Those who stayed were mainly peddlers and small merchants who concentrated in the dense North End, close to the docks where many worked. Many were married men who arrived alone and once established, sent for their families. With help from the Daughters of Israel, they were able to provide for and contribute to the community. Their children either expanded the family business or became professionals. S. Hart Green, Nathan's son, was admitted to the Bar in 1901 and became the first Jewish member of the Manitoba Legislature. Eli Boyaner, the first Jew born in Saint John, was an optometrist. Bessie Marcus was the first Jewish teacher and Jean Rosenthal the first nurse. At its height in the 1920s, the community of eight hundred (the ninth largest in Canada) amalgamated the synagogues, had youth organizations allied with the Zionist and women's movements and a Hebrew School with one hundred students, and created a YMHA (H for Hebrew).

Historian Robin McGrath writes that the presence of Jews in Newfoundland before the late nineteenth century was a mixture of fact, speculation, and folklore. It is "unlikely that … any of the early settlers in Newfoundland were Jews."[1] Speculation abounds that *conversos* on Portuguese ships went on land. A Sephardic Jew, Joseph de la Penha, was granted Labrador, perhaps by King William, for saving his life, but Penha did not act on the claim. Other early settlers to Newfoundland may have included the Ezekiel, Toques, and Levi families, who assimilated and converted. There is also record of a Lyon family in St. John's in the mid-nineteenth century, who was said to be engaged in "Jewish trades" like silversmithing and watch making.

But the first well-documented individual was Simon Solomon (1767–1839), who is regarded as the first Jew to settle in 1792, but two years later, also converted. An entrepreneur, he was the first postmaster in the colony. His progeny seems to have ended in 1897 with the death of Eliza Solomon, perhaps his granddaughter. So, it is not until the advent of the great migration from East Europe that a Jewish presence can be documented. It begins with Israel Perlin (1871–1945) who came from Russia in 1891. A peddler at first, he established a wholesale dry goods company in 1905 that employed travellers across the island. Perlin founded the first congregation, married Adelle Adams, a Russian Jew, raised six children in a Jewish home, though they assimilated as adults. Perlin was joined by David Borenstein, a coastal trader, Max Pink, a peddler, and the Blumenthal brothers who sold portraits and pictures. Joseph Burnstein from Poland established a clothing shop on Water Street in St. John's in 1900.

Immigrants were drawn to the island as peddlers, merchants, and teachers. Laz Rosenberg, originally from Lithuania, but who had manufactured war uniforms for the British Army in Leeds, started Rosenberg and Company in Newfoundland in the 1920s. Otto Sidel, from Russia via Liverpool, arrived in 1908 as a peddler, and his brother-in-law, Isidor Wilansky, created a clothing enterprise. Rev. Joseph Plotsky was the first rabbi, arriving in 1909, followed by Rev. E.B. Ershler, but the community was too small to support a second rabbi. Services were initially held in Blumenthal's furniture store, then various spaces, until the Henry Street Synagogue was built in 1930, a modest two-story clapboard structure with a false front, attached to a row house. We have evidence of a Jewish presence in Bell Island, Burin, the Gulds, Twillingate, Badger, and Grand Fall Station by 1921. Unfortunately, we are unable to determine the number of Jews. This is largely because until 1949, Newfoundland was a colony of Great Britain, and thus not subject to the Canadian census. An estimated two to three hundred were centred in St. John's, in the 1920s.

THE PACIFIC

Until the mid-nineteenth century, there was scant settlement by non-Indigenous peoples between Lake Superior and the Pacific coast. The first recorded contact by Europeans with the northwest was Spanish explorers in 1774–5, followed by James Cook in 1778 and George Vancouver in 1792, which solidified the British claim to the territory. In the following year, Alexander Mackenzie reached the coast overland, inaugurating a period of exploration that reached the Arctic, and within a generation a network of posts from Lake Superior to Fort Vancouver had been established by the Hudson's Bay Company. Simultaneously, traders came from the California coast in search of seal fur. These first Europeans to set foot on the Pacific slope encountered one of the most skilled and developed Indigenous cultures in North America. It is estimated that the population along the coast numbered approximately one hundred thousand, representing some thirty peoples, each with distinct languages, complex ceremonies, tools, transportation, art, and clothing. By 1840, the immigrant population had almost tripled. Until 1849, the jurisdiction of the territory belonged to the Hudson's Bay Company, but the administration was haphazard. With the rapid American expansion to the Pacific Coast, Britain and the United States negotiated the border, and Britain installed a colonial administration in Victoria in 1849. Nine years later, Queen Victoria bestowed the name British Columbia on the colony.

With the discovery of gold in the Fraser basin in 1858, there was a surge of entrepreneurs, itinerant workers, con-artists, and those hoping for a quick fortune. Boomtowns such as Barkerville and Yale came and went, and Victoria in short time became the major centre from trade, commerce, and supplies for the prospectors. These developments were catalysts for the rush of American Jews looking to capitalize on the prospects.

Within five years, Victoria became home to the second largest Jewish community in British North America, with 242 residents, representing almost 5 per cent of the population. Almost all were of British and German ancestry. Many arrived from San Francisco, where they were involved in similar commercial activities in response to the gold rush there a decade earlier. They immediately undertook the establishment of the necessary communal structures: a congregation (1858); the Hebrew Benevolent Society (1859); a cemetery (1860); and Temple Emanu-El Beth Shalom (1863), which remains the oldest continuously operating synagogue in Canada. The cornerstone ceremony was attended by the political and social elite of the town.

This small group dominated the retail trade and provisions to prospectors in the colony. In short time, there were twenty-two Jewish-owned clothing and dry goods stores, fourteen grocers and thirteen tobacconists in the town. Others diversified into sealing and shipbuilding enterprises. Among the prominent were the dry goods merchant Kady

Gambitz, the tobacconist Gustave Sutro, the grocer Lewis Lewis, and the indefatigable Joseph Boscowitz and the mysterious Morris Moss. Boscowitz arrived in 1858 seeking an opportunity in the fur industry. Initially a dealer, he became one of the leading sealers on the coast, establishing a shipping network, and a processing plant on Johnson Street in 1882. He remained active until his death in 1923, at the age of 89. Moss arrived in Victoria in 1862 at the age of 21, from London, via Panama and San Francisco. A handsome dandy, he immediately cut a swath in town, but he was quickly drawn to the adventure of the sea and the wilderness. With the help of Indigenous people, he ran pack trains to the miners in the boomtowns, became a government agent and a justice of the peace. In 1867, Moss became a fur trader in Bella Bella, but not content, he looked for claims near Alaska, and then turned his attention to sealing. His schooners antagonized the Americans who had claimed a monopoly and nearly precipitated a war. Returning to Victoria, he married Hattie Bornstein, twenty years his junior. Still restless, Moss went to the state of Washington in search of mining prospects and disappeared. Local historian Cyril Leonoff writes, "News was received of his death in Denver, Colorado four years later [1896]."[2]

Another notable character was Frank Sylvester, born Francis Joseph Silberstein in Liverpool, England in 1842 to German immigrants. In his infancy the family migrated to New York, and in 1856 to San Francisco with his father Henry who opened stores with his son-in-law Martin Prag. Young Frank, determined to establish himself, was one of the first Jews to arrive in Victoria in 1858, shuttling between San Francisco and the gold fields, as a provisioner of goods to the miners. Finally settling in Victoria in 1864, Sylvester worked for an auctioneer during which time he was shipwrecked carrying a supply from San Francisco. While three men drowned, the rest of the crew and passengers, including women and children, were saved. Sylvester established close relations with non-Jews but remained true to his faith. He remained an important figure in local life until his death in 1908. He was the father of eight children, the youngest of whom, Rebecca Florence, died in 1979 at the age of 90.

Recent research by historian David Koffman has revealed that American immigrants controlled the curio trade in the American West. Curios, or artifacts created by Indigenous peoples, were extremely popular in the nineteenth century. The trade was centred in Omaha and Santa Fe and expanded to Victoria during the gold rush. Koffman documents that there were seventeen Jewish curio traders listed on Johnson Street, the main commercial artery of the pioneer town. When the craze ended, some of the traders shifted to tourism, notably Frederick Landsberg, who created the Royal Tour in 1902.

The impact of Jewish settlers was not limited to the commercial sphere. A few made significant contributions to the bourgeoning political system. Selim Franklin was elected to the colonial legislative assembly in 1860; Henry Nathan (1842–1914) was a member of the inaugural British Columbia legislature in 1870 and the first Jew to sit in the House of Commons in 1871. Franklin and Nathan were active proponents for the establishment of provincial status after Confederation. On the local level, Lumley Franklin (Selim's brother) was elected mayor of Victoria in 1866. As the boom and bust of mining and sealing subsided, Victoria and its Jewish residents were replaced by Vancouver by 1900 as the centre of British Columbia's commercial life.

Before leaving Victoria, however, a curious incident occurred there during the Jewish High Holidays (the Jewish New Year) in the fall of 1895. Ray Frank, born Rachel in San Francisco, was invited by Congregation Emanu-El, to officiate at all the services. The curiosity is that women were not even allowed to come to the *bimah* (pulpit), a practice that is still adhered to in Orthodox congregations, meaning that they were not considered fit for ordination. Her invitation was due to her leadership in social and educational initiatives throughout the American West, including delivering sermons at the Chicago World's Fair and at synagogues in the Reform Movement. She was incorrectly referred to as the first female rabbi, even though she refused to apply for ordination. This event has been popularized in the play, *The Girl Rabbi of the Golden West*, by Jennifer Wise which premiered at Temple Emanu-El on its 150th anniversary in 2013.

In the wake of the Victoria experience, Jewish settlement spilled over into the interior of British Columbia. New Westminster and Fort Langley served as supply centres for the fur trade and miners. Frederick Heinze, the "copper king of Montana," built a copper smelter in 1895 at Trail Creek Landing and sold it to the Canadian Pacific Railroad three years later for $1.2 million.[3] The five Oppenheimer brothers, who came from Germany via San Francisco, had stores in the boom towns of Yale, Fort Hope, and Barkerville. The Oppenheimers were in the forefront of merchants who supplied miners flocking to the Yukon during the

Klondike Gold Rush in 1897. The base for the gold rush was in Dawson City, where some sixty Jews settled. Shortly thereafter a cemetery was erected. Max Hirshberg, who had lost his supplies in an avalanche and was then detained by blood poisoning making it too late in the season to travel by dog sled, rode a bicycle from the Yukon to Alaska while wearing a fur robe, until another delay due to a broken chain. J.S. Baron, who came from Winnipeg with a stock of merchandise, endured two fires that destroyed his supplies. Louis Brier made a fortune in the Yukon and donated his estate to building a Jewish retirement home, orphanage, and hospital in British Columbia. Diamond Tooth Lil, born Honora Ornstein, came from Montana to the Klondike to entertain patrons at houses of ill repute. She died penniless in 1975.

The Oppenheimer brothers also had stores in Vancouver. Most notable among them was David (1834–97), who was colloquially referred to as "the father of Vancouver"[4] and was mayor of the city from 1888 to 1891, at a time when there were eighty-five Jews resident there. The cemetery opened in 1887, and the first burial took place five years later. Religious services were held in Zebulon Franks' store. In 1894 Temple Emanu-el was established as a quasi-Reform congregation under the leadership of Louise Mahrer, the daughter of the rabbi of same-named synagogue in Victoria, and Samuel Gintzberger, who came from Switzerland to mine and hunt seals before settling in Vancouver. In 1907 the Orthodox *B'nai Yehuda* (Sons of Judah) congregation under the leadership of Franks was established and its synagogue, the *Shaarey Zedek* (Gate of Righteousness), was built a decade later. Rachel Goldbloom (1865–1931) emigrated from New York to Vancouver and, it was said that she was a "one-woman philanthropic organization." The Jewish population grew alongside religious institutions and commerce;[5] by 1914 the Jewish population in Vancouver had swollen tenfold.

In comparing the Jews of the Atlantic with those of the Pacific region at the turn of the twentieth century, we find one similarity – a small number of settlers, less than a thousand in each region, mostly in two cities, Halifax and St. John on the east coast, and Victoria and Vancouver on the west coast. Otherwise, these groups did not share a common history or a common future. The Atlantic region was where Jews first arrived in Canada, but did not stay, whereas in the Pacific, settlement began a century later. While the Jewish population plateaued in the Atlantic in the 1920s, it has grown steadily in the Pacific. Currently, about 2,000 Jews live on the east coast, while some 25,000 have settled in the along the Pacific rim, the vast majority in Vancouver, home to the third-largest Jewish community in Canada. The factors behind these developments will be addressed in a later chapter.

TORONTO

Following the creation of Upper Canada (Ontario) via the Constitutional Act of 1791, its governor, John Graves Simcoe, chose the site between the Don and Humber rivers for defence and transportation. The village, York, became a point of destination for the leaders of this frontier province. These leaders, an oligarchy dubbed the Family Compact, were stolid Anglicans who controlled the affairs of the province. Poor immigrants, Scottish, English, and then Irish, came in increasing numbers to the middle of the nineteenth century. In 1834, with some nine thousand residents, York was renamed Toronto, but it was hardly an attractive site. Mrs. Jameson, the wife of the attorney-general of the colony, described it as "most strangely mean and melancholy. A little ill-built town, on low land, at the bottom of a frozen bay, with one very ugly church, without tower or steeple; some government offices, built of staring red brick, in the most tasteless, vulgar style imaginable....[6] She spent less than one year in Toronto. The only significant ethnocultural minority were Black people who had been slaves to the elite until their emancipation in 1833, as well as American slaves who arrived via the Underground Railway prior to the Civil War. Scholar Daniel Hill estimates that by the mid-1850s, there were close to 1,000 Black people in the city, out of a total population of 47,000.

Early Toronto was not alluring for immigrants with means, who more readily settled in the United States. The pre-eminent historian of Toronto's Jews, Stephen A. Speisman, wrote that there was no basis for a permanent community until the 1850s. In the preceding two decades, the records show that a few Jews, such as Arthur Wellington Hart, the grandson of Aaron, the scion of the Quebec Jewish family, came and left. The Rossin brothers came in 1842, followed by Judah Joseph and the Nordheimer brothers. Judah Joseph's son died, causing Joseph and Abraham Nordheimer to purchase a half-acre on Pape Street for the first Jewish cemetery in Toronto in 1849, when there were thirty-five Jews resident. Among them were merchants in "fancy goods" and jewellery. The Rossin House was the first luxurious hotel, where the Prince of Wales stayed in 1860; the Nordheimers were successful piano dealers. But these notables receded from historical memory as the Rossins departed after the hotel burned down and the Nordheimers intermarried.

In the 1850s, English immigrants were instrumental in building on the Jewish presence. Most notable was Lewis Samuel, an observant Jew who helped start the Hebrew Congregation, which met at Coombe's Drug Store on Yonge and Richmond streets in 1856, when there were 65 Jewish adult males registered in town. The congregation's name was changed to "Holy Blossoms" in 1871. More Jews moved from the United States due to an economic downturn in the early 1870s. Most joined Holy Blossom (as it came to be called) necessitating the building of a synagogue. The imposing structure on Richmond Street could hold four hundred people, the approximate Jewish population of the city in 1875. This ambitious project was the symbol of a nascent community, signifying the wealth and influence of notables like Samuel and Alfred Benjamin, his business partner. Samuels opened a hardware store with his brother Mark, and with connections to suppliers in Quebec and New York, as well as access to capital in Liverpool via his family, his enterprises expanded into commodities such as metal and lumber.

This fledgling community expanded in the 1880s as Jews moved from smaller towns in Ontario, from Germany, and from the United States. German Jews easily assimilated, but frequently married out of the faith. Wealthier Jews lived in gracious homes on Simcoe, Center, and Edward streets. Apart from synagogues, though, there was little social life. Some newer arrivals established the second major synagogue, *Goel Zedek* (Righteous Redeemer), in 1883 on Richmond Street. While those with less capital included merchants supplying the needs of the community – food, clothing, and housewares. The 1881 census lists 534 Jews, making Toronto the second largest centre in Canada. Although they were virtually invisible in a city that had rapidly grown to 86,000, they were the first non-Anglo-Celtic Europeans to become established in the city.

In the last two decades of the nineteenth century, the boatloads from eastern and east-central Europe grew the country's Jewish community to 1,425 in 1891 and 3,090 in 1901. In Toronto, there was a division between the wealthy ones of German and English background, such as the Samuels and Benjamin clans, ensconced at Holy Blossom, and their poorer brethren from the Russian and Austrian empires. Holy Blossom, nominally traditional, could not hold back the demand by a faction that wanted to adopt a more liberal approach. It gradually adopted elements of the Reform movement, which originated in Germany and was finding a growing following in the United States. As such, women were no longer segregated in the sanctuary, and a woman's choir was created. The schism between the traditionalists and the modernists was a curious mix, but it did not deter the members from raising the funds for a new grand edifice on Bond Street in 1895, where the mayor and Anglo notables attended the opening. The Goel Zedek Synagogue, the other spiritual home of this class, built an even grander building on University Avenue in 1906. While they were able to integrate into the Anglo world because their British tone made them acceptable to the community at large, their faith and ethnicity denied them entry into the elite societies, such as the Granite Club and the Rosedale Golf and Country Club, an exclusion that persisted until the 1980s. In response, they created their own circles, including the Toronto Jewish Literature and Social Union in 1892 and, in the following year, the National Council of Jewish Women.

Sigmund Samuel and Leo Frankel were among the most prominent figures in Toronto. Samuel (1868–1962) whose father, Lewis, is mentioned above, was raised in an assimilated home, schooled at Upper Canada College and the Toronto Model School, and was a bar mitzvah at Holy Blossom. Sigmund expanded the family's industrial holdings, by purchasing Algoma Steel in Sault Ste. Marie, Ontario, and manufacturing hardware. His legacy is enshrined in two Toronto institutions: the Royal Ontario Museum's the Sigmund Samuel Gallery of Canada and a library for undergraduate arts, established in1954, at the University of Toronto. Dubbed "Sig Sam" by subsequent generations of Toronto students, it is a fixture on Queen's Park Circle (since renamed the Gerstein Science Information Centre after another Jewish philanthropist). Samuel's autobiography was posthumously published in 1963.

Leo Frankel was born in 1864 in Biblis in central Germany, the eldest of nine children. Leo, in search of better opportunities, left for New York, where there were family connections, and in 1881 came to Toronto where he and his brother, Maurice, opened a junk shop selling scrap metal. In 1885, they established Frankel Brothers Limited, which dealt in metals and steel. In time his other seven siblings immigrated to Canada and joined the family business. The Frankels quickly cut a swath within the Jewish elite from their home at 504 Jarvis Street, a grand mansion purchased in 1906. Frankel's enterprises incorporated smaller metal and steel fabricators, and he became president of the National Electric Heating Company, a member of the Toronto Board of Trade, and a founder of both the Oakdale Golf and Country Club and the Primrose Club, as Jews were denied membership in the tony Anglo establishments. His tenure from 1908 to 1927 as president of Holy Blossom Temple saw the congregation shed its Orthodox allegiance and become the largest Reform congregation in Canada. Frankel was involved in the Federation of Jewish Philanthropists (FJP) and a fundraiser for the Toronto and York Patriotic front during World War I, and contributed in his quiet manner. His wife Lena was also an important figure: as Superintendent of the Religious School at Holy Blossom, and engaged in the Red Cross and the National Council of Jewish Women. She died in 1923 at the age of 56, while Leo lived for another ten years.[7]

Most of the immigrants were impoverished, traditional, Yiddish speakers. While their world is described in greater detail in Chapter 4, for our purposes it is instructive to glimpse at their conditions. Most settled in the St. John's Ward, known colloquially as "the Ward," a rectangle in the city centre, extending from Yonge Street in the east to University Avenue in the west, and from College Street in the north to Queen Street in the south. Here were a warren of streets and lanes, tucked behind grand avenues, the sites of frame cottages built in the middle of the nineteenth century. Lacking sanitation, electricity, and refuse collection, life in the Ward offered little more than did the villages of eastern Europe. As the first Continental European ethnocultural minority in the city, Jews establish the template for many subsequent immigrants – living with extended family members and renters in squalid dwellings, doubling as stores or workshops, where many worked. Others pulled carts laden with rags and bits of metal, peddlers of junk. Although they received some aid from the Hebrew Benevolent Society, the great synagogues were alien to them. Instead, they prayed and studied in store-front rooms, *shtiblech* in Yiddish, meaning "little rooms."

The process of adaptation depended upon the period of arrival, the place of origin, the degree of family and/or community connections, and socio-economic and cultural levels. For those like the Samuels, who came from England with financial connections to their homeland and elsewhere in North America, the transition in early Toronto was fluid. For some like the Frankels, who had to learn English and came from rural backgrounds, their heritage in commerce allowed them to quickly ascend to leadership positions in the community. For the majority who fled from the economic backwardness and existential threat due to repression and persecution, Toronto did not provide a better life in material terms, but it was a haven from oppression and an opportunity to pursue economic mobility.

ONTARIO

In the second half of the nineteenth century, Ontario emerged as the dominant province in Canada. In 1851, Canada West, as it was called until Confederation, had a population of 952,000, about 40 per cent of the colony. It was overwhelmingly rural, with 86 per cent of its inhabitants living in farms and villages. As the Prairies were not yet populated by immigrants, Ontario had the choicest land for agriculture, where half of its exports were grain and flour and 60 per cent of its residents were farmers. After Confederation, new sources of economic growth were on the horizon. Railroads opened the interior. The major beneficiaries were local towns with a commercial base that emerged as centres of industry and manufacture. Toronto was the predominant recipient, but others, notably Hamilton, London, Windsor, and Ottawa, formed most of the second tier of urban Canada. Mining attracted immigrants and rural dwellers, drawing settlers to the northern reaches. Whereas there were some one hundred thousand urban dwellers in 1851, their number had grown thirteenfold fifty years later, accounting for 43 per cent of the population. About half of urban workers were employed in factories, mills, and mines while a significant minority were engaged in commerce and in the service sector. This rapid economic growth was fuelled by immigration, from the 1850s to the 1870s, largely from the British Isles, while in the final two decades the majority came from Continental Europe. By 1901, there were almost 2.2 million Ontarians.

Given this scenario, there were ample opportunities for immigrants with experience and ability in the commercial and manufacturing sectors. These included Jews who settled throughout the province. While the numbers and impact were insignificant with respect to the larger picture, they set the foundations for communities across the province, such as Cornwall, New Berlin (Kitchener), Brantford, Timmins, and Sudbury. In 1851, the Jewish population of Ontario was estimated at 106, a decade later it was at 614, doubling each decade thereafter. In 1901 there were 5,321 Jews in the province, of whom some 2,000 lived outside Toronto.

A pattern of settlement and adaptation was soon apparent. Jewish immigrants came to these towns as traders and pedlars, others as provisioners to farmers and millers. As they gained a foothold, Jews predominantly became merchants and small manufacturers. On the main streets their stores sold hardware, textiles, and food. Their workshops produced clothing, cigars, and furniture. Few Jews participated in the industrial working class, a small number were farmers, and fewer were miners or loggers. One can identify a standard pattern in the evolution of Jewish life. Upon arrival, they first prayed in private homes and as their number grew, in a rented room or a hall. They might acquire a Torah through donation from a benefactor or from Toronto or Montreal, employ an itinerant *shochet* (meat slaughterer according to Jewish ritual) and teacher. Where numbers warranted, they would purchase a house as a place of worship, study, and assembly (synagogue), and a plot of land for a cemetery. Conditions, however, were tenuous. Some settlers could not make a living and left for Toronto, Montreal, or the United States. One instance of this were early settlers in Lancaster and Alexander in eastern Ontario who departed, leaving little trace of their lives there. The twin attractions of assimilation and intermarriage that hounded Jewish life historically were ever present. A snapshot of some of these settlements is representative of these patterns.

After Toronto, Hamilton was the most economically developed city in Ontario. By 1871, its population of twenty-two thousand was exceeded only by Montreal, Toronto, and Quebec. In that year, one finds a Jewish presence of 131 people, largely of German origin, with a benevolent society, *Anshei Shalom* (People of Peace), which created the first Reform synagogue in Canada in 1882. The Reform Movement originated in

Germany in the early nineteenth century as a counter to traditional Orthodoxy. Reform was marked by its insistence that Jews had to be productive and involved members of the whole community, meaning that they had to have a secular education, have fluency in the vernacular, and accommodate to modern dress and manners. Reform synagogues seated men and women together, created a ritual that included music and prayer in the vernacular, and its members were largely unable and unwilling to speak Yiddish. In Hamilton, some were not comfortable with this radical departure, and created the more traditional *Beth* (house) *Jacob* Congregation. Two significant organizations, the Lady's Aid Society for immigrants, and the Jewish Community Centre (JCC), were markers of the emergence of the community. The JCC, established in 1890, is the oldest in Canada. In 1901, there were 485 Jews, making it Canada's third largest community. It represented about 0.8 per cent of the city's population, approximately the same proportion as that of the Jews of Toronto.

Jews first came to London, Ontario in the middle of the nineteenth century. One of the most influential residents in the city was a converted Jew, Isaac Hellmuth, an Anglican bishop who was a founder of Huron College, which preceded the establishment of the University of Western Ontario. Some early Jewish settlers left for Detroit, which presented greater opportunity and had a much larger community. Nonetheless, by 1891, there were 144 Jews, who had established a cemetery, *Or Shalom* (Light of Peace) and synagogue, *B'nai Israel* (Sons of Israel). In 1901, the community numbered 206 souls, 25 of whom attended the first Zionist convention in Canada. B'nai Israel's first rabbi, Isaac Phillips, arrived in 1899, and in later years was the community shochet until his death in 1931 at the age of eighty.

Historian Bill Gladstone provides an extensive portrait of the first settlers, three of whom deserve mention. Isaac Waterman, a German, arrived in 1858. He and his brother Herman became prominent as oil refiners, and Isaac became a co-founder of the Imperial Oil Company of Canada in 1880. He was a major figure in local politics and institutions. He married an Anglican, and was buried in an Anglican cemetery, even though he had not converted to Christianity. Waterman's colleague, William Spencer, however, did convert. He built refineries in Woodstock, Petrolia, and London. Another company founder was Jacob Lewis Englehart, born in Cleveland, who participated in the extension of the Northern Railway. A town on the route was named after him. As with Spencer, he was a convert.

But the North American beginnings of the Wonsul family, discussed in the introduction to this chapter, was much more typical of the poor immigrants from the German and Russian empires, whose primary occupations were as peddlers; dry goods, iron and rag merchants; cigar makers; dressmakers; pawn brokers; and music teachers. They lived and worked proximate to London city centre, at the intersection of Richmond and Simcoe streets. Similarly, Abraham Fox, whose father, Joseph arrived from Poland via New York City, founded Dominion Pawnbrokers in 1887. Next door, his rival Isaac Levy, and on the other side his uncle Tommy, were the competition. Jake Harris (né Yertsky or Paretsky – c. 1870–1940) arrived with his parents and siblings in 1886 and became a junk peddler. In short time he became a scrap iron dealer and soon after a major iron recycler. Harris was a fervent support of Wilfrid Laurier's Liberal Party and attended the party convention in 1905. London was the centre of the cigar industry in Canada, and one of the largest firms was Brenner Brothers whose factory employed many of the six hundred members of the cigar maker's union in 1914, making the family perhaps the most prominent Jewish clan in town that had not converted.

Of Ontario centres, a few others are of note. Windsor was home to 171 Jews in 1901. One of the first settlers, William Englander, ran a grocery store and served as an immigration officer. Religious services were first held in 1893 and the synagogue, Shaarey Zedek, was opened a decade later. Cornwall, where Aaron Horovitz served as a two-time mayor, had a long-standing Jewish community dating to 1858. As in many other small centres, Jews established themselves, but their offspring left for better opportunities. In Cornwall, Jacob J. Phillips was a prominent figure. His son, Nathan, born in 1891, left to study law in Toronto, and in 1954 became its first non-Protestant mayor. Henry Sadowski was mayor of Massey, a village in northwest Ontario. His son Ben was one of the central figures in Toronto's Jewish community in the mid-twentieth century.

Jewish life in middle-sized and small cities in Ontario presaged the pattern of settlement and adaptation throughout Canada in the first three decades of the twentieth century. Although the major centres of Toronto and Montreal are duly afforded the bulk of our attention, we must be cognizant that the foundations of Jewish life were spread across Canada. From this brief overview, we learn that this pattern created diverse communities – even in London with its 206 Jews in 1901 – that reflected social and economic distinctions, as well as religious differences, which in some cases led to conversion. We also can determine that this settlement was not necessarily permanent due to the attraction of larger communities in Canada and the United States.

Further, we understand that these foundations involved a relative handful of Jews, some five thousand in Ontario and approaching one thousand in British Columbia and in the Atlantic region, according to the 1901 census. Within the context of the number of immigrants who came to these shores in the second half of the nineteenth century, Jews were almost invisible. It was, rather, the short period from 1901 to 1914 that witnessed the Great Migration from eastern and central Europe, the largest wave of newcomers in Canada's history, and established a significant Jewish presence in Montreal, Toronto, and Winnipeg, as well as active communities in most of the smaller cities in the Dominion. The factors explaining this development, and the settling of the last frontier of sub-Arctic Canada, the Prairies, are the subjects of the next section.

SETTLING THE LAST FRONTIER – THE PRAIRIES

The last frontier to be settled in Canada, by both Jews and gentiles, was the Prairies. Jewish immigration to 1881 was limited almost exclusively to Montreal and the cities and towns of Ontario. The events of that year in Russia not only changed the horizon for Jews there, but also created the impetus for Jewish settlement west of Ontario. While most of the immigrants migrated to the new towns, our discussion here is limited to those who chose to settle on the land. Life in Winnipeg, Edmonton, Calgary, and the smaller cities that grew due to overall immigration is discussed in later chapters.

The response to the anti-Jewish outbreaks in Russia in 1881–2 initiated a furious response from the Jewish Diaspora. In London, a group of influential Jews met at the official residence of the Lord Mayor, the Mansion House, where they created a committee by that name, and collected more than one million dollars in the 1880s for relief. Similar committees were created in Berlin and Paris. In New York, the Hebrew

Immigrant Aid Society, which later changed its name to the Jewish Immigrant Aid Society (JIAS), was formed and continues to provide services to today. One of the thrusts of the committees was to appeal to western nations to allow Jews to immigrate. This was an auspicious occasion for Canada to become involved, as its High Commissioner to London was Alexander Galt. Next to Macdonald, Galt was the "grand old man" of Canadian politics. Forty years earlier he was a land speculator, then a railroad financier, a father of Confederation, and minister of finance, until he landed in London. Galt attended the first meeting at Mansion House where he learned of the promotion by Americans to bring Jews there. Writing to Macdonald, he stated that, "what was good for them, could not be bad for us" as quoted by J.D. Sack, an early scholar of Canadian Jewry. Aside from providing an outlet for Russian Jews, Galt was considering the earlier immigration of 340 Jews to Winnipeg, the vast majority of whom continued to work on the Canadian Pacific Railway (CPR). Macdonald responded that "they would be a superior class of people." He continued that "the Old Clo [Old Clothes – referring to pedlars] movement is a good one. A sprinkling of Jews in the Northwest would be good. They would at once go in for peddling and politicking...."[8]

Consequently, the Mansion House Committee financed 240 Jewish refugees who arrived in Montreal on April 4, 1882. Twenty-four ventured to Winnipeg, where they were greeted by the thirty-odd who had not gone to work on the CPR. Two years later, twenty-seven additional Russian Jews were sent by the committee to what would become Saskatchewan, in an isolated location far from railroad access. Called Moosomin, this first colony of Jewish farmers, most of whom had no experience, not surprisingly, was a failure. Ultimately, a fire destroyed the colony in 1889. In 1886, four migrants with farming experience came to Wapella, where they established a settlement leading to the arrival of a contingent, financed by the philanthropist Herman Landau. There, the conditions were much better and eventually the colony took shape. Journalist Erna Paris relates the story of Maggie Wasserman who was born in Wapella in 1896. In Wasserman's unpublished diary, she writes: "If each event in my life were registered truly as it happened, how many people of this generation would believe? ... The sky and the whole outdoors as far as I could see was mine to investigate. Population was very sparse. I loved it."[9]

These initial colonies could not have been created without aid. But the federal government under Macdonald and his immediate successors were not motivated to go beyond their initial involvement. Into the breach stepped two new sources: a group of Montreal Jewish leaders, and a remarkable individual, Maurice Hirsch (1831–96). The Young Men's Hebrew Benevolent Society (YMHBS) had been established in Montreal in the 1840s to aid Jewish immigrants from central Europe. Faced with the oncoming wave of Jewish settlers, the leaders of the community, including Lazarus Cohen, who had come from Germany in the 1850s, tried to raise funds for services, including transportation to the Prairies. But they had left their meeting with Prime Minister Abbott (1891–2) disillusioned at his refusal of government support.

Meanwhile, Hirsch, born in Germany, who had amassed holdings in banks, railroads, and industries, making him one of the world's wealthiest individuals, was moved by the poverty of Jews in eastern Europe and the Ottoman Empire. His philanthropy led to the creation of the Jewish Colonization Association (JCA) in 1891. The Jewish contribution continued with the creation of the Canadian Committee of the JCA, led by the next generation of Montreal leaders, including Lazarus Cohen's son Lyon, and Samuel Jacobs, who would become the first Jewish member of parliament.

Another factor accounting for the colonies was Prime Minister Laurier's immigration policy. Laurier was moved by the assault on Russian Jews in 1903–4 and welcomed their arrival. In 1904 alone, upwards of 375 Jewish settlers arrived who would cultivate some twenty thousand acres. And it was not only in the Prairies that one would find Jewish farmers. In Quebec, colonies were established in Ste. Agathe and Ste. Sophie, and in Ontario in Georgetown and Pontypool. One should add that these colonies, and the overwhelming agricultural revolution in the Prairies in general, served as an impetus for Jewish commercial interests. As in the cities, these commercial interests began with itinerant peddlers, and led often to retail and wholesale establishments.

Scholars of this development are united that the most successful colony was Edenbridge in central Saskatchewan. Established in 1906, its name seems to have come from "Yidden bridge," that is, "Jewish bridge," that they built over the Carrot River, dividing the colony into north and south sections. The initial settlers were of Lithuanian origin, who first went to South Africa, and then were lured by the promise of homesteads, which were no longer available in the United States. The leaders were the Vickar brothers, Sam, David, and Louis, who arrived with forty others. Once founded, relatives joined them, so that by 1910, the colony had 138 settlers, who farmed on the south side. A year later, a new group came, from Russia via London, and occupied the north side. Their most vocal spokesperson was Mike Usiskin, known colloquially as Uncle Mike.

In short time, the two groups found it difficult to cooperate. The "Africans" were more traditional, as demonstrated by their erection of a synagogue. The "Londoners" were imbued with the radicalism that was festering in Russia and had little truck with "old world" customs. Each had its own community centre and school, with the Londoners subscribing to radical publications and the Africans to mainstream ones. Yiddish was the operational language of the first generation of settlers. Families lived in shacks, isolated from each other, separated by forests and swamps that were alternately frozen and passable in winter, when there was no farm production, and the opposite in the summer. Dependent upon one another, as were farmers in general, decisions were to be made cooperatively, but the frequent meetings often broke down into both internal disputes and disputes between the two factions. Despite the division based on religious observance and political ideology, by the early 1920s the colony numbered 218 and had an average equity of almost six thousand dollars per homesteader. It declined during the Great Depression but lasted into the postwar era with a skeletal group, the last of whom left in 1965.

The Vickars could be considered the royalty of Edenbridge. Sam and Dave expanded their holding from the original 160-acre homesteads to more than 1,400 acres. They were presidents of the congregation and alternated as the reeve of the municipality. Sam's son Norman was born in 1916 and left the colony after high school for the nearby town of Melfort, becoming its mayor in 1970. Six years later, he was elected to the provincial legislature and became its minister of industry and commerce. Norman's older brother Ed moved to Winnipeg and became a successful businessman.

Mike Usiskin, however, is Edenbridge's most well-known resident, largely because of his book, written in Yiddish, translated as *From Oxen to Tractors*, which was written but not published, in 1945. His niece, Marcia Usiskin Basman, translated it as *Uncle Mike's Edenbridge: Memoirs of a Jewish Pioneer Farmer* in 1983. Born in 1876 in a village in what is today Belarus, he taught himself to read Yiddish, Hebrew, and Russian. In 1906, he migrated to London, joining other Russian Jews in the Whitechapel district, one of the worst slums in England. Yearning for freedom in a natural, communal setting, he joined his brother Dave in Edenbridge. While he never married, he was revered by the children as their teacher and was called Uncle. Here are two excerpts from his memoir. The first is an evocation of his radical thought.

> Dear Friends, do you know what it means to be the slave of a slave? Have you ever met people who place less value on a whole human life that they do on the tiniest screw of a machine? ... Have you ever had to listen to God fearing folks who preach of the good things to expect in the hereafter while taking what they can do for themselves in the present?[10]

The next deals with the conditions in the early years of the colony.

> The house where this child was born was not more than a shack. That night the temperature dropped to 40 degrees below zero. The winds were so strong that heating the place made little difference to its comfort. The doctor and the nurse were one and the same person, a woman somewhat deaf, about seventy years of age, and unable even to write her own name.... Our joy was boundless when we heard the news of the successful birth. A person never knows what sort of things he will have to struggle with in his lifetime, but as long as he continues to really participate in life, the possibilities are limitless.[11]

Uncle Mike left Edenbridge for Winnipeg in 1941 and spent the last nine years of his life living with Dave's family.

The agricultural colonies of the Prairies are integral to the Jewish experience in Canada. While relatively insignificant in the wave of the Great Migration, their existence merits historical memory. Without being unduly sentimental, by telling their story, we learn of the courage of the settlers, the aid provided by European and Canadian supporters, the collectivity of the project, and the internal divisions carried over from eastern Europe.

By the turn of the twentieth century, the contours of Jewish settlement in Canada were in full view, from the Atlantic to the Pacific, representing the diversity of the nascent community. Jews were present in all nine provinces, and while settling primarily in Montreal, Toronto, and Winnipeg, they had also established a presence in the agricultural colonies of the Prairies, in the opening of the Pacific, in the main streets of smaller towns, and in the Maritimes. While a small number were manufacturers, the majority were struggling workers adapting to their new environment. In so doing, they were relying on their historical experience as minorities for whom adaptation was an inherited trait.

PART B

Building a Community, 1900–1945

The author's maternal grandparents: Razel and Yehoshua Rosenbaum, Warsaw c. 1910, victims of the Holocaust

Source: Franklin Bialystok

CHAPTER THREE

The Great Migration

Max Dessau was born in Belchatov, in the Kingdom of Poland, which was part of the Russian Empire, in 1888. It was a town that underwent industrialization in the late nineteenth century, became prominent for its weaving factories. It was considered a *shtetl* (Yiddish for small town), even though there were much smaller Jewish settlements in the region. Dessau left school early to be apprenticed to a tailor. In his late teens, he left Poland hoping to join his brother, Laibish, in Toronto. Laibish, on his journey, had obtained a passport with the surname Tohn (pronounced tone). It is unclear why and how this took place, but this was not a rare occurrence during the Great Migration. Thus, Max Dessau, now Max Tohn, arrived at Pier 17 in Halifax, the major entry point for European immigrants, on his way to Toronto in about 1909. He found work as a presser in the sweat shops in downtown Toronto, where the *shmata* (Yiddish for rag) trade flourished. Tohn married Chaika Gudofsky, who came from Russia with her family. They raised three children, and he remained a presser for the next half century. He died in 1984, survived by his children, seven grandchildren, and eleven great-grandchildren. We will catch up with Max Tohn in another context in a subsequent chapter, but at this point, this short introduction to his life is emblematic of some forty million stories of those who escaped poverty and oppression in Europe at the turn of the twentieth century in the hope of finding a better life. About 10 per cent of these migrants found a haven in Canada, of whom about one hundred thousand were of Jewish origin. This chapter describes their collective Jewish experience, from their conditions in eastern and central Europe, to their settlement in Canada.

From 1881 to 1914, Canada experienced its heretofore most dramatic demographic and economic transformation. Its economy, historically dependent upon natural resource extraction in farming, fishing, and lumber, diversified into mining and secondary and tertiary industries. A transcontinental railroad, the CPR, was completed in 1885 and a network of smaller lines reached most of the nation's smaller towns. While much of the population was rural at the outset of this era, by 1914 almost 50 per cent of Canadians lived in cities. In the first decade of the twentieth century alone, Montreal's population grew by 50 per cent, Toronto's almost doubled in size, and Winnipeg's grew fourfold.

The most important catalyst for these developments was immigration. Approximately one and a half million people entered Canada between Confederation and 1896, but most of them were in transit to the United States. From 1896 to 1914, the net migration was three million in increasing numbers to the degree that in the last year before the outbreak of World War I, some four hundred thousand found a haven in Canada. In so doing, not only did the population explode, but so did its ethnic composition. In 1867, 90 per cent of Canada's three and a half million residents were of British or French descent. By 1914, there were almost nine million Canadians, of whom 84 per cent were British or French, leaving approximately one and a half million representing approximately fifty other ethnic groups. Of these, there were 126,000 Jews, who arrived almost exclusively from the Russian and Austro-Hungarian empires.

JEWISH LIFE IN EASTERN EUROPE C. 1800

By 1800 one could find Jewish communities across Europe, on the American eastern seaboard, in the islands of the Caribbean, in Brazil, throughout North Africa, and across Asia to India and China. About 75 per cent were concentrated in the Russian, Austrian, and Prussian empires. They were Ashkenazim, "German Jews," who spoke and wrote in Yiddish, an internal language that evolved in the states of southwestern Germany during the Middle Ages. Although Jewish roots in

Russia date back a thousand years, these Jews were the descendants of migrants from central Europe who began arriving in the twelfth century. They found refuge in Poland from the massacres in western Europe instigated, in part, by marauding crusaders. Protected by Polish monarchs and landowners, they flourished in the Polish-Lithuanian Commonwealth, which included parts of the present-day countries of Ukraine, Belarus, Lithuania, Hungary, and Russia.

Jewish fortunes declined from 1648 to 1772 in tune with the deterioration of the Commonwealth due to revolts in Ukraine and wars with Swedes, Russians, Germans, and Turks, from 1648 to 1772. Unable to withstand these pressures, the Commonwealth was partitioned over the subsequent twenty-three years to 1795. Most of its territory was absorbed by the Russian Empire, the southern frontier was taken by the Austrian Empire, and the western reaches by the Prussians. Most of the Jews were Russian subjects, although their experience differed depending on whether they lived in Poland, Lithuania, Russia, or Ukraine. A minority lived under Austrian control and a smaller remnant of Polish Jews remained under Prussian rule.

The population of central and eastern Europe was a mixture of ethnicities, languages, and customs of which the most prevalent were German, Polish, Ukrainian, and Russian, who lived, for the most part, in defined geographical zones, each with a strong national heritage. Germans, Poles, Ukrainians, and Russians also composed minorities in other lands, settled notably by Romanians, Hungarians, Croats, Serbs, Czechs, and Slovaks. They all had the following in common: they were Christians and had national homelands, languages, and customs. Jews were the singular exception in this mosaic.

Four central features separated Jews from other nationalities. The most significant was their religion. Although Judaism was the progenitor of Christianity, it was vilified, in large part because Jews did not accept the divinity of Jesus and were blamed for the Crucifixion. This was the religious basis for their expulsions, persecutions, and restrictions. This hatred of the Jewish people and of Judaism (antisemitism) led to periodic bursts of violence where Jewish communities were attacked and sometimes destroyed. Called *pogroms* (from the Russian, meaning to "wreak havoc"), they were usually planned outbreaks, organized by local officials. The second distinguishing factor is that Jews had no homeland. Since their dispersal from Israel by the Roman

Emperor in 70 CE, they were scattered among the Christian empires in Europe and, from the seventh century, in the Islamic states in North Africa and the Middle East. Third, Jews lived largely in isolation from Christians. This was both by design, where they suffered long-standing prohibition from owning land, confining them to villages and towns where they lived apart from the general populous, and by choice, so that they could practice their religion and customs within familiar surroundings. Finally, to pray all Jewish males needed to be literate, which was also useful for internal correspondence and commerce, and which required a measure of fluency in the language(s) of their settlement. In addition, it was not uncommon for women to be literate inasmuch as many participated in commercial dealings.

JEWISH LIFE INSIDE AND OUTSIDE THE PALE OF SETTLEMENT

Until the Partitions of Poland (1772–95), most the Jews in east-central and eastern Europe lived in the Polish-Lithuanian Commonwealth whereas, due to the historic anti-Judaic prejudice of the Czars, a smaller cohort lived in the Russia Empire. Consequently, with the Russian takeover of most of the Commonwealth, six hundred thousand Jews were inherited, a tenfold increase. The question for the Tsars was how to deal with this unfavourable situation. Broadly speaking, Jews were deemed to be a "harmful element" in the social order due to their "fanatical religious beliefs." It was determined that these "faults" were not innate but due to historical conditions, and thus the Jews could be transformed and ultimately converted to Christianity. To achieve this goal, severe restrictions were placed in the spheres of social interaction, economic opportunity, and religious observance. In so doing, the Tsars aimed to destroy the foundations of Judaism, which would lead to their Russification. This policy was consistent from the first partition in 1772 to 1881, after which it too took a more violent turn.

Empress Catherine II (the Great) was alarmed by the Jewish presence in the empire. She and her advisors created a Pale of Settlement in 1794 that determined where Jews could reside. This had devastating social and economic consequences. Almost all Russians were serfs, who had no individual or collective rights, and were subject to their masters, the landowners; Russian society had remained constrained for centuries. Consequently, unlike the other nation-states and empires of Europe, there was no opportunity for social mobility and little impetus for modernization. The limitations of Jewish settlement placed them between the serfs and the nobility, each of which was hostile to their presence, although each benefitted from Jewish merchants and artisans. The second harmful restriction was mandatory conscription for Jewish males between the ages of twelve to twenty-five. The period of military service was twenty-five years, and for Jewish boys an additional six years, the purpose of which was to weaken the community. Boys were kidnapped and often forced to convert. Additionally, military life was brutal, and Jews, in greater proportion, died from hunger, exposure, disease, and violence than did non-Jews. Initially, this punitive law was not effectively enforced, but during the reign of Nicolas I (1825–54) it was increasingly devastating as there were some seventy thousand Jews in service, about 5 per cent of its population, by the end of his reign.

Further Jews were subjected to the historic accusations of blood libel (ritual murder of Christian children), of the charge of deicide (the murder of Jesus), for spreading disease, and of criminality. These charges were levelled at them because of Church doctrine and as a way of justifying plagues, famines, and war. Beaten but unbowed, Jewish demographic growth reached historic heights. Within the Pale, they numbered just over one million in 1849, and almost one and a half million sixteen years later. Moreover, the Russian state was ineffective, open to corruption, and its policies of absorption and isolation self-contradictory. Thus, some Jewish children did not attend Russian schools, merchants circumvented the Pale's restrictions by moving to cities, and a small number fled westward. During the more tolerant reign of Alexander II (1854–81), an urban middle class emerged. It included bankers, industrialists, and shipping magnates. They were most visible in Odessa, a Black Sea port, an "open city," outside the Pale. As Russia slowly began to modernize, the urban middle class played a major role in building railroads and funding industry, and was prominent in the trade of liquor, grain, and sugar. Nevertheless, the economic conditions for the majority continued to decline.

The turning point for life in the Pale was in 1881. In the wake of the assassination of Alexander II, blame was placed on Jewish Anarchists, leading his successor, Alexander III (1881–94) to embark on a vicious campaign of reprisal. He discarded the policy of "transforming" the

Jews by proceeding to attack them in all respects. It began with widespread pogroms, 259 in the year following the assassination, destroying communities in whole or in part, which, combined with new restrictions on residence, resulted in the obliteration of rural livelihood. This forced Jews to flock to the towns and cities where there was little opportunity for employment. Conditions continued to worsen. At the turn of the century, another wave of pogroms, more destructive and aimed at cities rather than villages, swept across Ukraine. The most severe were in Kishinev in 1903 and Odessa in 1905. Overall, an estimated two thousand Jews were killed through 1906. Further, approximately half of the Jewish population in the Pale had no means of support and depended on the charity of the more well-to-do and from Jewish organizations in western Europe and the Americas.

Although central and eastern Poland were within the Russian Empire, the situation for the Jews there was less egregious than from those in the Pale. Although the Czar was the ruler, the Polish section, termed the "Kingdom of Poland," was semi-autonomous, and theoretically there was a possibility for Jews to become citizens. Of the 400,000 Jews in the kingdom in 1820 (growing to 1.1 million by 1880, about 10 per cent of the population), the majority lived in towns and villages, *shtetls*, ranging in population from hundreds to as large as several thousand inhabitants, a pattern that was also found throughout the Pale. The proportion of Jews resident in a shtetl varied from about fifty to over 90 per cent. Where there was a larger Christian contingent, the Jews lived apart, but dominated the central marketplace as shop owners, artisans, and peddlers. In 1794 most lived as they had for centuries, especially those who were disciples of influential religious leaders and scholars. Because there were no restrictions on movement (contrary to the Pale), and fewer prohibitions commercially, Polish Jews were able to withstand the primitive economic situation better than those in the Pale. Nevertheless, shtetl life was in decline with the advent of industrialization. Thus, from the middle of the nineteenth century to 1914, there was an increasing movement to larger towns and cities. By 1914, the Polish Kingdom's two largest cities, Warsaw and Lodz were each one-third Jewish, and the former was the second largest Jewish city in the world, after New York. In the main, Jews had become the core of the emerging industrial labour force. Consequently, Polish Jews were more likely to integrate into Polish life than were Russian Jews.

JEWS IN THE REMAINDER OF EASTERN EUROPE

Jews in the Austrian Empire, ruled since the Middle Ages by the Hapsburg Dynasty, lived among Slavs, Hungarians, Germans, Romanians, and a host of other nationalities spread across the empire. In the partition of Poland, Austria acquired the region termed Galicia, comprising the territory that is today western Ukraine, southern Poland, Moldova, and corners of Hungary and Romania, the home of 170,000 Jews. Galicia was the least developed region in the empire, historically bereft of German culture and language and isolated from central Europe. Jewish settlement there had its roots in the tenth century, and a distinct culture had evolved. Galician Jews, called *Galicianers* in Yiddish, developed a unique accent. Living in the most multicultural corner of Europe, they functioned in the major Slavic languages, as well as German, Hungarian, and Romanian. Unlike in Russia, however, Austrian authorities had less animus towards Jews, so that the restrictions on Jewish life there were less severe. Nevertheless, daily life was a struggle for bare existence. Even so the pace of growth exceeded even that of the Russian Empire. By 1900 there were approximately eight hundred thousand Jews in Galicia, 11 per cent of the total, living primarily in urban centres.

The Prussian Empire gained the adjacent Polish lands to the west in the Partitions. Historically, these regions had had a small Jewish population relative to the Russian and Austrian acquisitions. Jews there were more influenced by the *Haskalah* (Enlightenment), more prone to being members of the middle class, many were fluent in German, and therefore their experience in the nineteenth century was much less onerous than the Jews to the east. While antisemitism had not eroded, the Prussian kaisers, the military, and the nobility were far less energetic in enacting new restrictions and in harbouring ancient prejudices than in Russia. With the unification of Germany in 1870, Jews in the former Poland region became German citizens. German Jews were in the forefront of the small Jewish immigration to the Americas that began in the mid-eighteenth century, setting the pattern the future. By 1910 there were only 26,000 Jews in the partitioned region of Poland under Prussian control.

There was one major outpost of Jewish life in eastern Europe that was not party to the partitions – Romania. Jews had settled there during the reign of the Roman Emperor Trajan in the second century CE, but the bulk of the population consisted of those who escaped from the Pale in the early nineteenth century. Romania, with its language akin to French and Italian and its religion Roman Catholic, had become nominally independent from the Ottoman Empire in 1859, and its population considered themselves to be more Latin that Slavic. Still, Romania considered its Jews to be "other." As Balkan nationalism intensified in the last decades of the century and threatened Romanian autonomy, antisemitism intensified. Many Jews were financially bereft, their security uncertain, subject to indiscriminate pogroms. Of the two hundred and fifty thousand Romanian Jews in 1899, almost a third managed to flee in the next five years, including about five thousand to Canada.

JEWISH RESPONSES TO PERSECUTION

Jews living in the Russian Empire, whether inside the Pale or in Poland, were victims of the traditional antisemitism that had religious, economic, and social roots in the advent of Christianity; venal restrictions on their movement, place of residence, and occupations; and violent pogroms that destroyed their communities. By the late nineteenth century, there were five avenues of response: faith, nationalism, socialism, assimilation, and emigration. Each is discussed in turn, but with two caveats. The first is that aside from faith, the other responses were the product of modernization. Jews had suffered persecutions, massacres, and expulsions for centuries, yet they could not respond in the same manner as the Jews of eastern Europe at this time because the economic, political, technological, and industrial pre-conditions for these responses had not yet materialized. The second is that these responses were intertwined. One could embrace more than one of these responses. Every adult Jew who emigrated was an adherent of at least one of the other modes of response.

Despite the centuries of persecution in Europe, Judaism dictated all aspects of life including faith, laws, life cycle events, institutions, customs, historical memory, and adaptation. By the eighteenth century, *yeshivas* (seminaries) headed by influential rabbis with large followings flourished from Ukraine to Hungary. Despite the temptations of modernization, even in progressive cities like Warsaw, most Jews maintained a traditional life. Even though insularity and isolation receded as the twentieth century beckoned, Judaism remained immutable. Throughout their history, Jews had experienced much worse including expulsions and massacres in Spain, the destruction of communities by crusaders, and in their historical memory, slavery in Egypt and the destruction of Israel by the Romans. Having survived those, they could survive within and outside the Pale. While faith was the historic response by Jews to oppression, the advent of modernization and urbanization, spurred by the Industrial Revolution, offered alternatives more suited to the rapid changes in nineteenth-century Europe.

The overriding development that changed the course of European history from the French Revolution in 1789 to the outbreak of World War I was nationalism, the second response to persecution. Nationalism was the engine behind the creation of a unified Germany and Italy, the liberation movements of minorities living under the relatively benign rule of the Hapsburgs of Austria, those wishing to free themselves from the despotic but ineffective yoke of the Ottoman Turks, and the aspirations of national minorities in the Russian Empire. Therefore, the emergence of a Jewish national movement was a natural by-product. In essence, because Jews lived in scattered communities under the rule of gentiles, in conditions that were less than hospitable, they yearned for a return to their homeland, from where they had been exiled two millennia earlier. That land was Israel. Return was on the lips of those who worshipped every day: "If I forget you, O Jerusalem, let my right hand forget its skill!" (Psalm 137). But the reality was that this tiny outpost was ruled by succeeding empires and establishing a homeland there was relegated to prayers and dreams.

Oddly enough, the impetus for a return to Israel came from a secular rather than a religious source – the *Haskalah* – the Jewish Enlightenment that originated in Germany in the late eighteenth century. At the forefront were *Maskilim* (the Enlightened Ones), who posited that return was an antidote to both antisemitism and assimilation. They advocated that Hebrew, considered a holy language restricted for prayer, be resurrected as a modern, spoken language. In their passion to modernize Jewish life in tune with the changes taking place in Europe, speaking Hebrew and writing of secular works in that language were central to Jewish survival in a changing world. The movement was called Zionism, a return to the historic land, Zion, the name of a mountain near

Jerusalem. Russian thinkers Leon Pinsker and Eliezer ben Yehuda were early advocates; the latter created a modern Hebrew vernacular. Pinsker wrote that antisemitism had a deep psychological component that could not be erased, so that only through immigration to the homeland could the Jews be free. The initial Zionist group in Russia was the Lovers of Zion (*Hoveve Zion*) in 1882, but the breakthrough took place in central Europe a decade later. Theodore Herzl (1860–1904), a journalist in Vienna wrote *The Jewish State* in 1896, which spurred the Congress of Zionists a year later. The solution to the Jewish problem, its delegates determined, was a recognized and secure homeland. The Zionist message was electric. By 1901, there were 913 Zionist societies worldwide. In short order, some thirty thousand Jews immigrated to Palestine (as it was called by the Ottoman Empire who controlled the region). By 1917, ninety thousand Jewish settlers had arrived.

The third response to persecution, socialism, another outgrowth of modernization, was fuelled by commercial and technological advances resulting from the Industrial Revolution that had originated in Britain, swept across Europe, and reached eastern Europe in the second half of the nineteenth century. Industrialization changed the landscape of Europe, from rural to urban, from peasants to workers (the proletariat), and challenged the traditional bastions of monarchies, religion, and landowners. It gave rise to socialism, which split into two movements – moderates and radicals.

Socialism was a countervailing response to the refuge of faith. It was a catalyst to establish a Jewish national movement in eastern Europe rather than in Palestine and to alleviate the exploitative aspects of industrialization, by uniting the industrial proletariat in a political force to peacefully overthrow the old order. Socialism gained adherents in France and Germany and had a strong Jewish following across Europe.

The breakthrough for Jews in the Russian Empire came at a meeting in Vilna, a Polish city proximate to Lithuania and the Pale, in 1897. The delegates created a political movement called the *Bund* (alliance/league/political society), a union of Jewish socialists who would defend Jewish workers, combat anti-Jewish discrimination, and fight for the civil rights of all workers. It proposed that Jews required national and cultural autonomy, with Yiddish as the language of education and the right to use Yiddish in public affairs. The Bund caught on in the cities, where it organized strikes, created schools and welfare institutions, published newspapers and books, and tried to work with other socialist movements. Strictly secular, the Bund's appeal was to Jews who wanted to stay rather than leave for Palestine and strive for citizenship in their native lands. By 1914, it had created a political party that had representatives in municipal councils in Poland.

Almost from the outset, however, the socialist movement was split between moderates, who championed the democratic process of free elections, and radicals, who sought to overthrow the existing order via a revolution, led by the proletariat, which would create a classless utopian society that would live harmoniously and communally – the Communists. Its leading thinker was Karl Marx, a German, whose father had converted from Judaism. Marx and his Jewish associate Friedrich Engels had a rabid following in western Europe, but their greatest impact was in Russia, where socialism had a great appeal due to Czarist oppression, but where industrialization was in its formative stage. However, the nascent Social Democratic Party was split between its moderate and radical factions. Each one had a significant Jewish following. The difference was that most of the moderates (*Mensheviks*) maintained their Jewish heritage and identity, while the radicals (*Bolsheviks* ("majority men") shed all connection to their tradition. They were strict disciples of Marx, and overthrew the Czarist regime in November 1917 (the Russian Revolution). Among its leaders were a powerful group with Jewish roots, most significantly Leon Trotsky (b. Lev Bronstein), second in command to the leader, Vladimir Lenin. Jews were drawn to the radical alternative for the same reasons as they were drawn to Zionism or to the Bund – the promise of a better life.

The process of modernization gradually broke down traditional social barriers. For Jews everywhere, but especially in eastern Europe, the separation between them and the rest of society frayed most quickly in the towns and cities. The Jewish industrial elite that had arisen in Russia was an extension of what had begun a century earlier in central and western Europe where families such as the Rothschilds and the Warzburgs had become prominent in banking and industrial circles. Lodz, the second largest city in Poland, had emerged as a centre of textile production, second only to Manchester in the early twentieth century. There, leading Jewish families, such as the Poznanskis, employed thousands of workers, predominantly Jewish, in their factories. But as the social order was overturned, the desire for social mobility was unleashed. Rapid urbanization changed the landscape, especially for Jews, who had the advantage of literacy and a heritage of adaptation. Jews, historically disproportionate in cities and in the middle class, saw this as an opportunity for advancement, of being equal citizens in a nation-state – of being accepted as Poles, Russians, etc. It heralded a process of assimilation for many, which would render, they believed, the decline of antisemitism. We accept that assimilation is an elastic term, conveying a range of alternatives, from being part of the majority society yet maintaining religious and/or cultural traditions, to rejecting these traditions, to religious conversion. Clearly, Zionists, socialists, and radicals were, to a degree, assimilated, because their responses were reflections of the modern world.

Despite these rapid changes, the situation for most of the rapidly growing Jewish cohort in eastern Europe was increasingly dire. In 1914 there were about seven million Jews in east-central and eastern Europe, compared to five million in 1800, a staggering rate of increase, yet the proportion had dropped from 75 per cent of world Jewry in 1800, to 55 per cent in 1914, due to the emigration of almost four million people. Emigration had been virtually non-existent up to 1850. Over the next thirty years, the outflow increased to about two hundred thousand, but it was still a remote option. The dramatic events of 1881–2 in Russia following the ascension of Alexander III, in combination with economic and technological changes, produced an outflow of another 450,000 to the end of the century and another three million emigrated in the following fourteen years.

Emigration became viable because of modernization. Simply put, it was extremely difficult to leave the shtetl until the 1850s, because there were no accessible transportation links. As railroads were built, as Trans-Atlantic crossings were made easier and less costly with steam rather than sailing ships, and as a network of agents promoted the prospects of life abroad, the possibilities increased exponentially. We must add to this mix that as Jewish security plummeted in the Russian Empire, the impetus to flee was greatly accelerated.

In the last year of this period, 1913–14, some four hundred thousand Jews left lands where their forefathers had lived for a millennium. The majority went to the United States. New York was the major port of entry, where a million Jews settled. Others went to central and western Europe, mainly to Germany, Austria (proper), France, and England.

Argentina was a major attraction, and smaller contingents went to South Africa and Australia. A small but significant group went to Palestine. Canada was the destination for some 125,000, about 3 per cent of the total who emigrated.

The immigrants had two common features. First, they were poor, but not the poorest Jews, arriving mostly from shtetls rather than cities. Second, they carried the elements of the other responses to persecution with them to their adopted lands. Most were traditional in their faith and certainly in their customs; some were imbued by Zionism but chose not to go to Palestine; some were Bundists but realized that an autonomous Jewish society was wishful thinking; some were radicals but refused to abandon Jewish identity; and some were assimilationists, although the most acculturated ones were the ones least enticed by emigration.

In general families compiled their resources, borrowed what they could, and sent out one person, usually a young male adult if they did not have the means to leave together. As emigration increased, that person might go to where others from the same shtetl or region had found a new life. One significant example is the city of Bialystok in northeast Poland, which had the largest proportion of Jews in Europe. In the 1870s, a small number, often alone, left for New York. After finding employment, saving money, and borrowing more, the immigrant might send for other members of his family. By 1910, there were some seven thousand Bialystokers in New York, among a total Jewish population in the city approaching two million. This pattern, termed "chain migration" was characteristic for most emigrants across the European landscape.

Sam Goodman lived in the large shtetl of Opatow (Apt in Yiddish), in central Poland. He left his wife Fanny and two sons, Harry and Isha, aged three and one, in 1914, and came to Toronto. After World War I, he sent for his family, where Mildred and Ida, were born in 1921 and 1923. Fanny and her sons were among the million Jews who left between 1919 and 1925. By 1933, of the fifteen million Jews worldwide, less than half lived in eastern Europe.

In summary, emigration from eastern Europe was caused by two push factors: living under autocracies that rendered life intolerable for the masses and modernization. For Jews, there was an additional factor – antisemitism. Their exodus, while relatively minor compared to the total, but vastly disproportionate to the Jewish population, had dramatic consequences. It moved the balance of the Jewish world from the east to the west. It created a Jewish presence in the Americas, the Antipodes, and Israel, and it broke apart a millennium of existence that had been insular and maintained the traditional characteristics of Jewish communities.

CANADIAN IMMIGRATION POLICY 1867–1914

When the Dominion was established in 1867 neither the federal government nor the four provinces of Ontario, Quebec, New Brunswick, and Nova Scotia considered immigration a priority. In fact, both levels considered immigration to be within their purview but neither level had a coherent plan, other than the appointment of agents by the provinces to promote settlement. In 1874, immigration, a small division of the Department of Agriculture, took some measure of control from the provinces, setting up agencies in Britain and then in United States. It had two initiatives: to attract farmers and to repatriate Canadians from the US, especially French-Canadians, who had migrated in droves. Two years later, the Conservatives under Sir John A. Macdonald returned to power and unveiled the National Policy to unite the Dominion from coast to coast. It had three planks: protecting Canadian producers from foreign competition by raising tariffs; building a transcontinental railroad; and settling the country, especially the Prairies. The first plank was simple enough, requiring an act of Parliament. The second was difficult, as construction was mired in scandals, far more costly than projected, rife with geological obstacles, and suffered from a shortage of labour. But the network was completed in 1885 and branch lines came to dot the landscape. The third, immigration, had little success because of international and domestic factors.

Leaving Europe, especially the most economically backward and isolated parts, was prohibitively expensive until the 1890s. For those who managed to leave, their choice of destination was the United States. Following the Civil War, industrialization boomed creating jobs in factories and mines and the west offered excellent soil and a moderate climate. Indeed, it was so attractive that about half a million Canadians emigrated there between 1867 and 1900. At the same time, Germany prohibited the advertising of the benefits of immigration, France was concerned about losing its citizens in the wake of military defeat by Germany in 1870, and Russia prohibited departure entirely. In combination with intermittent economic depressions (note that they were not on the scale of the Great Depression of the 1930s), immigration until the end of the century, except to the United States, was relatively insignificant.

The domestic impediments to immigration exacerbated this situation. The federal government under the Conservatives from 1876 to 1896 favoured immigrants from the United States and British Isles, were satisfied with those from western Europe and Scandinavia, but resisted accepting peoples from the rest of Europe. As for immigrants from Asia, the government conspired to import Chinese slave labour to build the railroad, denied the entry of Indians, and western communities attacked Japanese migrants. Such schemes as government assistance and free transportation met with little success, as private agents stepped into the breach and were often unscrupulous. Reports filtered back to Europe that the best agricultural lands in the west had been allotted to the CPR, and the climate was unforgiving. Finally, a recession in the early 1890s crippled the Canadian economy.

Two developments in the late 1890s reversed this situation. First, the Liberals under Wilfrid Laurier came to power in 1896. Laurier's vision of Canada was much broader and proactive than that of his Conservative predecessors. His first minister responsible for immigration was Clifford Sifton, who combined the departments of Agriculture and the Interior. He broke the obstacle of settlement on the best agricultural lands by buying them from the Hudson's Bay Company and the CPR, thus creating the opportunity for immigrants to establish homesteads of 160 acres. Under his watch promotional campaigns were elevated, bonuses were paid for agents of steamship lines, and coordination was established with international and local organizations. When he left office in 1905, the immigration budget was one million dollars. Although Sifton was not enamoured of non-British newcomers, he yielded to the realization that they were needed to settle the west. As he famously put it, "I think a stalwart peasant in a sheepskin coat, born on the soil, whose forefathers have been farmers for ten generations, with a stout wife and a half-dozen children, is good quality."[1] Under Sifton, agents worked in Russia and Austro-Hungary promoting western settlement. Thirty per cent of European immigrants came from Galicia, many of them independent farmers. Aside from those of British and French ancestry, the largest nationality was German. The Liberals lost power in 1911, but their successors, the Conservatives under Robert Borden not only continued the aggressive immigration policy but accelerated it, so that in the last year before World War I, the budget had risen to two million dollars.

The second development that led to Canada being an attractive alternative, the so-called, last best west, was the industrial boom that lasted from the late 1890s through the war. The boom was a confluence of forces, including higher prices for staples, increased foreign demand, new strains of wheat that were more resistant to the elements, the development of hydro-electric power and pulp-and-paper plants, and a large demand for finished goods, especially clothing. These two factors, an assertive immigration policy and a vibrant economy, were the pull factors that attracted three million immigrants from 1896 to 1914, 4 per cent of whom were Jews from eastern Europe.

THE JEWISH COMPONENT OF THE GREAT MIGRATION

An overview of the Jewish component of the Great Migration reveals five characteristics. The first is that the rate of Jewish immigration to Canada from Confederation to World War I mirrored the degree of overall immigration. Thus, it began very slowly in the 1870s and 1880s, increased in the 1890s, and was of flood-like intensity from 1900 to 1914. In 1871, there were 1,333 Jews in Canada, rising to 2,445 a decade later. By 1891, the number had risen to 6,501. A decade later, there were 16,401 Jewish residents. Joseph Kage, an early scholar of Jewish immigration to Canada wrote that 1900 marked "the end of the formative phase of Jewish immigration and settlement."[2] The subsequent immigration flood brought some 138,000 Jews to Canada's shores, of whom about one-third left for the United States. In total, there were 126,000 Jews in Canada by 1914.

The second characteristic is that Jews were proportionately far more prone to settle in cities than other ethno-cultural minorities. The Jewish population in Montreal rose from 409 in 1871 to 45,802 in 1921; Toronto, from 157 to 34,770 for the same period; and Winnipeg from none to

14,837. Jews in Toronto constituted the largest ethno-cultural group, after Anglo-Celtics. In Montreal, they were the third largest group, after French and Anglo-Celtics, and in Winnipeg, third after Anglo-Celtics and Ukrainians. Jews had settled in 351 communities by 1911.

The third characteristic was that, while comprising less than 2 per cent of Canada's total, Jews had established the foundations for a nation-wide presence. Finally, the fourth and fifth characteristics related to the employment Jewish immigrants were most and least likely to undertake. Although Jews were disproportionately the ethno-cultural minority for the nation's population as a whole, they dominated employment in trade, textile, and fur manufacturing and in the professions by 1920, and were the least representative cohort in occupations relating to agriculture and other forms of natural resource extraction.

CONCLUSION

Canada's transformation at the turn of the twentieth century mirrored that of Canada's Jews during the Great Migration. Europe's poor downtrodden masses found a refuge in the West, and while conditions in the adopted countries were not always an immediate improvement, there existed the possibility for upward mobility for them and their descendants. The push factors for emigration were dire poverty under inflexible autocracies and the modernization of transportation, banking, and communication, which made the possibility of emigration an increasing reality. For Jews, the additional motivation was the pervasiveness of rabid antisemitism, that led to the emigration of some four million, representing about one-tenth of the total. Their decision to come to Canada was due to the pull factors of an aggressive immigration program, the economic transformation at the turn of the century, chain migration, and, for the minority that chose to become farmers, the opening of the Canadian Prairies for settlement. It is estimated that in the early 1920s, there were about three thousand Jewish farmers (including their families) in Canada. The story of the agricultural colonies is a small but significant chapter of the Great Migration. It speaks to the impact of the social change that was dreamt of by eastern European Jews and complicates the stereotype of newcomers as urbanized factory workers, peddlers, and shopkeepers.

Fur worker sewing

Source: Alex Dworkin Canadian Jewish Archives

CHAPTER FOUR

Yiddish Canada

J.I. Segal (1896–1954) and Ida Maze (1893–1962) were immigrants from Ukraine and Belarus respectively, both in the Russian Empire, who came in their youth to Montreal. They were two of the central figures in the immigrant community for a forty-year period ending in the 1950s. Segal, born Yaakov Yitzchak Skolar, was an essayist, poet, journalist, mentor, and teacher. He wrote ten volumes of poetry, the first of which was *From My World* in 1916. He wrote for the Montreal Yiddish daily newspaper, *Der Keneder Adler* (the *Canadian Eagle*), founded literary journals, taught in the Jewish People's School, maintained contact with the Yiddish literary world in Europe and New York, and was a bulwark in the Jewish People's Library. His role in literary Montreal was pivotal.

Ida Maze arrived in Montreal in 1906. She had little schooling but taught herself Russian and Hebrew. Active in the cultural life of Yiddish Montreal, she came to be known as the mother of Jewish writers, as their guide and sounding board, and her modest home became the hub for Jewish artists and thinkers until late in her life. A poet since her teens, her first volume appeared in 1935, titled *Songs of My Child.* Further collections were published to 1954 as well as in Yiddish language journals in North America and Europe. She was an ardent supporter of the Jewish Socialist movement, the Bund, yet welcomed rival advocates from the Zionist circles and from the radical political streams to her home, where she fed her visitors while they discussed, not always amicably, the latest news.

Segal and Maze were among the leaders of Yiddish Canada, the world of the Jewish immigrants who arrived en masse from the 1880s to the 1920s. Although they came from the Russian, Austrian, and Prussian empires before 1918, and the countries of central and eastern Europe that were created in the aftermath of the fall of the empires at the end of World War I, the immigrants were united by their faith, history, and language. Yiddish was a unifying adaptive force. It muted the differences regarding religious observance, politics, and culture, and lessened the isolation of those who were removed from the largest cities.

This chapter discusses the lives of the first two generations of Jews that arrived during the Great Migration with an emphasis on the evolution and characteristics of the communities in Montreal, Toronto, Winnipeg, and in some smaller urban spaces.

MAMA LOSHEN

Yiddish dialects reflected the influence of the vernacular. The main dialects were "Polish," "Russian," "Ukrainian," and "Lithuanian." With the process of modernization and urbanization, Yiddish rapidly became a literary language in the second half of the nineteenth century. Essays on politics and the sciences, poetry, prose, and drama, flourished as an assertion of Jewish nationality. Two of the most notable Yiddish writers were Solomon Rabinovich (1859–1915), who adopted the pseudonym *Sholem Aleichem* meaning "peace to all" and I.L. Peretz (1852–1915). Aleichem wrote in Hebrew and Russian as well, but his Yiddish stories, especially the ones about "Tevye the milkman," who was exasperated with God, his family, friends, and non-Jewish neighbours, were most popular. They were the basis for the play and movie, *Fiddler on the Roof*. Aleichem died in New York and his funeral procession attracted several hundred thousand followers. Peretz was Polish and joined a clique of Yiddish writers in Warsaw. His most popular stories were of "Brontshe the silent" who suffered the indignities of poverty without complaint. Throughout eastern Europe Yiddish newspapers proliferated, heralding a plethora in North America, notably *Der Forverts* (The Forward, also called *The Jewish Daily*) in New York in 1897, which is still in print. The fertilization of Yiddish written culture permeated the lives of the immigrants who transposed this modern mode of communication to their adopted countries. For them, Yiddish, the *mama loshen* (mother's tongue), was as central to their being as was Hebrew, the *lashon kodesh* (holy tongue), which was reserved exclusively for prayer.

DI YIDDISHE GASS

In Montreal, it was "the Main"; in Toronto, Spadina Avenue; in Winnipeg, Selkirk Avenue. For Jewish immigrants, these were the Jewish streets, *di Yiddishe Gasn* (pl), the spines that fused the immigrant communities in Canadian cities and towns. They were the heartbeat of Jewish life, from tiny shops to large stores, jammed with warehouses, small factories, street front artisan hovels, *stibls* (tiny synagogues), cafes and restaurants, with dwellings above, while the sidewalks were jammed with shoppers, *kibitzers* (people hanging out), peddlers, hawkers, and grifters. The warrens of surrounding streets were ill kept, many without internal plumbing, sewage control, or electricity until 1914. Within walking distance were the textile factories, scrap metal yards, and stores where the majority were employed. Those with means could travel the thoroughfares on street cars to escape to a nearby lake, river, or park.

Montreal

In 1900, Montreal had approximately 250,000 inhabitants, extending from the port to the mountain (Mount Royal). Newcomers congregated at the base of Boulevard St. Laurent, the main artery northward from the port. It was given the moniker, "the Main," separating French Canadians to the east from Anglo Canadians and immigrants to the west. Jewish arrivals settled in a rectangle roughly defined by rue Sherbrooke to the north, rue Notre Dame to the south, rue de Bleury to the west and the Main to the east; an area of approximately half a kilometre squared hosted the majority of the seven thousand Jews in the city and several thousand other newcomers. Exotic street names, like de la Gauchetière, belied the reality of the tenuous lives of their inhabitants. Within the rectangle were the St. Laurence Market and a pocket park, Dufferin Square. By the 1880s, clothing factories sprang up on the streets surrounding rue de Bleury, which greatly expanded their facilities over the next half century.

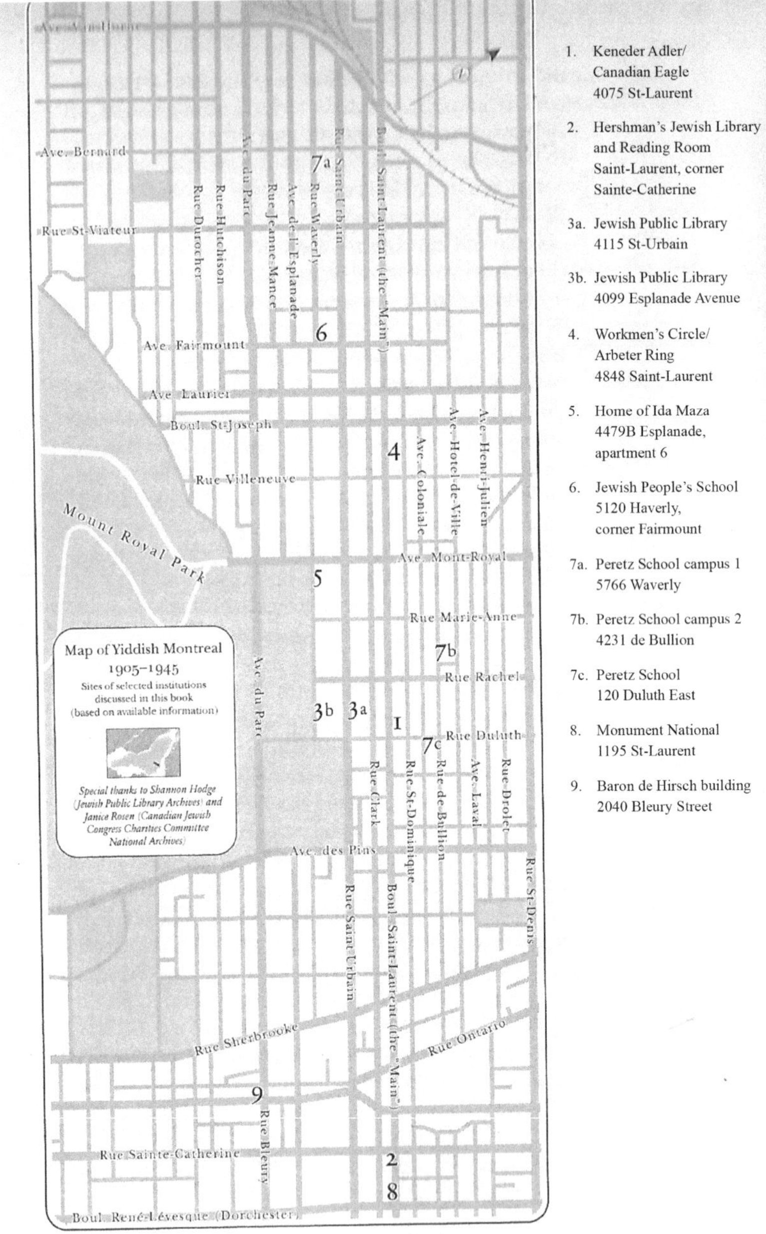

Map of Yiddish Montreal. Credit: Brian Ally, Zijn Digital

Map of Montreal

Source: Rebecca Margolis, *Jewish Roots, Canadian Soil: Yiddish Culture in Montreal, 1905–1945* (Montreal and Kingston: McGill-Queen's: 2011)

Israel Medres (1894–1964) was a staff writer for the *Canadian Eagle* from 1922 to 1947 and continued to contribute articles until his death. His compilation, *Montreal fun Nechten* (Montreal of Yesterday: Jewish Life in Montreal 1900–1920) was published in 1947 and translated into English in 2000. In "The Jewish Neighbourhood" he takes the reader on a walk through the rectangle. "The corner of St. Urbain and Dorchester was the very heart of the Jewish neighbourhood. Nearby was Dufferin Park ... where Jewish immigrants went to breathe the fresh air, meet the *landslayt* (friends from the old country), hear the latest news, look for work, and read the newspapers." He continues: "... there were hardly any Jewish children in Montreal. Many Jews had left their wives and children in Europe. Here ... they lived alone as boarders, saving their dollars to purchase steamship tickets to bring their families across the ocean."[1]

By 1920, Montreal had grown to some 600,000 inhabitants, including 45,000 Jews, marking them as the city's largest non-Anglo-Celtic minority. The immigrant community burst north along the Main, up the hill past Sherbrooke and beyond where it crested, thus inspiring the moniker, the Plateau. It extended east from the edge of the McGill University campus across the Main, and from Sherbrooke north to the edge of the wealthier suburb of Outremont, the Plateau has carved its place in the city's history and was the nexus of Canadian Jewish life. The living conditions ranged from crowded store-front tenements to the city's ubiquitous triplexes with iron staircases that led down to the sidewalks that remain a feature of Montreal's architecture.

Today one can find remnants of Jewish institutions from the interwar period, such as Schwartz's delicatessen on the Main, the Fairmont and St. Viateur bagel bakeries named after their respective streets, and Beauty's Luncheonette on rue Mount-Royal. Residents relaxed at the vast park, Fletcher's Field, now called Parc Jean Mance. Baron Byng High School on rue St. Urbain, was a rite of passage for two generations of Jewish teenagers. The more upwardly mobile children of immigrants migrated to Outremont and to the western suburbs in the interwar period. Mordecai Richler (1931–2002) vividly portrays the street life in the immediate postwar years. "On each corner a cigar store, a grocery and a fruitman. Outside staircases everywhere. Winding ones, wooden ones, rusty and risky ones.... No two stores were the same either. Best Fruit gypped on the scales, but Smiley's didn't give credit."[2] Hugh MacLennan (1907–90), author of *Two Solitudes*, late in life wrote: "The

Main astonished me, and it still does. I had walked the streets of many famous cities in England, Europe, and the United States, but this was something new. Most of the stores had Jewish names. It was probably the most creative Jewish area in North America.… The Main has been the most astonishing forcing house in Canada for culture and business."[3]

Montreal's immigrant Jews created a "third solitude," a transition zone between the two founding peoples of Canada, not only in terms of geography, but also with respect to religion, language, and culture. After New York, it was the most important centre of Yiddish life in North America.

Toronto

In 1881, Toronto was an Anglo-Celtic town whose English, Scottish, and Irish descendants constituted almost 90 per cent of the population. Among the remainder were some five hundred Jews. Twenty years later, Toronto Jews numbered three thousand, approximately 1 per cent of the city's inhabitants. They settled primarily in St. John's Ward, commonly called the Ward.

The first non-Anglo inhabitants were Black people, whose ranks included entrepreneurs and professionals, heralding the origins of the city's ethno-cultural diversity with the arrival of Chinese, Italian, eastern European, and Jewish immigrants. The Ward was bounded by Yonge Street on the east, University Avenue on the west, Queen Street on the south and College Street on the north, with an area of 0.57 square kilometres. Originally a forested suburb north of the city, by the mid-nineteenth century the Ward boasted mansions on University and Centre streets and Protestant churches representing Anglican, Baptist, and Methodist denominations.

But within two decades the Ward had been become an unsightly slum. Fuelled by the Great Migration, it was squeezed between the financial district to the south, the commercial strip on Yonge Street, the prominent homes and institutions on University Avenue, the legislature and the University of Toronto to the north. Municipal authorities were hard put to provide services to the neighbourhood. Its residents lived in shacks, teeming tenements, and "rear houses" that could only be accessed through basements. Yet, writes historian Charlotte Gray in the collection *The Ward: Life and Loss in an Immigrant Community*: "Its unpaved streets were lively with entertainers, local preachers, and small stores selling fresh vegetables. Women wearing brightly coloured shawls over their heads haggled in unfamiliar languages over prices."[4] By 1908

a **KENSINGTON MARKET**
b **THE WARD**

1 SITE OF FIRST SYNAGOGUE 1856-75
2 RICHMOND ST. SYNAGOGUE 1876-97
3 BOND ST. SYNAGOGUE 1897-1938
4 UNIVERSITY AVE. SYNAGOGUE, OPENED 1907
5 McCAUL ST. SYNAGOGUE, OPENED 1905
6 SIMCOE ST. (ASSOCIATED HEBREW CHARITIES, TALMUD TORAH, ORPHANAGE, ZIONIST INSTITUTE)
7 JEWISH DISPENSARY, OPENED 1909
8 LYRIC THEATRE 1909-C. 1923
9 STANDARD THEATRE (OPENED 1922)
10 BRUNSWICK AVE. TALMUD TORAH (OPENED 1924)
11 NATIONAL RADICAL SCHOOL
12 EITZ CHAIM TALMUD TORAH
13 SCHEUER HOUSE
14 OLD FOLKS' HOME
15 MT. SINAI HOSPITAL
16 ZIONIST BUILDING
17 LABOUR LYCEUM

Plan of the City of Toronto, Copp Clark, 1903, presented with The Canadian Almanac for 1903.

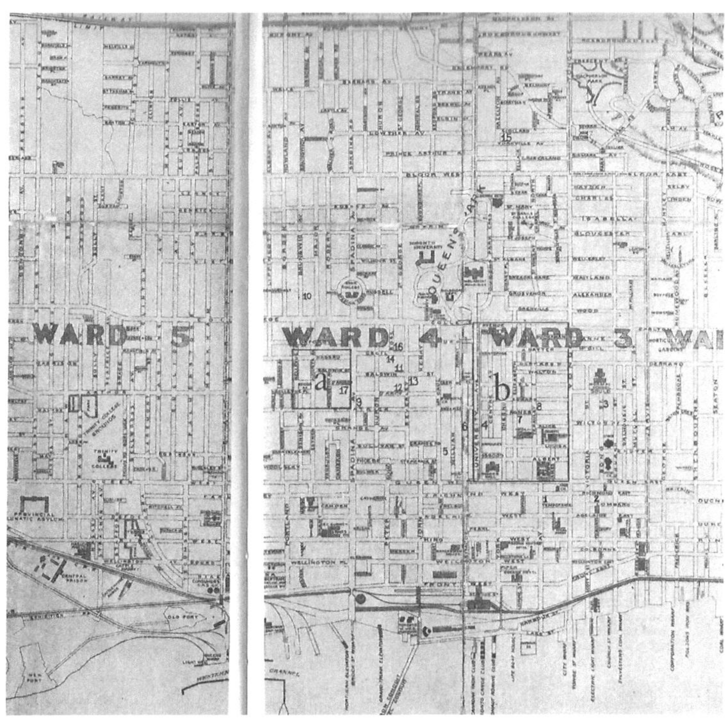

Plan of the City of Toronto, 1903

Source: Plan of the City of Toronto, Copp Clark, 1903, presented with The Canadian Almanac for 1903 in Stephen A. Speisman, *The Jews of Toronto: A History to 1937* (McClelland and Stewart: Toronto, 1979)

it housed eleven thousand people growing to eighteen thousand by 1917, rivalling the densities of the worst slums in London and New York. Of these, Jews were the primary ethno-cultural minority.

By 1921 the Jewish population had swollen to almost 35,000, approximately 6 per cent of the city, and Yiddish was Toronto's second most spoken language. The Ward was undergoing changes, as public officials, concerned about public morals and, more significantly, about the spread of diseases, were tearing down hovels and installing infrastructure, housing, and hospitals. Jews had already started to cross University Avenue a decade earlier to a neighbourhood that had been established in the late nineteenth century to house and provide for the growing industrial working class. Spreading westward, it reached Spadina Avenue. Toronto writer Rick Salutin writes that *spadina* derives from the

Ojibway language, in contrast to the neighbouring streets named after prominent Anglo founders, implying that the name alone welcomed "newcomers in a place where all non-native Ojibway speakers have only recently arrived. It's an equalizer."[5] Robert Baldwin, a prominent Upper Canadian reformer, laid out the avenue that eventually stretched from Lake Ontario to Bloor Street and beyond to the hill upon which Casa Loma was built in 1908. Baldwin wanted a large vista, so the street was initially 131 feet wide, and broadened to 160 feet. Salutin continues: "The width … dominated buildings on either side … The life of the street focused on the 'street,' and on the people in it."[6]

By the mid-nineteenth century the lower part of the avenue served the port and railway yards, and warehouses and small factories on Front and King streets. Further north it was sparsely populated, punctuated by churches, and between Agnes Street (renamed Dundas) and College Street, plots of land were developed and sold to the middle class in what was called Kensington. Thirty years later, Kensington was densely populated, and Spadina was a commercial strip, becoming Toronto's *Yiddishe Gass* by 1920, replete with stores, small synagogues, and restaurants. Jewish inhabitants lived in rented rooms, flats (with shared kitchens and toilets), in houses with extended families and/or tenants, and above stores. Within Kensington, a "Jewish market," was open on Thursdays and Fridays prior to the Sabbath. Between Queen and Front Streets, factories were erected along the Spadina corridor to serve the hungry Canadian market for ready-made clothing.

By 1941 Toronto's Jews numbered 49,045. The community had spread north from College Street to the Canadian National Railway (CNR) tracks, and west along College Street to Ossington Avenue. The more upwardly mobile segment lived on Palmerston Avenue, and north along the Bathurst Street corridor to Oakwood and Cedarvale neighbourhoods, and the wealthiest, to Forest Hill. But most Jews, whether they or not they lived and worked on Spadina, continued to be drawn there. After all, it was *di Yiddishe Gass.*

Winnipeg

While the agricultural colonies in the Prairies were significant, most of the Jewish settlement on the Prairies was in small towns, of which Winnipeg became predominant. In the wake of the fur trade, the British

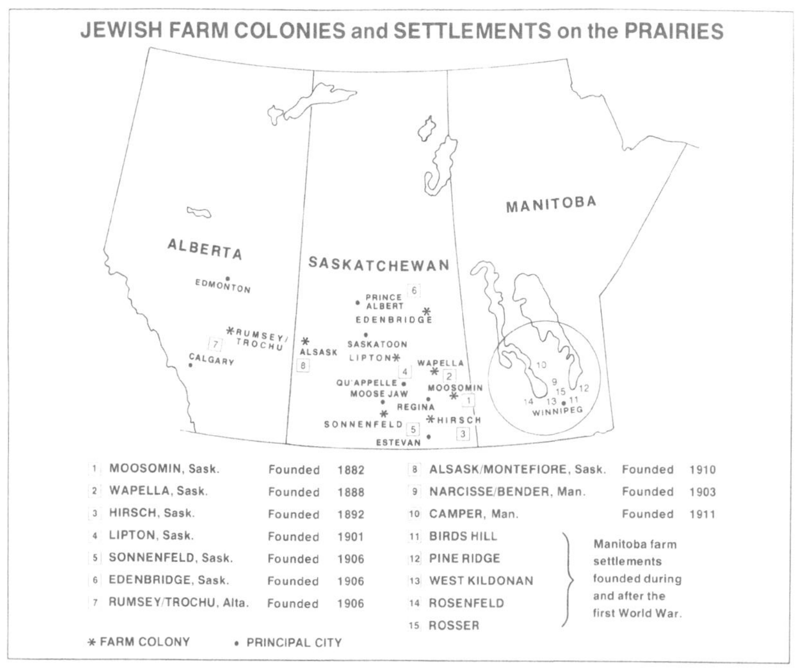

Map of agricultural colonies in the Prairies

Source: Irving Abella, *A Coat of Many Colours: Two Centuries of Jewish Life in Canada* (Toronto: Lester Orpen Dennys, 1990).

established a site, Fort Garry, at the juncture of the Assiniboine and Red rivers. With the first Riel Resistance in 1869, and plans for a transcontinental railroad, Manitoba became a province a year later, and Winnipeg was incorporated in 1874. In fact it was a solitary outpost, a collection of shacks, housing 3,700 inhabitants. Historian Allan Levine quotes Reverend George Young who wailed that it was "a mass of soft, black, slippery and stick Red River mud ... streets with neither sidewalks nor crossings."[7] But perhaps 150 years earlier, Ferdinand Jacob, possibly Jewish, arrived with the Hudson's Bay Company. In the 1850s, Maurice Samuel and Joseph Ullman, who were merchants in St. Paul, Minnesota, were active in the trade down the Red River. The first Jewish settlers may have been the Coblentz brothers, Edmond, Aachel, and Adolphe, from the Alsace region of German-speaking France, who came via Pennsylvania. They opened general stores in southern

Manitoba, were active in local affairs, and were buried in the first Jewish cemetery, called *Zedek* (Righteous). Their offspring intermarried and converted, a not unusual pattern, as discussed regarding some of the founding families of Quebec.

In early 1882 there were perhaps one hundred Jews in the town, who barely survived by peddling. In the spring 232 Jews boarded the SS Lake Huron from Liverpool, having made their way from Russia. Some disembarked in Quebec, but the majority went to Sarnia, where they continued by boat and wagon to Winnipeg. They were soon joined by another contingent of some 350 from Russia who worked in lumber mills and on the railroad, while some waited for farmland. Jewish settlement had barely doubled in the next decade, during which time Winnipeg had exploded with the completion of the CPR. But by 1901, it boasted 42,000 inhabitants, including 1,156 Jews, immediately constituting the third largest Jewish community in Canada and the country's third-largest city. By that point, the railroad, running somewhat parallel to the Assiniboine River, divided the city into north and south sections. The confluence with the Red River ("the Forks") was the corporate and commercial centre. To the west and south were the middle-class neighbourhoods. The North End, as it was called, was the home of the immigrants from eastern Europe – Ukrainians, in the main, other Slavic groups, Jews, and poor English and Scottish settlers.

Winnipeg proclaimed itself the "Chicago of the North," with 150,000 inhabitants by 1913. The Anglo elite reigned, but the city's economy was born on the backs of its immigrants, who were called "foreign trash," "heathens," and "vermins" by the local press and municipal leaders. Six per cent of the city was Jewish, crowded in the North End, dubbed by some "New Jerusalem," and by critics, "CPR Town." Bounded by the Red River to the east, Point Douglas to the west, and stretching toward Kildonan to the north, it was akin to the Ward in terms of living conditions. While Jews constituted but one of the ethno-cultural minorities there, they established Selkirk Avenue as the Jewish street. Unlike Toronto and Montreal's initial Jewish settlement areas, the North End remained the Jewish redoubt for most of the community through the interwar period. Conditions were severe. Indoor plumbing was limited until 1914, most of the houses were wooden framed, pervious to winter blasts, home to three times the number for which the houses were designed. Street life was boisterous, somewhat dangerous, and given the deplorable housing conditions, an escape, except in the most severe Prairie weather.

One man literally stood out in the Jewish community. Emerson Swift Mahon was born a Catholic in Grenada in 1891. He arrived in Saskatchewan c. 1912, worked on a farm, and joined the Canadian Expeditionary Force in World War I. There, he met Rabbi Herman Abramowitz of the Shaar Hashomayim Synagogue of Montreal, and persuaded the rabbi of his desire to convert, and after instruction, Abramowitz signed the conversion certificate. Upon his return, he settled in Winnipeg, graduated from the University of Manitoba in 1929, and although he received a teaching certificate, he became a porter with the CPR. Mahon was a member of Young Judea, married a woman of Russian-Jewish descent and amassed a large Judaic library. He is regarded as Canada's first black Jew. It is said that on Saturday mornings on the way to the synagogue, his hastened his children, in Yiddish, to hurry. Mahon died in 1963.[8]

By 1931 the city's 17,660 Jews constituted 8 per cent of the Canadian total, and the same ratio of Winnipeg's inhabitants, making it the "most Jewish city in Canada," with Yiddish the third language. Gradually, the more affluent moved to Kildonan and to the South End. We will examine the character of this community, and how it differed in some respects from those in Montreal and Toronto in a further chapter.

Other Jewish Streets

Montreal, Toronto, and Winnipeg's dominance overshadowed a Jewish presence on the streets of smaller cities and towns. Demographer Louis Rosenberg's study of the 1931 census revealed that the relatively small Jewish population had settlements of at least one hundred residents in forty-one communities.

Ottawa's first Jewish resident may have been Moses Bilsky (1829–1923) who arrived in 1857 from Lithuania, although there is no entry in the city directory for him until 1878. He settled in Lower Town, between the Ottawa River and Rideau Street, where Bilsky ran a jewellery/pawn shop enterprise. Adjacent was the ByWard Market, a ramshackle area with unpaved roads and numerous alleys, where most of the four hundred Jewish immigrants in 1901 lived and engaged in peddling, small commerce, and service occupations. One peddler, John (Yekuthiel)

Dover (b. 1871) arrived around 1890, and, in addition to peddling, also worked as a butcher, produce vendor, and merchant. His son, Harry (b. 1890) was perhaps the first Jew born in Ottawa. The Jewish population tripled in the next decade, and boasted 3,482 residents in 1931, the fourth largest community in the country. The more upwardly mobile moved to nearby Sandy Hill.

Most of London's 683 Jewish residents in 1931 lived south of the city centre along South Street, where some operated stores, notably the Ginsberg family (arrived in 1903) who opened a large grocery that delivered its produce in a horse-drawn cart. At the northern end of the neighbourhood, the Silverstein family opened a fish market, where they smoked some of the produce, on King Street in 1929. With one brief interval, it remained a family enterprise until 1988.

Vancouver's port was the arrival site for newcomers, whether by rail or water. Adjacent was Gastown, the first neighbourhood for many. European migrants were more drawn to eastern and central Canada, but the ones that made it to Pacific, 205 by 1901, joined the pioneers who arrived from the United States during the Gold Rush half a century early. The newcomers included the Oppenheimer brothers and Zebulon Franks. Abraham Goldberg's Vancouver Junk Company originated in 1912, Max Freeman opened the Hub, the "First Men's Wear Store in Vancouver" in 1908, and other notables had establishments on Gastown's streets – Hastings, Powell, and Water. By 1931, the Jewish community had swollen to 2,458 residents, who had largely settled on the other side of False Creek, on Main Street and the Kingsway, and to the more affluent Oak Street.

Edmonton was incorporated as a town in 1892 and its first Jewish resident arrived a year later. While the town grew, it did not attract Jewish settlers until just after World War I, when there were 821 individuals. Calgary's community followed a similar pattern with a growth from 1 in 1901 to 1,622 in 1931. Some five thousand Jews lived in Saskatchewan in 1931, of whom 1,500 were in Regina and Saskatoon. Defying the pattern of largely urban settlement, in addition to the farmers in the agricultural colonies, there was a substantial portion living in smaller towns. Melville, Prince Albert, and Yorkton had more than one hundred Jews, and nine other towns had more than thirty residents. Kamsack had the highest proportion of Jews of any town in Canada in 1931 – 197 out of a total population of 2,087 – almost 10 per cent. While the numbers seem insignificant, the common theme was each had a "Jewish street."

Sault Ste. Marie and Brantford, two medium-sized Ontario towns whose Jewish communities are profiled by two prominent writers. Morley Torgov (b. 1928) is a lawyer who moonlights as a novelist, and his detective books enjoy a wide readership. His memoir, *A Good Place to Come From*, tells of his upbringing in "the Sault." He writes of the thirty Jewish families (the high point was in 1921, with 115 residents out of 23,000) who primarily worked in the town's hub at Queen and Bruce streets. Most were merchants, such as Himmel's Ladies' Wear, Friedman's Department Store, Fishman's Men's Wear. "You heard Mr. Cohen and Mr. Mintz greeting each other in Yiddish outside the Royal Bank. Yet you were not conscious of being in the midst of a Jewish world. It was as if the Jews – even those who owned their own properties – were no more than temporary tenants who borrowed time and space on Queen Street.... Despite this apparent concentration, it is impossible to characterize.... this isn't a shetl"[9] as the small community was more acculturated than the ones in the large cities. Indeed, the synagogue was not built until the mid-1940s.

Gerald Tulchinsky (1931–2017), the foremost scholar of Canadian Jewry, veered from his scholarly output in a set of short stories, *Stetl on the Grand*, about growing up in Brantford in the '30s and '40s. In 1931 its Jewish population of 208 representing 0.65 per cent of the total, lived in the Albion Street neighbourhood, between the railroad and canal, amid other European ethnic minorities. They owned shops on downtown Colborne Street and scrap yards on Grand Trunk Street. His cast of colourful characters include Yankel Murafsky, whose grocery was the meeting place "for news and gossip on current local politics, on the state of marital or extramarital liaisons, on the chastity of the young women, on the gambling debts of the 'boys'.... and – for business."[10] Murafsky was one of the immigrants who spoke Yiddish and broken English. Tulchinsky's alter ego is Brantford-born Jake Tabachnik, a ghetto kid who stole apples, led a gang that fought with non-Jewish boys, and terrorized teachers. Jake's recollection of Billy Bucovetsky, a great athlete and student who enlisted rather than pursue his education, only to be killed in World War II, is moving. "The whole town mourned Billy. But not Jake. He didn't believe that Bill was dead.... The *shtarker* (tough guy) who whacked the Andersons....

No way. Billy dead. Naw! Billy was coming back. He knew it. He just knew it."[11]

ES A BISL

Food. It bonds families, marks specific geographic origins, delineates group and individual identity. And it speaks to the smells and attractions of the street. One speaks of "Yiddish food," and of "Jewish food," but to do so blurs the vast differences between the cuisines of Ashkenazi, Sephardic, and *Mizrachi* (literally "eastern," referring to those in north Africa, western Asia, the Middle East) Jews. The key factor in eastern European Jewish cooking is that it borrowed from and contributed to non-Jewish cuisine. Crepes (*blintzes*), dumplings (*kreplach*), breaded and fried chicken filets (*shnitzels*), cabbage rolls (*haluptches*) are among the ubiquitous staples of eastern European cuisine. Of course, the dividing line between Jewish and non-Jewish cooking is the laws of *Kashrut* (fit, proper, correct), notably the prohibition of pork and shellfish, mixing meat and dairy products, and the method of animal slaughter. On *di Yiddishe Gass*, one would find a plethora of cafes, delis, dairies, and restaurants. Each had their specific characteristics. Cafes were just that – hot drinks and cakes. Delis were primarily for lunch, serving beef brisket that was either smoked or pickled, depending upon the region in Europe. The other lunch option was a dairy restaurant or counter, that included fish, usually smoked and served cold, the most well-known being *lox* (salmon) and herring as well as cheeses, and the hot dairy foods, some of which are mentioned above. Not all Jewish delis were strictly kosher, but none would serve both meat and dairy. Restaurants were generally for dinner, and would serve multi-course meals: appetizers, soup, mains (meat or fish), and desserts. The Bagel, on College at Spadina in Toronto, fed generations of hungry residents and university students. Its waitresses were notorious for not serving dessert if all the previous courses had not been finished. Every person had a favourite establishment and fierce loyalties would be passed down to successive generations. Schwartz's deli on the Main in Montreal and United Bakers Dairy in Toronto (originally on Spadina) are now in their ninth decades and still boast lineups at lunch time. Arguments about the "best" preparation of bagels, brisket, and chopped (*gefilte*) fish, date back centuries.

Recent research by historian Ellen Scheinberg on the first delicatessen in Toronto is instructive. It was not only the first deli, but the first Jewish restaurant. It opened in 1900 by Sam and Sarah Harris, who met in Detroit in 1892. Located at a two-story building on 233 Queen Street West, west of the Ward, the establishment was on the ground floor and the couple and their three children lived on the second floor. As none of the kosher butchers in the city prepared smoked meat at that time, the Harris Deli imported the meat from Chicago on expedited train shipments, and bought bread from the Ruben Bakery, the first one in Toronto. Sandwiches cost five cents. The deli moved to 178 Queen Street West in a new structure built by the Harris family in 1910. With the rapid growth of the Jewish immigrant community, by 1921 there were twenty-one delis and twenty more a decade later.

Clearly, most people ate at home – whether their own, or at friends, or even at strangers (where it was mandatory to feed those who had family, or money). Mothers would insist that the guest, upon entering the home, to *es a bisl* (eat a little), and then proceeded to ply the visitor. Food was a unifying factor on the Jewish street and home, not dissimilar to its importance in many other immigrant communities.

MACHTN A LEBEN

Yiddish was the language of the Jewish street and home, but less so the Jewish workplace, where rudimentary ability to communicate in other immigrant languages, as well as French and English, may have been necessary. Jews worked in defined occupations in which they were overwhelmingly represented in comparison to Canadians as a whole, and from other immigrants from eastern Europe in particular. Their choice of how to make a living, *machtn a leben*, was a combination of the skills that were transported to their host country and the restrictions against their employment in some factories, most department stores, all banks and insurance companies, and in the professions, necessitating many to be self-employed, or in the employ of other Jews. The reality was that irrespective of their job, work was difficult, demeaning, irregular, and for most immigrants barely provided most of life's necessities.

Most of the immigrants, especially those who arrived in late nineteenth century, became peddlers. This was the transfer of a long tradition in the lives of poor Jews in eastern Europe. Peddling was an exceedingly difficult line of work, but it was self-sufficient, negating the obligation to follow the orders of a foreman or owner and allowing freedom to observe the Sabbath. Peddling required a little start-up capital and a cart, while the dense immigrant neighbourhood offered opportunity, as a storehouse of used clothes, metal scraps, usable garbage, and an eager clientele. But it was literally back-breaking work because, until one could afford to buy and keep a horse, the peddler had to pull the cart. Without a guaranteed income, it was a penurious existence. Peddling was often a family business, where parents and children worked in concert. This line of work was not limited to the city. Peddlers roamed the Prairies, the small towns of southern Ontario and along the St. Lawrence River in Quebec, and the back roads of the Maritimes. For the poor, the peddler was the main source for manufactured goods that could be mended, welded, and re-used into useful finished products. In 1889, peddlers in Winnipeg had to obtain licenses, and of those who did, half were Jewish. Given that there were only 630 Jews in the city two years later, the number was less significant than the ratio. Louis Rosenberg, a pioneer cartographer, in his monumental study, *The Jews of Canada*, based on the 1931 census determined that the almost two thousand Jewish "hawkers and peddlers" constituted 43 per cent of this sector across the Dominion.

It may be assumed that peddling was an entry into the bottom of the labour force that led to more lucrative employment. Indeed, some peddlers became travelling salespersons, or owners of shop and junk yards, from which a minority emerged as landlords and manufacturers. But, as historian Deena Nathanson has argued, leaving peddling meant taking another job, usually in the needle trades, a sector that had its own limitations.

The Shmata Trade

Rosenberg's study determined that close to half of Canada's 62,000 Jewish workers, worked in the textile, fur, and leather industries. Some 12,700 worked in the manufacture of clothing, as tailors, cutters, finishers, pressers, hat and cap makers, and sweepers, who were often children under the age of ten. Ninety per cent were wage workers, the remainder were managers and owners. In Montreal they constituted half of the Jewish workforce and 45 per cent of it in Toronto. Further, female labour in textiles was far more predominant than in other manufacturing sectors. In 1911, 60 per cent of the workforce was female, mostly young, and unmarried. Another two thousand Jews were employed in the manufacture of furs and leathers.

Louis Rosenberg determined that nineteen thousand Jews worked in commercial sales, and while he does not break down the types of sales, given the volume of Jews in the above industries, one can estimate that at least half sold textiles, from peddlers to department store owners. In total, approximately 40 per cent of Jews worked in the shmata trade. Four factors account for the preponderance of Jews in these fields. First, many were tailors and dress-makers in Europe, especially in the growing cities. Second, by 1914, 95 per cent lived in the cities and towns where manufacturing industries were located. Third, the explosion of ready-made clothing grew exponentially over the first four decades of the twentieth century and Canada's tariffs on imported manufactured goods stimulated the industry. Finally, Jews were prohibited from finding work in many other sectors of the economy, but were welcomed in this segment, as some of the owners and managers themselves were Jewish, and large-scale department stores such as Eaton's would hire non-Anglo immigrants in their factories (but not in their stores).

The factories were called "sweat shops," an apt moniker, due poor ventilation, dust, and dim lighting. Wages were inadequate, with one letter from a "working girl" stating that an experienced worker was paid $4 a week in 1914.[12] Many manufacturers opted to pay "piece work," where the worker was paid according to how many pieces of garment were sewn together. If a worker managed to buy a used machine, that person would work from home. Work was irregular. The fashions were seasonable, with periods without work followed by brutal schedules. Historian Ruth Frager writes that in Toronto in 1921, the average annual wage for males was $1050 and $670 for females, whereas the poverty line for a family of five was $1,655. As early as 1897, William Lyon Mackenzie King investigated the shops and reported that "work from early morn till ate [*sic*] at night will scarcely suffice to procure the necessaries of a bare existence,"[13] and that one man he interviewed worked eighteen hours a day. The situation remained exploitative through the Depression. Frager reports that the Royal Commission on Price Spreads in 1935 stated that the wages and working conditions "merit the most emphatic condemnation."[14] In the first five years of the Depression (1930–5), wages fell by 30 to 50 per cent. After twelve or more hours at the machine, amidst the din of the factory, labour exceeded physical and mental limits. The shmata trade barely provided the essentials of life for many immigrants, Jewish and non-Jewish, and the sweat shop was where they spent most of their waking hours.

A step up from the factory workers were contractors. Due to the fierce competition, manufacturers had to cut costs. One method was to sell contracts to middlemen, who gave the fabric to workers to produce the garments at home for a lower price than those produced in the factory. Competition among the contractors led many to financial ruin, while others were able to become small-scale manufacturers, representing the vast majority of the 894 Jewish owners and managers who constituted 14 per cent of the workforce in the manufacture of textiles in 1931.

While most of the manufacturing was done by major department stores and non-Jews, some major Jewish manufacturers stand out. In Montreal the oligarchy of the "uptowners," the descendants of the pre-immigrant economic elite, included community leader Lyon Cohen and A.J. Hart, a descendent of the notable family that had arrived in 1760. Sam Rubin was a latecomer, starting a men's wear factory in 1920. In the 1930s, he claimed that he employed four hundred workers, three-quarters of whom were Jewish. In Toronto Samuel Posluns' Superior Cloak Company moved its operation to Guelph, after a lockout of two hundred workers. David Dunkelman established Tip Top Tailors after an initial investment of $1,500 in 1910, and it became one of major producers of men's wear in Canada. In Winnipeg Moses Haid and Harry Steinberg developed the Western Shirt and Overall Company that sold to farmers and factory workers. Ben Jacob came from Russia in 1909 and teamed with John Crowley, a Catholic, to sell women's wear to Eaton's. By the 1930s the Jacob Crowley Manufacturing Company was the largest manufacturer of women's cloaks and suits in the city of Winnipeg.

Handlers

At the turn of the century, with most Canadians living in rural areas, shopping was essentially relegated to the urban dwellers. With rapid mechanization, the production of household goods, especially clothing, expanded exponentially. Major department stores, notably Eaton's, Simpson's and Hudson's Bay, had flagship stores that were the centre point of the country's main downtown districts. They had branch outlets in smaller cities and mail order catalogues. Most immigrants could not afford to shop there and relied on neighbourhood shops. This niche was partially filled by Jewish *handlers* (sellers). Merchandising was ingrained in Jewish life for centuries, a traditional occupation necessitated in part because they were town dwellers, and because other avenues were closed to them, primarily agriculture. In Canada sales were the largest sector of Jewish employment constituting 36 per cent of their workforce in comparison to 8 per cent of all Canadians in 1931. Slightly more than half of the Jewish component were listed as owners and managers. They sold everything needed for the household – clothing, furniture, utensils, toilets, food, newspapers, and medicines. Included within this category were those who bought "job lots" from manufacturers. These were end-of-line fashions and other items that would be sold in bulk, where clever shoppers went for lower prices.

Some Jewish immigrants expanded their operations and created specialized stores, notably women's fashions. These stores were ubiquitous in Canada's smaller cities. Gerald Tulchinsky and Morley Torgov note that this market was dominated by Jewish merchants in Brantford and Sault Ste. Marie. Torgov writes that the owners went to the factories on Spadina Avenue in Toronto twice a year to order the latest fashions. Other Jewish merchants in small Canadian towns also specialized in clothing stores. A smaller number became successful merchants whose operations became central to shoppers in the larger cities. On Selkirk Avenue in Winnipeg, Harry Oretzki from Russia opened a small store that evolved into a department store that employed clerks who spoke the languages of the North End. In Montreal Ida Steinberg opened a grocery store on the Main in 1917. Her son Sam expanded the enterprise and by 1933 there were ten stores across Quebec. By the 1990s, Steinberg's had the second most employees, after Bell Canada, in the province.

Archie J. Freiman (1880–1943) came from Lithuania to Hamilton in 1893. Six years later, he and Moses Cramer opened the Canada House Furnishing Company on Rideau Street in Ottawa, which rapidly expanded into two other locations. When Freiman opted to sell his merchandise on credit or installment, Cramer demurred, and was replaced by Archie's father Harris. Consequently, H. Freiman & Son created a new store on 67 to 73 Rideau Street in 1908 and signed an annual advertising contract with the *Ottawa Citizen* for $50. Archie became the sole owner a decade later, and the Archibald J. Freiman Department Store opened in 1918. He expanded his investments into other areas and established A.J. Freiman in 1923. He and his wife Lillian became central figures in Canadian Jewish life, whose contributions will be discussed further in a subsequent chapter.

Professionals

The children of the immigrant wave who were born or raised in Canada clearly had an easier path in adapting to Canadian life. The most important factor in this process was public education. We will look more closely at this in Chapter 6, but for this discussion, education was the path by which a small minority of this cohort was able to achieve the training to enter the professional class. Louis Rosenberg's study shows that in 1931, 5 per cent of Jews in the workforce were professionals, slightly less than the national average, but higher than other non-Anglo-Celtic ethnic minorities. Approximately 40 per cent of Jewish professionals were classified as self-employed, including musicians, lawyers, doctors, and dentists. The remaining 60 per cent were salaried professionals, including teachers, rabbis, and accountants. Of significance, the relatively large number of Jews entering the professions would have been higher, had they not been subjected to barriers because of their ethnicity and religion.

DERTSIUNG

Shloime Wiseman (1899–1985) and his contemporary and rival Yakov Zipper (1895–1971) were the directors of the two most important Yiddish secular schools in Canada. Wiseman came to Montreal in 1913 and began teaching in the Jewish People's School in 1916. After earning his degree from McGill University, he became the school's director in 1920 and maintained his position until 1971. Zipper arrived in 1925 when he joined the Peretz School. He became its director in

1934 until his death. Both men were passionate about Jewish education, staunch Yiddishists, divided over the age of introduction for the teaching of Modern Hebrew and were major contributors to Jewish newspapers. Zipper wrote a chronicle of his life starting in 1950. Wiseman was also the director of the Jewish Teacher's Seminary. The lives and commitment to secular Jewish scholarship shaped generations of Montrealers.

Jews are commonly regarded as "the people of the book." This expression is derived because the Jewish Bible ("Old Testament") and the Talmuds (the commentaries) are the portable covenant of the Jewish nation. It was incumbent for Jewish males to devote daily study and recitation of these texts. Hence, for almost two thousand years of Western history, where the vast majority was illiterate, Jews were the exception. The synagogue (from the Greek meaning "a place of gathering" or *Beit Knesset* in Hebrew) was also the place of prayer (*Beit Tfila*) and of study (*Beit Midrash*) or book (*Beit Sefer*). In Yiddish, the term *shul* (school) is also used to denote synagogue. Education (*dertsiung* in Yiddish) is the glue for the maintenance of Jewish tradition and for examining the universe. This section examines the transmission of religious and secular education in Yiddish.

Until *Haskalah*'s impact in eastern Europe in the nineteenth century, Jewish education was limited the study of the Torah and the Talmuds. The "Talmud Torahs" (schools) were in rooms (*kheyders*) in synagogues and, for the most learned, in academies (*Yeshivas*). The teachers were rabbis (*rebbe* – teacher in Yiddish), some of great erudition and scholarship, but most were of limited ability (*melamdnim* – teachers in Hebrew) who travelled from one community to the next. They taught in Yiddish, the colloquial language; the students read in Hebrew, the holy language. Children (all boys, some girls), began study as early as at age four, and boys were called to the Torah at thirteen – the bar mitzvah, the rite of passage to adulthood. With the advent of modernity, public education incurred on the preserve of the Talmud Torahs. Nevertheless, by the time of the Great Migration, education for the most observant had changed little; for those who were affected by urbanization and industrialization, they went to shuls,[15] learning Yiddish literature and Jewish history, and to public schools. For a small minority, Jewish education was either incidental or non-existent.

Montreal

Upon arrival, most immigrant children attended the local public schools, where the need to adapt to the realities of Canadian life was immediate. In Canada education was a power given to the provinces as a condition for Quebec's entry into Confederation and was formalized with separate Catholic and Protestant commissions. The former was run by the Church and excluded non-believers, while the latter was a public system, but maintained a "Protestant" curriculum. The Jewish arrival was a challenge for the Protestant schools and for the migrants. Officially, Jewish children were considered "Protestant" in 1903, but learned the Christian Bible, and their parents had neither representation on the commission nor employment in the system. Many of their parents were too poor to be taxed, so the school services became strained as the Jewish population grew. By 1904 Jews constituted 23 per cent of the enrolment, which doubled by 1917, and were a majority in two districts. As early as 1874 Jews lobbied for their own commission without success. Forty years later, this movement had grown exponentially, alarming both commissions. The dispute was resolved in 1931 with Jews still ensconced in the Protestant schools but excused from religious instruction and with the removal of the restriction against the hiring of Jewish teachers.

During this long process, a parallel system of Jewish education emerged to the degree that by the 1930s it was among the most formidable in North America. It began haltingly in the 1880s at the Shaar Hashomayim Synagogue, a preserve of the city's elite. In 1896 a Talmud Torah offering Modern Hebrew education was established and others followed. Unlike in eastern Europe, these were supplementary institutions where classes were held in afternoons and Sunday mornings.

Montreal, after New York, was a magnet for left-wing and nationalist Jewish immigrants. They had embraced socialism and/or Zionism in Europe and transported their ideological fervour to North America. For them, especially the left-wing immigrants, Yiddish – the language and the culture – was a passion. *Yiddishkeit* (Jewishness) was central to their being. Rebecca Margolis contends that they created "a new brand of Diaspora nationalism."[16] The project was to establish "National Radical Schools" in major Jewish communities. The first one was in New York in 1910, the first one in Canada was in Winnipeg in 1913. A year later, the Montreal school opened, and the schools changed their name in 1914 to the Peretz Schools in honour of the memory of the great poet, I.L. Peretz. Yet, it came as no surprise that immediately there was an ideological split in Montreal over the introduction of Hebrew – either in the third grade or from the outset, together with Yiddish. The dissenters created *Der Folks Shul* (The People's School) in 1915. A full day program began in 1927. The schools finally merged, due to financial factors and the retirement of their respective directors, Yakov Zipper and Shloime Wiseman.

Winnipeg

The National Radical School's emergence from the Jewish Youth Union of 1912 was a natural product of the devotion to Yiddish of the Russian immigrants. Although denounced by Rabbi Israel Kahanovitch, the director of the community Talmud Torah, the renamed Peretz school quickly grew and became the first full day parochial school in North America. Yet, for some, its curriculum was too moderate because it did not stress the working-class struggle. Their intense socialist orientation led to *Der Arbeiter Ring Shul* (the Workers' Ring School) renamed the Temple School in 1937. Both institutions maintained the prevalent secular Yiddish culture.

Toronto

The first Jewish school in Ontario was established by Edmund Scheuer (1847–1943) in Hamilton. He was born in Germany, spent time in Paris, and arrived in Hamilton in 1873 to open a jewellery store. Having been raised in the Reform movement, he joined Temple Anshei Shalom, the first Reform synagogue in the country, and started its school in 1876. Although enrolment was miniscule, it not only opened the doors to Jewish education, but to modern religious education. Scheuer moved his business to Toronto in 1886, joined Holy Blossom Synagogue, and directed Toronto's only Sabbath school for the next twenty years, partially filling a void at a time when historian Stephen A. Speisman contends that due to a dearth of qualified teachers, Toronto "Jewish education suffered a deplorable decline."[17] In response, a Talmud Torah established by two eastern European Congregations, Goel Zedek and *Beth Hamidrash Hagadol* (Great House of Study) opened on Simcoe Street, between the Ward and Spadina, in 1907. It reflected the growth of modern Orthodoxy, where Hebrew was taught, and Zionism was emphasized. The flood of Polish immigrants in the next few years brought about the motivation for a more traditional school, resulting in the *Eitz Chaim* (Tree of Life) Talmud Torah in the Ward in 1915, with Yiddish as the language of instruction. Scheuer re-emerged as the director of the Zionist Free School in 1908 that had opened its doors to immigrant girls. His textbook on pedagogy was the first of its kind in Toronto.

The Jewish National Radical School's establishment in 1914 led to the consternation of Toronto's Orthodox institutions, who accused the schools of being Godless, of Zionists for the school's lack of support, and of radicals because the schools did not inculcate socialist ideology. Predictably, the renamed Peretz School split, and its rival, the Folks Shul emerged. As in Montreal, Yiddish was the language of instruction, and Hebrew was introduced. Unlike Montreal, the Jews of Toronto did not have the same ardour for secular education. A full day program was never instituted. In 1922, the Simcoe Street Talmud Torah moved to Brunswick Street, in the expanding Jewish neighbourhood.

Smaller Cities

The pattern of traditional and secular schools in the three largest communities was followed in miniature across the country. Ottawa's Talmud Torah opened in 1924 and the Folk Shul a year later. It moved to instruction in Hebrew in 1929 but closed during the Depression. The opposite occurred in London, where the Talmud Torah was replaced by the Folk Shul. In smaller communities, classes were held in synagogues led by itinerant teachers. The divisions in the large centres were no less absent in small settlements. In the farm colony of Edenbridge the split between the traditional "Africans" and the radical "Londoners," created two schools in a community that that had approximately three hundred settlers at its height.

Education in Yiddish, in both religious and secular schools, was a fixture until World War II. It was rare for Jewish child not to attend a "Jewish school" at least once a week. For many boys, formal Jewish education ended at thirteen, and for girls earlier. Nevertheless, the exposure to

Yiddish on a daily basis, aside from the home and the street, was, for the children born or raised in Canada, an avenue of maintaining eastern European culture, whether they learned at a Talmud Torah or at a secular institution.

TSEITUNGN

The flourishing of Yiddish secular culture in eastern Europe was most evident in the proliferation of newspapers (*tzeitungn*) and periodicals devoted to literature, politics, and the arts. The first Jewish periodical appeared in Warsaw in 1823, and subsequent publications quickly evolved in the Russian Empire despite repression from the Czarist authorities. With the fall the Russian Empire and the creation of an independent Poland in 1919, the full scope of Yiddish publications representing the political and artistic spectrum reached its apogee in the interwar period. Warsaw was the second largest Jewish city (after New York), with some four hundred thousand inhabitants at the outset of World War II. According to historian Marian Fuks in his Polish language study (translated as *The Jewish Press in Warsaw*), in 1935 there were eleven Yiddish dailies as well as two Jewish dailies in Polish. In the Soviet Union, with three million Jews, Yiddish publications proliferated as they were free to publish under the Communist regime.

The transference of Yiddish life to North America during the Great Migration facilitated engagement with the press. In the United States, this development created a new perspective on its long history of Jewish journalism. Historian Jonathan D. Sarna in his *History of the Jewish Press in North America* notes that although the first newspaper in Yiddish appeared in 1686 in Amsterdam, the true development of Jewish newspapers was in the nineteenth century, written initially in English, and later in German as well. The publication of *Der Forverts* in New York in 1897 broke open the market for Yiddish readers. The paper originated through the efforts of some fifty Yiddish-speaking socialists. Its publisher was Abraham Cahan (1860–1951) who had come from Russia in 1880, mastered English, became a teacher, a journalist in the English language press, and editor of two Yiddish papers that were succeeded by *The Forward.* Cahan ran *The Forward* until 1946. Almost immediately, the paper was distributed throughout the main Jewish communities in North America and was the single most important purveyor of news written in Yiddish, a symbol of the American working class and its Jewish settlers. It currently publishes in Yiddish and English. Within a few years, rival Yiddish dailies appeared together with papers in major American cities, with a combined circulation of six hundred thousand. Considering that each paper was read by a few persons, most literate Jewish immigrants read at least one Yiddish paper on a regular basis as well as periodicals and books. In Canada the first Yiddish publication was a pamphlet during the federal election in 1887. Imported Hebrew type from New York produced calendars for the Jewish year, and in 1905 and 1907 two newspapers in Montreal published briefly. Canadian historian Irving Abella wrote, "The … Yiddish dailies … in Canada were not merely newspapers; for the newcomer they were an introduction to the New World; they were forums of debate, vehicles for self-expression … They were, for all intents and purposes, the university of the Jewish common man and woman."[18]

Der Keneder Adler

The *Canadian Eagle*, the longest and far most significant Yiddish newspaper, was a Montreal daily that began in 1907 and immediately became the most read Canadian Jewish newspaper, irrespective of language, to the 1940s. It existed until the 1960s. It was created by Hirsch Wolofsky (1878–1949) who, upon emigrating from Poland in 1900, had opened a fruit store on the Main. He was the managing editor from 1907 until his death, picking his writers, and promoting community institutions including the Jewish Community Council, Canadian Jewish Congress (hereafter CJC), and the Jewish General Hospital. The paper attracted Jewish writers internationally and published local writers. Wolofsky was a regular contributor and wrote three books in Yiddish. The last one, *Mayn Lebns Rayze* (My Life's Journey), appeared in 1946 and was correspondingly released in English, and into French in 2000 by historian Pierre Anctil, with the subtitle *Un demi-siecle de vie Yiddish a Montreal.*

The *Canadian Eagle* filled its pages "with international, local, and community news, essays and opinion pieces, serialized novels, fiction, short plays, and poetry. Its contributors included Simon Belkin, a noted authority on Jewish immigration, and H.M. Caiserman, the key figure in the formation of the CJC in 1919, as well as Israel Medres whose contribution is discussed earlier in this chapter.

From 1912–15 the newspaper's editor was a polymath, Rueben Brainin (1862–1939), who was a Hebraist writer, journalist, translator, essayist, and critic. He was born in Russia, where he was a featured writer in the Hebrew and Yiddish press. He moved to western Europe, became fluent in French, English, and German, and arrived in New York in 1909. During his short stay in Montreal, he helped establish the Jewish Public Library (JPL) and the National Radical School. After a contretemps with Wolofsky, he created a short-lived rival paper. Although he lived the rest of his life in New York, he remained attached to Montreal and was buried there.

Numerous writers contributed to the *Canadian Eagle* in both Yiddish and Hebrew. Unlike most of the Yiddish press, it represented the spectrum of Jewish political and religious views – Zionism as a cultural movement and a practical necessity, anarchism, socialism, and articles on religious texts and interpretations. Gerald Tulchinsky writes that Wolofsky "had broad liberal and progressive views and saw the primary role of his newspaper as a 'communal institution.'"[19] In part this was good business sense; in part it was to unite a diversified and marginalized immigrant community in a rapidly changing country.

Other Yiddish Newspapers and Journals

The *Canadian Eagle*'s moderation was criticized, and stimulated rival newspapers to spring up. In Montreal, an Orthodox publication *Di Yiddish Velt* (The Jewish World) and an anarcho-Labour-Zionist *Di Folkstsaytung* (The People's Newspaper) were published from 1912–15. Some five other publications met a similar demise, even though they attracted some of the *Canadian Eagle* contributors.

Winnipeg's rapidly expanding Jewish population in the first decade of the twentieth century provided the impetus for the second successful Yiddish paper in Canada – *Der Kanader Yid* (The Canadian Israelite) in 1910. It was a weekly that changed its name to *Dos Yiddishe Vort* (The Israelite Press) in 1913. It represented liberal and socialist views, and was regarded as a "folkspaper" that was not beholden to glorifying the community's leaders. It boasted the largest circulation of any Jewish paper in western Canada. The Israelite Press put out an

English column in 1938 and a full English section a decade later. It folded in 1981.

Initial attempts for a Yiddish press were unsuccessful in Toronto until 1912, when *Der Yiddishe Zhurnal* (confusingly named The Hebrew Journal) was established. It attracted readers because of its coverage of European news during the onset of World War I and of local events. Abraham Rhinewine (1887–1931), a socialist and a Zionist, was its first editor. He died while starting a competing paper. His successor was Samuel Shapiro, who was a good journalist but lacked Rhinewine's idealism and breadth of knowledge. Kayfetz remarks that "the *Journal* never pretended to be anything more than it was – a provincial daily serving the needs and interests of a very local public."[20] Stephen A. Speisman, the primary historian of Jewish Toronto, observed that Toronto in the twenties and thirties was not a cultured community compared to Montreal and Winnipeg. It put out an English page which in 1938 criticized the government's refusal to admit Jewish refugees from Nazi Germany.

In the interwar period, these relatively mainstream Yiddish papers were rivalled by ones that extolled communism as the sole authentic antidote to class struggle. They had a limited but dedicated following. The most important was *Der Kampf* (The Struggle) in Montreal in 1924, edited by Michael Buhay, a British immigrant. It met resistance from adherents to the less extreme New York communist daily, *Der Freiheit* (The Freedom), but the Canadian paper gained traction, moved its operation to Toronto, and reportedly printed five thousand copies in the middle of the Depression. It changed its name twice, ultimately becoming *Vochenblatt* (Weekly Paper) after World War II.

English Language Newspapers

Lyon Cohen and Samuel Jacobs were two members of the Montreal Jewish elite. Sensing the need for a Jewish publication that would defend Jewish rights and cement the growing community, they founded the *Jewish Times*, a bi-weekly in 1897. Its creation was spurred by growing antisemitism that was being inflamed during the trial of Alfred Dreyfus, a colonel in the French military who was accused of spying for Germany. The paper was strongly supportive of the Federal Liberal Party under Wilfrid Laurier. It reported broadly, from the impact of world events on the Jewish people to social items from Glace Bay. At its peak in 1904 it published ten thousand copies, but its circulation declined due to the *Canadian Eagle* and the feeling that it did not represent the "Yiddish masses." It stopped publication in 1912. Hirsch Wolofsky seized the moment to establish the *Canadian Jewish Chronicle*, with financial support from Mortimer Davis, the president of Imperial Tobacco, and other community leaders. It was a weekly that supported local institutions, Zionist organizations, and the establishment of the CJC. Its critics observed that it succeeded because it made Jewishness respectable. In 1938 it hired A.M. Klein, a young lawyer, as its editor. Klein, arguably the seminal Jewish intellectual in Canada, and of whom more will be written in subsequent chapters, transformed the publication into an eloquent publication until his departure in 1955. In the following years, the *Chronicle*'s standards and readership declined, morphed into other publications, and closed shop in 1974.

The *Chronicle*'s rival was the *Canadian Jewish Review*. It began in 1921 in Toronto, reflecting the positions of the Reform movement as represented at Holy Blossom Synagogue, which included opposition to Zionism and the promotion of social justice. It moved to Montreal in 1929 but after World War II, its popularity dwindled. The longest reign of an English language paper devoted to Jewish life in Canada is the *Jewish Western Bulletin* from Vancouver. Founded in 1925, its name was changed to the *Jewish Independent* in 2005. Among its array of contributors, Abraham Arnold (1923–2011), a journalist and historian of the Jews of western Canada, was perhaps the most prominent.

The significance of the Yiddish press in North America is that it was the main source of information – from analyses of world events, to scholarly articles on literature, to social columns – for most immigrants in the first half of the twentieth century. The success of the Yiddish press in Canada must be tempered with the reality that *The Forward* was often the preferred paper, yet its Canadian competitors lasted into the 1970s, some twenty years after most of the other Yiddish dailies in the United States had closed down.

KULTUR

The transition of Yiddish as a language of communication and personal correspondence to a literary one was rapid and had a dramatic impact on eastern European Jewry. The ability to depict the Jewish experience in poetry, prose, and theatre resonated with a population that was growing at twice the rate of Christian Europe and was increasingly literate, urbane, and multilingual. Yiddish culture, *kultur*, was inextricably linked to Yiddish in the school, the home, street and workplace. Cultural transmission to North America presented new challenges of adaptation and in meeting these obstacles culture was transposed into a European–American hybrid. Montreal's Jewish community created a cultural "utopia," in the words of scholar David Roskies.[21] Its output was only outmatched by New York, whose Jewish community by the 1930s had reached two million people. The following section examines the development of Yiddish culture in Canada's largest city.

The Jewish Public Library

There were three major developments in the transfer of Yiddish culture to Montreal – the Radical Schools, the *Canadian Eagle*, and the JPL. These institutions were created between 1907 and 1914, when the Jewish population tripled from approximately thirteen thousand to forty thousand. The incentive for the *folks-biblyotek* (people's library) came from the need to provide a place where one could borrow books and provide a centre for cultural activity. Yehuda Kaufman (1886–1975) and Reuben Brainin were the driving forces. Kaufman was a Zionist and helped found the Jewish People's School. Brainin wrote editorials in the *Canadian Eagle* lobbying the community for support for self-education and suggesting the library would consolidate the community. It opened in May 1914, with five hundred books and no budget. It raised funds by bringing in public speakers, including Sholem Aleichem, historically the foremost Yiddish writer. Even though Brainin and Kaufman left Montreal in 1916, the institution grew, with fits and starts, so that by 1930, its circulation had surpassed fifteen thousand and it moved into a large building on Esplanade Avenue in the Plateau. A year earlier, it anglicized its name from "Peoples" to "Public."

In the interwar period, the JPL was the central cultural institution, a nonpartisan meeting place, a repository not only for publications but also for archives, and hosted a variety of cultural and educational events. It moved in 1953 and is now housed in Cummings Square, the site of Montreal's Jewish institutions. In its second century, it remains a unique treasure for the public in general, and for students and scholars.

Poetry

The literary scene in Montreal was sparked by the establishment of the *Canadian Eagle* and by Jewish writers in Europe and New York who had created an international network. In Montreal approximately fifteen literary journals were founded before 1939. They published short stories and poems. Of the host of renowned poets, the focus here will be on J.I. Segal and Ida Maze, who are introduced in the beginning of this chapter, and Chava Rosenfarb.

Segal was the most prolific Yiddish writer in Canada. He came from a small Ukrainian town, Korets, in 1911 at the age of 15. He was briefly employed in the textile industry until he began writing in the *Canadian Eagle* and teaching in the People's School. His collected works over a forty-year period took up ten volumes. Segal's poetry opens our eyes to the struggle of immigrant adaptation. He identified himself more as a Yiddish poet living in Canada than a Canadian Yiddish poet. He was psychologically trapped between Korets and Montreal, a small-town boy who was bewildered by life in a Christian city. In "Strange," published in his 1930 book, *Lirik*, he wrote:

> In a strange city on a strange day
> How can one find a friend …
> In every little street a church bell rings,
> And all go in the gates,
> … And I will remain alone in the street,
> Alone here with the great sun,
> And so cold will be my heart,
> And my eye will be bent down,
> Over the emptiness of the world.

A selected collection of Segal's work has been translated into French by Pierre Anctil as *Jacob-Isaac Segal (1896–1954): Un poète yiddish de Montreal et son milieu* and Anctil's volume was in turn translated into English by Vivian Felsen as *Jacob Isaac Segal: A Montreal Yiddish Poet and His Milieu.*

Ida Maze's poetry evinced another aspect of adaptation – that of an immigrant woman, a wife, and mother. She was renowned as the doyenne of the Yiddish scene, as her modest apartment on Esplanade Avenue was an open house to the literati for some thirty years.

The poet Miriam Waddington was born in Winnipeg and as a young woman often visited Maze's "salon" (the term comes from the bedrooms of French aristocratic women prior to the Revolution of 1789, which had been the scene of intellectual discussion). She recalls that Maze supported the impecunious Yiddish writers as the eternal mother, providing much appreciated food and solace. Her work consisted of children's poetry and lullabies, motherhood, elegies to nature, and of her maturation. In "To Earth" from her collection *A Mother*:

> Heart to hear with you
> Embrace me, sweetest sleep;
> In your warm arms I'll dream
> How first and last can meet …
> Fall upon me, rain;
> My eyelids need your love
> And on earth, at last:
> Earth, set my heart at rest.[22]

In "I'd Like to Be" from her collection *Grow My Children*:

> I'd like to be, I'd like to be
> I'd like to be a hare
> To a hunter, a grandfather, an author, a
> I don't know what, myself.[23]

Chava Rosenfarb (1923–2011) presents yet another perspective of adaptation. Born a generation later than Segal and Maze, in Lodz, Poland, Rosenfarb was a survivor of the Holocaust. She began writing poetry and short stories as a child and in the Lodz Ghetto. After the war, some poems were rewritten from memory together with new works. Her fame preceded her arrival to Montreal in 1950 where she was feted by the great writers of the earlier period. Although she quickly became fluent in English, she wrote in Yiddish and translated some of her work. Rosenfarb is the last significant Canadian poet who wrote in Yiddish. Her three-volume novel about the Lodz Ghetto, *The Tree of Life*, is regarded as a classic. The following is from a collection that she wrote in Canada.

Praise

Praise the likeness of the day
standing still as a water –
a mirror without a reflection.
Through hours that slide
through its hazy-pale surface
like breath-carried skaters
are sharing the lighted eye of awareness,
erasing their footprints
before they are falling –
Praise likewise that day
you will never remember.[24]

Theatre

Modern Yiddish theatre had its origins in traditional Judaism. Religious liturgy and ritual were sung by a *Chazan* (cantor), Jewish weddings and parties featured *klezmorim* (musicians, but technically "instruments" from the Hebrew), and jesters. During the festival of Purim, recalling the saving of the Jews of Persia by Esther, a play (*spiel*) for all ages tells the story. Itinerant actors, singers, comics, and musicians travelled through the countryside providing entertainment and necessary divergence to the populace. The performance of Yiddish secular plays became widespread in the late nineteenth century and professional theatre companies became commonplace. The most well known was the Vilna Troupe, from the city that was a centre of Yiddish culture in Poland. The works of major Yiddish writers were turned into literary plays; Shakespeare and other notable playwrights' works were translated and performed. The most popular play was *Der Dybuk* by Shmuel Ansky, about a malevolent spirit that inhabits a young girl. First performed in Moscow in 1920, it quickly gained renown throughout the Yiddish-speaking world.

On New York's Lower East Side, plays and "historical operas" were written nonstop. Yiddish theatre appealed to all audiences, from the literati to the working poor and children. The merger between Europe and New York created a hybrid: the musical theatre. Jewish immigrants, including Irving Berlin, the Gershwin brothers, and Al

Jolson, were figurative in the origins of the Broadway musical and Tin Pan Alley.

Canada was an outpost of Yiddish theatre. The large centres relied on visiting companies from New York and Europe. Theatres in Montreal (the Monument National), Toronto (the Standard and the Lyric) and Winnipeg (the Queen's Theatre) regularly staged productions. By the 1930s Yiddish theatre was in decline having been superseded by Broadway and Hollywood. There was a renaissance of Yiddish theatre in Montreal in the 1960s that will be discussed in a later chapter.

Another aspect to traditional Yiddish theatre that created a hybrid was comedy. This was most evident in the contribution made by the children of immigrants, who integrated Yiddish comedy, based on one-liners, slapstick, and send-ups of stereotypes, into English. Comedians were a regular feature of Jewish summer resorts in the Catskills north of New York City, and in the Laurentians, Lake Simcoe, and Lake Winnipeg. The most well known of Canadian Jewish comedians was the duo of Johnny Wayne (b. Louis Weingarten 1918–90) and Frank Shuster (1916–2002) who performed on Canadian Broadcasting Corporation (CBC) radio and television for half a century and are profiled in a subsequent chapter.

Recreation

An important factor in the process of adaptation was recreation. Jews participated in recreational activities, from vigorous sports to social clubs. An aspect of Jewish nationalism was that a "new Jew" was in the offing, one who was willing to train (mostly his) body and well as intellect. Using the model of the Christian "Y," YMHAs (Young Men's Hebrew Association) were established in Montreal, Toronto, and Winnipeg. Offering more than the opportunity to play sports, they became community centres, where youth especially found a haven.

The first YMHA was in Baltimore in 1854. In Montreal it began in 1910 in a room in the Baron de Hirsch Institution and moved into a building in 1929 donated by Mortimer Davis, the tobacco tycoon. It rapidly expanded to 4,300 members, including 1,100 in the YWHA (Young Women's Hebrew Association) by 1940. In Toronto the Young Men's Hebrew Athletic Club began in 1901 as one of several other clubs for Jewish children. With concern about the children's health and antisemitic incidents at the YMCA, the clubs amalgamated and the YMHA was incorporated in 1930. From rented rooms in the Brunswick Avenue Talmud Torah, an athletic building was built next door in 1937 and a new JCC opened in 1953 at Bloor and Spadina.

A "Y" existed in Winnipeg in the 1890s, but without a facility. Historian Allan Levine describes an incident during a football game in 1915, where a member of the Y's team had to recite Kaddish (the memorial prayer for the dead) for his father at halftime. As it happened, Rabbi Samuel was a member of the team and led the service. The YMHA also sponsored soccer and baseball teams. It moved into a facility on Albert Street in the North End in 1939. Levine lauds the contribution of Sam Sheps who was its director for thirty years and the athleticism of Leibal Hershfield who was inducted into the Manitoba Sports Hall of Fame.

Many Jewish children loved sports much to the consternation of their traditional parents. Although more assimilated Jews participated in winter and summer competitions in Europe (Hungary's fencers, among the best in the world, included Jews), this diversion had not penetrated to the more devout. Two Canadian Jewish athletes had to overcome this, and other obstacles, in placing their names into the annals of Canadian sport.

Fanny "Bobbie" Rosenfeld (1904–69) came from Ukraine as an infant when her family settled in Barrie, Ontario. Her father had a junk business, and the family moved to Toronto in 1922. Bobbie, who had played sports in high school, joined the YWHA where she captained the basketball team that went on to be the city and provincial champion and a two-time national finalist. Turning to track, she dominated the 1925 Provincial Championship, with five firsts. In the 1928 Olympics, she set national records in three field events, won a silver medal in the 100-metre dash, and gold in 4x100 metre relay. Rosenfeld was considered the "superwoman" of women's hockey, a dominant baseball and softball player, and was a nationally ranked competitor in tennis, lacrosse, golf, and speed skating. She was forced to retire in 1933 due to arthritis. Rosenfeld was a modest woman who downplayed her achievements, as well as her Jewish heritage, to avoid antisemitism. At a time when women's athletics was frowned upon, she was a major figure in Canadian sport. Turning to journalism, she was a staunch advocate for women's sport, and a sport administrator, coach, and official. She was voted as Canada's Female Athlete of the Half-Century (1900–50).

Jewish boys' favourite sports were baseball and basketball. But their greatest impact was in boxing. Sammy Luftspring (1916–2000) was born in Kensington Market. He began boxing at the Y on Brunswick Street, wearing a Magen David (Star of David) on his trunks. In 1933 he was the Ontario amateur lightweight champion. Turning professional, he won the Canadian welterweight championship in 1938 and was ranked third in the world. An injury in 1940 ended his career. Luftspring was the most successful of a cadre of Jewish boxers, including his fellow Torontonians, the Yack brothers, Dave and Baby, and Montrealer Maxie Berger, who won the World Junior Welterweight title in 1939. Toronto and Montreal were boxing hotspots and the sons of immigrants had dreams of escaping the ghetto by gaining wealth and admiration through sport. Few succeeded. Rosenfeld was a Canadian athlete who happened to be Jewish, whereas Luftspring was a Canadian Jewish athlete, they were both the products of Yiddish Canada. Their individual adaptations to Canadian society reflect the panorama of responses by immigrants and their children.

We would be remiss if we did not mention the most important Canadian Jewish athlete of the nineteenth century – Louis Rubenstein (1861–1931). Born in Montreal to recent immigrants from Poland, Rubenstein was the foremost figure skater in Canada. In c. 1885, he won the gold medal in the World Championships. Following his retirement in 1892, he was a founder of the Amateur Skating Association of Canada and the National Amateur Skating Association of the United States. An accomplished bowler, curler, and cyclist, Rubenstein served as alderman in the St. Louis Ward from 1916 until his death. A memorial water fountain is dedicated in his honour in Montreal's Fletcher's Field, in the middle of the Plateau, where two generations of Jews were introduced to athletics.

CONCLUSION

Historian David Roskies, in the compendium *An Everyday Miracle: Yiddish Culture in Montreal,* called Yiddish Montreal a "utopian experiment." He contends that the word *folk* was the key to this coalition of traditionalists, nationalists, reformers, and radicals from "downtown" who preserved Yiddishkeit in a city divided geographically, economically, religiously, and linguistically by the two founding European peoples. This "third solitude" used Yiddish as, in Roskies' term, "a vehicle of national liberation."[25] Utopias, of course, have, at best, a short life. In 1931 Yiddish was the mother tongue of 96 per cent of Canada's Jews. Ten years later it was 77 per cent, reflecting the adaptation of those immigrants who no longer spoke to their children in Yiddish, and no net migration during that decade. If Roskies is correct that this was an experiment, then it was a singularly successful one in North America. The experiment sustained an immigrant community for forty years, and established institutions such as the JPL and the secular schools that are thriving a century after their foundation.

Yet, Yiddish Canada was far from a monolith. The immigrants represented the diversity of Jewish life in the early twentieth century, from traditionalists who tried to live as if they were still in shtetls, to those who had assimilated. Stratifications in class, education, and religious observance exposed the different paths of adaptation. While Yiddish as an everyday language is now spoken only by some traditional Orthodox followers, and otherwise is a rather exotic academic pursuit, for half a century it was a unifying force for a disparate ethno-cultural minority.

Shearith Israel synagogue on Chenneville Street, Montreal

Source: Canadian Jewish Heritage Network

CHAPTER FIVE

Organizations

Lyon Cohen (1868–1937) was arguably the most prominent Jewish figure in Canadian life from the 1890s to the 1920s. As an industrialist, publisher, community leader, and philanthropist, his mark on many of the organizations that arose in this period was instrumental in their development. He was born in Poland, the eldest son of Lazarus and Fanny, and came to Ontario as a child. The family moved to Montreal, where Lazarus quickly established interests in coal, brass, and construction. Lyon became president of the Freedman Company, one of the largest clothing manufacturers in Canada. He founded the *Jewish Times* in 1897, was the president of numerous relief and welfare societies including the FJP of Montreal, and of the Shaar Hashomayim Synagogue. Cohen was vice-president of the Zionist Organization of Canada (ZOC) and the initial president of the CJC.

Throughout their history, Jews have organized themselves, initially as a people of faith bound by a set of laws governing virtually all aspects of life and worship, and then into communal structures that oversaw education, rites of passage, health, provision for the sick, indigent, and aged, and dietary laws. From their dispersion by the Roman Empire in the first century of the Common Era, consigned to distant lands under rulers who were rarely benevolent, these structures evolved into ones that also dealt with relations with their host societies. With the advent of the Great Migration the range of Jewish organizations in eastern Europe had accelerated from the religious realm to include social, cultural, and political concerns. The transposition of Jewish life from Europe to the New World intertwined with the process of adaptation. Therefore, the Jewish organizations that evolved in Canada in the first half of the twentieth century were a combination of the religious and ethical ones from time immemorial, and the ones honed by the trends of modernization and urbanization in Europe, with those that merged with Canadian values. Communal organizations were necessary to solidify Jewish life in their new home. Their formation reflected the diversity of the community.

Adapting traditional and modern European structures to the Canadian reality was a difficult and, at times, a fractious development. There were four dimensions to this problem. First, it immediately posed a predicament in that the first Jewish settlers were predominantly middle class, anglicized, and sought to acculturate. Comfortably ensconced, this Canadianized cohort was numerically significant in 1881, but was only a tiny minority forty years later when there were 125,000 Jews in the country, of whom the vast majority were traditional and working class. Responding to their integration pitted the establishment against the newcomers: the former had the means but not necessarily the trust and skills to connect with the immigrants, while the latter had the needs but resented the establishment's control over the community. Second, immigrants displayed a broad diversity of religious, social, cultural, and political expressions. These fissures complicated the quest for communal unity. Third, Canadians, especially those whose roots were from western Europe, tended to look down on "foreigners." Jewish communal organizations were created in part as a reaction to obstacles against their integration into Canadian society and as an avenue of melding into Canadian society. Fourth, international developments, most significantly the two World Wars and the Great Depression, had catastrophic consequences on the Jewish world, primarily in Europe, that necessitated a concerted effort by Canadian Jews to provide relief and to create a communal voice that would be heard by Canadian leaders.

Establishing organizations to meet the needs, yet keep the traditions, was a delicate undertaking. It required coordination, understanding, and most of all money. It took almost half a century to reach a measure of achievement in this feat, entailing a process that, while imperfect, required a monumental effort and ultimately was a guarded success. By 1945 most Canadian Jews felt they belonged to a national community, which, because of its diversity, had a range of organizations that provided relatively effective communal services and articulated the concerns of its members. Collectively, Canadian Jews had achieved a modicum of success in adapting to the realities of life in Canada.

SYNAGOGUES

An old joke: "How many Jews live in this town?" "One hundred." "And how many synagogues are there"? "One hundred and fifty." The proliferation of synagogues, not to mention the social, cultural, ideological, and benevolent societies in the emerging immigrant communities, was a testament to the diversity of the Jewish people. While faith, history and culture welded "the nation of Israel," these traditions were marked by interpretations and disputes from the outset. The creation of synagogues from the 1880s to the 1930s is one reflection of these internal divisions.

The focus of the synagogue is as a community organization rather than a place of worship. Its maintenance and services required a communal effort. Every synagogue has an executive of volunteers that oversees finance, building maintenance, programs, outreach, education, religious services, and welfare. Larger synagogues have an administrator and staff in addition to at least one rabbi and cantor. They were often part of a network of institutions of the same denomination, locally and internationally. They also provided venues for Jewish communal events.

There was a consistent pattern in the erection of synagogues in Toronto and Montreal to the mid-twentieth century: ones established by early settlers, followed by a second one built by the next wave of immigrants. These dominated the Jewish landscape until the Great Migration, when less imposing structures proliferated in immigrant neighbourhoods. In addition, one would find small congregations on the Jewish streets that blended in with other establishments. These shtiblech were ubiquitous. With a few notable exceptions, synagogues in Canada were Orthodox, that is, traditional in ritual and custom. This did not mean that they were homogenous. The divisions that emerged in eastern Europe, reflecting different approaches to scholarship, liturgy, and local customs, were transported to the Diaspora.

Orthodoxy was challenged by modernization. The Reform movement originated in Germany in the early nineteenth century, as a product of the Jewish Enlightenment, and gained traction in the United States, but made little headway in Canada. The Conservative movement arose in New York in the late nineteenth century as a median between Orthodox and Reform but was even less attractive to Canadian Jews than Reform until the 1940s. In general terms, those who joined the established synagogues tended to be wealthier and more adaptive to Canadian life than their counterparts. Irrespective of size, they were fundamental to Jewish life.

Not all Jews belonged to a synagogue, although some belonged to more than one. But virtually all Jews belonged to at least one Jewish organization. Nevertheless, it was rare for even those who were not observant to not celebrate the High Holidays, to not provide some measure of Jewish education (at least for boys), to not to keep a kosher home and for the majority, to not abstain from work on the Sabbath. All marked significant life events (marriages, bar mitzvahs, deaths) in synagogues.

Montreal

We have referred to *Shearith Israel*, dubbed the Spanish and Portuguese Synagogue, the first Jewish institution in Canada, dating from 1776, and its rival, Shaar Hashomayim, the first Ashkenazi synagogue, established eighty years later. They not only dominated Jewish life but were centrepieces in the city. Their rabbis and founders were integral in Montreal's social circles. Factions from these institutions seeking a more modern approach in line with their acculturation to Canadian society founded Temple *Emanu-El Beth Shalom* (God is with us, House of Peace) in 1882. It was the first (and remains the only) Reform congregation in Quebec. Its rabbi, Samuel Marks, came from the United States. A new building was erected ten years later on Stanley Street ("uptown") on land donated by tobacco mogul, Sir Mortimer Davis. Twenty years later, mirroring the elite's economic success, it moved to an impressive structure in Westmount, the preserve of the Anglo and Jewish elite.

The first expansion was the surge of synagogues around the Main during the Great Migration. In 1945, some thirty congregations were still active, not to mention the countless shtiblech. Of note were: *Beth David* (the Romanian Shul) in 1886 on the site of the former Spanish and Portuguese Synagogue; *Beth Yehuda* (the Russian Shul) in 1890; *Shaar Tefilah* (Gate of Prayer, aka the Austro-Hungarian Shul) in 1892; *Chevra Tehilim* (Society of the Psalms, aka the Russian and Lithuanian Shul) in 1903; *Chevra Shas* (Society of the Six Books, aka the Lithuanian Shul) in 1890. One can see that the region from which the immigrants came was a central factor in creating a congregation. Typically, the first building was modest structure reflecting the economic circumstances of its congregants. In time a more imposing home may have been erected. Chevra Shas, for example, moved four times in thirty years, before settling on St. Urbain Street in 1920. After 1945, some of these congregations followed the migration of Jews to the suburbs.

The migration of *Hasidim* (the righteous) in 1941 marked a turning point in Montreal's Jewish community and signalled the re-emergence of Traditional Orthodoxy. The Lubavitch movement, named after the town of the founding rabbi, heralded the move of followers of other rabbinic dynasties. They tended to live segregated from one another and from the general community.

Yudel Rosenberg (1859–1935) was one of the most important religious scholars of his time but is relegated to a footnote in Canadian Jewish history. He was born in Poland and became a rabbi in his teens. He undertook the study of the Torah and Talmud and was admired for his scholarship. Yet he was also influenced by the Jewish Enlightenment (*Haskalah*) by reading current Hebrew works. Rosenberg led congregations in Lodz and Warsaw, Poland's two largest cities. He came to Toronto in 1913 and moved to Montreal six years later as chief of the Rabbinical Court. Of his voluminous publications, his translation of part of *The Zohar*, the medieval text of the *Kabbalah* (Jewish Mysticism), from Aramaic to Hebrew was most notable. His "Letter to the Sabbath Queen" in 1924 was an admonition to those Jews who forsook the holiness of the Sabbath for personal matters. As historian Ira Robinson has written: "Through him, we may come to understand not merely the pressures of the modern world upon Orthodox Judaism.... But also the beginnings of the sort of creative response to these pressures which ultimately enabled Orthodoxy to emerge as a viable force within Judaism of the late twentieth century."[1] Rosenberg's contribution to Canadian Jewry is, in fact, worthy of more than a footnote.

Toronto

A similar pattern of congregational development to that of Montreal took place in Toronto, albeit beginning a century later. The major distinction between the two communities was that Toronto's two major synagogues eventually deviated from Orthodoxy, and ultimately, the religious landscape there was somewhat less Orthodox than in Montreal. Holy Blossom's grand edifice was built by the community elite attracting members from smaller Ontario communities. Reflecting their rapid adaptation to Canadian life and in concert with the growing Reform movement in the United States, some of the members sought to modernize the liturgy by adding English, ending segregated seating according to gender, and incorporating music. This created a rift, especially when an organ was installed in the sanctuary, and when they failed to find a Jewish musician, they hired a Christian. Some members left in disgust to its rival, the Goel Zedek Synagogue. A new rabbi, Solomon Jacobs, was hired in 1901 but was unsuccessful in mending the rift. His successors, Barnett Brickner, and Maurice Eisendrath, undertook outreach to Christian denominations, a program of aid to Torontonians especially during the Depression, and advocated for social justice at a time when there was widespread discrimination and lack of services for the destitute. Eisendrath was a force, not only in Jewish circles, but across the span of city's political and social networks. During his tenure (1929–41), the synagogue adopted the customs of American Reform. Head coverings were removed for services, sermons were given at non-denominational Sunday services, and worship was almost entirely in English. Bar mitzvahs for thirteen-year-old boys were secondary to confirmations at sixteen. Bat mitzvahs (for girls) began in the 1950s. He persuaded the Congregation to move from its downtown base to the upscale Cedarvale/Forest Hill neighbourhood in 1938, even though it meant raising funds during the Depression. His commitment to social justice was acknowledged when he was awarded the Gandhi Peace Award in 1961. Four years later, he walked alongside Martin Luther King on the "Selma to Montgomery March," a turning point in the American civil rights movement.

The Goel Zedek Synagogue was founded in 1883 by Polish immigrants. Two years later, they purchased a Methodist church on University Avenue adjacent to the Ward, and later moved down the street to an imposing edifice in 1907, attracting some traditional members of Holy Blossom who rejected its flirtation with Reform. The leaders were less traditional than the founders and joined the American Conservative movement. In 1951 it amalgamated with the Beth Hamidrash Hagadol Congregation (aka the McCaul Street Shul) to create *Beth Zedek* Synagogue (House of the Righteous). Five years later, the amalgamated congregation moved into a new edifice, down the hill from Holy Blossom on Bathurst Street. Today, its six thousand members form the largest congregation in the country.

Like the history of Montreal, there was a rapid development of synagogues in the immigrant neighbourhoods: first in the Ward and then in the Spadina neighbourhood. Stephen A. Speisman explores their origins and development in his seminal book *The Jews of Toronto.* In 1939 there were approximately thirty synagogues, of which four currently remain. Some relocated to the suburbs, while others were sold to churches and community centres. Of note was the Beth Jacob Congregation (aka the Poilisher [Polish] Shul). Its wealthy congregants hired Benjamin Brown (1888–1974), the first Jewish synagogue architect, to build a Byzantine-style structure on Henry Street at Cecil Street known as the "Henry Street Shul" in 1922. Its imposing façade, complete with onion domed cupolas, can still be seen from Spadina, three blocks away. Appropriately, as the neighbourhood changed its complexion after 1945, it was sold to a Russian Orthodox congregation. A common practice was to colloquialize formal names with the congregants' geographical origins, including Shaarey Zedek (Gates of Righteousness, aka the Russisher Shul) and *Adath Israel* (Congregation Israel, aka the Rumanian Shul), *Anshei Minsk* (the People of Minsk), *Anshei Kiev* (the People of Kiev), or to the neighbourhood, such as Beth Jacob (the Beaches Shul) and *Knesseth Israel* (Assembly of Israel, aka the Junction Shul).

Historian and community leader Ben Kayfetz wrote of a "rabbinic dynasty on Cecil Street" in the Spadina district during the 1930s that was headed by Reb Moishele (Rabbi "little" Moses) from his *hoif* (house/dwelling) that also served as a synagogue. His four sons each had a stibl nearby with their own group of followers. He describes "the swarms of worshippers who flocked to the West End Veteran's Hall on College Street" as his hoif could not contain them all, and "the men and women who danced with Avrumele (one of the sons) on Clinton Street"[2] – scenes reminiscent of the shtetls of eastern Europe.

Winnipeg

Shaarey Zedek was the first congregation, created in 1880 and erected on King Street in the North End a decade later. It was followed by *Beth El* (House of God) and the Sons of Israel in 1884. The former is described in some texts as a Reform congregation, and in others as a Conservative one. They quickly realigned. Beth El joined Shaarey Zedek and Sons of Israel merged with *Rosh Pina* (Cornerhead). To add the confusion, Shaarey Zedek split in 1903, creating an off-shoot, *Shaarey Shomayim* (Gates of Heaven), only to re-merge ten years later. In addition, there were fourteen smaller Orthodox congregations by 1914. The splits reflected different Orthodox liturgies based on regional origins. Reform did gain a toehold, and, as Arthur Chiel (1920–83), rabbi of the Rosh Pina Synagogue, writes in *The Jews of Manitoba*, the Conservative movement made an imprint after World War II.

The key religious figure in the community was Israel Kahanovitch (1872–1945) who came from Belarus via the United States in 1907 as the rabbi of the Orthodox Beth Jacob Congregation and ultimately became chief rabbi of western Canada for thirty years. He was steadfast in his resolve to combat the politically radical forces in the community that sought to secularize Jewish education. Even so, he worked with his adversaries to create the United Hebrew Charities in 1912 and was a force in the creation of the Old Folks Home. He was recognized by Parks Canada in 2016 as "a person of historical significance," and a "seminal figure in the social, cultural and religious life of Western Canadian Jews," according to historian Allan Levine.[3]

Two Small Communities

Synagogues in smaller cities and towns were the central institutions in all Jewish communities. Saint John, as discussed in Chapter 2, emerged as the largest in the Maritimes before World War II, with 848 members in 1921 representing 1.8 per cent of the city's residents. Its first congregation, Achavath Achim (Brotherly Love) built a synagogue in 1898, when the community numbered approximately two hundred souls. It cost $10,000, a huge sum that relied on contributions from local Christians and from the Jewish communities in Boston and New York. A second synagogue opened in 1908 on Hazen Avenue, known as the "Deutche (German) Shul," which split due to disagreements between its Russian and central European members. By 1920 the three synagogues, amalgamated, bought a church, and established the Shaarey Zedek (Gates of the Righteous). It was Orthodox, the denomination that was ubiquitous in small towns.

Owen Sound, at the entrance to Georgian Bay in Ontario, was a frontier boom town at the turn of the twentieth century due to its port and railhead. A synagogue opened in 1904 when there were only a few Jews who had opened businesses in the downtown area. Its population crested at seventy-two in 1921, which was sufficient to support an itinerant rabbi-teacher. Its current synagogue, *Beth Ezekiel*, was purchased in 1946 on a site that had been a church. Still in operation, it is designated as a historical site.

CHARITIES

In the first quarter of the twentieth century, synagogues remained the most significant Jewish organizations in Canada, but some Jews were not members and/or not pious. Yet, the commandments to tend to those in need and to love the stranger as oneself, that is, the act of *tsedakah* (charity), a central tenet, was respected regardless of religious adherence. It was mandatory throughout history not only because of Jewish heritage but because the state did not provide social welfare until the early twentieth century. A fraction of the upper middle class in Britain and the United States undertook the effort to provide for those most in need. They created fraternal societies and Christian organizations. Women were especially important in these endeavours. We see the impact of these groups on the nascent Jewish community in Canada, which coupled the commandment to charity with Victorian sensibilities to respond to the needs of impoverished immigrants. These charities expanded their activities during the Great Migration. Yet it was the immigrants themselves who undertook much of the responsibility for welfare, creating communal institutions and associations based on places of European origin and linked to social and ideological groups. The spectrum of these charitable organizations was vital to the betterment of Jewish life in the Diaspora.

Benevolent Societies

Montreal's Hebrew Philanthropic Society founded in 1847 the first Jewish charitable organization. As the need increased with immigrants from central Europe, a group of thirty men, drawn from the two major synagogues, founded the YMHBS in 1863. In the 1890s the Baron de Hirsch Society in Montreal promoted Jewish agricultural settlement of the Prairies and training for trades, and its building housed several other charitable organizations. The Anglo-Jewish Association was founded in 1880 in Toronto and Montreal to aid British Jews in dealing with the large migration from eastern Europe.

Winnipeg's Hebrew Benevolent Society emerged in 1884 in response to the first Russian immigrants. Its equivalent in Toronto had been founded in 1882 by members from Holy Blossom Synagogue. Generosity was tempered by Victorian attitudes that relief should be limited to avoid fostering dependence. Nevertheless, these societies provided a framework for the creation of future communal institutions that provided services to the mass of immigrants arriving in the subsequent decades.

Women's Organizations

The role of middle-class Jewish women in providing welfare and creating institutions to care for the elderly, indigent, and sick in their midst was indispensable in the overall effort. In Montreal, the Ladies' Hebrew Benevolent Society was founded in 1877 to oversee the burial of Jewish poor and those who succumbed to tuberculosis, and to establish orphanages. In Toronto, the Toronto Hebrew Ladies Sick and Benevolent Society was organized in 1868 to provide loans, funeral expenses, and support for bereaved families. It changed its name to the Ladies Montefiore Hebrew Benevolent Society two years later and expanded its activities.

Mount Sinai Hospital

A crying need for Jewish immigrants was proper medical care. Hospitals were, in fact, inhospitable institutions. They were regarded as places where one went to die. Women were particularly averse to them, preferring home care, and for those in labour, support from the Jewish Maternity Aid Society. Hospitals did not provide kosher food, their staffs did not understand Yiddish, they tended to be intolerant of immigrants in general, and they would not hire Jewish doctors, despite the high number of graduates. At the University of Toronto's Medical School, Jewish enrolment rose from 2 per cent in 1910 to an astonishing 25 per cent in 1932. Upon graduation, however, the graduates faced extreme discrimination. They would not be hired as interns by local hospitals, necessitating finding residencies in the United States. Jewish doctors opened their facilities in immigrant neighborhoods, especially because Anglo-Saxon practitioners would not accept impoverished immigrants. Consequently, four women started *Ezras Noshim* (Ladies Aid) in 1913 to perform the divine commandment of visiting the sick and providing care to children and households. The organization quickly attracted new members and they were able to raise the funds for the first ethnically distinct home for the aged in Ontario in 1917.

Ezras Noshim then embarked on a project for a Jewish hospital initiated by a midwife, Dorothy Dworkin, the formidable community leader Ida Siegel, and Slova Greenberg. By 1922 the society had raised $12,000 in down payment for a former private hospital on Yorkville Avenue. Its obstacles, however, were not confined to converting the building to a general hospital, but also to gaining the trust of immigrants and the acceptance of the Jewish elite. These impediments were overcome with support from Jewish doctors and Ida Siegel's influence in the F JP. Nevertheless, the board of the hospital, which admitted only four women, insisted on the transfer of control from Ezras Noshim. The hospital opened its doors to Canadians, irrespective of origin, and became a welcome place for all immigrants. As journalist Lesley Marrus Barsky points out,[4] Mount Sinai's creation was due to the efforts of Jewish women and Jewish doctors in finding a solution to the exclusion of the community by the Anglo establishment that dominated Toronto. In Montreal, where discrimination closed the doors to Jewish doctors like it did in Toronto and throughout Canada, the Jewish General Hospital was established in 1934, with a bequest from business magnate Sir Mortimer Davis who had died in 1928.

Hadassah

During World War I, Canadians rallied to the cause both in the field of war and at home. Jewish women contributed on behalf of Canadian combatants and to the Jewish settlement in Palestine which was then under Turkish control. Their efforts brought influential women together in the Canadian Red Cross and veterans associations. It also led to the founding of the Canadian Women's International Zionist Organization (WIZO)/Hadassah (the Hebrew word for compassion) organization in 1921. WIZO had begun in Britain and Hadassah in the United States. The charity first attracted middle-class women across the country who formed local chapters, and soon immigrant women came on board. It was initially designed to raise funds for settlers in Palestine, especially regarding education and agricultural development. Over time, it also became involved with childcare, health, and women's issues in Canada. Hadassah's impact in Winnipeg, for example, was notable. Within the first four years, ten chapters had been formed with one thousand members. Almost immediately, Hadassah became the pre-eminent Jewish women's organization in Canada and worldwide. This reflected the commitment by middle-class women to welfare, and to the rapid acculturation of immigrant women. At its height in 1967, it had sixteen thousand members in 304 chapters in Canada alone. A feature of Toronto's community calendar was the Hadassah Bazaar held on the grounds of the National Exhibition. Thousands of Torontonians flocked to buy used clothes and household items and to munch on Jewish delicacies. Female students at North Toronto Collegiate in the 1970s would skip school to shop for bargains and munch on exotic food. Very few were Jewish.

Lillian Freiman (née Bilsky, 1885–1940) was a philanthropist and communal activist. Born in the logging town of Mattawa, Ontario, her family prospered and moved to Ottawa, as perhaps the first Jews to settle there. When eighteen, she married businessman Archie J. Freiman, and the couple moved in the highest social circles in the capital. Archie came to head the ZOC. Lillian threw herself into the war effort

Lillian Freiman

Source: Alex Dworkin Canadian Jewish Archives

volunteering for the Canadian Veterans Association and numerous Ottawa social welfare initiatives as well as Jewish welfare. In 1918 she chaired the city's response to the flu pandemic that killed more people worldwide than did the war. She campaigned to bring in 2,000 Jewish war orphans, but the government permitted fewer than 150, a harbinger of future government policy regarding Jewish refugees. Freiman emerged as the leader of WIZO/Hadassah and barnstormed across the country raising funds from Canadians of all faiths for Palestine, especially the initiative to bring European youth, living under the spectre of antisemitism, to the colony. Her untimely death at fifty-five was a blow for all Canadians.

In contrast to Freiman's standing in the social elite, Annie Ross (1911–98) was born in a Russian village and arrived in Winnipeg in 1921. Growing up in the impoverished North End, she set her sights on medicine but lacking the financial resources, entered the nursing program at Winnipeg General Hospital, the only Jewish woman in a class of sixty. She was hired by the Mount Carmel Clinic in 1948, having advanced her training to Xray and lab analysis. She became the executive director and served in that capacity for thirty-seven years, advocating a holistic approach to health that encompassed physical, emotional, and social well-being. Historian Allan Levine notes that "Ross's combative spirit and endless energy ... won her numerous awards, including the Order of Canada."[5]

Fraternal Organizations

A common feature of middle-class life in the United States in the nineteenth century was joining a fraternal organization. These attracted men who created chapters linked to national organizations that espoused the principle of serving the community while inculcating a spirit of male friendship that included sports and other forms of recreation. They not only fostered male bonhomie but cemented business relationships. Among the organizations were the Odd Fellows, Shriners, and Masons. One could say that they were the "LinkedIn" of that time. While these organizations were aimed at English-speaking Americans, they came to be popular with established Jews who desperately wanted to fit into the mainstream. Yet, the needs of Jewish immigrants were not the raison d'être of these societies. To meet this specific need, a small group of recent German Jewish immigrants in New York met to deal with the appalling conditions of Jews in America. They called themselves "Sons of the Covenant," translated from the German. Soon after they adopted the Hebrew translation, *B'nai Brith*, and opened lodges across the country.

B'nai Brith made its foray into Canada in 1875. Its first lodge, number 242, was founded by members of Holy Blossom and served the same purpose as the Hebrew Benevolent Association, with essentially the same membership, but linked to its American partner. In time lodges sprang up throughout the country and were especially active in smaller communities. While B'nai Brith served Canadian Jews in similar ways to other charities, it also found new avenues of providing a measure of comfort. One example was establishing summer camps for boys and girls, serving southern Ontario in 1909, Montreal in 1921, Ottawa in 1944, and Winnipeg in 1954. In the interwar period, the organization responded to antisemitic acts, advocated on behalf of the community in matters of social welfare, and was heralded as being a grass roots collective. It was the first national Jewish organization in Canada, albeit one that was linked to its American forerunner and to its contemporaries in other countries.

Landsmanschaften

Most immigrants were not attracted to membership in the benevolent societies due to the barriers of social class and language. Instead, they turned to their European roots, where their place of origin and/or political orientation served to bring them together. The concept of chain migration, whereby immigrants from the same place follow one another to their new home, was central to the process of settlement and adaptation. When a significant number of arrivals from the same town, city, or region settled, they created mutual benefit societies. For others, the link was political ideology. In some cases, it was a mixture of the two. The first of these were called *landsmanschaften* (societies of people from the same place). They were established throughout the immigrant Diaspora and were a vital facet of communal life. They operated on the basic principle that members would contribute what they could to a collective "bank" and that the proceeds would be lent to those in need at extremely low rates of interest. They undertook to help the newcomers with housing, employment, and education, and visited and served those in need. "Lodge doctors" provided their services to their members. Their social role brought members to one another's homes, local halls, and in some cases, to small synagogues that they established. Most established plots in Jewish cemeteries.

Clearly, mutual benefit societies based on place of origin could only exist where there were enough settlers. Consequently, they were a prominent piece of the adaptation process that was limited to Montreal, Toronto, and Winnipeg. Winnipeg established thirty-two societies between 1906 and 1920, and a further twenty-one by the late 1930s. Writer Erna Paris notes that "the *landsmanschaften* were central to the psychological well being of the community ... provided their members ... a soothing balm for frazzled nerves ... [where] at meetings one could catch up on the latest news from the old *stetl*, sigh over or laugh at a common remembrance."[6] In Toronto, immigrants from the Polish town of Ilza created the Drildzer (the Yiddish name for the town) Society in 1921. The town was so obscure that one would have difficulty finding it on a map, yet it was almost entirely Jewish until the migration. Its members built its first synagogue, *Anshei Drildz* (People of Drildz) in the Spadina neighbourhood in 1932. The society still exists, as do many other landsmanschaften, primarily to maintain connections between the families of the founders. They raise funds for the community and for Israel, and host speakers about Jewish topics. Only the oldest members, the children or grandchildren of the first cohort, may still be conversant in Yiddish. With the arrival of Holocaust survivors, some of the societies were reinvigorated.

ZIONISM

The impact of Zionism in Canada was immediate and widespread creating two main organizations that coalesced to become the ZOC in 1919. From 1920 to 1934 it was Canada's sole national Jewish association.

Three central considerations materialize from the study of Zionism in Canada to 1945. The primary one is that the movement had widespread appeal. Its detractors were communists, Bundists, and, the Reform movement, who argued that Zionism would undermine the acceptance of Jews into Canadian society. The second reflection is that the ZOC was the product of the integration of two disparate groups. The first were members of the Jewish establishment, the children of immigrants who arrived from the 1850s to the 1880s and had attained social and economic status. It espoused general Zionism, a movement that was free of political ideology. The second group were the new immigrants, who were primarily concerned with the plight of the working class and were drawn to the relationship between socialism and Zionism. The third consideration that materializes is that the primary goals of Canadian Zionists were to promote the movement to Canadian political leaders, to support a Jewish state in Palestine, to join forces with the American Zionist Organization, and to raise funds for immigration to Palestine.

The initial driving force came from Clarence de Sola (1858–1920). His father, Abraham, was the renowned spiritual leader of Montreal's *Shearith Israel*. Clarence was a businessman who represented manufacturers and contractors. He had close ties with the Liberal Party, and it was during the tenure of Wilfrid Laurier that de Sola was appointed consul to Belgium. Although he mixed with the Anglo establishment, he remained devout and dedicated himself to aiding refugees who had fled the pogroms in Russia. On the heels of the First Zionist Convention in 1897, de Sola founded *Agudath Zion* (Zionist Society) of Montreal, and became president of the Federation of Zionist Societies in Canada (hereafter referred to as "the Federation") a year later. De Sola felt that, in the words of historian Gerald Tulchinsky, "Zionism could bring order out of the chaos and disunity which had held back Jews everywhere for many years."[7] He resigned his position in 1919 due to internal and external challenges and because of declining health.

Like de Sola, the leaders of the Federation were Montreal "uptowners." The most prominent were Lyon Cohen, Samuel Jacobs, and Sir Mortimer Davis. Cohen, an industrialist, factory owner, and publisher, was indisputably the most well-known Canadian Jew of his generation. Jacobs (1871–1938) was a lawyer, a member of parliament for twenty years, a noted orator, and according to Gerald Tulchinsky, "one of the most influential Jews of Canada."[8] Davis (1866–1928) was the president of Imperial Tobacco, the only Canadian Jew to have been knighted, and among the wealthiest Canadians. Historian Henry Srebrnik, in his valuable work, *Creating the Chupah,* notes that the Federation had a bureaucracy with annual conventions sending representatives to the World Zionist Congress." By 1907, there were chapters in forty-two cities and town in Canada."[9]

It was most effective in communities outside of Toronto and Montreal, which contributed 60 per cent of the membership, although they represented only 30 per cent of the Jewish population. Zionist societies were particularly noteworthy in the Prairies. Yorkton, Kamsack, and Prince Albert had societies by 1916, even though there were fewer than one hundred Jews in each of these Saskatchewan towns. From 1903 to 1905 the Federation debated choosing between "practical" Zionism and "political" Zionism. The former maintained that the homeland had to be Palestine. The latter argued that if the Palestine option proved to be not feasible, then another "territory" would have to be chosen. The Federation sided with the first option.

The Federation, however, did not meet the expectations of many poor immigrants. They regarded the Federation as an enclave of "uptowners" and its General Zionism as not addressing the fundamental concerns of the working class. They looked to the growing movement of Labour Zionism in Europe, which synthesized nationalist and political aspirations, claiming that class consciousness would give rise to national consciousness. Their organization, *Poalei Zion* ("Workers of Zion" – hereafter referred to as PZ) vied with the Federation and stopped attending its annual convention in 1909. Its own convention met on a Sabbath in 1910, which was the final break with the Federation.

World War I brought the division between the Federation and the PZ to a head. The immediate issue was loyalty to Britain. The anglicized Federation was devotedly pro-British. Others were more favourable to Germany, where the Jewish Enlightenment had begun, and Austria, the home of Zionism. Complicating the scene were the momentous events of 1917 – the Russian Revolution, and what it would portend for the safety of Jews, and the declaration by Lord Balfour, the British foreign secretary to Baron Rothschild, a leader of the British Jewry who stated,

"His Majesty's government view with favour the establishment in Palestine of a national home for the Jewish people."[10] Finally, the imperative to create a "congress" of Canadian Jews, one of whose goals was to provide a united voice to the Canadian government that, in the event of an Allied victory (which would include the demise of the Ottoman regime), serious consideration would be made to provide a homeland in Palestine. These developments motivated the Federation and PZ to press for the creation of the CJC in 1919, which ultimately unified the two factions.

Henry Srebrnik persuasively argues that de Sola's resignation in January 1919, just ahead of the convention that created the CJC, was due to the revolt of younger Montreal uptowners against the establishment. They were joined by community leaders Louis Finkelstein from Winnipeg, Archie Bennett from Toronto, and Archie J. Freiman of Ottawa, who sought to heal the rift with the immigrant community. These leaders realized that in 1919, with rising antisemitism in Canada and pogroms in Russia that had taken at least one hundred thousand Jewish lives, there was an existential threat to the remainder that overrode social and political divisions. With the consolidation between the Federation and the PZ at the convention in 1921, Freiman was elected president, and Davis and Cohen were honorary president and honorary vice-president, respectively. Freiman, a generation younger than Cohen and Davis, reflected the changing of the guard. In that year, there were 8,585 registered Zionists, in over three hundred communities, who had raised almost half a million dollars in the previous two years.

Unfortunately, from this height, the renamed Zionist Organization of Canada (ZOC) foundered. The postwar recession and the drop in immigration reduced fundraising. The organization embarked on ill-considered projects, the most damaging of which being a commitment to raise one million dollars to buy a stretch of land in Palestine that could not support agriculture. Despite pressure from Chaim Weizmann, the head of the World Zionist Organization (WZO) to accelerate contributions to the settlement, fund raising declined during the Great Depression. The ZOC's woes were exacerbated by divisive extremists. On the right were the "revisionists" who railed that the leadership in Palestine was too timid in retaliating against Arab attacks.

They gained adherents in the Jewish Diaspora largely due to the appeal of its leader, Vladimir Jabotinsky, a multilingual and fiery orator who toured Canada. On the extreme left was *Hashomer Hatzair* (the Young Guardians) that sought to merge Zionism with communism to create an ideal classless society. Buffeted by the Depression and these internal divisions, the ZOC survived, but its contribution to the Jewish settlement was limited and its influence on Canadian immigration policies was inconsequential.

Until the outbreak of World War II, the ZOC restricted its activity to fundraising. It did not promote immigration to Palestine, although it aided the small number who chose to do so. It played no role in determining Zionist thought and planning. Even its leaders rarely visited the *Yishuv* (the name given to the Jewish entity before it became Israel). Freiman only went once, although the organization would have expired without his leadership. When he died in 1944 at the age of 64, the situation was rapidly changing. At the end of the war, with the British Empire in disrepair, accompanied by the Cold War between the Soviet Union and its allies against the Western democracies, in tandem with the creation of the United Nations (UN), and the newly independent Arab states, the Zionist project faced an existential crisis. The threads of this story are continued in Chapter 8.

The significance of the Canadian Zionist movement to 1945 is that it succeeded in attracting the support of most of the Jewish population. Its rapid ascendance from 1897 to 1921 marked two important features of immigrant adaptation. The first was that the "uptowners" were the first non-Christians to gain a small measure of political influence, a major accomplishment for an ethno-cultural minority in Canada. They met with prime ministers, worked with the leaders of the Jewish Diaspora, and put Canada's Jews on the Jewish map. Second, the generations of Clarence de Sola and Archie J. Freiman achieved stature as Canadians, which was rare for those outside the orbit of the Anglo and French elites, although it had a marginal effect when it came to influencing the brazenly anti-Jewish immigration policy. Even so, the CJC folded after only three years, leaving the ZOC the only national organization of Canadian Jews from 1920 to 1934.

CANADIAN JEWISH CONGRESS

It would be tempting to state that a national Jewish community came into existence over a three-day period in March 1919, at the Monument National Theatre where 209 men were elected by 24,886 men representing local organizations as delegates to the meeting to create the CJC. They came from the five largest cities, with the remainder representing their province or region. In Toronto, for example, one hundred candidates competed for forty seats in a campaign replete with advertising and cars taking voters to the polls. Indicating the emergence of immigrants as a political force, most of the candidates were Yiddish speakers. The delegates represented the ideological spectrum of the community from General Zionists to Bundists (socialists). The enthusiasm and heightened expectations of those days, however, were illusory. Congress faltered and dissolved three years later. It was reinvigorated in 1933 but did not assert itself as a national force in the community for another five years. The factors leading to its creation, its initial period of operation, and its ascendance just before the outbreak of World War II are found in Chapter 6.

The idea of a Jewish Congress first appeared in 1908 when the PZ appealed for a "World Jewish Parliament." Four years later, Reuben Brainin, the editor of the *Canadian Eagle*, began to advocate for a national congress. It led to an alliance of left-wing groups that was opposed by the Federation. The alliance hosted a meeting of delegates representing two hundred groups in Montreal in February 1916, calling for a Canadian "congress" as part of an international organization that would represent world Jewry at the peace conference after the war, meet with the Canadian government to press for continued immigration, support Jews in war-torn Europe and Palestine, and cooperate with the Federation.

The impetus for these developments was the precarious situation for Jews in Europe and Palestine during World War I. Eastern Europe, where most Jews still lived, was the zone of confrontation between Germany and its allies against Russia. Jews were caught between the warring factions, their loyalties divided, their members serving in the armies of all the combatants. The Ottoman Empire, a German ally, included

Palestine, fomenting apprehension over its fate if Germany triumphed. The Balfour Declaration gave Jews hope that there might be a homeland in Palestine, but the Jewish colony was imperiled by a rising Arab nationalism that led to anti-Jewish riots. To complicate the unease, the Russian Revolution led to a bloody civil war that did not end until 1922. In its wake, Jews were the targets of the competing factions, unleashing the largest pogroms since the seventeenth century.

The events of 1917 and the defeat of Germany and its allies the following year created a momentum in the Jewish Diaspora to build a unified voice in preparation for the peace conferences. It began with the founding of the American Jewish Congress in December 1918, which was attended by Canadian observers. Soon after, congress committees in Toronto and Montreal prepared for the Canadian version. The Federation joined the movement, and the range of ideological groups took the initiative to register their voices. Every adult Canadian Jew was eligible to vote upon paying 10 cents to register. The ballot was secret.

At the Monument National Theatre, on Montreal's Main, Lyon Cohen gave the keynote address and was elected as the chair. He spoke of the condition of eastern European Jews and the endorsement of the British Government to create a national homeland in Palestine.[11] Cohen's support of the movement removed some of the obstacles raised by the Jewish elite. His vice chairs, from Montreal, Toronto, and Winnipeg, were community leaders. Cohen and his cohort were elevated to the positions of president and vice-president respectively following the congress.

CJC resolved to cooperate with other Jewish congresses and the World Zionist Organization in persuading the Paris Peace Conference to recognize the historic claims to Palestine and in calling for the removal of ethnic discrimination in the new states being formed by the League of Nations from the defeated German, Austrian, Russian, and Ottoman empires. CJC determined that Jews were a national entity in Canada, but a more radical proposal that Jews be recognized as a national minority was not adopted. The CJC was sensitive to the rising wave of nativism and isolationism that would curb Jewish immigration. In response, it created the JIAS, which became the central agency to facilitate immigration and provide aid to the settlers. JIAS (the word "society" was eventually changed to "services") not only outlived CJC's first iteration but continues its important work to the present.

Despite the heady few months following its founding, cracks began to appear. The initial enthusiasm waned as the postwar recession, labour unrest, and protest parties rocked the Dominion. Fund raising was inadequate. H.M. Caiserman, the congress secretary and a moving force behind its creation, worked without a salary. As loyal as he was to the cause, as a recent immigrant, he did not have the clout to stop its dissolution. The reality was that after the inaugural meeting, an organizational structure was not created to effectuate the aims of its founders.

Meanwhile the aims of the World Jewish Congress to influence the peace makers came to naught. While minority rights in the new nations were promised, they were not fulfilled. The British Mandate in Palestine had to mediate between the small number of Jewish settlers and the Arab majority. The collapse of the Russian and Ottoman empires unleashed an orgy of bloodshed, much of it directed against Jewish communities. In Canada, the new Liberal government headed by William Lyon Mackenzie King took power in 1921 and inaugurated draconian immigration restrictions.

With congress dormant and the ZOC relatively ineffectual, the national voice was mute through the rest of the 1920s. With the collapse of the global economic system in 1929, Canadian Jewish organizations had to deal with the daily survival of its constituents. International developments, as they affected the Jewish world, were put on the back burner. This changed in January 1933 with the seizure of power by the National Socialist Workers Party (Nazi) in Germany. The alarm within world Jewry was palpable. In Canada it was exacerbated by the rapid rise in antisemitism. The trigger was a protest in April 1933 by young French-Canadian intellectuals, supported by public opinion and the French language media, in favour of the Nazi takeover, and led by Raoul Dandurand, a senator and former president of the League of Nations. This visceral reaction led to a reconvening of CJC in 1934. Its purpose was no less than to advocate on behalf of Canadian Jewry in the face of discrimination, to lobby the Canadian government to relax its immigration restrictions, and to take a hard line against Germany.

The reinvigorated congress was dominated by its patrons in Montreal. It had lofty goals that included regional organizations in Toronto and western Canada, and it tried to control the work of the Jewish federations there. But, as before, there was little money, with only a skeletal staff lodged in Montreal. It foundered until 1938 when two developments changed its course. The first was the death of its president, Samuel Jacobs, a former member of parliament. The search for a successor led to the door of Samuel Bronfman, one of the wealthiest individuals in the country, a man of unbounded determination and an irrepressible ego. Despite a checkered business past he took control and would not brook any opposition. The second was the creation of the Joint Public Relations Committee (JPRC), a venture undertaken by community leaders from CJC, B'nai Brith, and the ZOC. In short order, the JPRC worked with other ethnocultural organizations and church groups, thereby heightening the posture of CJC so that at the outbreak of World War II, CJC had become the primary association advocating on behalf of Canada's Jews. The unsung force in congress was Montreal's Hannaniah Meir (H.M.) Caiserman (1884–1950) a multilingual labour leader, Zionist, and the general secretary of the CJC from its founding, through its re-establishment, until his death, for a period of thirty-one years. He was also an essayist and compiler of the works of Canadian Yiddish writers. He travelled to Europe after World War II to orchestrate the relief and rescue of Jewish survivors, and to Latin America and Palestine to report on Jewish life there. He was an indefatigable force, dedicating his life to these causes.

FEDERATIONS

By 1914 the interwoven fabric of Jewish welfare provided by synagogues, charities, and fraternal and political organizations resulted in a chaotic situation for the burgeoning Jewish communities in Toronto and Montreal. The divide between the established middle class and the mass of working-class immigrants was the root of the problem. The former had the means and therefore wanted control; the latter had the needs but not a voice. The conglomerate of Jewish organizations, each with their agenda(s), relied on raising funds to provide services. The Great Depression caused those funds to dry up and the need for welfare to grow. Complicating the situation was that fundraising and providing services were largely done by volunteers. This proved to be wholly inadequate, but hiring professional social workers was opposed by the organizations that were still operating on the Victorian or European models of charity from above. Further complicating the picture was the re-establishment of the CJC in 1933, with its national office in Montreal, and smaller centres across Canada, which demanded a major role because of its role in providing financial support to the federations. The changing demographic composition of immigrant neighbourhoods and the crushing impact of the Depression resulted in the creation of a new organizational structure – local Jewish federations.

Jewish federations originated in the United States in the late nineteenth century. They were the product of two social movements. The first social movement was created by the absence of state intervention in providing social services for the neediest, inspiring local groups to fill the need. While fraternal organizations came to the fore, the increasing demand came to be met by organizations staffed by professionals rather than volunteers. Social work became an academic field and by 1873, with the founding of the National Confederation of Social Work, the basis for the provision of social services emerged. The second social movement leading to Jewish federation formation was the inability of existing communities to respond to the needs of the numerous newcomers. American Jews numbered two hundred thousand in 1870, were multiplied fivefold by 1900, and thirty years later, totalled approximately four million. Consequently, Jewish federations that arose in the 1890s adopted the principles of the local networks – fundraising and allocation under the direction of professional social workers and administrators. During the Great Depression, 85 per cent of American Jews received aid from Jewish federations.

THE TORONTO MODEL

The most comprehensive examination of local federations is Jack Lipinsky's work, *Imposing Their Will: An Organizational History of Jewish Toronto, 1933–1948*. Its thesis is that a unified Jewish federation was imposed by the socio-economic elite despite the objections of the immigrant community. In the 1920s the proliferation of synagogues, fraternal organizations, and charities that vied for power and influence represented cultural, religious, and economic forces antithetical to and disrespectful of the needs of immigrants.

The first local networks were in Toronto: the FJP in 1916, with male representatives from the two dominant congregations, and the Ladies' Montefiore Society, which dated to the Victorian era, but both lacked an up-to-date infrastructure. Further, CJC's creation in 1921 of the JIAS, which was primarily responsible for settlement, "was and remains central to this issue but its inception was a further impediment to FJPs attempt to consolidate control and highlighted [its] considerable inadequacies in other areas."[12]

During the Great Depression, the FJP was overly reliant on a small group of affluent donors. It had adopted the American model of professionalism, but many of the social workers were not native Yiddish speakers and consequently were viewed as outsiders by the immigrant community. Wider community organizations, including the Family Welfare Bureau, were also in dire straits due to the global economic collapse, and could not contribute to the FJP. Meanwhile the core fraternal associations continued to cater to the requirements of their own members.

The turning point was hiring Martin Cohn in 1932 as director of the FJP. He exemplified the progressive wedge that reshaped communal organizations.[13] His task was compounded with the resurrection of CJC in 1933, whose Montreal leadership was dismissed in Toronto. It was only when CJC teamed with B'nai Brith Canada to create the Public Relations Committee in 1938 in response to the virulent antisemitism that had arisen in Canada that CJC found its niche. In the meantime, Cohn countered by appealing to the wealthiest families, the uptowners, to use their influence to unify the community. Consequently, United Jewish Welfare Fund (UJWF) of Toronto was created and constituent organizations could join for a nominal fee of $5. In Lipinsky's words, the UJWF had "imposed its will" on the community. In 1944, affiliated with the city's Community Chest, thereby overcoming the parochial divisions of the previous generation.

The UJWF was able to impose its will for two reasons. The first was the impact of the Great Depression. It became clear that multiple aid societies could not rise to the challenge of the economic collapse. While many survived, some until today, the need for a professional organization that was part of the larger civic community could not be denied. The second factor was that by 1939 Jews were no longer a predominantly immigrant community. More had been born or raised in Canada than in Europe, and many had adapted to the Canadian lifestyle. While they still participated in the spectrum of Jewish religious observances, political orientation, and class and gender consciousness, they were unified in their aspiration to play a part in the local, national, and international challenges that faced Canadians as a whole.

The Toronto model was mirrored elsewhere. Montreal established the first federation in 1916, the FJP, to centralize administrative services, including the fee collection and accounting that oversaw a dozen constituent agencies, such as the Jewish Public Library, a health clinic, and the Montreal Mount Sinai Hospital for tuberculosis care. Its scope expanded to a home for the aged, the Jewish General Hospital, an enlarged YM-YWHA, and the Jewish Vocational Service. In 1941, the Combined Jewish Appeal was created as the vehicle for raising funds for the Federation.

Winnipeg's situation was like that of Toronto, with a division between the middle-class South End and the working-class North End. They were brought together to create the United Hebrew Charity in 1910 to dispense services to immigrants. Eventually, in 1937, it morphed into the Jewish Welfare Fund, which received contributions from about 20 per cent of the Jewish population of the city. It oversaw a spectrum of smaller institutions and relief organizations including the Canadian Jewish Orphanage founded in 1912, the Home for the Aged founded in 1919, and the Mount Carmel Clinic founded in 1926. Yet, it was CJC that united the two social classes. With its reconstitution in 1933, its elected officials from Winnipeg created the Western Canadian Jewish Congress Committee.

Calgary's Jewish population of 1,600 in 1931 represented 2 per cent of the Canadian total, following the pattern of Jewish settlement of the Prairies at the turn of the twentieth century. Nestled in the downtown commercial district, its residents established the Beth Jacob Synagogue in 1911 and the House of Israel in 1935. A Talmud Torah and a Peretz School served the children of the religious and non-observant Jewish families by 1928. The community was an outlier in that its Jewish Community Council remained in place until the 1960s.

Edmonton's Jewish community was somewhat smaller, with 1,400 residents in 1941, 1.5 per cent of the total. Its *Beth Israel* Congregation had its origins in 1906 when there were a handful of pioneers. Beth Shalom, the first conservative congregation in western Canada, was founded in

1928, although its synagogue was not built until 1933. The Edmonton Jewish Federation was established in 1937 to oversee fund raising and communal welfare. Jewish organizational life in Vancouver was remarkable in its breadth and depth.

Despite a rather meager 2,450 residents in 1931, representing less than 1 per cent of the city, the community boasted eleven major organizations including the Vancouver Jewish Community Chest, organized in 1924 as the first central fundraising body. The Toronto federation model was also adopted in midsize Ontario communities. The Hamilton Jewish Federation was established in 1934 as a fundraising arm for community relations, education, and welfare. But, as in Winnipeg, its connection to CJC was more vital, largely due to the tension between the community and the Christian majority over religious instruction in public schools and exclusion from public recreation. London's Jewish Community Council was formed in 1933 to link twelve Jewish organizations including the first cemetery and synagogue, which had been established in the 1880s. Windsor's Jewish Community Council was founded in 1938 to coordinate fundraising and projects as well as to mitigate a division between religious and non-observant Jews, which continued to fester until the 1950s. By 1945 its predominant goal was to raise funds for Israel. An exception to the Toronto model was Ottawa's *Va'ad Ha'Ir* (community council), which was created in 1933 as a union of the city's synagogues to oversee religious education and fundraising.

CONCLUSION

Jewish organizations are historically woven into Jewish life. From synagogues and ideological and welfare societies, to congresses at the international and national level, to local federations, Jews are joiners. This arises from their faith, the commandment to help others, the need to protect themselves in inhospitable surroundings, and, in modern times, the call to embrace political and nationalist ideals. The creation of Jewish organizations in Canada was a chance to meld tradition with modernity, during a period of rapid growth when the community had grown tenfold between 1901 and 1931. It required them to adapt, whether as descendants of first settlers or recent immigrants. The plethora of organizations reflected the diversity of the community in all its religious, political, and nationalist and cultural elements. With the solidification of the ZOC and CJC, and the consolidation of social services under the auspices of local federations, it can be argued that a national community, bolstered, rather than hindered by its diversity, had been erected by the 1940s.

The Ward/Kensington. Sample ward house c. 1910

Source: Ontario Jewish Archives

CHAPTER SIX

The Socio-Political Landscape: Workers, Liberals, Reformers, Radicals, Rogues

From the Great Migration through World War II, Canadian Jews were buffeted by national and international developments at an accelerated rate. Many came from a highly politicized environment with rigid ideologies and practices that would be tested in the turbulent interwar era. Politics were enmeshed in the workplace, on the street, within families, in religious practice, and in gender and ethnic affiliation. Jews were more drawn to the Liberal Party than to the Conservatives, and more likely to support reform and radical political alternatives than Canadians in general. Further, there were those who did not abide by the accepted mores of most Canadians. This range of the political landscape was a product of adaptation and was representative of the increasing diversity of the community.

Canadian Jews' participation in Canadian politics and social movements stemmed from their European heritage in combination with their occupations, social class, gender, and ethnic identification. They struggled to merge ethnicity with nationality, to blend the political traditions of Europe with the Canadian environment, to adjust to the restrictions placed upon them because of their otherness, and to contend with the imposition of a rigid and patriarchal social and religious hierarchy that stultified all Canadians.

The chapter opens with Jewish participation in organized labour, its connection to political developments, and its role in class, gender, and ethnic identification in the urban workplace. It continues with Jewish participation in the political arena, as liberals, reformers, and radicals. It concludes with those who chose to disassociate themselves from mainstream Canadians, who existed on the margins of society as criminals, who straddled the law, and who engaged in pursuits contrary to the norms of traditional Jewish life. The term "rogues" is applied to this cohort.

THE LABOUR MOVEMENT

Workers organizing for their rights have a long historical heritage in Western civilization, beginning with the guilds in the Middle Ages. Although the Canadian economy at the time of Confederation was still primarily based on staples (extracting natural resources), workers in specific fields, such as mining, shoemaking, and needle trades, had been joining together to protect their interests since the 1840s. Workers' societies, associations, and unions, mainly among those in skilled trades, had been created. Their conflict with management often led to strikes, which were sometimes violent, but progressively became a feature of Canadian life. With the onset of industrialization, women and children were increasingly relied upon as sources of cheap labour, especially in the shoe and clothing industries. By the 1880s, women represented 15 per cent of the workforce. In that decade, working-class militancy had coalesced under the Order of the Knights of Labour, which sought to organize all workers. By 1902 the Order had organized locals in 83 Ontario towns, 64 in Quebec, and across the Prairies to the Pacific coast. Organized labour helped elect a reformer, W.H. Howland, as mayor of Toronto in 1885. Yet, unity was ephemeral, riven by workers collaborating with manufacturers, the impact of socialism, and ethnic and religious hostilities within the workplace.

Labour's growth was accelerated by the Great Migration. Jewish participation in secondary manufacturing was an important component as many Jews drew on their experiences as industrial workers in Europe where they had been imbued with the zeal for reform. As immigrants settled almost exclusively in cities, almost half found employment in the clothing industry.

Unions competed among themselves to attract workers. The most prominent clothing unions originated in the United States. They included the Journeymen Tailors Union of America, founded in the United States in 1883 and in Toronto in 1891; the United Garment Workers (UGW) (1891, 1894); the Amalgamated Clothing Workers (ACW) (1914, 1915); and the most powerful, the International Ladies' Garment Workers Union (ILGWU) (1900, 1903). Canadian rivals did not emerge until a generation later. The Industrial Union of Needle Trade Workers (IUNTW) was established by the Communist Party of Canada (CPC) in 1928. The much smaller National Clothing Workers of Canada (NCWC) began in 1934.

In Toronto by 1914 there were three divisive issues that had an impact on organized Jewish labour. The first was that some of the employers were Jewish. Among them were those with similar activist principles, as many had once been workers and had accumulated the capital to go out on their own. They often belonged to the same Jewish organizations as their employees. The establishment of the Labour Lyceum (the Jewish workers home) was made possible by contributions from unions and Jewish manufacturers, despite class distinctions between the two groups. Nevertheless, disputes arose, and when strikes were called, some Jewish manufacturers hired strike breakers. Others would not hire Jews because they were regarded as more militant than non-Jews.

The second divisive factor was the conflict between Jewish and non-Jewish employees. Some non-Jewish owners fomented animosity between the two groups. In some strikes, only the Jewish workers walked out, for which they were maligned by their fellow workers and in the local press. The third factor was the competition between the IUNTW and the other unions. The IUNTW fought for its place in the labour movement by adopting a "dual union policy," whereby its members could work together with those of other unions in the same factory. This created divisions among Jewish workers (most of the IUNTW was Jewish, but most of the non-Jews belonged to the American-based unions). In one instance, Max Tohn of the IUNTW was delivering copies of the Jewish Communist newspaper, *Der Kampf* (the struggle), at the Shiffer-Hillman factory in Toronto in 1931, which had a dual union membership. The predominant union there, the ACW, sought to have Tohn fired. When the communist faction threatened a walkout, the owner relented. In defiance of this decision, the ACW faction went on strike. After two months, the owner capitulated to the ACW demands and the communists were locked out. Historian Ruth Frager relates this story in her seminal work, *Sweatshop Strife: Class, Ethnicity and Gender in the Jewish Labour Movement in Toronto*: "the fight between the Communists and the anti-Communists obviously provided the owner ... with a fine opportunity to play off one group of unionists against the other. Since both groups were dependent on courting the boss's favour, he was in a good position to manipulate the situation to his own advantage."[1]

Organized labour made its greatest impact when workers went on strike. With respect to Jewish workers in the needle trades, two instances in particular stand out, the first in Toronto and the second in Montreal.

Timothy Eaton emigrated from northern Ireland and established a dry goods store in St. Mary's, Ontario in 1860 and then a clothing outlet on Yonge Street in Toronto. His innovations included providing refunds, expanding his enterprise into a general store, and creating a mail-order enterprise (the "Eaton's Catalogue") whereby the company became Canada's dominant commercial enterprise. By 1911, it had seventeen thousand employees, and its flagship store in Toronto was adjacent to four factories in the Ward. Eaton's was the primary cloakmaker in the city, and most of its employees were Jewish. While the company boasted that it had modern ventilation and fire prevention facilities, its detractors claimed that workers in the clothing factories stood at their machines for sixty hours a week, and women and children replaced higher waged male workers. Conditions rose to a head in February 1912 when sixty-five employees staged a sit-down strike and were fired. In sympathy, under the direction of the ILGWU, most of the workers, especially Jews, struck in solidarity, but most non-Jews remained on the job. Even pro-labour publications, while supporting the strike, excoriated the Jewish workers as foreign troublemakers and that "a dirty Jew is about the dirtiest specimen of humanity in the world."[2] In addition, the suffragette movement was unwilling to support the strike because of the Jews. Given these fissures, the strikers were forced to return after four months with little gain and Eaton's refused to hire any more Jewish workers. Yet, labour militancy only grew. Ruth Frager notes that there were thirty-eight strikes in the needle trades between 1918 and 1936 in Toronto, with between seventy-five and two strikers. In approximately half of these disputes, the strikes were successful.

Sadie Hoffman came to Canada from Russia as a child in 1905. Influenced by her radical sister, she marched during the Eaton strike. At the age of thirteen, she started work in a box factory and then sewed uniforms during World War I. She joined the ACW but left it for the fledgling Communist Party in 1923. Her commitment involved unionizing workplaces, picketing (for which she was arrested), and mobilizing women over consumer issues. Hoffman helped establish the Jewish Women's Labour League (*Arbeiter Froyen Fareyn*). Her contemporary, Molly Fineberg, came to Toronto at the age of twenty. Like Hoffman, when she had her own family, she left the workplace but was active in organizing strikes; however, she broke ranks with Hoffman's radical political orientation. Fineberg was an important figure in the Workers' Circle (*Arbeiter Ring*), which represented Bundists, the Jewish socialists. Another leading figure was the activist, Leah Stern, unusual in that she was an Orthodox Jew.

The Eaton's strike was one of a rash of protests in the clothing industry in 1912. In June, agitating for better working conditions and higher wages, Jewish clothing workers in Montreal walked out. In this instance, many of the manufacturers were Jewish. Supported by the left-wing Zionist workers and Jewish socialist workers movements, the workers were organized by the UGW. In response four manufacturers moved their factories to small towns in Quebec, while some others employed strike breakers and gangsters, many Jewish, creating long lasting diversions. The strike ended with a partial victory, reducing hours without lowering wages.

Tulchinsky writes that "H.M. Caiserman was the real inspiration for the strike."[3] Caiserman, introduced in the previous chapter, was, in 1912, a twenty-six-year-old recent immigrant from Romania. He quickly became a leader in UGW locals in Montreal, which were aligned with the Labour Zionists (*Poalei Zion*), and when the strike broke out Caiserman was joined by important Jewish professional and cultural leaders, including Reuben Brainin, the editor of the *Canadian Eagle*, and Peter Bercovitch, a lawyer who became a member of the provincial legislature.

The height of labour unrest in Canada occurred in the wake the Russian Revolution of 1917 and because of the postwar economic recession. The overthrow of the Czarist regime by the Bolsheviks produced a "red scare" in western Europe and North America, marked by a fear that such an occurrence would be replicated by radical "foreign" agents, creating an anti-immigrant backlash. The slow reorganization from a war-time to a peace-time economy accelerated the economic downturn. Wages were slashed and workers were laid off. On May 1, 1919, Winnipeg building trades workers walked out, followed by workers in many other fields. The momentum was rapid, resulting in a General Strike within two weeks. As many as thirty-five thousand workers participated, approximately 20 per cent of the city's population. In response, a Citizens' Committee of one thousand was formed, condemning the action as a "deliberate, criminal and fantastic attempt to make a revolution,"[4] especially citing the predominantly immigrant North End, even though the instigators were British-born reformers. A special police force and the Royal North West Mounted Police raided labour halls and homes to arrest suspected leaders. In this action, one person was killed and thirty were injured.

Much of the anti-immigrant hysteria was levelled against Jews, both because of their large representation in the labour force, and because "Bolshevism" was thought to have been an instrument in the non-existent "international Jewish conspiracy" to control the world. Further, antisemitism within the labour movement had arisen as Jews emphasized their Jewish as well as their class identity. The police raided the Liberty Temple, a centre of Jewish Marxism, and the Chief Press Censor of Canada tried to close left-wing Yiddish newspapers. These anti-Jewish feelings existed, even though at least one Jew was on the Citizens' Committee, while several were on the Strike Committee, notably A.A. Heaps. Heaps, a socialist, and three Jewish communist figures were arrested. One of them was Louis Kon (born Konarski, he used aliases including Koniatski and Kohn), who had participated in the general strike in St. Petersburg in 1905 as part of the abortive attempt to overthrow the Czarist regime. He was described in police files as a fanatical Bolshevist yet Kon never joined the Communist Party. Subsequently he worked as a trade intermediary for the Canadian and Soviet governments. In sum, the General Strike initiated an anti-immigrant offensive that allowed the government to deport "foreigners" without trial, and to impose severe immigration restrictions against European minorities. In the words of historian Allan Levine, "The General Strike polarized city politics for decades to follow, as it did the Jewish community."[5]

One of the foremost Jewish labour leaders was Max Federman (1902–91). He arrived in Toronto in 1920, having been a union member in Germany. Working in the fur industry, he joined and then led the International Union of Fur and Leather Workers. As a committed socialist, he spent decades battling communist infiltration in the unions, including his own, which split along these political lines, in 1934. He was regularly denounced in the Yiddish language communist paper *Der Vochenblatt* ("the Weekly Paper") as a working-class renegade. Aside from his contribution to labour, Federman persuaded the government to allow five hundred furriers and tailors, who were Holocaust survivors, into Canada. He was an ardent Zionist, served on numerous labour organizations, and was active in the Cooperative Commonwealth Federation (CCF) and its successor, the New Democratic Party (NDP).

The divisions within Jewish labour in Canada were not confined to the internecine conflict between reformers in the mainstream unions and radicals in the IUNTW, nor between the workers and the owners. They were exacerbated over the role of women, the issue of class solidarity with all workers, and the struggle to maintain Jewish identity in a pluralist society. In short, the intersection among political orientation, gender roles, class consciousness, and ethnic concerns was posted on a delicate balance.

Ruth Frager's study of the Toronto clothing industry deftly analyzes these tensions in *Sweatshop Strife*. She argues that Jewish workers saw themselves as part of the working class, and that their leaders and most of the rank and file considered strikes to be not only necessary to improve their conditions, but to fundamentally reform society. Further, the labour movement not only addressed economic exploitation but antisemitism, thereby linking class and ethnicity. Indeed, this commitment attracted radicals who viewed the Soviet Union as embodying these principles. While Jewish women played a vital role, they were not attracted to the women's movement in general because of its domination by middle-class Anglo women. Frager writes: "the emphasis on both class consciousness and ethnic identity inhibited the development of feminist perspectives."[6] Further, to have elevated this emphasis would have fragmented the Jewish labour movement, which already had to deal with the competing political ideologies and the chasm between Jewish workers and Jewish owners. Frager concludes: "Although the immigrant Jewish activists were often unable to overcome these divisions, they fought courageously.... They strove for justice for working class people and for Jews. The socialists among them fought for nothing less than a new Garden of Eden that proved out of reach."[7] With respect to the mix of class, ethnicity and gender, ethnicity was predominant.

According to historian Irving Abella: "When the history of labour in Canada is finally written, the Jewish labour movement will stand out in its contributions to the betterment of Canadian society. Without a doubt it was the conscience of the Canadian labour movement."[8]

POLITICS

Liberals

For the first fifty years following Confederation, Canada was a two-party state – the Conservatives and the Liberals. The former ruled for thirty-four years, largely under the leadership of John A. Macdonald, while Wilfrid Laurier led the Liberals to power at the turn of the twentieth century. The emergence of smaller parties began in World War I and grew though the Great Depression of the 1930s. While none gained even the status of the Official Opposition (save for the Progressives, who were a splinter group of Liberals, Conservatives, and United Farmers), they garnered support based on their regional and/or social class affiliations, and on their political ideologies, which were outside the mainstream, on both ends of the political spectrum. While their influence at the federal level was muted, they were successful in the provinces, forming governments at various points in the period from World War I to the present in all but New Brunswick, Prince Edward Island, and Newfoundland.

During the Great Migration, the Liberal party was favoured by most immigrants. Under Laurier, the Liberals from 1896 to 1911 created a brisk program to bring immigrants to Canada, largely to settle in the Prairies, but also to provide labour in primary and secondary industries. The Conservatives were associated with the Anglo elite, and while they had some support in French Canada, that waned after Macdonald's defeat in 1891. Most of the Jewish immigrants supported the Liberals, not only because of their aggressive campaign to promote immigration, but because they were associated with liberalism, the political ideology that promoted progress and liberty. Jews who had been mired in eastern Europe under the oppressive regimes of the Russian, Austrian, and Ottoman empires and had arrived on Canadian shores where the promise of better life and freedom beckoned made the Liberal Party their natural choice.

The dominance of the Liberal Party in the Jewish community can be measured by the election of Jewish members to provincial and national legislatures. Montreal's Peter Bercovitch (1879–1942) was elected as a member of the Legislative Assembly (MLA) from 1916 to 1936, and as a member of Parliament (MP) from 1938 to 1942; his counterpart, Joseph Cohen (1891–1973), was an MLA from 1923 to 1936. Samuel Jacobs was an MP from the Cartier riding in Montreal from 1917 until his death in 1938, as well as the most prominent Jewish politician in the interwar era. He was the only Jewish member of the House of Commons until the election of Toronto's Samuel Factor (1892–1962) in 1930, whose tenure ended in 1945. Winnipeg's Jewish community helped elect Solomon Hart Green (1885–1969) to the provincial legislature from 1910 to 1914. Winnipeg's William Tobias (1892–1941), who was an MLA from 1927 to 1932, was the only elected Jewish Conservative representative in Canada until after World War II.

The longest serving Jewish politician in Canadian history is David Croll (1900–91). Born in Russia, he and his family migrated to Windsor, Ontario. He served as the city's mayor from 1931–4, during the heat of the Depression. Elected to the provincial legislature as a Liberal in 1934, he became Canada's first Jewish cabinet minister. He broke with the party's leadership over its opposition to the United Auto Workers strike against General Motors in Ottawa in 1937. His statement, "I would rather walk with the workers than ride with General Motors"[9] was a landmark declaration in labour history. He remained in the legislature as a member from Windsor and then from Toronto's Spadina riding until 1955. From that point to almost his death, Croll was a senator, the first Jew in Canada to be appointed to the Upper Chamber. He was instrumental in the Trudeau government's decision to increase family allowances and formulate a child tax credit. He became a symbol of the reformist wing of the Liberal party.

Reformers

The advent of fringe parties in Canada began in the first decade of the twentieth century, with socialist parties that had microscopic support, and a farmers' lobby that that led to United Farmers parties that gained power in Ontario and Alberta. The first breakthrough in radical left-wing politics was the establishment of the CPC in 1921, which became part of the Communist International in 1924. It was aligned with the Soviet Union, although that relationship became more complex during the reign of Joseph Stalin from 1927 to his death in 1953.

The Great Depression accelerated the rise of protest parties. On the right, the creation of the Social Credit Party in Alberta was a loose mixture of agrarian protest and proto-fascism, which excoriated the economic control by central Canadian business and banking interests. It captured the government of Alberta, where it ruled for forty years. The

CCF emerged in 1933 as the authentic voice of democratic socialism, a true reform movement, in contrast to the mainstream Liberals. The party was founded in Regina, at the height of the Depression, and led by James Shaver Woodsworth (1874–1942), a Methodist minister who preached a social gospel that called for the Kingdom of God "here and now," which emphasized improving the lives of poor and immigrant families. His social activism led him to adopt socialism. He addressed meetings in Winnipeg during the General Strike and organized the Manitoba Independent Labour Party (ILP), winning a seat in parliament in 1921 as the representative of Winnipeg North Centre. The ILP merged into the CCF. In Regina, its manifesto laid out it plans for a democratic socialist society that united all sectors of the working class. Its immediate appeal was in Saskatchewan and to a lesser extent in Manitoba, both ravaged by the Great Depression. At the founding of the CCF 27 per cent of the labour force was unemployed. Although it had limited success in supplanting the Liberals in federal and provincial constituencies that had a sizeable Jewish population, the CCF captured the hearts and minds of a minority of immigrants and some of their descendants. The North End of Winnipeg was a hotbed for left-wing politics due to immigrants from eastern Europe, notably Jews, Finns, and Ukrainians, as well as workers from the United Kingdom. The General Strike accelerated their commitment to reform and radical movements. Jews became active in politics at all levels. Jack Blumberg aka "Fighting Jack" came from England and was elected as alderman in 1919 at the age of 25, joined the ILP, and served on various committees and organizations, including the role of acting mayor. Marcus Hyman came from Poland via England as an Oxford scholar and lawyer in 1913. He represented unions during the General Strike, joined the ILP, and was elected to the provincial legislature in 1932, and then in 1936 as a member of the CCF. The Bund, through its *Arbeiter Ring* and the *Poalei Zion*, despite their differences, found political expression in the ILP-CCF. J.A. Cherniak, a lawyer, was a founder of the Zionist Folk School, and although unsuccessful in local races, was a force in ILP-CCF politics through the interwar period.

The most significant Jewish reformer was Abraham Albert (A.A.) Heaps (1885–1954). Born in Leeds, England, of Polish descent, he arrived in Winnipeg in 1910, worked as an upholsterer, and was elected as a Social Democrat to the Winnipeg City Council from 1919 to 1925. He was acquitted of seditious libel during the General Strike. Heaps won the 1925 election representing Winnipeg North, joining Woodsworth in the House of Commons. They were instrumental in persuading the Liberal government to adopt an Old Age Pension in 1927 in return for their support. Heaps remained in the House of Commons until his defeat in 1940. He was one of three Jewish members through this period. It is notable that Heaps and Woodsworth were able to work with the Liberals but were reviled by the Canadian Communist Party. Political scientist Nelson Wiseman opines that the origin of democratic socialism in Canada came from the British Labour Party, rather than continental socialist movements.[10] Heaps, Blumberg, and Hyman were indoctrinated in England rather than in eastern Europe.

The most noteworthy Canadian Jewish socialist was David Lewis (1909–81). Born David Loyz in a small town (shtetl) in present-day Belarus, his father, Morris, was a devoted member of the Bund. Although David attended Jewish religious school (*cheder*), his family was not religious. The unease at the end of World War I due to the civil war following the Bolshevik revolution, during which hundreds of thousands of Jews were killed, was the catalyst for their emigration. The family came to Montreal in 1921 where Morris' brother lived. He had changed his name to Lewis, so Morris followed suit. David grew up in the immigrant neighbourhood on the Plateau. His father's political leanings were highly influential. He attended meetings of the Bund, and quickly overcame his late entry into the English language by excelling in school. Admitted to McGill University, he was attracted to socialist circles populated by Anglo-Canadians, in the mould of Woodworth. After three years at Oxford as a Rhodes Scholar, Lewis returned to Ottawa where he was a patent lawyer by day and national secretary of the CCF by night. In time, his part-time job became his avocation, as he remained secretary to 1950. In 1961 he was a founder of the NDP which succeeded the CCF. He was an MP from Toronto York South, and succeeded Tommy Douglas as party leader from 1971 to 1975.

Radicals

The CPC was an outgrowth of smaller socialist groups that coalesced in the advent of the Bolshevik takeover of Russia and the Winnipeg General Strike. The party was accepted by the Communist International in 1921, thus automatically acceding to the dictates of Vladimir Lenin. It was initially an underground organization due to the War Measures

Act imposed to curtail anti-government activity and began operations in 1924 when the act was lifted. Its core membership came from the labour movement. After Lenin's death in 1924, Soviet policy was in flux due to the competition between Joseph Stalin and Leon Trotsky for control. With Stalin's accession, the Trotskyites in Canada were ousted from the CPC. Tim Buck, an avowed Stalinist, became the party secretary in 1929 and remained so to 1962.

The CPC was subject to "Moscow Rules" but their implementation in the vast panorama of Canada was not an easy task. Unlike the Soviet Union, which was an authoritarian regime led by Stalin and his confederates, the CPC's membership was miniscule and diverse geographically and ethnically. It alienated itself from the mainstream political left by proclaiming that the greatest threat to the working class was the democratic socialists, especially the CCF. The CPC was controlled by Buck and his Anglo cohorts from Toronto, in a rebuke to the French-speaking wing. A large segment of the party was made up of Ukrainians and Finns and to a lesser degree, Jews. These fragments conducted party business in their native languages and created their own social and cultural networks. Yet, aside from the mode of gaining power, a major difference between the reformers and the radicals, was that for the former, social transformation was an evolutionary project, while for the latter, it was an all-consuming matter.

The true believers in the CPC chose to know little of the fierce autocracy under Stalin, where opponents, real and imagined, were murdered or imprisoned, where a forced famine killed millions in Ukraine, where long-term plans for industrialization had disastrous consequences, and where an overbearing personality cult dominated all aspects of life. When Stalin signed a nonaggression pact with Hitler days before the outbreak of World War II, the CPC did an about-face in supporting the move. In response, the Canadian government outlawed the party, arrested some of its members, and only reinstated the party, under the name, Labour Progressive Party (LPP), when the Soviet Union joined the Allied forces.

Jewish attraction to communism stemmed from their oppression under the Czarist regime, and the Marxist doctrine of universal brotherhood. As such, they believed that the Bolsheviks would liberate them from antisemitism and end class conflict. This enthusiasm was transmitted by a fraction of the Jewish Diaspora to Canada, which had welcomed the birth of the Soviet Union. However, while Jews played a role in the leadership of the CPC, they never numbered more than five thousand supporters. At its height in the 1945 election, the LPP, captured 2.1 per cent of the popular vote.

While Jewish participation in the movement was small, it was influential. Maurice Spector (1898–1968) came to Toronto from Ukraine, and, while a student at Osgoode Hall Law School, helped draft the first CPC program, and became its leading speaker at its founding. He edited the party paper, *The Worker*, and went across the country raising awareness and advocating world revolution and independence from Britain. But Spector was a devotee of Leon Trotsky. When Stalin consolidated his power in 1928, and Trotsky went into exile and was assasinated in Mexico, Spector was expelled.

Sam Carr (1906–89), born Schmil Kogan, came to Winnipeg in 1924 and settled in Montreal, where he was an organizer of the Young Communist League with Fred Rose. He served twenty months in prison when the party was declared illegal in 1931. Nine years later, when the party was again outlawed, he fled to the United States, and returned to Canada in 1943. His fortunes fell in the wake of the Igor Gouzenko Affair. Gouzenko, a cipher clerk in the Soviet embassy, defected in 1945, revealing that a Soviet spy network in Canada intended to gain information about the atomic energy program. Carr and Rose, who had been elected as an MP that year (the only Communist parliamentarian in Canadian history), were found guilty of conspiracy. They were imprisoned and then exiled to their home country of Poland. Carr eventually returned and joined the United Jewish Peoples' Order (UJPO), a fraternal organization. Rose never left Poland.

As a corollary, it is instructive to note the impact of the government's treatment of immigrants who were not only active but also those who were suspect. Most notable is the case of Leopold Infeld (1898–1968), who was born in Poland, studied physics in Berlin with Albert Einstein, and became a professor at the University of Toronto in 1939 (perhaps the first Jewish professor in the department). Like his mentor, Infeld became a peace activist after the detonation of nuclear bombs in Japan in 1945. For this, he was accused of harbouring communist sympathies, was fired, returned to Poland, after which he was stripped of his Canadian citizenship. Infeld was one of eleven signatories to the Russell-Einstein Manifesto against the use of nuclear weapons and was the only one not to receive a Nobel Prize.

Journalist Joshua Gershman (1903–88), born in Ukraine, supported the Bolsheviks. In an interview with historian Irving Abella in 1973, he stated: "They [the Bolsheviks] drove out the various counter-revolutionary bands and the *pogromists* [Jew killers].... We sided with the October Revolution and the Communist party."[11] He came to Winnipeg in 1921 to join his father, worked in a fur factory, and joined the CPC in 1923. He moved to Toronto three years later and in 1927 became a professional revolutionary. He organized strikes on behalf of the IUNTW in Toronto and Montreal after which he became the editor of the Yiddish language paper, *Vochenblatt* in 1940, and joined UJPO. He remained a committed communist through the post-Stalin era because he "agree[d] with the Communist party practically on every question but on the Jewish question or on the national question."[12] Abella wrote that in May 1977 Gershman "was officially censured by the Central Committee of the Communist Party of Canada for ... his attacks on the Soviet Union for its callous treatment of its Jewish population."[13] In protest, Gershman resigned, ending a fifty-four-year commitment to the party.

Joseph Salsberg (1902–98), colloquially known as "J.B.," was the most significant Jewish activist in the CPC. He was born in a shtetl in Poland to a traditional Jewish family. His father ventured to Toronto and became a peddler. When he had the funds, he sent for his wife and son (a common practice by immigrants) in 1912. J.B. left school at the age of thirteen to work in a leather goods factory, earning $3 for a forty-nine-hour work week, and rising to the levels of designer, cutter, and dyer, where his wage increased tenfold. Despite his lack of formal education, he was an autodidact, a vociferous reader of Yiddish and English literature, especially political theory. He joined the United Hatters, Cap, and Millinery Workers International Union, and rose through the ranks to become a union organizer in Montreal. While his father wanted him to be a rabbi, Salsberg was attracted to socialism and Jewish nationalism, and joined the Labour Zionist movement, much to his father's consternation. But his instincts were more radical, and in 1926 he joined the CPC. His biographer, Gerald Tulchinsky, writes: "This was more than a significant shift to the left. It was a radical break with the past and a momentous adoption of communism and all that it implied at the time."[14] The implication was dedication to the Soviet Union and to the struggle for a world revolution. But it also related to his Jewish upbringing.

For the rest of his life, Salsberg struggled to blend his ethnicity with his politics. This continually put him at odds with Buck and the CPC, resulting in his dismissal for a short time. While he never deviated from the struggle for the working class, he remained a committed Jew who did not disavow his faith nor his ethnicity. Salsberg entered the political arena by running for the position of alderman for Ward 5 (the Spadina neighbourhood). He was defeated in his first two attempts, achieving victory in 1938, but losing it the following year. With the crackdown on the CPC, Salsberg went into seclusion, emerging when the LPP was legitimized by the government. In 1943 he turned his attention to the provincial legislature, winning the seat in the St. Andrew riding, and becoming the only Communist to ever hold a provincial seat. For the next twelve years, he was a tireless advocate for human rights. He was a popular figure in the House of Commons, a friend of the Premier Leslie Frost (a conservative), joined the CJC, and was the most well-known Jewish personality in the city. His was defeated by Allan Grossman, a conservative and fellow Jew, in a nasty campaign in 1955.

Salsberg remained a devoted disciple of the Soviet Union. While he had heard of a widespread campaign of antisemitism that became public in 1948, he remained unbowed, refusing to believe the news. With Stalin's death in 1953, the new leader, Nikita Khrushchev, revealed Stalin's "crimes" in 1956. This was a catastrophic blow to communist sympathizers worldwide. Salsberg broke with the CPC when it refused to support his proposal that the new regime create a Jewish section. For the remainder of his life, he was active as a public speaker and writer in the Yiddish and English press. In Tulchinsky's words, "Salsberg's involvement in the movement had arisen from his transforming engagement with Jewish socialism, the search for Jewish emancipation within Marxism (and) the concept of working-class self-emancipation."[15]

The resignations of Gershman and Salsberg speak to two points. The first is that Marxist ideology, when put into practice, was subverted for the total domination of the nation-state at the behest of its leaders. The Soviet regime enslaved its citizens, instigated famines and deportations, created client states in east-central Europe, and helped precipitate the nuclear race. The blind adherence of its devotees in the West speaks to the power of the ideology, the dream of a classless society, of a world revolution. That illusion was challenged in the 1956 revelations and was ultimately disposed of with the collapse of the Soviet regime in

1991. The second conclusion is that, ultimately, ethnicity triumphed over ideology. The mistreatment of Soviet Jews was the final straw for the Jewish members of the CPC. Currently, the CPC is anachronistic. At its central convention in 2016, there were some seventy to eighty delegates in attendance.

ROGUES

Inevitably, there is a segment of the population that does not conform to the mores of conventional society. In the Jewish community in Canada, especially from the 1920s to the 1960s, immigrants and their offspring were maneuvering within the rigid confines of Anglo society, and in Quebec within the strictures of the French-Canadian Catholic Church. Some chose to flout conventions. We term these individuals as rogues, outside of the mainstream of Canadian society in general. This discussion posits that there were three elastic categories of rogues – criminals, those who straddled the law, and those who led nonconformist lives.

Criminals

Jewish criminal activity in Canada from 1923 to 1937 is documented in Louis Rosenberg's monumental study, *Canada's Jews: A Social and Economic History of Jews in Canada in the 1930s.* He cites scholarly "investigators" who attributed greater criminal activity by "foreigners" (the designation given by the Canadian government) than by "native" Canadians to three factors: a disproportionate number of younger males (who tend to criminality more than do females) due to their recent arrival; a lack of knowledge of laws, which differed from their country of origin; and a period of "social maladjustment" following their arrival. In addition, Rosenberg adds a fourth point, that much higher crime rates occurred in urban settings, by a magnitude ranging from 4.7 per cent in 1927 to 2.7 per cent in 1937. Within this context, with Jews being by far the most urban-based immigrant group, Rosenberg provides the following profile. First is the number of criminal convictions per one hundred thousand people. In 1923, for all Canadians, the figure was 145; for "foreigners," 490; for Jews, 139. In 1933, the comparative numbers were 276, 515, and 317. The rise in criminal activity in the decade under Rosenberg's study can be attributed to the Great Depression and increased proportion of Canadians living in urban areas. As such, Jewish criminal activity was roughly consistent with that of all Canadians, and about 30 per cent that of other "foreigners," adjusting for rural-urban distribution.

Rosenberg then breaks down the categories of indictable offenses. The largest activity was "theft," where in 1937, there were 106 actions per 100,000 nationally, and 69 committed by Jews. The only major category in which Jewish activity exceeded the national average was in "gambling and lotteries." In 1937 nationally there were 24 cases per 100,000 people, whereas 57 Jews were indicted on the same basis. The other category that jumps out is "Opium and Narcotics Drugs," which, while marginal, shows a disproportional Jewish involvement of 14 indictments per 100,00 in 1937, in contrast to 8 indictments nationally. In total, there were 486 criminal indictments against Jews in 1937, a significant rise over the preceding three years. In spanning a fourteen-year period ending in 1937, Rosenberg finds that one Jew was indicted for murder and one for manslaughter.[16]

One finds that criminal activity was conducted in isolated incidents, by outlaws, and by organized criminals. Jewish participants were found in all these categories.

Our focus is on some of the most notorious individuals, as related by sociologist Stephen Schneider in *Iced: The Story of Organized Crime in Canada* (2016). The importation and sale of illegal narcotics began to escalate in 1918, from European manufacturers of morphine and heroin, where they were legal but had limits on their export. Nevertheless, additional quantities were diverted to international black markets, including Montreal, from where they were distributed to the rest of the country. A Royal Canadian Mounted Police (RCMP) investigation determined that an average of 250 cases annually was distributed during the 1920s in Quebec alone. Max Farber, born in Poland in 1892, made his reputation in London, where Scotland Yard described him as "an exceptionally cunning scoundrel."[17] Based in Montreal he imported drugs from Germany and bribed customs officials to clear boxes of soap laced with opium. The bounty was then dispensed through wholesale drug firms and opium dens. One of his clients was Harry Davis, who was born in Romania and arrived in Canada in 1907. Davis headed an enterprise that purchased large quantities and trafficked them through the night clubs and betting emporiums that dotted the city. His associates included

Jewish immigrants such as Eddie Baker, who was born in Russia in 1898 and arrived two years later. He sold the drugs in Montreal's notorious Red Light district and operated a mail-order enterprise across the country. Baker was indicted and served a three-year sentence, after which his stature diminished. After Davis served a six-month sentence in 1928, he emerged as the biggest trafficker in Montreal, until he was snared by the RCMP again in 1933. At his trial, his associates, "Fat" Charlie Feigenbaum and "Sammy the Wop" Arcadi, turned state's evidence against Davis, and he received a fourteen-year sentence. A year later, Feigenbaum was murdered by hired guns from Detroit. In 1946, a year after his release, Davis was killed by a Louis Bercowitz, a minor crime figure, who pleaded self-defence and was convicted of manslaughter, thereby avoiding execution. An estimated five thousand people attended Davis' funeral.

It is no overstatement that Montreal was not only the vice capital of Canada, but also a major centre for organized crime in North America. There were some two hundred casinos, which collectively contributed $5000 a week to corrupt police and city officials, who either turned the other cheek, or staged pre-arranged raids on the operations where minor miscreants were fined. Barney Shulkin, for example, was arrested ninety-seven times and never went to jail. One of the kings of the underworld was Harry Ship (1913–98), who operated gambling enterprises throughout the city. He was a mathematical wizard, who had enrolled at Queen's University but did not graduate. His casinos, notably the Chez Paree, welcomed not only the underworld, but politicians, police and judges, business leaders, and performers, such as Frank Sinatra. In a crackdown on the rackets following Davis' murder, Ship was sentenced to a six-month term. He faded from the underworld in the 1950s as the mafia gained control of organized crime.

Italian crime syndicates, originating from the provinces of Sicily and Calabria, had become well established in the United States by the early twentieth century. They gained a foothold in Canada, largely due to the imposition of temperance acts by several provinces, including Ontario in 1916, that prohibited the sale of alcohol. But these controls were not uniform across the country, including in Quebec, which had overturned this legislation in 1919 followed by Saskatchewan and Alberta in 1927. The Eighteenth Amendment to the American Constitution imposed prohibition of the production, sale, and consumption of alcohol in 1920, a disastrous decision in social and economic terms that remained in force for twelve years. Due to Canadian rulings in 1920–1 that overturned the manufacture and export of liquor, criminal enterprises seized the opportunity to smuggle liquor into American outlets, mostly via the Great Lakes. "Dry provinces" relied on smugglers and on home-based "moonshine" operations.

Bessie Starkman was born in Poland in 1889 and married Harry Tobin in Toronto in 1907. Living in the Ward, she eked out a living as a seamstress in the Eaton's factory. Rocco Perri, born in Calabria, came to Toronto in 1912, where he rented a room in the Starkman-Tobin home. Bessie, smitten with the dapper Perri, abandoned her family and ran off with him to Hamilton where they opened a grocery store, behind which was a house of ill repute. Their activities soon branched out to bootlegging and selling home brew. Perri ran the operation, but Starkman was the brains behind the enterprise. Capitalizing on the huge market in the United States, they created a network of bootleggers, with a fleet of trucks and fishing boats that ferried alcohol across Ontario and the Great Lakes. Perri boasted that they sold one thousand cases of whiskey per day, at a profit of one hundred dollars a case. They isolated themselves from the actual operation because they had "soldiers" who did the work, and in whose names the vehicles and boats were registered. Further, their payroll included police and customs officers on both sides of the border. Rival gangs were bought off or their leaders murdered. Arrested several times, they either paid fines or were released for lack of evidence. Their high life in Hamilton, where they lived in a nineteen-room home, was a marked contrast from the lives of ordinary workers. When they entered the narcotics trade, their fortunes turned when Bessie refused to pay off the suppliers. She was murdered in 1930. In the following years, Rocco escaped from explosions to his home and car, and was eventually arrested as a wartime enemy alien. Called "Canada's answer to Al Capone" by Stephen Schneider,[18] Perri disappeared after his release in 1944. Bessie Starkman's epitaph was that she was the most notorious Jewish female criminal in Canadian history.

The takeover of organized crime by the Sicilian and Calabrian syndicates was a factor in the diminution of Jewish involvement in criminal enterprises. Nevertheless, in the postwar period, there were some notable exceptions. A prominent criminal was William (Willy) Obront who was born in Montreal in 1924. In his youth, he was a petty thug working his way up as loan shark and club owner. He emerged as an associate to the Cotroni clan, which controlled the mafia in Quebec, providing funds for their illegal operations and becoming the syndicate's chief banker. Obront accelerated his empire though stock market manipulations and selling tainted meat ("Obie's Meat Market") to restaurants, including establishments at the World Exposition (EXPO) in Montreal in 1967. In 1974–5 alone, he laundered over $18 million for the syndicate. Fearing the heat of investigations into organized crime, he fled to Florida and then to Costa Rica, from where he was extradited to Canada. Sentenced to four years, he re-emerged as a drug trafficker and was sentenced to a twenty-year term. In 2002 at the age of 78, he was released. He dubbed himself "the Boy Wonder," and this moniker was attached to a shady figure by Mordecai Richler in his novel *The Apprenticeship of Duddy Kravitz.*

Maxwell ("Max, Maxie") Bluestein (born Baker) controlled gambling operations in Toronto. First convicted in 1934, and then charged with assault against an associate in 1946, he established gambling clubs in Toronto and its environs, from where bets were placed on sports, and where craps (dice) games were held. But Bluestein's criminal empire was an island in southern Ontario, where the Maggadino clan of Buffalo had taken control of organized crime, from its headquarters in Hamilton. There, a Maggadino "soldier," Johnny Papalia, pressured Bluestein to merge his holdings with the mafia. When Bluestein refused, he was brutally assaulted outside the Town Tavern in downtown Toronto on March 21, 1961, in front of scores of denizens from the underworld. This was, in the opinion of Stephen Schneider, "the seminal event in the history of organized crime in Ontario."[19] In "Toronto the Good" the incident received enormous coverage, and those old enough can still recall the event. Despite the mass number of witnesses, at the trial of Papalia and his fellow toughs, no one could recall the attack. Perhaps it was Papalia's superiors who convinced him to plead so as to take the public eye off their ventures. He was sentenced to an eighteen-month imprisonment. But Bluestein's criminal endeavours continued. In 1973, while in prison, he killed his associate David Stillman, for which he was committed to a mental institution. He died at home in 1984.

Straddling the Law

Two of the areas of criminal activity where miscreants tended to operate on the edges of the law were the production and sale of alcohol, and betting on horse racing. The operators and their clients came from all segments of Canadian society, irrespective of class, ethnicity, or gender. In the burgeoning Jewish communities, betting parlours, and "gin joints" were as ubiquitous as synagogues. There were two ends of liquor distribution – home brews and major corporations.

Howard Moscoe was a longtime municipal politician in the Toronto suburb of North York. He contributed a short essay to the collection, *The Ward.* His grandmother, Gertrude (Gussie) Shumacher, settled in the Ward in 1908. Her husband, Pesach (Percy), was a peddler. Gussie opened a grocery store, acting as a front for the sale of homemade brew, which was dispensed by the shot. Moscoe was told that "… [Gussie's brother] Shmuel was a bootlegger, but (religiously) observant, so on the Sabbath, Bubby (Grandma) took over."[20] No shrinking violet, in 1925 Gussie assaulted a woman who had snitched to the police. She was fined $50, sentenced to a week in jail, and given a suspended sentence of two years.

Sammy Luftspring was the son of Polish immigrants. His father Yossel (Joey) was a boot maker, but was stricken with tuberculosis, necessitating a three-year stay in a sanatorium. Abetted by his wife, they sold homemade liquor from their home, a two-storey frame cottage on a lane off Baldwin Street, in Toronto's Kensington Market, which also housed Sammy's six siblings and grandparents. From the age of six, Sammy was the lookout for police who occasionally staged raids. Otherwise, they were paid off, either in product or cash. The product was a mixture of pure alcohol, brown sugar, flavouring and colouring agents, and tea. Customers sat at the kitchen table paying 25 cents for a one ounce shot. The operation ended in 1940, when his mother died, and cocktail lounges were legalized by the province.

At the other end of the production and sale of alcohol were the distillers. The most successful producer was Seagram's, which was owned by the Bronfman family. The Bronfmans are the most prominent Jewish family in Canadian history. In brief, Yechiel (Ekiel) Bronfman was the patriarch of a family that owned a mill and tobacco plantation in Russia. Bronfman, his wife Minnie, and three children fled Russia in 1889 because of pogroms. A fourth child, Samuel, was born on the voyage and three more children were born in Canada. Unable to grow tobacco on the harsh plains of Saskatchewan, Ekiel worked on the CNR, then in a sawmill, and soon became a dealer in wood, fish, and horses. Ekiel established a synagogue in Brandon. His second son, Harry, aged sixteen, saw the opportunity to sink the family savings into a local hotel that profited from liquor sales to thirsty travellers. This began a string of establishments across the Prairies, managed by his brothers Abe and Sam, as well as real estate ventures in downtown Winnipeg. When prohibition was enacted in Saskatchewan (1915) and Manitoba (1916), the family moved into the still legal business of manufacturing liquor and sold the product via mail order. With prohibition in the United States, the Bronfmans were among those with the means to buy existing distilleries and open new ones, creating conglomerates that controlled all aspects of the trade. The family, now headed by Sam, moved its operations to Montreal, where he founded Distillers Corporation in 1924. Four years later, he bought the Seagram's Distillery in Waterloo. He then was able to sell to bootleggers run by criminal syndicates in the United States. Harry, who ran the trade from Saskatchewan, was arrested in 1929, but the case was dismissed due to the absence of witnesses. The four Bronfman brothers were charged by the federal government for evading payments of duty on liquor in 1934. But the RCMP could not find evidence in the company headquarters and they were acquitted. With the passing of Prohibition, the company became the most successful producer of alcohol in the world. Seagram's sales sailed past the $1 billion plateau in 1965. Sam, and to a lesser degree his brothers and their progeny, emerged not only as captains of industry, but as dedicated community leaders and philanthropists.

Although gambling was illegal, there was a gray area in the law regarding betting on horse races. One could legally bet at the racetrack, but not anywhere else. As most working people could not get to the track on a regular basis, they placed their bets with bookmakers in person or via telephone. The list of races and the odds on each horse were posted in *The Racing Forum*, but the odds changed by the minute. The changes were sent to bookmakers who relayed the information to betters. A network of bookmakers took the bets and charged bettors a percentage of the winnings.

As with alcohol, gambling in all forms was, and remains, appealing to all walks of life. In immigrant communities there were known hangouts for gamblers and bookies. One story is recounted by Bob Bossin in *Davey the Punk: A Story of Bookies, Toronto the Good, the Mob and My Dad.* Davey was born in Toronto in 1905. As a child he came under the watch of Harry Orpen, a gambling proprietor in downtown Toronto. Davey had the unusual ability to memorize the gamblers and their bets. By the 1930s, he served as a "lay off man." That meant that if too much money was being bet on one horse, he would "lay off" the action by finding other gamblers to bet on other horses. Bossin operated in innocuous houses in the suburbs that did not raise the suspicion of the police. During infrequent raids, the telegraph and telephone lines were confiscated, but as no papers were found, and Davey could not be charged. Although his operation was linked to organized crime, he had little direct contact with the mob. Tired of being harassed, Bossin closed shop in the 1950s, when his son Bob was a child. He died of a heart attack in 1961 at the age of 58.

Completely outside the realm of bootlegging and bookmaking is the story of a married couple, Ben and Alice Edelson, and her friend Jack Horwitz. Members of the small middle-class Jewish community in Ottawa in 1931, Alice, the mother of seven children, had been carrying on with Jack, who was a husband and father. Ben had long known of the illicit relationship, but despite Alice's promises to curtail it, she and Jack continued their affair. The three met at Ben's jewellery shop to settle the matter. But as the men fought, Ben reached for a gun and killed Jack. Historian Monda Halpern relates the story that shocked polite society in *Alice in Shandeland* (*shande* is Yiddish for shame or disgrace). Ben was acquitted because the blame for the incident was placed on the adulterous Alice. She would never really know absolution. As friends gathered at the Edelson home to celebrate the acquittal, Alice, according to the *Ottawa Journal*, wasn't there. Eventually Alice became an assiduous volunteer for Jewish women's organizations, organizing fundraising and providing anonymous donations to underprivileged women. Her contribution was acknowledged at her death in 1972 but Halpern concludes that she was never able to regain her standing in the community.

Outside the Mainstream

At the end of Chapter 4, we learned of Jewish athletes, whose careers violated the norms of the Jewish community. Rather than conforming to the expectations of their families, they exposed their bodies to athletic competition. They included boxers associated with criminals which added more reprobation to their reputation. Sammy Luftspring's manager was Harry Orpen, a notorious titan of gambling in Toronto. The connection between boxing and criminals in the Spadina neighbourhood is portrayed in Karen X Tulchinsky's novel, *The Five Books of Moses Lipinsky.*

Goodwin (Goody) Rosen was born to Russian immigrants in 1912, and grew up in Toronto's Parkdale neighbourhood. Passionate about team sports, he excelled in baseball, playing for the Elizabeth Park teams that had originated in the Ward. The teams, dubbed "Lizzies," won many city championships at all youth levels from their home at Christie Pits. His brothers Jake and Willie were, respectively, a boxer and a ball player. Rosen turned professional in 1931 and signed with the Brooklyn Dodgers six years later. Playing centre field, in 1945 Rosen was one of the National League's leading players, finishing third in batting average and second in hits and runs. He was the first Canadian-born player to be named to the All-Star Game. After two poor seasons he retired and turned his talents as a player-manager in the Intercounty Baseball League in Ontario. Inducted into the Canadian Baseball Hall of Fame in 1984, Rosen died ten years later. He was the only Canadian Jewish big leaguer until Adam Stern's brief tenure for the Boston Red Sox in 2005.

Perhaps the most "rogueish" non-criminal was Morris Abraham "Two Gun Cohen." He was born in London, England in 1887 to Orthodox parents who struggled with his fighting and petty theft as a child. They exiled him to Saskatchewan in 1905, where he tried ranching and peddling, but found that smuggling liquor, pimping, and swindling was more profitable. In a Saskatoon Chinese restaurant that doubled as a gambling den, he disarmed and knocked out a would-be bandit, earning him the plaudits of the Chinese community. He learned the language and championed the rights of this discriminated nation. After serving in World War I in France, partly with a Chinese labour battalion, Cohen went to Shanghai, where he became a bodyguard for Sun Yat Sen, the leader of the Chinese Nationalists. He was promoted by Sun's successor, Chiang Kai-Shek, to the rank of general. Always carrying two guns, he trained the Nationalist army in resisting the Japanese invasion. Captured in Hong Kong and imprisoned for three years, he avoided execution when the British negotiated his release. On his return, he married a much younger wealthy divorcee, from whom he drained her savings in one year. In 1945, at the inaugural gathering of the UN, CJC

President Sam Bronfman used Cohen's influence to successfully negotiate China's support for the creation of the state of Israel. Cohen's admiration of the Chinese people and culture stemmed from his contention that they were the only people that never persecuted Jews. Rejected by the Maoist regime for his tie to the Nationalists, he decamped to England, where he died in 1970.

CONCLUSION

Throughout the twentieth century Canada's Jews mostly supported centre and left-wing political parties and movements. While most of Canada's Jews favoured the Liberal Party, a minority felt that the party's pro-immigration platform had turned toward greater restrictions after World War I, and that there was little differentiation between the Liberals and Conservatives in rejecting the needs of working-class Canadians. This minority determined that an alternative, democratic socialism would provide greater benefits and security to the working classes by reforming the political process. An even smaller minority, concluding that gradual change would inevitably be absorbed by the mainstream political parties, looked for salvation in communism. The main arena for political choice was in the urban workplace, notably in the labour movement.

Although there was sharp drop in the settlement of Jews from the mid-1920s to the late 1940s because of restrictive government policies and international events, the adaptation of those who did come, and those who had arrived in earlier waves, was marked by a continuum from those who retained the links to the "old country" to the majority who acculturated to the societal norms of their "host country." The broad spectrum of support for mainstream, reform, and radical political and social movements was indicative of the complex diversity of the Canadian Jewish community that was augmented by those who lived on the margins of "acceptable society." Arguably, this period in the story of Canadian Jews produced a motley cast of characters, from strait-laced politicians, to rabble rousers, con artists, crooks, and athletes. This speaks as much to the rapid transformation of the Canadian urban landscape as it does to variety of paths taken by immigrants adapting to a nation that was not comfortable with their presence.

AVIS

Les Juifs ne sont pas désirés ici, Ste-Agathe est un village canadien français et nous le garderons ainsi.

NOTICE

Jews are not wanted here in Ste. Agathe, so scram while the going is good.

Antisemitic posters

Source: Alex Dworkin Canadian Jewish Archives

CHAPTER SEVEN

"The Line Must Be Drawn Somewhere": Shades of Antisemitism in Canada, 1760–1945

WHAT IS ANTISEMITISM?

In the history of the Canadian Jewry, the spectre of animosity directed at the community has been an ever-present factor, reaching its zenith in the 1930s. Hatred of Judaism and Jews (antisemitism), culminating in the Holocaust (the genocide against European Jewry during the Nazi era), began two thousand years ago. The term was first coined by Wilhelm Marr (1819–1904), a German who had a rather unsuccessful career in business and journalism, as hatred of Jews and Judaism, in a pamphlet titled *The Way to Victory of Germanism over Judaism* in 1879. He mistakenly associated the language group termed Semitic (which includes Hebrew, Arabic, and Aramaic) with a racial group of the same name. His assumption was tied to the false proposition that biology determines group behaviour. Marr drew on the medieval stigma that Jews had "inferior blood" and therefore were an inferior race. This reasoning led, during the Nazi era, to the formulation that Jews had to be excluded from the human species. Antisemitism is an absurd term whose literal meaning is hatred of one who speaks a Semitic language.[1]

Racial biology took hold in the mid-nineteenth century and had wide appeal in Europe and North America. It posited that visible physical characteristics divided humans into races of which there was a hierarchy. The superior race was the "Aryan" one, which again confused a linguistic group, Aryan, which includes the Germanic languages, with physical features. In this characterization, Jews constituted a separate race, at the bottom of the classification. Their biology determined their behaviour, which included, among many unseemly characteristics, an aptitude for business, cunning and deviousness, tribal identity, and disloyalty to their state. Thus, even if a Jew converted to Christianity, his "blood" was the determining factor in his identity, marking him an enemy of other races. The Nazi party, which emerged after World War I, took this specious "scientific" interpretation one step further, by determining that Jews would bring about the destruction of the Aryan race, and therefore had to be eliminated from the rest of humanity. The invocation of visible characteristics as the basis for racial classification conveniently justified colonialization. Human classification according to these pseudo-biological categories was the underpinning of modern racism, of which antisemitism is the category reserved for Jews. In fact, race is a social construct, rather than a scientific one.

The coalescence of historic antisemitism, which had its roots in Christianity in the proposition that Jews were responsible for the Crucifixion, and modern antisemitism, which posited that they were a subordinate race bent on world domination, led to the most significant publication of antisemitic indictment of modern times – *The Protocols of the Elders of Zion*. The book, serialized in a Russian newspaper in 1903, was supposedly the minutes (or protocols) of meetings of Jewish leaders around the world to plan global domination by manipulating the world economy, controlling the media, and fomenting revolutions and wars. It was soon translated into many languages and circulated worldwide. In fact, the *Protocols* was written by extreme nationalist elements tied to the Czarist secret police as a clumsy plagiarization of a French political satire in which Jews are not even mentioned. Its impact was enormous in instigating antisemitism worldwide and was widely referred to by the most rabid antisemites, including those in Canada, and was a major influence for the formulation of Hitler's world view. In the last half century, the text has been cited as proof of Israel's intention to destabilize the world.

There are several shades of antisemitism in Canada. Antisemitism in Canada has been subject to regional differences based on class, religion, and ethnicity, creating different shades of anti-Jewish invective. Irrespective of these differences, they collectively contributed to anti-Jewish discrimination, culminating in the refusal to respond to the plight of European Jewry during the Nazi era. The historic and modern invocations of the practice are the framework for this discussion.

1760–1867 OVERVIEW

There is little evidence of overt antisemitism in British North America, due primarily to the tiny Jewish population of about one thousand at Confederation. Chapter 1 discussed the disallowance of Ezekiel Hart to assume a seat in the Assembly of Lower Canada in 1808 for refusing to swear his oath on the Christian Bible. The Hart affair was due more to the need to have a French-Canadian hold the seat rather than anti-Jewish animus. Twenty years later, when the tiny Jewish community petitioned to have the right to hold property for communal purposes there was no opposition from French Canada. Further, in 1831, the community pushed for the protection of their rights. Supported by the assembly, the bill was given royal assent the next year, "professing the Jewish Religion [be]entitled to all the rights and privileges of other subjects of His Majesty in this Province [Lower Canada]."[2]

After the failed rebellion of 1837 in Lower Canada propagated by *patriots* in the assembly, the Roman Catholic Church launched an attack on liberalism and republicanism that implicated Jews. While this had little impact at the time, this regressive policy, termed *ultramontane*, became fixed, with dire consequences for the Jewish community. The Protestant majority in the colony, on the other hand, had little negative comment. The credit rating agency R.G. Dunn intoned in 1863 that M. Feintuch, who had applied was "a Jew of the regular type,"[3] implying that he was shady, an opinion that was reinforced in other applications. Nevertheless, at Confederation, when there were approximately one thousand Jews in the Dominion, there was little discrimination. Henry Nathan, for example, was elected to the House of Commons in 1870, and Selim Franklin, his counterpart in Victoria, to the provincial legislature in the same year.

Shade One: Anglo-Protestant Supremacy

Through the nineteenth century, English Protestants undertook widespread missionary activity. While this was predominantly to convert the colonized peoples of Africa and Asia, a small contingent focused on Canada. Their message was summarized by a Congregationalist minister, Reverend Henry Wilkes, in Montreal in 1851. His sermon intoned that the Old Testament was specific about the traits of a messiah, of which Jesus was the embodiment. Jewish rejection of Jesus in this context was "(a) perversion of a misguided rationalism," relegating Judaism as an outmoded faith. Therefore, Christianity was considered to have superseded Judaism. The ideal Jew, then, was one who converted. This was the central theme of Anglo-Protestant supremacy. While not inherently antisemitic, it added a layer to the prevailing view that Jews were fundamentally inferior.

The efflorescence of Anglo-Protestant supremacy in Canada was in the second half of the nineteenth century. It was invoked to primarily decry the danger of a Roman Catholic domination of the new nation, rather than to combat Judaism. Rooted in the split between Catholics and Protestants in the Reformation was the belief that each branch sought to destroy the legitimacy of the other. In Canada, with the mass migration of Irish Catholics in the middle decades of the century together with the increasingly strident tones of ultramontanism in French Canada, Protestants felt that the new nation would become captive to the Vatican. With the rise of Quebec nationalism, sparked by the Métis uprisings of 1870 and 1885, the Manitoba Schools Act in the 1890s, and French-Canadian condemnation of Britain in the Boer War (1898–1902), the backlash against Catholics reached a feverish pitch, sparked by the Orange Order (named after William of Orange, the British Monarch who subdued the Catholic majority in 1690 and comprising descendants of Protestant immigrants from northern Ireland), who were especially hostile. The Orange Order was influential in the political and commercial development of English Canada, notably in Ontario, until the mid-twentieth century. Anti-Catholic resentment was directed at all Canadians who were not of Anglo-Protestant heritage, including Jews.

The most noteworthy figure in the initial promotion of Anglo-Canadian antisemitism was Goldwin Smith (1843–1910). Born in England, Smith was professor of modern history at the University of Oxford. In 1867, he joined the history faculty at Cornell University and then moved to Toronto four years later. Until his death, he was considered the most prominent intellectual in Canada, termed the "Sage of the Grange" (his home in Toronto), known for his prolific output of essays and articles. His anti-Jewish animus was sparked by his hatred of Benjamin Disraeli, who was born into a Jewish family, but was converted in his childhood. Disraeli was a prominent figure in the British Conservative

Party and served as prime minister on two separate occasions. In 1848 Smith began writing critical articles that came to focus on Disraeli's Jewish birth. Disraeli responded by calling him a social parasite. McMaster University professor Alan Mendelson in his book *Exiles from Nowhere: The Jews and the Canadian Elite* explains that Smith's hatred of Jews evoked the antisemitic tropes of the period: a rejection of humanity, statelessness, tribalism, and Christian triumphalism. He writes:

> Genteel antisemitism … was not a simple matter of racism. It was an elaborate edifice in which traditional racial stereotypes were transformed by the doctrines of Christian triumphalism and supersessionism … Smith's "achievement" was to translate supersessionism into a kind of economic and sociological analysis (whereby) modern Jews were a parasitic remnant, who could never be patriots, because their only country was their race, which was "one with their religion."[4]

Gerald Tulchinsky notes that "it is impossible to estimate the true effect of (Smith's) antisemitic declarations on public opinion or public policy."[5] This is due to several factors. The first is that Smith was an intellectual, not a politician. He did not rouse crowds and had no intent or interest in creating a movement. The second is that his antisemitism was polite, not so much in his pronouncements as in their social impact. In his years in Canada, Jews were restricted from joining the cozy confines of the Anglo-Protestant elite, namely their clubs and associations. This concealed discrimination did not affect the vast majority of Canadian Jews, especially the immigrants. The Jewish elite, in turn, created its own inner sanctums. Third, Smith's writings did not reach the average Anglo-Protestant worker. Widespread literacy had not penetrated across the country to many native English speakers. Finally, the daily antisemitism that most Jews encountered was from fellow residents and workers, especially from other European immigrants and from French Canadians.

Yet, Tulchinsky's point has merit. Smith was extremely influential in the Anglo-Protestant elite. He corresponded with Macdonald and Laurier, was a close friend of William Lyon Mackenzie King's father, who was a frequent visitor at the Grange together with his sons. His anti-Jewish views resonated with three generations of formidable Canadian intellectuals, and more significantly, with Canadian political leaders.

Smith's contemporary, George Munro Grant (1835–1902), was an ordained Presbyterian minister who traversed the Dominion writing a diary of his experiences. He became principal of Queen's University in 1877, was a frequent contributor to *Grip* magazine, and the *Globe* newspaper. He was the foremost promoter of Christian triumphalism, the belief that because Christianity superseded Judaism, it had been victorious. Hence, his mission was to Christianize the world. This was prescribed in his 1894 publication, *Religions of the World in Relation to Christianity*. In real terms, Jews may have been among the thirteen "non-Christian" students at Queen's University but far more telling is that the trustees and officials had to be professing Christians. Historian Michael Brown concludes that a "national university" where Jews were excluded meant that "Jews were not part of the nation."[6]

Grant's progeny, directly and through intermarriage, included some of the leading Canadians of the twentieth century: Vincent Massey (1887–1967), the first Canadian-born governor general, and George Grant (1918–88), the renowned philosopher of the post–World War II era. Each exercised antisemitism in their political and academic appointments as will be discussed below.

Shade Two: French Canada, Religion, and Nationalism

The triumph of the British forces in 1759–60 over New France was perceived as catastrophic for the sixty thousand Quebecois. They feared that eventually they would be swamped by English-speaking Protestants, leading to the loss of their heritage. Although they were somewhat mollified by the Quebec Act that protected Roman Catholicism and use of the French language, their fears never were abated. The great majority remained insulated from the British presence in the villages and farms. National survival meant that threats, perceived or actual, had to be countered. The Roman Catholic Church was the bulwark for the preservation of the two pillars of national identity – faith and language – which included education and health. Yet, the threat was not only religious, in the guise of Protestantism, but secular, especially with the advent of industrialization. Hence, a growing nationalist movement arose, whereby survival would be protected through political means. In this regard, a third pillar, race, was identified. Consequently, through the nineteenth century, the political realm became increasingly significant in preserving survival. From the *Patriotes* in 1837, to the *Bleus* in the Conservative Party at Confederation, to threats of English domination posed from Confederation, to World War II, varieties of nationalist expression arose, voiced by powerful politicians and clergy. While not always agreeing on a course of action, the Roman Catholic Church in Quebec and the nationalists projected the fear that the nation may not survive. For them, the threat was magnified by the arrival of non-French immigrants to Quebec specifically, and to Canada in general. The group that posed the greatest threat was the Jews. This shade of antisemitism is explored from three perspectives: Jews in the minds of French Canada, Jews in the lives of French Canadians, and French Canadians in the lives of Jews.

In the first century of Jewish life in Canada, few French Canadians knowingly encountered Jews. When they did so, Jews were usually perceived as Anglos. Rather, the Jew that existed in their minds was based on traditional religious stereotypes. Foremost, they were Christ killers, having inherited this calumny, which proclaimed that all Jews shared the guilt for the Crucifixion. Second, Jews were committed to kill Christians through blood rituals and the spread of diseases and pestilence. Third, that Jews were bent on destroying Christianity by controlling economic affairs. Fourth, that as Jews were condemned to live without a homeland they were a silent but effective enemy of host nations. These traditional views were heightened by two developments in the nineteenth century: ultramontanism and growing antisemitism in France.

Ultramontanism ("beyond the borders") is a term applied to the supremacy of the Pope's words and writings. In response to the failed rebellion in Lower Canada in 1837, clerics viewed the *Patriotes* as "liberals," bent on upsetting the traditional order. In 1864 Pope Pius IX promulgated the *Syllabus of Errors*, including the one that the Pontiff could not condone liberalism. This strengthened the resolve of the Church to control the education of Roman Catholics across the land. Religion scholar Ira Robinson writes "the papacy in the nineteenth century was vehemently opposed to the very aspects of the modern world that had revolutionized the civil and political status of Jews and enabled their equality."[7] Ultramontanism was also influenced by racial biology, spreading the view that Jews were in a secret cabal with the Masonic Order to destroy Christian civilization.

Antisemitism's growth in France in the late nineteenth century contributed to how Jews were perceived in the minds of French Canadians. It was a reaction to ill-fated liberal revolutions earlier in the century. Politicians who adopted antisemitism found it a successful route to power. The country was engrossed in Édouard Drumont's *La France juive* that spoke of a Jewish takeover. In 1894 it was heightened when a Jew, Alfred Dreyfus, who was a French captain, was arrested for treason for having passed on secrets to Germany. His trial and conviction split the country between conservative and liberal factions. Although Dreyfus was finally exonerated, the impact of Drumont and the Dreyfus affair on French Canada resulted in several articles, notably by Paul Tardivel in the influential newspaper *La Vérité*, in support of the conservative forces, which coalesced with the views of Church leaders.

The concept of French Canadians as a race reached its fruition through the writings of the nationalist politician, Henri Bourassa, and the ultramontane cleric, Lionel Groulx. Bourassa (1868–1952) served in the Canadian parliament and Quebec legislature for almost forty years. A prolific writer, he founded the intellectual daily *Le Devoir* in 1910. Bourassa was outspoken in his opposition to Canadian participation in the British Empire, especially during the Boer War and World War I, ironically sharing the views of Goldwin Smith. He created the *Ligue nationaliste canadienne* in 1903 to protect French-Canadian institutions, primarily the maintenance of French as a language of instruction outside Quebec. He supported the Roman Catholic Church with respect to faith and maintaining the social order but opposed its involvement in politics. Termed the father of French-Canadian Nationalism, he was not ambivalent about the Jewish question. In 1906, for example, he railed against "a system which peopled the West with a mixture of foreigners, neglecting prospective French and Belgian colonists in favour of Jews from Poland and Russia."[8] During the Conscription Crisis in 1944 he declared: "We don't want to see thousands of young Canadians die overseas to save international Jewry's finances."[9]

Lionel Groulx (1878–1967) was a priest, historian, and, following Bourassa, a champion of French-Canadian nationalism. He held a chair in history at the Université de Montréal for more than thirty years. He saw the conquest as a catastrophe and Confederation as a threat to his nation. Unlike Bourassa, Groulx did not uphold human rights and liberalism, but was strictly protectionist of traditional French-Canadian values. He was a force in *Action française*, the most significant nationalist movement in Quebec. Historian Esther Delisle attacks him and his legacy as being inherently racist. Adopting the views of French writers, he argued that not only physical, but socio-psychological characteristics were transmitted through blood, and when this is done by two people of different "races," the stronger one will degenerate. He wrote in *L'appel de la race* ("Calling the Race") that "peoples who have arrived at a high degree of civilization have always avoided mixing with foreigners."[10]

In the minds of those French Canadians who resonated with Groulx's pronouncements, the most invidious foreigner was the Jew. As the Jewish population in Quebec swelled from about one thousand to forty-eight thousand in 1921, forming the third largest ethno-cultural community in the province, the fears mounted that the nation was at risk. The coalescence of traditional religious antisemitism and modern pseudo-biological race theory created an unhealthy climate as Jews became a daily presence in the lives of many French Canadians, notably in Montreal, where 6 per cent of the populace was Jewish.

Jews and French Canadians converged at the turn of the twentieth century due to the Great Migration, industrialization, and urbanization. At Confederation, 15 per cent of French Quebec lived in urban areas; by 1921, this had swollen to 52 per cent. Montreal's population grew from 107,000 in 1871 to 618,000 in 1921. The non-French-Canadian cohort decreased from 38 to 27 per cent, while the French population grew from approximately 65,000 to approximately 370,000. They provided much of the labour force for the port and rail development and in secondary manufacturing. Living almost exclusively east of the Boulevard St. Laurent ("the Main"), they created neighbourhoods that were virtually exclusively French speaking. Their contact with Jews was effectively limited to those, like themselves, who were recent migrants. Contact occurred in public places and in factories. Jews and French Canadians shared the Plateau with smaller groups of immigrants from eastern Europe. As much of the small commerce was in the hands of Jews, their exchanges occurred daily. While French children attended schools under the Catholic Board and Jewish youngsters under the Protestant Board, they played in the same streets and parks. Yet, as Ira Robinson states, "proximity meant conflict as well as comfort." Quoting the poet Irving Layton, who grew up on the Plateau, "without fail, every Easter, they would descend on the embattled Jews with bottles and bricks, and we'd be waiting for them on the roofs, like an army, with sticks, and stones, with anything."[11] Proximity also reinforced stereotypes for both communities. This was not reserved for Montreal, or French Canada. Similar hostilities, while not as regular or aggressive, occurred in working-class neighbourhoods where Jews and other ethnic groups shared living space.

In factories, especially the rapidly expanding textile trade, Jews and French Canadians worked side by side. This was especially the case for young women. It would have been rare to hear English spoken on these shop floors. We assume that the conversations between the two groups were limited due to linguistic barriers, but presumably each learned some of the other's language. At a different level of contact were French Canadians and uptown Jews. Many of the household workers in wealthy Jewish households – maids, cooks, nannies, chauffeurs, and maintenance staff – were French Canadians. What were their relations? To what did degree did their interactions re-enforce predominant stereotypes?

At another level were the interactions between Jewish and French businessmen and professionals. Again, these were initially limited due to the barriers to upward mobility instigated by the Anglo oligarchy. Victor Goldbloom (1923–2016) was the grandson of immigrants. His father, Alton, was the first pediatrician in Quebec. The family lived on Crescent Street in central Montreal. The short span of the street from Sherbooke (the major east-west street in Montreal) to St. Catherine (the main shopping street) housed seventy-five doctors, of whom only one was French. After learning French so that he could take care of French-speaking children, he required the same of his children. Victor and his brother Richard followed into their father's profession.

Jewish daily life was marked, in part, by a struggle to combat the calumny that was expressed by some French Canadians to their presence in the city. Several incidents illuminate this conflict. In 1910 Joseph-Edouard Plamondon, a lawyer and journalist for *La Libre Parole*, addressed a Catholic youth organization in Quebec City. He charged Jews with many of the traditional antisemitic accusations that arose in the Middle Ages – ritual murder, usury, the Crucifixion – and cited the Talmud as the source for these hatreds. He called for the eradication of their equal rights and for their expulsion. Consequently, Jewish homes and businesses in Quebec City were vandalized and individuals were beaten. In a civil suit launched by two Jewish residents, Plamondon was acquitted of libel. This was overturned in an appeal, leaving the outcome ambiguous. Nevertheless, it was a turning point in the public condemnation of Jews in Canadian history.

A second incident was public education in Quebec. The Catholic boards would not accept non-Catholic children. Hence, Jews registered their children in the Protestant system, where in Montreal, they constituted 40 per cent of the enrolment by 1919. Yet Jews were not allowed to sit on school boards nor were they hired as teachers. When Jews called for their own board, they were attacked by Catholics and called "enemies" who did not have the same rights as Christians.

A third incident was the appointment of Dr. Samuel Rabinovitch as an intern at the Hôpital Notre Dame. He was a graduate of the Université de Montréal, because of McGill's strict quota on Jewish students. His appointment led to a strike by non-Jewish interns, who were joined by those in other Catholic hospitals. Although some French leaders opposed this action, the predominant response was support for the strikers, marked by angry letters including those that argued that Jews were bent on domination in all fields and that they should be formally ghettoized. Rabinovitch, like most Jewish graduates, was then forced to intern in the United States.

In sum, there was not a unified French-Canadian nationalist organization. The main players, apart from Groulx's *Action française* and Bourassa's *Ligue nationaliste canadienne*, were *Jeune-Canada* and *Le parti national social chrétien* (LPNSC). *Jeune-Canada* was created by young French-Canadian intellectuals in 1933. There is dispute as to its antisemitic tone. Historian Esther Delisle claimed that it was an important force, whereas Pierre Anctil points out that its antisemitic rhetoric was pronounced only once. The LPNSC was avowedly fascist. Its role is further discussed below.

There is no question that French-Canadian nationalism was the response to fear of the loss of the pillars of the community – language, religion, and race. Apprehension of Jewish control was deeply seated in traditional and racist antisemitism, and the Jews were an easy target, victimized as well by Anglo Protestants and some euro-ethnics. Their presence, notably in Montreal, was viewed as a palpable threat. Ira Robinson concludes: "Whether antisemitism was worse in Quebec than elsewhere in Canada is debatable; its reality was not."[12]

Shade Three: Western Nativism

Nativism is a term that describes hostility to immigrants by the dominant ethno-cultural majority. In Canada, Protestant immigrants from the British Isles and to a degree from Scandinavia, were considered "native." For everyone else, Catholics, Jews, eastern and southern Europeans, Asians, and those of African heritage, whether native born or immigrant, were regarded as a menace. This animus was also directed at Canada's actual natives, the First Nations. Nativism in the Canadian west took a decidedly different turn than in Ontario, Quebec, and the Maritimes. There, it was expressed through agrarian protest leading to the establishment of political parties, of which the Social Credit Party was by far the most successful and enduring. Further, opposition to non-Anglo-Protestant immigration in the new provinces established in the Prairies after Confederation was exacerbated by the crippling impact of the economic woes of the interwar period, culminating in the Great Depression. These two intertwined developments were the fodder for western Canadian antisemitism.

The opening of the Prairies for settlement in the "last best west" attracted immigrants from across the European continent, eastern Canadians, and Americans. Europeans arrived after an arduous trans-Atlantic crossing and a slow journey by train from eastern Canada. They and other migrants were then faced with the reality of an unforgiving climate, isolation, and a paucity of resources. Their travail was heightened by the accumulation of a crippling debt to establish their livelihood on a farm. But the non-Anglo-Protestant newcomers faced an additional obstacle: the recalcitrance from some of their fellow immigrants who were "native" Canadian and American immigrants to their arrival and settlement, which altered the region's ethnic balance. By the 1920s Anglo Protestants were in the minority in Saskatchewan and their numerical superiority was declining in Manitoba and Alberta. As discussed in Chapter 3, Jewish migration was initially negligible. In 1901 there were some two thousand, across the three Prairie provinces, with the majority in Winnipeg. Twenty years later, it had grown to twenty-five thousand, constituting about 1.3 per cent of all inhabitants.

The seeds of agrarian protest were in the United States. After the Civil War, the huge migration to the Midwest and Prairies established the country's agricultural underpinnings and constituted a significant portion of its exports. Yet falling grain prices, the devaluation of silver, periodic depressions, and rapacious borrowing rates led to widespread protest. Numerous parties and movements arose leading to violent incidents and demonstrations. Although they spanned the political spectrum, from the racist Ku Klux Klan (KKK), which had its largest contingent in Indiana, to democratic socialists, they shared the belief that there was a conspiracy to deny them a livelihood. These sentiments gravitated to the Canadian West.

In Canada, agrarian discontent led to the creation of the United Farmers movement, which was decentralized as a collection of provincial parties rather than as a national party. While short lived in eastern Canada, it was successful in the Prairies. The United Farmers of Manitoba was formed in 1920, on a platform of cooperative marketing bodies, creation of a central bank, and regulation in transportation. Supporting farmer candidates, it won the election in 1922 in cooperation with the Progressive Party, but soon withdrew, as it came to reject this political affiliation. In Saskatchewan the movement was absorbed by the provincial Liberals. Unlike in the other farmers' movements, they moved towards socialism and joined the CCF in 1935.

The United Farmers of Alberta (UFA) had the longest standing impact. It formed the government from 1921 to 1935, having originated as a lobby group. It was directly influenced by the American agrarian parties, in part because 22 per cent of the population in 1911 was American born. Its creator, the American Henry Wise Wood, assumed three tenets of the American populists: i) the harmony of the "productive classes," ii) the belief in the eternal struggle between evil and good, and iii) a conspiratorial theory of history. From this last point emerged the doctrine of the primacy of money, which was dominated by an alliance between bankers and Jews. In a 1965 edition of *Agricultural History*, American historian Irwin Unger wrote: "To populists the Jew was a non-producer, a mere manipulator of money, a parasite and at the same time representative of the sinister and forbidding power of international finance."[13] Yet, according to historian Howard Palmer, "antisemitism did not emerge in the UFA, but it did so with a vengeance in Alberta's second populist movement, Social Credit."[14] Even the KKK in Alberta focused its attacks on Catholics, and only intermittently against Jews. This was also the case in Saskatchewan, where the KKK had several thousand adherents, many of whom were also aligned with the ultra–Protestant Orange Order.

The Great Depression ravaged the Prairies. While Canada's agricultural economy declined by 68 per cent from 1928 to 1932, in the Prairies the figure was 92 per cent. In Alberta, the per capita income dropped from $548 in 1929 to $212 in 1933. Historian Janine Stingel writes: "Semi-starvation was not uncommon, and in some areas of Alberta the need for food forced people to pickle gophers."[15] Farm debts soared; especially as mechanized farming had taken hold in the previous decades. Interest was the crop that never failed. Credit created a cycle of dependence that ultimately led to bankruptcy. Blame was placed on "the east," the Ottawa-Montreal-Toronto triangle, which dominated the country's economy.

While the UFA had transformed itself from a protest party to an establishment monolith, with more in common with the socialist CCF than with its constituents, a more strident movement, Social Credit, emerged. Its founder, C.H. Douglas, was an un-orthodox dreamer and schemer who preached of an illusory monetary theory to subsidize producers, spread the profits, and wrest control from the banks. Further, he spoke of the Jewish conspiracy to dominate the world. He influenced some UFA politicians, but his major convert was William Aberhart, a radio evangelist, whose reputed audience numbered three hundred thousand, about half of the province at the height of the Depression.

Aberhart inculcated the doctrine and methods of American populism – huge rallies, thunderous rhetoric, simplistic solutions, and empty promises. In the 1935 election, the UFA received but 11 per cent of the vote, and Social Credit swept to power winning fifty-six of sixty-three seats. It was the beginning of its iron grip in Alberta, one that lasted until 1968. Douglas had infected the movement. His "second bible" was *The Protocols of the Elders of Zion.* In his delusions, he wrote in 1943 that "Hitler received exactly the same kind of support from powerful Jews as did the Kaiser."[16] Historian Janine Stingel states that Aberhart, while adopting Douglas's monetary fallacies, created his own brand of Social Credit, a mix of fundamentalism and conspiracy. Yet, by many accounts, Aberhart was not a diehard antisemite. Both Palmer and Stingel opine that he had ambiguous feelings about the Jews. Aberhart died in 1943 and his successor, Ernest Manning, ruled Alberta for the following twenty-five years.

On the surface, Manning was not an antisemite. He did not utter the word "Jew" in a derogatory fashion. But it did not take much to understand what he meant. He spoke of "a positive anti-Christian conspiracy, seeing to destroy everything which can be identified with the true Christian way of life."[17] He employed innuendo, creating, in the words of historian Bob Hesketh, "a veil of respectability" for antisemites.[18] Manning was a consummate politician who understood how to couch the party's racist views. This task put him squarely into conflict with the Douglasites, who controlled the party organ, *Today and Tomorrow*, which revealed the crimes of "the international Jewish conspiracy." The most outspoken figure was Norman Jaques, an MP (the national Social Credit Party was officially created in 1944), who read sections of *The Protocols of the Elders of Zion* in the House of Commons. Jaques, according to historian Howard Palmer, "amalgamated all the major foes of Social Credit – international finance, socialism and internationalism – and identified them as either predominantly or exclusively Jewish."[19] Ultimately, Manning purged the party of this group in 1947, recognizing that, in his mind, the greatest threat was socialism.

Palmer argues that Manning suppressed antisemitism in the movement. Stingel takes a different perspective: that he sanitized Social Credit's philosophy, in part because the revelations of the Holocaust cast a negative light on antisemitism, and because the discovery of oil in the province necessitated a less radical stance. Manning never refrained, however, from invoking the international Jewish conspiracy. Stingel writes: "Social Credit's extensive anti-Semitic [*sic*] propaganda campaign may not have physically harmed one Jew, but it adversely affected the entire Canadian Jewish community at a time when it feared for the fate of its European brethren and ultimately its own."[20]

Shade Four: Fascism

Antisemitism reached its peak in Canada in the interwar period due to the domestic factors cited above and was further exacerbated by international developments. The peace conferences in the wake of World War I, and the Bolshevik Revolution, recreated Europe. The Russian, German, Austrian, and Ottoman empires had fallen, Germany was subjected to exceedingly harsh losses, and the rising discontent helped fuel economic and political chaos. Extreme nationalist movements arose, and they took power across the continent, first in Italy led by Benito Mussolini in 1922, Germany under Adolf Hitler in 1933, and Spain under Francisco Franco in 1936. In the first two, they overthrew weak democracies, and in Spain, the royalty. These movements, termed fascist, after the Italian word *fascio* for a bundle of rods, indicating strength through unity, infected the continent. They were fuelled not only by the postwar political vacuum and economic collapse, but by the emergence of the Soviet Union under Josef Stalin igniting the long-held fear of the spectre of international communism. The impact of these developments reverberated in Canada.

There is no definitive boundary separating fascism from Anglo-Protestant supremacy, French-Canadian nationalism, or western-Canadian nativism. Lionel Groulx, for example, exhibited strong fascistic characteristics, but was not a supporter of the fascist party that arose in Quebec, nor was Norman Jaques, the extremist Social Credit MP, aligned with western fascist movements. Nevertheless, fascism gained a foothold in Canada. In part, it was because there were German and Italian Canadians who were sympathizers under the aegis of the home countries' agent provocateurs and consulates in Canada, and in part, because of fascism's appeal to a sliver of Anglo Protestants and French Canadians. These shocks ultimately propelled a Jewish response, marked by the rebirth of the CJC. Fascism's appeal was dealt a blow when Canada went to war in 1939.

In the 1930s, there were almost five hundred thousand Canadians of German ancestry, with the largest concentrations in southwestern Ontario and in rural centres in the Canadian west. The National Socialist message was carried by German government agents who infiltrated the communities. They subsidized German language schools, printed yearbooks, monographs, and articles, and created organizations, including a tiny Nazi Party. The German Labour Front assisted workers and the Canadian Society for German Culture (*Deutscher Bund*), led by Germany's unofficial ambassador, Karl Gerhard, was particularly effective in Saskatchewan, boasting almost one thousand members. The largest newspaper, *Deutsche Zeitung*, alleged that "a certain segment of the Canadian Press (attempted) to poison public opinion and to stir up racial hatred."[21] With respect, Italian and German Canadians did not flock to join these groups. The message of fealty to the homeland had a certain resonance, and many would have enjoyed the ethnic festivals, but foreign provocateurs played a marginal role in Canadian society. After the declaration of war, some of their leaders were eventually interned in camps across the country.

The foremost Canadian fascist was Adrien Arcand (1899–1967), a Montreal journalist who proclaimed himself the "Canadian Fuhrer." He was inspired by extreme French-Canadian nationalism and Adolf Hitler. He wrote and published several inflammatory journals that were shut down by the government in 1933. Undeterred, he immediately created *Le parti national social chrétien* (LPNSC) and started a newspaper, *Le Patriote.* Its language was inflammatory: "Jewry because of its very essence, because of its destructive instincts, because of its ancient atavism of corruption, because of its exclusively materialistic feelings, constitutes the real danger for the peoples whether materially or spiritually. Therefore, the Jewish Question needs to be at the foundation of any true fascism, of any serious movement of national regeneration."[22] He referred to Jews as cockroaches and insects, taking his inspiration from *Der Stürmer*, the organ of the Nazi party in Germany, and from traditional antisemitic tropes. Arcand remained a shadowy figure until his death. His avatar was Ernst Zundel, a German immigrant, who emerged as the largest distributor of antisemitic propaganda in the world in the 1970s.

While the membership of the LPNSC was miniscule (six thousand at its height), Arcand commanded wide attention. Some of Montreal's twenty thousand Italian Canadians were sympathetic to his call, but it was in the political realm where Arcand cast a shadow. The formation of the ultra-nationalist *Union nationale* party, led by the firebrand Maurice Duplessis, upset the traditional Liberal monopoly in the 1936 provincial election. Except for four years during World War II, it held power until 1960. The Union nationale was hysterically anti-communist and invoked a Padlock Law in 1937 to shut down any establishment that propagated communism. But the wording was deliberately vague, so that it was applied to any organizations and individuals that were considered a threat to the province, including political opponents. Duplessis was wily enough to ignore Arcand and mollify Groulx while implementing some of their hysteria to secure his domination of the province.

While there was fascist sentiment among a minority of Canadians of French, German, and Italian heritage, its impact on Canadians of

Anglo-Protestant background may have been as profound. In Winnipeg, William Whittaker, a British immigrant, established the Canadian Nationalist Party in 1933, shortly after the Nazi seizure of power in Germany. It attempted to replicate its German forerunner, employing its uniforms, tactics, and symbols, notably the swastika, but embellished its rallies with Union Jacks. Its organ, *The Canadian Nationalist*, employed antisemitic tropes, including global conspiracy and the equation of Judaism with communism. Its appeal went beyond the Prairies to Ontario, where a wing, the Canadian Union of Fascists, emerged. As such, Whittaker undertook an association with Arcand in 1937, creating the National Unity Party. It called for a leadership convention the following year in Toronto. In the interim, Whittaker died. The convention, at Massey Hall, drew some fifteen hundred people, while the counter demonstrations at Maple Leaf Gardens and at Queen's Park had a tenfold greater attendance. As the prospect of war grew, Arcand remained the only major fascist figure in Canada.

THE CHRISTIE PITS RIOT

The most singular fascist-inspired event was at Christie Pits, a park that was the site of a baseball ground, adjacent to a European immigrant neighbourhood in Toronto. On August 16, 1933, a riot erupted during a game between a largely Jewish team and one composed of Anglo Canadians. In the stands, when Anglo supporters unveiled a huge flag displaying the swastika, they were attacked by Jewish spectators. As news spread throughout the neighbourhood, supporters of each group, fellow European immigrants siding with the Jews, and Anglos with their cohort, rushed to the Pits. An estimated five thousand people participated as police were slow to respond, and when they appeared, they let the riot continue. Fortunately, there were no fatalities, but countless people were injured, and there were several arrests.

The context for the riot pointed to three factors. The first was that Toronto was a "British" city, dubbed the Belfast of Canada, because of the power of the Orange Order that controlled the municipal institutions, including the police, and whose views received a warm reception by the *Toronto Telegram*. Second, the city, according to sociologists Cyril Levitt and William Shaffir, was "a loose federation of wards and neighbourhoods, and the concept of territory were clearly demarcated in the different cognitive maps of the city held by various ethnic and religious groups."[23] Christie Pits was a border zone between the large immigrant community made up of Jews, Italians, and other Euro-ethnics, and working-class Anglos. The third factor was the seizure of power by the Nazis in Germany. This spawned swastika clubs in Anglo neighbourhoods. The main one was in the city's east end, the Beaches. On Sundays, it swelled with citizens from across the city, many of them immigrants, which greatly annoyed the local denizens. They vented their displeasure by singling out the Jews. Although they did not instigate the riot, they set the tone for local groups, including the "Pit Gang" that unfurled the flag. The riot was the touchstone event of antisemitism in an unseemly decade.

Canadian fascists were unable to create a viable national movement because they did not have an effective leader who could span the ethnic and linguistic divides, but predominantly its attempt was doomed because vocal, strident antisemitism was not acceptable, even to those who harboured antisemitic attitudes. Canadians were more comfortable with genteel antisemitism, of the sort that prohibited Jews from entering the halls of financial, corporate, academic, and professional institutions, and that excluded Jews from resorts, clubs, and organizations.

IMPACT, ADAPTATION, AND DIVERSITY

The Christie Pits Riot was an extreme magnification of the daily physical encounters against not only Jews, but against and among other ethnocultural minorities. These were essentially limited to young males in ethnic border zones. Philosopher Howard Adelman who grew up in the Bathurst-College Street neighbourhood in Toronto relates: "I can recall gang fights in [the] school yard of King Edward Public School."[24] The gangs were small, tied to specific streets, such as the Lippincott Gang, the Beanery Boys, and the Jersey Gang. Taunts of "Christ killers" and physical attacks were certainly a manifestation of anti-immigrant hostility. For many working-class Jewish boys, antisemitism was omnipresent. Attacks on Jewish peddlers were ubiquitous. Yet, antisemitism possessed a much greater obstacle to Jewish adaptation and participation in Canadian life than these incidents. Genteel antisemitism was far more pervasive and iniquitous than open and rabid hatred.

Antisemitism was routine. It was present in the workplace, in the educational systems, in housing, and in access to recreational facilities. The T. Eaton Company was very content to employ Jews in their clothing factories but would not hire them to work in stores. It must be stated that the same restriction was placed against other non-Anglo ethno-cultural groups. Jews were denied positions in public institutions. The Protestant Board of Education in Montreal would not hire Jewish teachers, even though Jews represented a significant portion of the student body. Municipal jobs, such as garbage and maintenance work, were closed. Demographer Louis Rosenberg wrote: "In seeking employment in public bodies, Jews must be so outstandingly brilliant that his [*sic*] qualifications swamp the obstacles raised by his birth."[25]

Jews were prevented from owning homes in certain neighbourhoods because of restrictive covenants. They were imposed by municipal jurisdictions in neighbourhoods usually populated by middle- and upper-class Anglos. As with employment, Jews were among ethno-cultural minorities who were denied access. Similar restrictions, as in the Toronto Beaches and in the Laurentian resorts north of Montreal were to be used by "Gentiles Only."[26] Signs bearing this slogan clearly made the point.

Social and institutional antisemitism had a greater impact on the bourgeoning Jewish middle class than the working class. The latter, while struggling to make a living, tended to be self-employed or worked for other Jews, as discussed in Chapters 4 and 6. Workers relied on neighbours, families, and union members in times of need and might have been eligible to secure credit from landsmanschaften. Clearly, during the Great Depression, many lost their jobs and homes regardless of the communal support. Middle-class Jews, however, were impacted more grievously by antisemitism precisely because they had to find a niche within the Canadian mosaic. Writer James Gray quotes an unnamed journalist about the situation in Winnipeg in the 1930s: "None of the city's chartered banks, trust companies, or insurance companies would knowingly hire a Jew.... The oil companies, banks, mortgage companies, financial and stockbrokers and most retail and mercantile companies except for the Hudson's Bay Company, discriminated against all non-Anglo-Saxons."[27]

Jews born or raised in Canada, adapted to Canadian life more rapidly than other non-Anglo immigrants. In general, they did so because the Jewish condition for two thousand years included the necessity to adapt to adverse conditions and because they were not living in their homeland. In addition, all Jewish males had to be literate throughout their history, and multilingual. Ashkenazi Jews spoke Yiddish and at least one European language and many came from cities and towns, allowing them to adjust to their new environment. Thus, there was rapid socio-economic mobility in comparison to most other non-Anglo-Celtic immigrants.

By the 1920s, children of Jewish immigrants who were born or raised in Canada were eager to enter the middle class. The middle class was a new phenomenon in Canada. Until the turn of the twentieth century, most Canadians worked in unskilled jobs, mainly in rural areas. With the rapid industrialization and economic boom, manufacturing production grew tenfold between 1901 and 1929. The workplace became increasingly bureaucratized with layers of management in major industries. Concern about public health, the advent of professional social work, the need for basic applied scientists, and rapid urbanization that required an expansive and trained civil service accelerated the growth of the middle class. In fact, as historian Paul Axelrod writes, it was not only expansion but the replacement of the old middle class. This "new middle class," he writes, was propelled by "the prospect of a decline in their ('the old') social status unless they adapted to new economic and vocational realities."[28] In addition to the traditional professions of law and medicine, business, engineering, teaching, sales, dentistry, and pharmacy were among the professions that now required advanced training. The middle class grew by 120 per cent from 1901 to 1941, in contrast to the total population, which grew by 34 per cent.

The interwar period marked the acceleration of the diversity, in the socio-economic realm, of Canadian Jews. Louis Rosenberg's monumental study of the 1931 census shows that about half of gainfully employed Jews over the age of 10 were in middle-class jobs, in comparison to 40 per cent a decade earlier. Further 60 per cent of those who were Canadian born were in this cohort, reflecting the rapid adaptation of immigrant children. The majority were in "lower middle class" occupations, especially in merchandising and clerical positions. Five per cent were "professionals," consistent with the national average, but double the average in music, law, medicine, and dentistry, and vastly disproportionate to other immigrants from Continental Europe. This underscores their accelerated adaptation. It also signifies that there was a growing socio-economic diversity at play, essentially between those who were employed in unskilled and semi-skilled labour and in small commerce on the one hand, and essentially a younger cohort, born or raised in Canada, that were in the process of elevating themselves in the workplace.

Entry into middle-class jobs necessitated education, high school degrees for the lower middle class and university for the professions. Aside from the well-worn stereotype of Jewish parents obsessed with their children's social status, education has historically been fundamental to Jewish life. Jewish participation in public education in the immigrant communities accelerated the process of adaptation. A recent study of Clinton Street Public School in Toronto by political scientist Robert Vipond indicates that from 1920 to 1952, most of the students were Jewish, peaking at 70 per cent in the early 1930s. The most notable secondary institutions were Baron Byng High School in Montreal, Harbord Collegiate in Toronto, and St. John's Technical High School in Winnipeg. The bonds and friendships that emerged there lasted through the lifetimes of many of the students.

Despite the hardships of the Depression that deprived Canadian children of further education, those of Jewish heritage who were able to excel academically and find the means to attend post-secondary institutions did so. In 1941, Jewish students constituted 11.3 per cent, 7.2 per cent, 1.9 per cent, 11.4 per cent, and 4.2 per cent of the student body at Dalhousie University, the University of Toronto, University of Western Ontario, the University of Manitoba, and the University of Alberta, respectively. In contrast, Jews made up 1.5 per cent of the Canadian population. The figures for Dalhousie and Manitoba are skewed because most of the students in medicine and some in law came from the United States due to the strict quotas there.

While post-secondary enrolment is a testament to the process of adaptation, many more Jews were prevented from entering the halls of academe because they were Jewish. The doors were closed to them and to racial minorities by the white, Anglo-Celtic, Protestant, and Catholic elite. Paul Axelrod contends: "Jews were perceived as a particular threat to the composition of the campus, and extraordinary actions were taken ... to limit, and in some cases to reduce their presence."[29] McGill University stands out in this respect. In 1924–5, Jews made up

24 per cent of the arts faculty, 15 per cent in medicine, and 40 per cent in law. This greatly disturbed administrators and major donors. Consequently, quotas and higher standards for entry than for gentile students were imposed. As Ira MacKay, the dean of arts put it: "The simple obvious truth is that the Jewish people are of no use to us in this country … a race of men (that) does not fit in with a high civilization in a very new country."[30] The impact was significant. By 1939, Jews represented 12 per cent of those in the arts, 12 per cent in medicine, and 15 per cent in law. Obviously, they were of "some use." One of the outstanding young scholars was A.M. Klein, who graduated from McGill but was forced to study law at the Université de Montréal, a Catholic institution. A similar situation occurred at the University of Manitoba. For those who did graduate many were denied the opportunity to enter the workforce. Law, engineering, and architectural firms were largely closed to Jews. In turn, these graduates either found employment with Jewish-owned firms, or started their own. In the Depression, this proved to be difficult and many turned to more menial employment. Jewish doctors and physiotherapists were not accepted in hospitals. Racial minorities were subject to similar, if not more extreme obstacles.

Antisemitism on campus tended to be less visible than on the street. Jewish students created their own spaces by forming associations, fraternities, and, in the case of the University of Toronto arts and science students, finding a comfortable home on campus. Their invisibility on campus was not due to their acceptance. The University of Toronto kept a tally, because, as its president, H.J. Cody, remarked: "a small group of Hebrew race [*sic*] were entering university without adequate funds."[31] Yet, unlike McGill and Manitoba, there were no established quotas. Students had to belong to a college, and as all colleges save the University College (UC) were denominational, that became their "Jewish" home. A study by this author found that in 1941–2, there were 161 "Hebrews," representing 17 per cent of the UC student body. But their impact was disproportionate to their number. Some were elected to the Literary and Athletic Society that organized college activities, including the annual UC Follies. In the late 1930s, the Follies featured Johnny Wayne and Frank Shuster, who would become Canada's most well-known comedians in the ensuing decades. In recent years UC has recognized "Alumni of Influence." Of the twenty-two who graduated by 1945, eight are Jewish. In addition to Wayne and Shuster, they include

Bora Laskin, who became the chief justice of the Supreme Court, Louis Rasminsky, who was the governor of the Bank of Canada, and Rose Wolfe, who served as the chancellor of the university.

THE JEWISH COMMUNITY RESPONDS

Adaptation to antisemitism was not only undertaken by families and individuals, but by the Jewish community. The interwar period marked the creation of a national community under the aegis of the reconstituted CJC, as discussed in Chapter 5. The communal response came to a head in 1933 in response to William Whittaker and Adrien Arcand's blatant provocations, on four fronts. The first was a bill introduced by a Manitoba MLA, Marcus Hyman, against group libel in response to Whittaker. Hyman was a central figure in the Anti-Fascist League in Winnipeg. The bill was passed unanimously in March 1934 as the Manitoba Defamation Act leading to an injunction that closed Whittaker's publications. The second was the Committee on Jewish-Gentile Relations, chaired by Rabbi Maurice Eisendrath of Toronto's Holy Blossom Temple and Dr. Claris Silcox of the United Church of Canada. They produced a series of publications to educate Canadians about Jews. This was typically Canadian – a polite measure to redress a national condition. The third was much more aggressive: a boycott of German products that was part of a coordinated campaign in alliance with non-Jews marked by lobbying, publicity, and research. It was in effect until the outbreak of World War II.

The final response was the resurrection of CJC in January 1934, prompted by the Nazi seizure of power in Germany and home-grown antisemitism. Concern was heightened with the accession of the Social Credit Party in Alberta and the Union nationale in Quebec in 1935–6, and the remilitarization of Germany. In response, CJC joined with B'nai Brith Canada in creating the JPRC. Among its initial actions was a committee to institute court proceedings against purveyors of antisemitism, promote legislation for court challenges, and align with like-minded gentiles including Afro-Canadian organizations and churches. Working with Dr. Silcox, J.J. Glass, a member of the committee and a Liberal MPP from Toronto, crafted the Discrimination Prevention Act in March 1943. Shortly thereafter, the Liberals lost the provincial election and Glass was defeated by J.B. Salsberg of the LPP. Salsberg supported the Conservatives in return for passage of the bill. The Ontario Racial Discrimination Act became law in 1944. It was a watered-down version of the original draft, limiting the provisions to discriminatory publications, broadcasting, and signs. Nevertheless, it was the first step in ameliorating discrimination in Ontario.

THE SHADES COALESCE: SHUTTING THE IMMIGRATION DOOR

The period from the turn of the century to World War I was the high point of Canadian immigration. While the most favoured immigrants were of Anglo origin, followed by those from Scandinavia, there were no outright restrictions against other Europeans. This relative leniency was rapidly reversed in 1919 and grew increasingly restrictive in the ensuing thirty years. The most grievous obstacles were against the entry of European Jews. This was the due to two interrelated factors. The first was international developments. In the immediate aftermath of World War I, the chaos in the reconstitution of nation states created political and economic turmoil. This was exacerbated by the Bolshevik revolution in 1917 and its triumph in the ensuing civil war. Prime ministers Robert Borden, Arthur Meighen, R.B. Bennett, and William Lyon Mackenzie King were reluctant to allow European immigrants of the "less favoured categories" entry to Canada unless they were farmers. The "Red Scare" led to the deportation of Canadians considered to be revolutionary. In the 1930s, the Great Depression and the overthrow of democracies and monarchies in Europe by fascist movements were obstacles for non-Anglo Europeans in finding a refuge in Canada. The second factor was entrenched racism. As documented, Canada was controlled by the Anglo elite in politics, business, and academia. It was abetted by French-Canadian nationalists who were dedicated to preserving their language, religion, and race. Both groups, at their extremes, constituted the nativist and fascist movements.

The coalescence of these two factors created the conditions under which Jewish immigration was gradually restricted. The Nazi seizure of power in Germany in 1933, their takeover of Austria and Czechoslovakia in 1938, their subjugation of Poland in 1939, their conquest of western Europe in 1940, and their invasion of the Soviet Union in 1941, unleashed the mass murder of European Jews. Given the directive to keep Canada "white," there was no political will for Canadian political and business leaders to respond to the pleas by the country's Jews to provide a haven for the Jews of Europe.

This proved to be the blackest mark in the history of Canadian immigration policy. From 1900 to 1915, almost one hundred thousand Jews immigrated to and settled in Canada, representing about 4 per cent of the total. A further forty thousand arrived until 1931, constituting another 1.7 per cent. Yet, from 1932 to 1945, the figure dwindled to some eight thousand, slightly less than 2 per cent. Concurrently, European Jewry numbered some nine million in 1939, of whom approximately two-thirds were murdered by Nazi Germany and its accomplices during World War II.

From 1919 to 1923 immigration officials restricted skilled and unskilled labour, raised the monetary requirements, instituted passport and visa barriers, narrowed the definition of family reunification, and moved inspections from ports of admission in Canada to points of departure in Europe. In 1923 the noose was tightened as unsponsored immigrants (those without family ties in Canada) and "races that cannot be assimilated without social or economic loss to Canada" were barred.[32] Tellingly, Europeans were divided into three groups: preferred (northern and western Europe, including Germany), non-preferred (central and eastern Europe), and special permit (Italy, Greece, and Bulgaria). Although almost all Jews who were potential immigrants lived in the non-preferred countries, they were the only ethnic group placed under special permit. This permit was issued by the federal cabinet, meaning that it could be granted if the applicant had political influence. Clearly, this was a great hurdle. Further, as historian Harold Troper comments: "In distinguishing Jews from non-Jews of the same citizenship, Canada predated the Nuremberg laws[33] by more than ten years."[34] The only Jews who were permitted were those with first-degree relatives (parents, children, siblings, spouses) in Canada. These draconian measures, which came into effect in 1926, prevented admission. The architect of these restrictions was Frederick Charles Blair, then deputy minister of immigration. From 1923 to 1931 approximately twenty thousand Jews arrived, almost all as first-degree relatives. From that point, until the late 1940s, Jews were almost unilaterally refused entry under any grounds.

The situation for German Jews became hazardous, especially after the Nuremberg Laws in 1934. With a population of half a million, and a thousand-year history, many were desperate to leave. But entry to England was difficult, even more so to the United States, and impossible to Canada. With the outbreak of World War II, and the rapid advances made by the German forces, by 1941 some five million additional Jews were now under German control. Three million more were added with the invasion of the Soviet Union. This created the greatest refugee crisis in history.

Historians Irving Abella and Harold Troper wrote a groundbreaking study of this period. *None Is Too Many: Canada and the Jews of Europe, 1933–1948* was released in 1982. Its impact was devastating in academic circles, but more importantly among Canadians in general. It revealed that there was a well-orchestrated policy by the Mackenzie King government to prevent the entry of Jewish refugees. It was moulded by Blair, who became director of immigration in 1936. Abella and Troper state that "the term 'refugee' was a code word for Jew." Blair declared: "Pressure on the part of Jewish people to get into Canada has never been greater than it is now, and I am glad to be able to add, after 35 years experience here, that it was never so well controlled."[35] Blair believed that there was a conspiracy to rescind the immigration policy.

Blair was the prime figure in creating the policy, but the government had the option to not enforce it. Yet it did so fully, despite lobbying by the CJC, thousands of letters from Canadian Jews, offers of payment by wealthy European Jews to be allowed entry, and coordinated campaigns by gentiles and Jews. An early indication of the government's obstinacy occurred in May 1939. The S.S. St. Louis, a passenger ship, left Hamburg with 937 Jewish passengers, and set sail for Cuba. Reaching its destination, the Cuban authorities denied entry, and quickly thereafter, so did the rest of Central and South America. Blair remarked to another bureaucrat that Canada could not "open its doors wide enough"[36] to take in the hundreds of thousands of Jewish people who want to leave Europe. Blair's retort was: "the line must be drawn somewhere."[37] As the vessel turned northward, King happened to be in Washington for meetings with Franklin Roosevelt, who also refused entry. King was pressed by some Canadian leaders to accept the vessel as Christian charity, but he joined Roosevelt's chorus. Ultimately, the ship was forced to return to Europe. Some passengers were accepted in western Europe and Britain. Two hundred and fifty-four were not as lucky.

The debate as to whether King was an antisemite has been argued for decades, and certainly more so since *None Is Too Many* became the slogan for Canada's discriminatory immigration policy. King was greatly influenced by Goldwin Smith as a young man, but also wrote of the travails of Jewish and immigrant workers in Toronto. On a trip to Germany, he was impressed by Hitler, but spoke in cabinet to "view the problem (of the Jews) from the way in which this nation will be judged in years to come."[38] The main point is that King was arguably the most adept and consummate politician in Canadian history. He clearly understood what was needed to maintain power. He appointed Ernest Lapointe minister of justice, and the untitled master of the Quebec Liberal caucus. Lapointe believed that communists, not fascists, posed the greatest threat, and that they were controlled by Jews. King understood that there was little love lost for Jews across the country, and with the entry of the Social Credit Party on the national scene, knew that he had to hold a strong line to consolidate his power in western Canada. Allowing Jews, even a small number of orphans that had been promised entry, would cost him at the ballot box. There was no political will to reverse immigration policy, and more importantly the nation's focus was a war in which Canadians were fully engaged.

King was the product of the Anglo elite. The Liberals could not hold power without French Canada and a foothold in the Prairies. Canadian Nativists, among the most fervent antisemites, were tolerated. Fascists were no longer in vogue, but they had made an imprint. Canada's record of accepting only five thousand Jewish refugees[39] during the Nazi era was the lowest, proportional to its population, of any country in the Western hemisphere. The coalescence of the four shades of antisemitism produced the most devastating chapter in the history of Canadian immigration.

There was no justification for antisemitism in Canada. But there was a context – Canada was a nation that was steeped in bigotry. The iniquities suffered by Jews pale in comparison to the treatment of many other ethno-cultural minorities. The most egregious and reprehensible treatment has been of First Nations. They were dispossessed of their land and not given the right to vote until 1965. In recent years, the documentation of the cultural genocide that was perpetrated upon them has brought a heightened sense of awareness of this crime. Immigrants from South and East Asia came in the fifty years after Confederation under difficult conditions. A ship, the Komagata Maru, arrived from India to Vancouver in 1914 but was refused entry by provincial officials and was forced to return. This effectively ended Asian immigration until after World War II. Chinese were dragooned into hard labour and denied basic rights. Each immigrant paid a head tax of $100, which was tripled in 1903. It was removed in 1923, largely because the new restrictions effectively curtailed all further immigration. Japanese Canadians were interned in detention camps during World War II, their livelihood destroyed, a generation lost, and its descendants emotionally scarred. Most Eastern and Southern European immigrants worked in the most menial jobs and were prevented from ascending the economic ladder. During World War I, some Ukrainians and Hungarians were interned because they were identified as "Austrian" as their territory was part of that country's empire. Some German and Italians faced the same fate in World War II. Finally, although citizens of the British Empire faced no obstacles in coming to Canada, that was only true of those who were white. There were virtually no newcomers of African and Asian origin. And those African Americans who found refuge in Canada were subjected to intense discrimination.

None Is Too Many shook the complacency of Canadians who, in the era of multiculturalism, basked in the glow of living in a fair and decent country. But there was a second context that was not discussed about the abysmal record of affording European Jews a haven. At the time of its publication in 1984, many Canadians could identify the Holocaust as a historical event. But that was not the case in 1933, or in 1939, because the orchestrated mass murder had not yet occurred. When it did, from 1941 to 1945, the rescue of European Jewry, in any tangible sense, was impossible. Germany and its allies and acolytes controlled the European continent until D-Day in June 1944. By what means could Jews be rescued? Further, there was no historical precedent for saving a nation. There was no international body to create a liberation force, nor statutes upholding universal human rights. The Holocaust was *sui generis*. While these caveats do not excuse Canada for not responding to the call – one that may have saved thousands in the early years of the war – they provide a perspective of the immensity of the task at hand.

CONCLUSION

Antisemitism in Canada was imported by European immigrants as it was a feature of Christian civilization. It originated in the early Christian period, casting Jews as Christ killers, and effloresced in the Middle Ages. Antisemitism added a second layer with the creation of pseudo-scientific racial biology, which promulgated the menace of a global conspiracy.

While antisemitism was incidental in the first century of the Canada's existence, when there were few Jews, it accelerated under the weight of Anglo-Protestant supremacy and French-Canadian ultramontism. In the interwar period, nativist and fascist movements ratcheted up the hatred. These four shades coalesced in the restrictive immigration policies of the federal government from 1919 to the late 1940s.

The Jewish response was familial and communal. Jewish immigrants and their children, born or raised in Canada, adapted to the restrictions placed upon them in employment, housing, education, and recreation by employing one another, creating a myriad of self-help societies, starting their own businesses, and striving to overcome the obstacles to acceptance by post-secondary institutions. Communally, they resurrected CJC as a viable national body, but under the weight of racist immigration restrictions, the CJC and other community entreaties were unable to budge the government's refusal to rescind those restrictions. Consequently, Canada firmly closed its door to European Jewry, consigning them to destruction.

Settlement reached its height in 1914, slowed through the 1920s and early 1930s, and was halted from 1933 to 1948. In adapting to the situation, some Jews moved into the lower middle and middle class, although that ascendance was mitigated by the impact of the Great Depression. Nevertheless, the community became increasingly diverse along these socio-economic dimensions.

World War II was a watershed for Canada and thereby for Canadian Jews. The immediate postwar years marked a rapid transition whose ripples continue to percolate through Canadian society.

PART C

THE COMMUNITY MATURES, 1945–2000

Arrival of immigrants

Source: Alex Dworkin Canadian Jewish Archives

CHAPTER EIGHT

"Into the Mainstream": From Immigrants to Canadians

THE JEWISH CONTRIBUTION TO CANADA DURING WORLD WAR II

It is a common assumption that historically Jews are not noted for their military service. This supposition overlooks the origins of the Jewish people during which they fought amongst themselves and against the great empires of the pre-Christian era. Historian Derek Penslar writes that, from the late 1700s to the end of World War I, military service was of enormous concern to Jews throughout the world and was a vehicle for emancipation and social acceptance. Penslar continues that "modernity introduced Jews to the ethical dilemmas of the use of force and challenged their historical self-representation as a people who shunned war."[1] Jews served in the armed forces of France, Germany, and Austria, and were unwillingly dragooned into the Russian army. They were active on both sides of the American (1861–5) and Russian civil wars (1919–22) and volunteered for the Republican forces during the Spanish Civil War (1936–9).

The Canadian story supports Penslar's assertion. During the Seven Years War between Britain and France, Alexander Schomberg captained the British frigate that repulsed the French in their attempt to recapture Quebec, for which he was knighted. Aaron Hart, the "father" of Canadian Jewry, served with the British at the surrender of Montreal that ended French rule, and then helped repel the American invasion of 1775. Some of the descendants of the original Quebec settlers participated in the British militia during the War of 1812. From the 1837 Rebellion in Lower Canada to the Boer War, we see a Jewish presence. In World War I, Jews volunteered for the Canadian Expeditionary Forces (CEF). Including those who were conscripted, 1,682 saw action, which represented 38 per cent of Jewish males over twenty years of age in contrast to 31 per cent of all Canadians. Seventy-six were decorated for bravery. One hundred and twenty-three lost their lives, including Myer Tutzer Cohen (1891–1917), killed in the battle of Passchendaele, for which he was posthumously honored with the Military Cross. An unidentified man died in Toronto in 1919 and his grave was marked as "Unknown" at the Pape Cemetery. Many years later, his identity was discovered. He was George Sorblum, who had come from New York City to enlist in the CEF.

Harvey Freeman (b. 1928) of Toronto comes from a military family. His grandfather served for thirteen years in the Austro-Hungarian army prior to his arrival to Canada. His uncle, Lou Krugel, served in the Canadian artillery in World War I. During World War II, seven cousins were members of the Canadian and American forces, one of whom, Sydney Brown of North Bay, Ontario was a bomb airman. His plane, a Wellington Bomber, was shot down over Germany on April 15, 1943, on his 27th mission. He was 24. The crew's bodies were buried in a German cemetery under the sign of the Cross. After the war, his family engraved the headstone with a Star of David. Sydney's brother, Zave, served in the infantry, and died of his wounds six weeks before the war's end at the age of 19. He is buried in the Canadian War Cemetery in Groesbeck, Holland. Freeman himself joined the Canadian militia after the war where he distinguished himself as a bag piper. Freeman's daughter, Tamar, chose the military for her career. She was a field medic and did tours of duty in Afghanistan in the first decade of the millennium.

Louis Tohn (1922–2005), the youngest child of immigrants, graduated from Harbord Collegiate in Toronto in 1941. He longed to enrol in chemistry at the University of Toronto, but his family needed another wage earner. With his academic prowess, he was hired by a small firm, Stark Electronics. As the war effort escalated, the Canadian government created the War Supply Board. Stark was contracted to manufacture electronic components for military aircraft, necessitating moving the factory from downtown Toronto to a larger facility in Ajax, east of

Toronto. Tohn was elevated to a position as an administrator. After the war, Stark struggled to adjust to peacetime production and eventually went out of business. Tohn married Ida Goodman in 1947. During the war she had worked at Tip Top Tailors, founded by David Dunkelman in 1909, which emerged as a leading producer of women's and men's fashions. As with Stark, its operations had been retooled to manufacture military uniforms.

The Brown brothers, Tohn, and Goodman are examples of the Jewish contribution to the war effort, in battle and on the home front. It is not an overstatement that World War II united Canadians and was the spur for the major political and economic developments that carried through the postwar era. The Canadian Jewish contribution was a galvanizing force and the necessary catalyst for the community's evolution in the remainder of the twentieth century from the working class to the middle class, as represented by its socio-economic elevation and its migration from the traditional Jewish neighbourhoods to the suburbs.

At the outbreak of World War II Jewish enlistment in the Canadian Armed Forces was not vigorous. Some were students, others already professionals, some with families, and others were discouraged by their families. The dean of Canada's military history is Jack Granatstein. In an article in honour of Gerald Tulchinsky, Granatstein opines that Jews should have had a special urgency given that the enemy was Germany and her allies.[2] The situation changed because of two factors. First, the CJC created the national War Efforts Committee (WEC) in 1940, to provide public relations, mobilize the community, and provide a network of support for Jewish soldiers. Second was the German invasion of its ally, the Soviet Union on June 22, 1941. Left-wing Jews, who were reticent about joining because of their pacifist political leanings, were now spurred to enlist. Further, the revelations, however irregular and imprecise, about the conditions and mass murder in the ghettoes and camps of eastern Europe, animated Canadian Jews. Ultimately, 16,641 men and 279 women enlisted. This represented 39 per cent of military-age Jewish men, in contrast to 41 per cent of all Canadians. The actual number of Jews may have been higher as some did not declare their religion in case of capture. Most Canadians in service were of British origin. We do not have the records of other ethno-cultural minorities, which might have provided a more useful comparative analysis of the Jewish response. The Jewish death rate was 2.6 per cent (427 men and

1 woman, Rose Goodman, who was killed in training) compared to the overall rate of 4.1 per cent. Part of the explanation for the disparity was the high proportion of Jewish service personnel who had higher education, for which some were assigned desk jobs.

Tulchinsky's research on this subject has led the way. Among the servicemen that he highlights are Mitchell Sterlin (1922–43) and Ben Dunkelman (1913–97). Sterlin, from Montreal, joined the Royal Canadian Regiment. He commanded 16 Platoon, D Company in defending the Ortona Crossroads in southern Italy, but a shortage of ammunition forced a withdrawal. He was killed in a fire fight and posthumously honoured by the regiment. Dunkelman, from Toronto, applied to join the Royal Canadian Navy in 1939, but was rejected because of his faith. Jews comprised just 0.6 per cent of the navy's forces, in comparison to 2.6 per cent of the Royal Canadian Air Force (RCAF) and 1.4 per cent of the Canadian Army. He enlisted in the army in 1939 as a private and progressed to the rank of major. He landed on the second wave on D-Day (June 6, 1944), and fought through the campaigns from France to Germany. He received the Distinguished Service Order. He joined a legion of foreign volunteers, the *Machal*, that joined the Israeli Forces in 1948 War of Independence. He became a brigade commander and helped break the siege of Jerusalem.

Journalist Ellin Bessner has done extensive research on this subject. In her book, *Double Threat: Canadian Jews, the Military, and World War*, she argues that Jewish soldiers were subject to antisemitism in the ranks, and, if captured, would face certain death. She has documented the service of seventy men who were killed in the Normandy invasion. They include Bombardier George Meltz of Toronto, Queen's Own Rifles, who was killed by a sniper at the age of twenty-five; Rifleman Israel Freedman of the Royal Winnipeg Rifles, age twenty-one; Lawrence Reider of Kitchener, Essex Scottish Regiment, age twenty-three. Fred Harris, twenty-three, of Toronto, Queen's Own Rifles, of whom his friend, Barney Danson, wrote that "he was killed right on the beach."[3] Danson eventually was minister of national defence in the 1970s.

The 2018 edition of the journal, *Canadian Jewish Studies/Études juives canadiennes* is devoted to the impact of the events of 1944 on Canadian Jewry. Historian Richard Menkis's article, "'There Were Cries of Joy, Some of Sorrow': Canadian Jewish Soldiers and Early Encounters with Survivors,"[4] is particularly relevant to this discussion. As Allied forces fought their way through Normandy and into the Low Countries, they found Jewish survivors. A chaplain, Gershon Levi, commented: "she [an old French woman] was a symbol of Jewish suffering and martyrdom – the first Jewish person liberated in Europe."[5] In the last months of that year, coinciding with the High Holidays and Chanukah, servicemen worshipped with survivors. In Brussels, Private H. Wisenthal wrote: "These Jews have been in hiding for two years … Only a quarter of the population survived."[6] David Heaps, son of the politician A.A. Heaps, wrote to his father from Antwerp: "A few escaped (shooting, drowning) … hidden for almost the entire time since 1940."[7]

Historian Mark Celinscak writes of encounters between soldiers and survivors during the liberation of the Bergen-Belsen Camp in Germany in April 1945. Two of the Canadian liberators were Maurice Victor and Alan Rose. Victor, raised in Winnipeg by immigrants, was a neurologist in the Royal Canadian Medical Corps. He related: "I have racked my brain since then, trying to recall what we did not know about the horror in Europe, back in the warm safety of North America."[8] Alan Rose, who became the vice-president of the CJC, remarked: "I intended to be an architect, but I decided then [at Bergen-Belsen] … to restore the remnants of Jewish life."[9]

Service eroded distinctions of social class, ethnicity, and religion. Canadian forces fought as one. The reports of Jewish chaplains, headed by Gershon Levi, reported few incidents of antisemitism. But the situation was not positive for all who volunteered. Jews were not welcomed by the navy, and despite their proportionately high enlistment in the RCAF, they were rarely trained as pilots. An RCMP report on enlistment in Saskatchewan noted that "despite antisemitism … Jews continue to enlist."[10] Another RCMP report from 1941 noted that of the fifteen Jewish families in Kamsack, Saskatchewan, thirteen men volunteered, including all five sons of the Alfman clan.[11]

On the home front, where many of the troops were stationed until hostilities increased, the War Efforts Committee and Jewish communities welcomed their countrymen and women. Brantford was an army base and Halifax and St. John were bases for the navy. Communities rallied to provide kosher food, religious services, and support for families of troops. Many of the recruits had little Jewish education, including knowledge of Yiddish. Consequently, their comrades and chaplains wrote letters to their families.

Until recently, scholars overlooked the remarkable contribution of the Women's War Efforts Committee (WWEC). Recent research by Jennifer Shaw Lander unveils the contribution by Jewish women, first in challenging the patriarchal CJC leadership, and then in articulating their full-fledged devotion to providing for the needs of Canadian servicemen in Canadian bases, whether Jewish or not. The WWEC was formed on January 7, 1940 and disbanded in 1946; its last act was assisting Holocaust survivors.

In 1939, the gross domestic product for Canada was $5.6 billion. The Depression was still ravaging the nation. Unemployment remained high, and the government had done little to allay the impact. Its expenditures were $680 million, a mere $60 per capita. The war effort reversed this dire situation. The King government ended controls on profits that had been put in place during the Depression. It created the War Supply Board and a Department of Munitions, headed by its minister, C.D. Howe. Twenty-eight Crown corporations were established, and the government subcontracted the war effort to firms, like Stark Electronics and Tip Top Tailors, which drastically lowered unemployment. By 1943, over one million men and women worked in war industries, and another two million were in essential civilian employment working in agriculture, mining, food processing and communications. The war industries did not discriminate in whom they hired. The number of Jews in wartime industries is unknown, but given the high proportion who lived in the industrial centres, their relatively elevated education, and the majority who were already working in manufacturing and sales before the war, one can speculate that their contribution was significant.

World War II was calamitous, most tragically for European Jewry. Nevertheless, with the Allied victory, the spectre of fascist domination of Europe and South and East Asia was eliminated. For Canadians, it united the country and set in motion a new economic and political model. For Canadian Jews, the majority of whom were born in Canada before 1939, the war accelerated their transformation from identifying themselves as immigrants to viewing themselves as Canadians. Their contribution was the precursor to the community's geographical and socio-economic transition in the postwar era. Canadians in general, from those who worked in defence plants to the smaller number who served in the armed forces, their return home set off the most significant social changes in Canadian history.

THE GREAT TRANSITION, 1945–1971

McGill University sociologist Morton Weinfeld wrote a provocative analysis of Canada's Jews, *Like Everyone Else ... But Different*, in 2001. The title is an apt description of the postwar generations of Canadian Jews. Celebrating Canada at the centennial of Confederation in 1967 was a telling comment as to how much had changed economically, socially, and in terms of Canada's pride of its place in the world. The World Exposition in Montreal was a national celebration, a testament to this rapid transformation. Yet, as Weinfeld relates, the national transition was integral for the Jewish community, accelerating its transformation more rapidly than it had for most other immigrant groups. This was due to two factors. First, the community's adaptation to Canadian life had been in many respects historically faster and smoother than for other ethno-cultural immigrant groups. Second, the generation born or raised in Canada during the interwar period was ready to grasp the opportunities provided by Canada's rapid economic growth, and the gradual erosion of some of the barriers preventing Jews from entering institutions of higher learning, professions, and certain neighbourhoods.

Ultimately, most Jews gradually crossed the threshold into mainstream Canadian society between the end of World War II and the celebration of Canada's centennial. Canada's Jews for the most part shed their self-image as immigrants and came to identify themselves as Canadians.

The marker of this development was mobility – geographic and socio-economic mobility that propelled the bulk of the Jewish community into Canada's urban middle class. Coincidentally, some ascended to positions of prominence in the professions, business, the academy, culture, and politics.

GEOGRAPHIC MOBILITY

At the end of the war, there was concern that the economic boom created by the war effort would stagnate. Industry would have to be retooled for peacetime production and Europe was devastated and had to be rebuilt quickly. Yet, this gloomy prospect was overturned by an international effort, led by the United States. Europe was rebuilt and international trade was liberalized growing sixfold in a generation, with an emphasis on manufactured goods. Most important was the imperative to create the UN.

In Canada from 1948 to 1968, the gross domestic product rose at approximately 7 per cent per annum, unemployment was relatively stable, and inflation, except for the late 1940s, was kept in check. The construction, mining, and financial sectors grew and employment in agriculture declined, largely due to mechanization. Oil was discovered in Alberta, the St. Lawrence Seaway was constructed, and consumer spending rose dramatically. A key factor for this growth was the baby boom. A recession from 1957 to 1961 was succeeded by the longest sustained boom in modern times that extended to 1973.

The impact of the economic boom was felt most dramatically in Toronto, Montreal, and their hinterlands, and in Alberta. The loosening of wartime price controls and rations in combination with higher wages, created an accelerated demand for consumer products. While during the Depression and war, residential construction had ground down to almost a halt, what young, urban, Canadian families most desired now were homes. Consequently, entrepreneurs, many of them with few financial resources, became contractors. Farms were bought, severed into neighbourhoods, and turned into streets, where one could purchase a modern home. Financial institutions were willing to take back mortgages, and suburbia exploded. The 1961 census revealed that suburbs had grown 8.5 times faster than cities since 1950. This upsurge forced municipalities to provide services, namely public transportation, sewers, and public facilities, especially schools.

For Canadian Jews, this development was more intense than for Canadians in general, as they were the most urban-based ethno-cultural community in the country. In 1951, 25 per cent of Canadians lived in the ten largest cities, in contrast to 91 per cent of Jews. The combination of the postwar economic and baby booms, the dearth of affordable new homes for two decades, and available agricultural land adjacent to cities, led to the geographical transformation of Jewish communities.[12]

Toronto was the fastest growing city in North America from 1945 to 1967, so it is only fitting that this discussion begins at the point where sixty-six thousand Jews resided in 1951. Bathurst Street, running north from Lake Ontario to the farm belt an hour distant by car, was adjacent to the downtown community. In the interwar period, a large segment moved north and west of College Street, into slightly more commodious dwellings than in the old Spadina/Kensington neighbourhood. Concurrently, the more well-to-do migrated into the Town of Forest Hill and to Cedarvale in the Borough of York. Eglinton Avenue served these neighbourhoods and marked the northern boundary of development along Bathurst. But the postwar exodus along Bathurst Street rapidly transformed farmlands into subdivisions. By 1950 suburban tracts had extended to Wilson Avenue, in the centre of the Borough of North York; a decade later to Sheppard Avenue, and by 1960 to Steeles Ave, at the border of Metropolitan Toronto, some thirteen kilometres from College Street. Bathurst Street was, and remains, a ribbon of Jewish life, perhaps unparalleled elsewhere. In 1941 there were 3,655 Jews in the suburbs, representing 7 per cent of the city's Jewish population. A decade later, there were 21,533 suburbanites, almost one-third of Toronto's Jewish population.

The case of Louis Tohn and his wife Ida, née Goodman, introduced in the beginning of the chapter, is illustrative of this transition. They were married in 1947, but the housing shortage necessitated moving into the Goodman home, a narrow row house on Robert Street, built in the 1890s, close to College and Spadina. Their first child was born a year later. They shared the dwelling with Ida's sister and brother-in-law and their two children, and Ida's parents. There were no affordable homes until 1951. They purchased a small bungalow on a sixty-foot lot in the Downsview neighbourhood of North York, across Wilson Avenue from the Canadian air force base. Their street was populated by mostly Jewish and Italian families. There were no sidewalks and open sewers connected to back yard ditches that had not been updated for several years. Their new home was eleven kilometers from Robert Street. Twenty years later, it was the geographical midpoint of the Jewish community. A survey by this author of the one hundred thousand Jewish residents in 1971 estimates that at least 90 per cent lived outside the confines of the old immigrant neighbourhood. In a period of sixteen years, some seventy thousand Toronto Jews had become suburbanites.

Until the 1970s Montreal was not only most populous Canadian city, but also the most dominant, as it had been since its founding in 1760. It was home to half of the country's Jewish population of approximately with 70,000 residents in 1945 and 105,000 in 1967. It was the epicentre of Jewish culture, finance, and the home of the community's national organizations. Its historic Jewish neighbourhood of the Plateau did not undergo as drastic a transition as did Toronto, in part because the migration had already begun in the interwar period. Mordecai Richler's groundbreaking novel *The Apprenticeship of Duddy Kravitz*, published in 1959, provides a picture of the Jewish community of the 1940s. His evocative prose is so colourful, that one can almost smell the smoked meat and taste the bagels. He satirizes the old neighbourhood of his youth on rue St. Urbain, and the puffed-up wealthy Jews of Westmount. Although the transition to the suburbs was not as rapid as in Toronto, by 1971, there were approximately twenty-three thousand Jews in the inner suburb of Côte des Neiges, and almost the same number in the newer Côte St. Luc. The adjoining municipalities (with approximate figures) of Snowdon (13,000), Notre Dame de Grâce (NDG) (6,700), and Ville St. Laurent (10,000) were other major destinations. Westmount, the traditional reserve of wealthy Anglo Montrealers, maintained a steady core of about five thousand Jewish residents through the postwar era, as did the newer outpost of Hampstead. Among the outer suburbs, the West Island community started in the 1960s, and grew over the following three decades.[13] But, while Toronto's Jewish population moved into surrounding farmland, Montreal's inner suburbs had been in existence before 1945. Thus, the phenomenon of suburbia was not as dislocating there as it was in Toronto.

Winnipeg was historically Canada's third largest city, and correspondingly had the third largest Jewish community. Its population of nineteen thousand between 1945 and 1971, constituting 3 per cent of the city's population, had marginal growth. Its historic immigrant community of the North End was densely packed, colourful, and retained the traditions of the first settlers. In the interwar period, there was some movement northward and westward to slightly better conditions. The preferred destination was West Kildonan, which boasted bungalows on large lots. The development of Garden City in the postwar period offered larger homes. In 1961 there were some seven thousand Jews resident there, representing 35 per cent of the city's Jewish population.

The transition to the more upscale South End began in the 1940s to the River Heights neighbourhood. It accelerated in the period under discussion, eventually to include the community of Tuxedo, which initially discouraged Jewish residency. Permission had to be obtained in writing from the town council and was awarded only to "acceptable" individuals. Despite laws passed in 1950 to prohibit such covenants, they remained in force for approximately another decade. Nevertheless, the migration to other South End districts quadrupled between 1941 and 1971, to approximately six thousand, and Tuxedo became the largest neighbourhood. The North End eventually became a small Jewish outpost as synagogues, businesses, and schools closed. Much after the fact, the Asper Jewish Community Campus opened in the South End in 1997. While Spadina and the Plateau have retained their character as vibrant multicultural enclaves that now attract walking tours of the old Jewish sights, the North End has sadly become an urban ghetto.

In 1945, the Vancouver Jewish community numbered some forty-five hundred. It grew by almost 50 per cent by 1971, making it the fourth largest cohort in Canada. The city and region became an attractive destination for Canadians and immigrants in the postwar era, as its population grew fourfold from 1945 to 2001. Among those who came were Jews. The foundation of the community was the poor East End with some one thousand dwellers in 1911. Too small to have a Spadina, the Main, or Selkirk Avenue in Winnipeg, the cramped streets teemed with Jews and other immigrants from Asia and Europe. The flight to Vancouver began in the 1930s and sped up in the following decade. The first new neighbourhoods were Fairview and Mount Pleasant on the south side of False Creek and along the Oak Street corridor, where two major synagogues were built. As historian Cyril Leonoff wrote, "with increasing affluence, and the opening up of new residential districts in the 1960s and 1970s, the population has continued to shift southward and westward."[14] The JCC and Home for the Aged were built at Oak Street and Forty-First Avenue as the surrounding communities of Oakridge, Kerrisdale, South Cambie, and Shaughnessy had attracted Jewish families. By 1972, 57 per cent of the community's ten thousand residents lived there. Nearby, the wealthier districts of Kitsilano, Arbutus Ridge, and West Point Grey had a growing Jewish presence. The further flung suburbs of Richmond and Burquest (Burnaby/New Westminster) became favoured destinations as did the North Shore. In 2011, they housed 55 per cent of Vancouver's twenty-six thousand Jews.

Ottawa's Jewish community initially settled in Lower Town, a stone's throw from the Houses of Parliament. Its heart was the Byward Market, and its main artery was Rideau Street. It was an ethnic mix of French, Irish, Italian, and Jewish residents. The three thousand Jews in 1921 represented less than 2 per cent of the city's population, but they were the majority in Lower Town. In 1945, most still lived there and in nearby Sandy Hill. The more well-to-do had decamped to the Glebe, a fashionable district along the Rideau Canal. After the war, the suburb of Alta Vista, to the south of the Glebe, was a destination point, and in subsequent decades Ottawa West, Nepean, and Barrhaven South, all of which were on the opposite side of the Rideau River and far from downtown, became home to approximately half of the Jewish population of six thousand in 1967, making Ottawa the fifth largest Jewish community in Canada. By 2001, it had experienced the third largest increase, after Toronto and Vancouver, with eleven thousand residents. Today, Byward Market is a tourist destination, a mix of fresh produce, meat and fish, and upscale restaurants and shops. There is little indication of its Jewish origins.

SUBURBAN LIFE

Jewish geographic mobility was a microcosm of the Canadian experience. The farms and forests of Scarborough (Toronto), Burnaby (Vancouver), St. Laurent (Montreal), Kanata (Ottawa), and Hamilton Mountain, were transformed into subdivisions and plazas. By the end of the 1950s, 150,000 new homes were being built annually, of which more than 70 per cent were single family detached dwellings. The average frontage was fifty feet. The Goodman property in downtown Toronto, referenced above, was, by comparison, twelve feet wide. Migration was fuelled by the insecurities of life marked by almost two decades of economic stagnation. Canadians wanted to enjoy life, peace, and prosperity. While suburbs rapidly expanded, 85 per cent of Toronto's employees continued to commute to work in the central core. Expansion was chaotic. Municipalities did not have a fully integrated process that brought together planners, developers, builders, and marketers. Little consideration was given to social infrastructure. Schools, rapidly built, quickly became overcrowded, there were few parks, and even fewer amenities for those unable to afford a home. In response, Toronto, with thirteen independent municipalities (including Toronto) harmonized the services in 1953, incorporated the six smallest ones into seven in 1967, and completed the eventual consolidation of Metropolitan Toronto in 1999.

Prosperity and isolation demanded that families had to have private transportation as municipal services were slowly expanded. The first subway in the country was not built until 1954, in Toronto, on the Yonge Line, with a stretch of only seven kilometers. Consequently, the family car was ubiquitous, as a necessity and as a status symbol. In 1960, two-thirds of Canadian households owned one and one-tenth had two. Suburbs and cars were markers of success. The family home was rapidly transformed by modernization and standardization – central heat, fridges, flush toilets, lawn mowers, and televisions were indispensable. By 1975, 75 per cent of Canadians lived in houses. Writer and broadcaster Pierre Berton, arguably the most recognizable face and voice of the period, wrote *The Comfortable Pew* in 1965, reflecting on this gross materialism. In commenting on the book Owram wrote, "although Canada was a Christian nation in 1950, it was, less of (a) commitment than a stabilizing force, a desire for conformity."[15]

The transition, it can be argued, was even more intense for Jewish Canadians than for most Canadians, because of the rapid dislocation from the immigrant enclaves that had experienced little change in half a century. The most visible impact was the absence of street life. Suburbs were essentially residential. One had to walk, or preferably drive, to the newly constructed avenues, that featured ubiquitous mini plazas, totally lacking character. People no longer hung out on the street, or met in cafes, local synagogues, or fraternal societies. The vast distance between the centre and the suburbs led to their mutual transformation. Spadina Avenue by the mid-1950s, was a mix of Jewish, ethno-European, and increasingly Chinese businesses. Many of the places of worship closed or were sold, such as Toronto's Beth Jacob Synagogue, the "Great Synagogue" built in 1922 on Henry Street. Its neo-Byzantine architecture is still visible from Spadina along the corridor of Cecil Street. Aptly, it was sold, to a Russian Orthodox congregation. Holy Blossom Temple, the first congregation in Toronto, moved to the Cedarvale district on Bathurst Street in 1938. Goel Zedek, the second largest, merged with Beth Hamidrash Hagadol, aka the McCaul Street Shul, to create the Beth Zedek Congregation, built down the hill from Holy Blossom, in 1955.

The new synagogues not only reflected the geographic transition but the shift to less traditional modes of worship, primarily from Orthodox to Conservative, and to a lesser degree, to Reform. Until the birth of the Reform movement in Germany in the 1820s, Jewish traditions had remained unchanged. Canadian Jewry was a small outpost until the Great Migration. All rabbis were immigrants, all congregations were Orthodox, and there were no seminaries. Changes came more slowly than in Britain and the United States. By 1945, there were Reform congregations in Hamilton, Toronto, and Montreal. The creation of the Conservative movement at the turn of the twentieth century in the United States as a liberal alternative to Orthodox did not penetrate Canada, with one exception (Shaar Hashomayim in Montreal), until after World War I. But by 1936, there were nine Conservative congregations, and some 140 Orthodox synagogues. The following section profiles some of the influential rabbis whose teachings and leadership signified the changing atmosphere of Canadian Jews.

RABBIS

Orthodox

Abraham Aharon Price (1900–94) was born in Poland and ordained in 1919. He went to Berlin in 1923, then to Paris, and New York, and arrived in Toronto in 1937 as spiritual leader of the Chevra Shas Congregation and dean of the Yeshiva until 1985, where many of his students were ordained. He authored ten volumes of studies and become the city's chief rabbi. In 1942 Price learned of the internment of European Yeshiva students by the British government in Canadian camps as enemy aliens. He convinced the authorities that the students did not pose a threat and orchestrated the release of some fifty to study at his Yeshiva. In 1948, he sponsored another group from Prague. Price was active until his final years as a scholar and teacher. His collection of more than three thousand works was donated to the University of Toronto.

Pinchas Hirschsprung (1912–98) was born in Dukla, an idyllic village in Galicia, a province of the Austro-Hungarian Empire, located in today's southeastern Poland and western Ukraine. In his youth, he was sent to a Yeshiva in Lublin, in east-central Poland, where he quickly became a noted scholar, who could recite the Talmud from memory. He was ordained in 1932. While his daily language was Yiddish, he spoke Polish, had knowledge of German and Russian, read Latin, and was conversant with philosophers from the Greeks to Freud, despite objections by his contemporaries that these activities were not worthy of a rabbi of his stature. At the onset of the war, German troops rapidly advanced through Poland, and transported Jews to larger towns. With great sadness, Hirschsprung escaped from a transit and came to the Soviet border.[16] As there was a pact with Germany, the crossing was difficult, but his ability to speak Russian and find refuge in synagogues allowed him to eventually reach Vilna, in Lithuania. With the help of Chiune Sugihara,[17] the Japanese consul in nearby Kaunas, Hirschsprung was given a transit visa through the Soviet Union to Japan in April 1941, two months before the German invasion. From there, he sailed to Shanghai, and then, with the aid of the JIAS, to Vancouver. Arriving in Montreal, he joined the *Merkaz Hatorah Yeshiva*, became rabbi of Congregation *Adath Yeshurun*, and joined the Jewish Community Council. He established the first Jewish school for girls, by collecting funds door to door. Most notably he was the chief rabbi of Montreal from 1969 to his death. Hirschsprung was renowned for his humanitarianism. He was accepting of people irrespective of their faith. At his funeral, religious and civic leaders from all walks of life paid homage to his life.

David Hartman (1931–2013) was born in New York and ordained at Yeshiva University in 1954. He was the spiritual leader of Congregation *Beth David Tifereth Jerusalem* (Splendour of David's House Jerusalem) in Montreal from 1960 to 1971. Hartman's major contribution was in interfaith dialogue and in breaking the barrier between secular and religious Jews. He studied with Charles Taylor, the renowned philosopher at McGill University, where he earned his doctorate. In 1972, he established the Shalom Hartman Institute in Jerusalem that included schools for boys and girls, a centre for religious research, and a seminar series for clergy of all faiths. It also organized Christian academics and clerics to spend a year in Jerusalem studying Jewish theology. He merged the study of Jewish philosophy, which had been limited to Jewish studies, with mainstream academia. Hartman stated: "University is fine for intellectual pursuits, but it can't make Jews. You need an institute to help make Jews."[18]

In Montreal, the Spanish and Portuguese Synagogue, the first Jewish house of worship in Canada, moved from downtown Stanley Street to Snowdon in 1947. Howard Joseph has been the chief rabbi since 1970. Currently he is rabbi emeritus. Congregation Beth David Tifereth

Jerusalem moved from the Plateau to Hampstead in 1965. New congregations were founded on the West Island, St. Laurent, and Côte St. Luc in the 1960s. Two stalwart institutions in Westmount, Shaar Hashomayim, founded in 1857, and relocated in 1924, and Emanu-El Beth Shalom, the first Reform congregation, built in 1911, are still in situ, neither having been a "downtown" synagogue. In Winnipeg, the venerable Rosh Pina Synagogue moved from the North End to West Kildonan 1951. Two main centres of learning, Talmud Torah and the Peretz Folk School followed suit shortly thereafter. The other founding synagogue, Shaarey Zedek, moved to new quarters in the South End in 1950.

Conservative

Wilfred Shuchat (1920–2018) was born in Montreal and, following his graduation from McGill University, was ordained at the Jewish Theological Seminary (JTS) in New York. Returning to Montreal in 1946 two years later, he was appointed rabbi of Congregation Shaar Hashomayim, the second oldest synagogue in Canada, founded in 1846. His tenure lasted forty-five years, after which he was appointed rabbi emeritus, a position that he held until his death. Shuchat has been a major figure in the Conservative movement, awarded for his contribution to adult education, and for his years as editor of a weekly column in the *Montreal Star*. He was chosen to head the committee for the design of the Jewish Pavilion at Montreal's Expo 67.

Stuart Rosenberg (1922–89) was born in New York, was ordained at the JTS in 1945, and received his doctorate from Columbia University. He was rabbi of Toronto's Beth Zedek Congregation from 1956 to 1973. In its new building on Bathurst Street, it became the largest congregation in Canada. He was appointed honorary fellow for life at the JTS in 1976. He was arguably the most well-known rabbi in Canada as a frequent contributor to newspapers across the land including a weekly column in the *Toronto Star* called "Lines on Life." He visited the Soviet Union in 1961, being the first Canadian to meet with Russian Jews, and became active in the movement to agitate for their right to emigrate a decade later. Rosenberg wrote twenty books, among them a two-volume study, *The Jewish Community in Canada* in 1971. Reflecting his commitment to Jewish-Christian Dialogue was *Bridge to Brotherhood – Judaism's*

Dialogue with Christianity in 1961. At the time of his death, he was rabbi of Congregation *Beth Torah* in Toronto.

Erwin Schild (1920–) was born in Cologne, Germany. While he was a Yeshiva student, he was interned at the Dachau Concentration Camp in 1938. After his release, he escaped to Holland and resumed his studies in England. But, in 1940, he was arrested as an enemy alien because of his German heritage and transferred to an internment camp in Quebec from where he was released due to the efforts of Rabbi Price. Schild was admitted to Rabbi Price's Yeshiva and was ordained in 1947. He was appointed rabbi of Congregation Adath Israel in downtown Toronto and served until 1989. Currently, he is rabbi emeritus. Adath Israel moved to the suburb of Downsview in 1958, the first and largest of several Conservative congregations in North York. By 1990, almost twice as many Canadian Jews identified themselves as Conservative than Orthodox. Rabbi Schild cut a swath in Toronto, becoming actively involved in Christian-Jewish Dialogue, for which he was recognized by being inducted to the Order of Canada in 2001, one year after having received the Order of Merit of Germany. He was a long-standing member of the CJC. He has penned four books, the last two being autobiographies, *The Very Narrow Bridge* (2001) and *The Crazy Angel* (2017), on his ninety-fifth birthday and sixtieth wedding anniversary.

Reform

The Reform movement has grown in the postwar era, to the degree that one-third of Canadian Jews identified themselves as such in 1990. Although numerous eminent rabbis have made significant contributions, two stand out.

Abraham Feinberg (1899–1986) was born in Bellaire, Ohio, where he was stirred by discrimination against African Americans. He took the pulpit at Holy Blossom in 1943 where he remained until 1961, after which he was rabbi emeritus, before returning to the United States. He wrote three controversial books: *Storm the Gates of Jericho* (1964), *Hanoi Diary* (1968) following his visit to Vietnam, and *Sex and the Pulpit* (1981). He was in the Canadian spotlight as a frequent contributor to newspapers and magazines, notably *Saturday Night* and *Macleans* and as a panelist on CBC television. He was most well known for his advocacy for world peace and social justice. Feinberg hosted the Reverend Martin

Luther King and sponsored interfaith dialogue. Feinberg was called the "the red rabbi" by his critics, including some of his parishioners, members of Toronto's Jewish elite, who were discomfited by his unconventional pursuits. During his tenure at Holy Blossom, he oversaw a remarkable program of Jewish education for all ages. Feinberg is the most controversial religious leader in Canadian Jewish history.

Emil Fackenheim (1916–2003) was born in Germany. As a student at the Reform Seminary in Berlin, he was arrested on *Kristallnacht* (the night of broken glass) on November 9, 1938, sent to the Sachsenhausen Concentration Camp, from which he escaped, and made his way to Britain. As with Rabbi Schild, he was released from an internment camp in Canada, to serve Temple Anshei Shalom in Hamilton. He received his doctorate in philosophy from the University of Toronto in 1948, was professor there and taught concurrently at Holy Blossom Temple, until 1984 when he moved to Israel. Fackenheim is the preeminent thinker about the impact of the Holocaust on faith, history, and morality. He wrote nine books and about one hundred articles, but to summarize his work would be to minimize it. He is well known for his reconstruction of a Jewish identity that faces the Holocaust honestly without abandoning God or Jewish tradition. Fackenheim believed that the Holocaust must be understood as imperative for perpetuation of Jewish existence and for the State of Israel. In the Torah, there are 613 commandments (laws), to which Fackenheim added one more: "The authentic Jew of today is forbidden to hand Hitler yet another, posthumous victory."[19] Gunther Plaut (1912–2011) was a rabbi, scholar, and devotee of interfaith dialogue. Plaut was raised in Germany where he received his doctor of laws degree in 1935, and then immigrated to the United States where he entered Hebrew Union College, graduating in 1939. He enlisted in the army as a chaplain and was in the frontline in the liberation of Belgium. In April 1945, his unit came to the Nordhausen facility cum slave labour camp, where the deadly V2 bombs were being manufactured. In his autobiography, *Unfinished Business* (1981), he wrote: "That afternoon I saw a sight that I won't forget for as long as I live … concentration camp Dora … where there were about 4,000 dead and 400 scarcely alive … I didn't know that Dora-Nordhausen was the first camp to be liberated, [that] it was a 'minor' installation. Nordhausen breached my protective shell as nothing else had done."[20]

His tenure as rabbi at Holy Blossom Temple, from 1961 to 1978, marked a symbiosis of Abraham Feinberg's dedication to dialogue and to human rights, with profound scholarship and community activism. He was a prolific author and editor of some thirty books, of which the most significant was the fourth edition of *The Torah: A Modern Commentary* (1985). As president of CJC, he was a marked contrast to his predecessor, the irrepressible and vulgar Samuel Bronfman, and considered to be the representative of the Jewish community. Among his other posts, he was vice-chair of the Ontario Human Rights Commission. Plaut was made a member of the Order of Canada in 1978 and elevated to companion (the highest level) in 1999, the same year that he received the Order of Merit of Germany. He was a senior scholar at Holy Blossom until his death.

THE MODERN JEWISH FAMILY

A central aspect of the rapid postwar transition was the composition and life of the average Jewish suburban family. There are five salient points. The first is that it was no longer multi-generational. Due to the economic situation from the late 1920s to the end of the war, most immigrant families lived together – the initial immigrant parents, their children, and their grandchildren. But during the postwar transition, most of the migrants were young families, while most of the original immigrants remained in their prewar homes, albeit with more space. Thus, family connections were strained. One pattern that emerged was the Sunday drive to visit grandparents who had remained in the immigrant neighbourhoods.

This disjointing factor was magnified by the second point: language imbalance. For most of the children born or raised in Canada before 1945, Yiddish was the mother language. But that was true of only 30 per cent in 1961 in contrast to 91 per cent in 1931. The figure is, in fact, an exaggeration due to the arrival of the Holocaust Survivors and their children born after the war, who by 1955, represented approximately 15 per cent of the community; Yiddish was the mother tongue for the most. As 60 per cent of Jews in 1961 were born after 1935, we can estimate that almost one half spoke Yiddish first, leaving a small coterie of those under twenty-five for whom that was not the case. For most Yiddish

Rabbi W. Gunther Plaut

Source: Alex Dworkin Canadian Jewish Archives

speakers, especially those born or raised in Canada before 1935, Yiddish was mostly spoken at home with their elders, or as a second language. In the suburbs, Yiddish, if it was spoken at all, was a code for parents who did not want their children to understand their conversations. Therefore, one can conclude that the cultural bonds of being a Canadian were closer between the interwar generation born or raised in Canada and their offspring than with their immigrant parents.

The third point is that, by 1961, 83 per cent of Jews under the age of thirty-five had been born in Canada. Of the remainder, 5 per cent had been born in Britain, the British Commonwealth, or the United States. Thus, aside from the Holocaust survivors, the majority of whom were older than thirty-four, young suburban families had no memory of having been immigrants of prewar Europe. This precipitates the fourth point: the rapid rise of marriages, divorces, and intermarriage. The marriage rate in 1961 was 65.5 per cent nationally, but 72.4 per cent among Jews. Seventy-two per cent of Jewish males under the age of 34 and 93 per cent of females were married in 1961. But Jewish divorce rates also outpaced the national picture, as seven out of one hundred Jews were divorced in contrast to four Canadians. Further, intermarriage, which historically had been a major scandal, soared from 5.3 per cent in 1933 to 18.5 per cent by 1963. The final consideration is family size. While among Jews, it was slightly higher in 1961 than thirty years earlier, it was still lower than for all Canadians. The baby boom, discussed below, resulted in 39 per cent of Canadian families with two or more children, in contrast to 27 per cent of Jewish families.

GROWING UP JEWISH

From the late 1930s to 1944, there were approximately 22,000 births annually in Canada. There were 300,000 in 1947 alone, and from 1952 to 1966, at least 40,000, per annum. In total, there were 6.7 million births between 1946 and 1961. In his wide-ranging account, *Born at the Right Time: The Phenomenon of the Baby Boom*, historian Doug Owram describes this rapid transformation of Canadian life, especially the experience of childhood and adolescence in the immediate postwar era. He writes that between 1945 and 1962, these births "have been among the most potent forces shaping Canadian cultural, political, and economic life ever since."[21]

Conclusions vary as to the exact duration of the boom. Owram proposes 1946 to 1964, maintaining that the first half, to the mid-1950s, had the greatest impact. Statistics Canada uses 1947 (when all the soldiers had been repatriated) to 1966. For Jews, it is advisable to take a longer view, from those who entered adolescence c. 1945, to the youngest siblings born at the tail end in the early 1960s as the basis for this discussion.

In 1888, a two-story, eight-room building on Clinton Street, just north of College Street in Toronto, was built to educate the children of a growing community, immediately west of the downtown core. The houses were marginally larger and were bought by working-class Anglo Canadians. The school had several expansions, until the current building was erected in 1966. Until 1920, 90 per cent of the students were British or Canadian born, but the expanding Jewish population along College Street changed the school's character. Within a decade, half were Jewish, cresting at 74 per cent in 1934 and remaining the majority until the early 1950s. By 1960 only 5 per cent of incoming students were Jewish, symptomatic of the migration to the suburbs. Robert Vipond's seminal study, *Making A Global City: How One Toronto School Embraced Diversity*, is a primer on growing up Jewish (as well as Italian, and the range of ethnicities in the neighbourhood to the present). Despite a major expansion, the school quickly became overcrowded, with some forty students per class. The curriculum, with only minor changes until 1967, stressed rote learning, drill and discipline, and corporal punishment was administered for misdemeanors, whether behavioural or academic. Ontario education was grounded in developing "Christian values." The Lord's Prayer was recited daily in all schools, until the late 1960s, and there were bible readings from both Testaments. Compulsory religious education was introduced in 1944, the basis of which was that Christianity was the morally superior faith. Clinton, and the adjacent public schools with the most Jewish students, had "a gentleman's agreement" to not enforce this edict. Indeed, Clinton appears to have been somewhat more sensitive to students of immigrants than the norm, according to Vipond's research.

In 1945, only 61 per cent of Ontario's students were enrolled in high school, and only 46 per cent remained past the age of sixteen. Jewish children were an outlier. For example, of males who attended school between the ages of five to twenty-four, Jews were overrepresented elevenfold in 1951 and sixteenfold in 1961 in comparison to the national average. The Montreal suburb of Outremont in 1961 had 75 per cent of its males and 63 per cent of its females at school aged fifteen to nineteen, compared to 61 per cent and 55 per cent respectively across Canada. More telling, 37 per cent of those aged twenty to twenty-four were in school, in comparison to 11 and 4 per cent, respectively for Canada. In 1961, one-third of the town of Outremont was Jewish.

The catch basin secondary school for Clinton Street Public School was Harbord Collegiate; for the Montreal Plateau, it was Baron Byng High; and for Winnipeg's North End, it was St. John's Tech. Some students who reached adolescence in the early years of the baby boom went on to become political, cultural, and business luminaries. By 1950, the shift to the suburbs necessitated the erection of new schools, to which students mostly cycled or were driven, and where the focus shifted away from school to extra-curricular activities, where being Jewish was the attraction. In suburban Toronto, Forest Hill Collegiate and Vaughan Road Collegiate already had a Jewish contingent before the War. In the 1950s and 1960s Bathurst Heights, Mackenzie, and Fleming followed suit, succeeded a decade later by Newtonbrook and A.Y. Jackson. All were part of the North York Board of Education. In Winnipeg's South End, Kelvin Tech and Grant Park High School were the destinations. In Montreal, in addition to Outremont there were high schools in each of the municipalities: Northmount in Snowdon, Wagar in Côte St. Luc, Westhill in NDG, Westmount, and Chomedy. Some of the boys from upper-crust families attended the private St. George's School.

Many Montreal children attended Jewish schools that were part of the Protestant Board of Education, and hence publicly funded, as detailed in Chapter 4. Some these elementary schools fed into Jewish high schools. Among the religious schools, Adath Israel (later called the Hebrew Academy) and Herzliah were modern Orthodox, and Merkaz Hatorah and the Lubavitch Yeshiva (Beis Yaacov for girls) were traditional Orthodox. The secular Jewish People's School (folk shul) and the Peretz School fed into the Herzliah High School. In other large communities outside Quebec, full day parochial schools were an alternative, albeit one that charged tuition and relied on support from local Jewish federations. More popular were "after school schools," some with classes four times a week and on Sundays, others less often, where Yiddish tended to be the language of instruction until it was gradually replaced by Hebrew. They were run by synagogues and Zionist and left-wing organizations. In smaller communities, Jewish education continued apace, although the range of schools was much more limited.

Forest Hill was an incorporated village, with its own bylaws and municipal jurisdiction, one of the thirteen municipalities, of which Toronto was one. Built in the interwar period, it was largely the preserve of wealthy Anglo Canadians. There was a noticeable Jewish presence, mostly relegated to the borders of Bathurst Street on the west and Spadina Avenue on the east in the 1950s. The south side was more upscale with fewer Jews. The less prestigious part, north of Eglinton Avenue, became primarily Jewish after the war. Most worshipped at either the Reform Holy Blossom Temple, or the Conservative Beth Zedek Synagogue. As many Christian children attended private schools, the Forest Hill elementary schools and high school were heavily Jewish. Writer Erna Paris (b. 1938), in "Growing Up a Jewish Princess in Forest Hill,"[22] recalls that she didn't know Hebrew or Yiddish, despite her Sunday morning classes at Holy Blossom. Her *nouveau riche* family was puritanical in outlook, devoted to education, not only as the gateway to status, but for its own worth. Life was "insular and unreal, unconnected to the WASP reality of Toronto, to the rural reality of Canada."[23] Life was centred on the village, shopping, and noshing on Eglinton, unconnected to the pain and suffering of Jews elsewhere, including those swept up in the Holocaust. Jewish princesses didn't "go all the way … to save themselves for Mr. Right."[24] Girls were educated but rarely became professionals. Paris spent a year in France, married a French Catholic at Holy Blossom, and, reflecting upon her return ten years later, saw her female cohort as having "hesitated" to be swept up by the changes of the sixties, choosing to continue the lifestyle in which they grew up, succumbing to early middle age.

Sharon Abron Drache (b. 1943) is a prolific writer of fiction and literary reviews. "Ruhama Fishbein and Me" is a short story of two Jewish girls in their last year at Forest Hill Collegiate. The story revolves around their relationship with a new student, Rosalie Case, who has moved from Sudbury. Its theme is the mindless materialism of teenage girls in the late 1950s. Ruhama drives a baby blue Austin Healey convertible, given to her for her sweet sixteen, because "it's too far to walk to school." Even so, the car was somewhat déclassé compared to the "Mercedes, Jaguars, Cadillacs, and Buicks (God forbid there should be one Pontiac)," in the school lot. She and Ruhama wore designer outfits – "A-line khaki-coloured skirts, starched white blouses ... highly polished brown loafers with a shining bronze penny ... purchased in Buffalo"[25] on their mothers' semi-annual treks. Rosalie, by contrast, is overweight and clumsy. In Sudbury, her parents have a sailboat. Ruhama retorts that her father has a thirty-two-foot cabin cruiser on Lake Simcoe. A year later, Ruhama is at Michigan State, Barbara at York, and Rosalie at Cambridge. This over-the-top satire, which could have taken place in Westmount, Tuxedo, or Vancouver's West Point Grey, invites the reader to consider one extreme of the socio-economic diversity of the postwar generation.

In contrast to Forest Hill were children born to immigrants. Rosalie (Rivke in Yiddish) Sharp, née Wise, was born in Toronto in 1936, a year after her parents' marriage in Montreal, shortly after their arrival from Poland. They lived on Grange Street, near Spadina and Dundas, and two years later moved to North Toronto, where they opened a dry goods store, where her father sewed, and her mother sold. They lived in a back room. The neighbourhood was a venerable upper middle-class Anglo landmark, settled in the late 1800s. Her parents lived, in Sharp's words, "as if they were still in a shtetl speaking Yiddish,"[26] while Rivke replied in English. Rosalie sang Christmas carols at school and listened to *Onward Christian Soldiers* at her friends' homes. While they had ballet, music lessons, and vacations, Rivke trekked to Yiddish school downtown. She led a double life, hiding her contact with her Christian classmates from her family. Toys were rare, clothes were homemade and in constant repair. Her mother was paranoid about attacks from "the *goyim* [gentiles]." When news of the Holocaust was made known, the family was traumatized. There were no survivors from their families, and in their hometown, Ozarow, where two thousand Jews had lived in 1939, none had returned in 1945. Rosalie worked summers, from the age of twelve, for a Chinese greengrocer. The family moved to a five-room bungalow in 1948 and her father ventured into small real estate acquisitions. In high school she fell in with a small group of Jews, began to date, and at the age of seventeen met Isidore (Izzy) Sharp, born in Canada. They married two years later. Izzy went on to become one of Canada's foremost property developers, through his Four Seasons Corporation, and Rosalie continues to be a major volunteer fund raiser.

Julia Koschitsky (b. 1944), née Podolski, was the younger of two daughters of a family that had lived for generations in Berlin. Her parents managed to flee to Britain in the wake of Kristallnacht, the large-scale destruction of Jewish property on November 9, 1938. They settled in Cardiff, Wales, and ten years later made their way to Toronto. Her story, in a collection titled *Growing Up Jewish*, relates her childhood and adolescence in north Toronto. While her parents were more acculturated than the Wise family, she was made very aware of her faith and ethnicity: "I had to learn how to decline going out with non-Jews.... explaining to our principal.... why I could not attend school"[27] during Jewish holidays. One of a handful of Jewish students at Northern Secondary School, she partially integrated, as a cheerleader, into the school culture. She married another immigrant, Henry Koschitsky, whose family survived the Holocaust by fleeing to the Soviet Union. Henry and his brother Saul, manufacture roofing materials. The family is a major benefactor to public institutions in Toronto and Israel and Julia is a significant leader in community organizations.

Boomers led much more organized lives than had their parents. Increasingly, extracurricular activities took precedence. Jewish kids, in addition to Jewish education, belonged to youth groups from synagogues and Zionist organizations. The B'nai Brith Youth Organization, organized by chapters for teenage boys and girls, was an attractive destination for teenagers. It was international, staffed by professionals, but the chapter activities were organized by the members. The Southern Ontario Region , which included chapters from western New York State, as an example, had approximately thirty chapters for each gender. In the early 1960s, there were some thirty members in each, so that a rough estimate was that almost two thousand teenagers were engaged. Boys belonged to Aleph Zadik Aleph (three Hebrew letters) and girls to the more prosaically named B'nai Brith Girls. Another draw for Jewish youth was the JCC, not only for sports but clubs, the arts, and as a meeting place.

Another socializing force was summer camps. While they began at the turn of the twentieth century, their popularity soared after the war. Their origins were diverse: from all three religious movements – Orthodox, Conservative, and Reform, from the varying strains of Zionist ideology, and from non-profits supported in part by Jewish federations and organizations, such as B'nai Brith. In addition, there were privately owned camps that catered to Jewish youth, ranging from the most basic to most lavish. For some children, their experience had a lasting positive imprint; for others, it was a tedious ordeal, or a soul-destroying one because they were not accepted by the dominant social leaders. By many accounts, Camp Kadima (Hebrew for forward) in Lunenburg County in Nova Scotia was a summer haven. It opened in 1943, initially underwritten by Halifax residents, drawing children from the Atlantic provinces, Ontario, and the United States. For children from small towns, it was their first exposure to other Jewish children and culture. Kadima's seventy-fifth anniversary in 2018 drew alumni scattered across North America.

The University of Toronto was founded in 1828 as King's College under the aegis of the Anglican Church. Based on the Oxbridge model of colleges, other Christian denominations built their own institutions. The exception was UC which accepted students from all faiths. The early story of Jewish students is outlined in Chapter 3. The heyday of Jewish life was in the period under discussion. Alan Borovoy, a graduate of Harbord Collegiate, who went on to become one of the most prominent human rights advocates in Canada, graduated from UC in 1953. At first, he recalls, there was a "feeling of inhibition" by Jewish students, but by his last year "there was a free-flowing relationship across ethnic boundaries."[28] Two years later, Martin Friedland was elected the president of the Arts and Literary Executive, the student body that ran the extracurricular activities. Ultimately, Friedland became a professor in the law school and the author of the university's history.

The door was wide open for the boomers. Between 1958 and 1973, 58 per cent of the UC executive was Jewish. Historian Michael Bliss (UC 1962), who was Christian, wrote that the Junior Common Room was called the Jewish Common Room, and not in a disparaging fashion. The activity most associated with Jewish students was the annual *Follies*, a series of comic and musical sketches. The apex was in 1964, which could have been termed the "Jewish follies." Paul Hoffert wrote the score and went on to found the band Lighthouse, compose for Hollywood movies, become an eminent scientist, and an expert in online content distribution. Earl and Hart Pomerantz wrote the prose, and Lorne Lipowitz directed the *Follies* that year. Lipowitz and Hart went on as a comedy team at CBC. A few years later, Lipowitz, who had changed his name to Michaels, went to New York with his wife, Roz Shuster, the daughter of comedian Frank, and they created *Saturday Night Live.* Politician, lawyer, and human rights activist Bob Rae (UC 1969) also joined the *Follies.* Paul Shaffer (UC 1971) went from the *Follies* to musical theatre, and eventually to television, where he led his band as David Letterman's sidekick for thirty-three years.

In 2012 UC selected one hundred Alumni of Influence and adds more each year. Currently, there are approximately two hundred. Of those, ninety-six graduated between 1953 and 1973, spanning the baby boom. Of those, fifty-two were Jewish. Since its Jewish heyday, UC students have come to mirror the diverse social composition of Canada. Until the 1980s it was uncommon for Jewish students to go to universities that were not in, or near, their hometowns. Since then, local schools have no longer been automatic choices. Allie Cuperfain (UC 2011) relates that in her graduating class of 180 at the Community Hebrew Academy in Toronto, only nine enrolled at the University of Toronto, of whom four chose UC.

The University of Toronto and other major metropolitan universities moulded two generations of Canadian Jews, from the 1930s to the 1970s, who, in turn had a significant impact on student life, the Jewish community, and ultimately, Canadian society.

CULTURE

The ascendance of Canadian Jews into the mainstream of Canadian life in the postwar era was apparent, not only in geographic and economic mobility, but also in the nation's cultural evolution. Until 1945 Canadian literature, music, drama, and entertainment were pale vestiges of their British heritage. There was little, aside from the paintings of the Group of Seven, that was uniquely Canadian. The emergence of a distinctive Canadian culture was due, in part, to the Jewish contribution. This "Jewish impact," especially in entertainment and music was not immediately apparent. It was adapted from its European roots, finding a new expression, initially in Yiddish and then in English. It was most dramatic in the United States, where, starting at the turn of the twentieth century, Jews were front and centre in popular music, the creation of Hollywood and Broadway, and in literature. In Canada, this contribution took hold after the war by writers, with exponents of diverse musical traditions, and in popular culture primarily through the medium of television. Three of the leading contributors in each field follow.

Literature

MONTREAL

The output of Montrealers A.M. Klein, Irving Layton, and Mordechai Richler heralded the emergence of literature outside the Canadian mainstream in the postwar years. Montreal was the country's cultural centre, drawing on its diverse heritage. Two of Canada's preeminent postwar writers are representative of the Jewish contribution.

Until well after his death, A.M. (Abraham Moses) Klein (1909–72) was the least well known of the major Jewish writers from Montreal. He was born in Ukraine and came to Montreal as an infant. Raised in a traditional home on the Plateau he undertook study for the Rabbinate. But it was the great Yiddish writers who evoked traditional Jewish life that captivated him. He was a polymath, who absorbed languages, history, philosophy, the classics, politics, and economics. Klein attended Baron Byng High School in Montreal's Plateau where his friends included David Lewis, the future politician. As a teenager, he was fluent in Yiddish, Hebrew, French, and English, and read Latin. At McGill University, he encountered poets and literary critics who were absorbing the progressive works of Americans and Europeans. Klein fell under their influence, and, with Lewis, founded a literary magazine that projected the avant-garde literature of the period. He graduated from law at the Université de Montréal, and opened a small office, which proved to be unsuccessful, due to his lack of entrepreneurial skills.

He turned his attention to writing poetry based on his European roots, the juxtaposition of faith and persecution, Montreal's beauty and intercultural richness, and the destruction of European Jewry during World War II. He won the Governor General's Award for poetry in 1948. The next year, following a trip to Israel, he wrote his only novel, *The Second Scroll.* Influenced by the Torah and Talmud, by the Holocaust and the state of Israel, and fixated on James Joyce's works, the book tells of the author's search for his uncle, Melech Davidson ("King David's

Son"). Davidson's life is a chronicle of European Jewry in the first half of the nineteenth century, mirroring Klein's journey in search of himself and the dilemma of the Jewish tragedy.

Klein supported himself as a speech writer for community titan, Sam Bronfman, as the editor and frequent contributor to *The Canadian Jewish Chronicle* from 1932 to 1955, as a fervent Zionist who went on speaking tours after his Israeli visit, and as a woefully unsuccessful candidate for the CCF in the 1949 election. His obsession with Joyce's unsuccessful search for the meaning of life foretold his rapidly growing depression. From 1956 until his death, he was a recluse. Klein, whose roots were in Yiddish Canada, but whose life reverberated with the modern world, was the bridge between his parent's generation and the postwar era, that is between Yiddish Canada and Jewish Canada. Klein was the preeminent Canadian Jewish intellectual of his generation.

Until recently, Klein's oeuvre and impact on Canadian culture has largely been the reserve of scholars. Sherry Simon and Norman Ravvin, writing in a 2011 introduction to *Failure's Opposite: Listening to A.M. Klein*, a collection of articles from a symposium on Klein's influence, posit that although Klein predated the more well-known Montreal writers – Irving Layton, Mordecai Richler, and Leonard Cohen – they were not his disciples. Their world was linked to the rough and tumble of the Jewish neighbourhood, their influences were European and American, and their lives pulsed with the rapid social and moral developments in the postwar world. Consequently, Klein's contribution to Canadian culture has not received sufficient attention. Fifty years after his passing, it is worthy of public awareness and appreciation.

Irving Layton's (1912–2006) upbringing mirrored that of Klein. He was born Israel Lazarovitch in Romania to a traditional Jewish family and came to Montreal at the age of one. He went to Baron Byng, voraciously read the English Romantic poets, Shakespeare, and Darwin, and befriended David Lewis. But his demeanour and response to the travails of immigrant life was the opposite to that of Klein. He rejected religion, fought French-Canadian kids, was thrown out of school for his rebellious attitude, but not before completing his junior matriculation with the help, ironically, of Klein, who tutored him in Latin. His first poem appeared in Klein and Lewis' magazine. He led a peripatetic life until he enlisted in the Canadian army in 1942. Returning to Montreal he received an MA from McGill in economics; he published his first collection of poems. Layton was a remarkable teacher who brought out the best of his students, beginning at Herzliah High School, then at Sir George Williams University (now Concordia), and as a tenured professor at York University from 1969 to 1978.

Layton was an *enfant terrible,* unkempt, outspoken, and profane, who shattered the delicate decorum of CBC television in the 1950s on the debating program, *Fighting Words.* He published some fifty volumes of poetry over a period of forty-seven years. Although he was of Klein's generation, because of his long and active career and his vociferous countenance, he is regarded as a contemporary of Richler and Leonard Cohen, who were born in the 1930s. He was respectful of Klein, for whom he wrote a requiem and an epigram, contemptuous of Richler, and mentor to Cohen. His poetry ranged from attacking formal religion, Western civilization, especially antisemitism, and praising of the military strength of Israel. He was strongly influenced by figures as diverse as Friedrich Nietzsche, Walt Whitman, Theodore Adorno, and Holocaust survivor and author, Paul Celan, who ultimately took his own life. Layton would not take fools gladly. He was an angry man, a detached father, an unfaithful husband, but a respected and demanding teacher and a devoted friend.

Mordecai Richler (1931–2001) was born in Montreal to Lilly, the daughter of Rabbi Yudel Rosenberg, and Moses, a scrap-iron dealer. This religious heritage, however, did not resonate at home. His parents had a tempestuous marriage and eventually split. Raised on rue St. Urbain on Montreal's Plateau, he attended Baron Byng High School where he was alienated from the staunchly Anglo-Protestant cultural scene. He wrote: "To be a Jew and a Canadian is to emerge from the ghetto twice."[29] Deeply influenced by the "lost generation" of artists and writers of the 1920s, he left for Paris, returned to Montreal, then decamped in London as a screen writer in 1954, where he married and raised his family. But, alienated from uptight English sensibilities, the family returned to Montreal. Richler felt comfortable in his favourite hangouts and at his country home in the Eastern Townships.

Richler wrote ten novels between 1954 and 1997, three children's stories (The *Jacob Two-Two* series), eight collections of essays, and numerous articles in journals and newspapers. He received several literary awards, including the Governor General's Award for *Cocksure* and

Hunting Tigers Under Glass in 1969 and for *St. Urbain's Horseman* in 1972, and the Giller Prize for his last work, *Barney's Version* in 1997.

His most well-known works revolve around the street hustlers of St. Urbain, Westmount snobs, repressed Brits, and unfulfilled Jewish men trapped in mundane lives. Some assume alter egos as Nazi hunters in Paraguay (*St. Urbain's Horseman*) and committed revolutionaries in the Spanish Civil War (*Joshua Then and Now*). One family, a stand in for the Bronfmans, traces its Canadian lineage to a fur trapper in the Arctic (*Solomon Gursky Was Here*); a young con-man alienates his sage grandfather and French-Canadian girlfriend (*The Apprenticeship of Duddy Kravitz*); and an old man who tries to clear his name for an accidental death that he did not commit (*Barney's Version*). Women are portrayed only to illuminate male frailties.

Richler's works were provocative. *Duddy Kravitz*, was his most significant novel as its publication in 1959 was a scalding satire of Quebec society – Jews, Anglos, and French. It upset mainstream Jews because Duddy represented the grasping, amoral Jew caricatured by antisemites. A generation later, Richler was the bane of French-Canadian nationalists. In his collection of essays, *Oh Canada! Oh Quebec! Requiem for a Divided Country* (1992), he lambasted the progenitors of the movement for the restricted language laws imposed on all Quebecers. Richler broke down the door for Canadian writers from ethno-cultural minorities, not that that was his impulse, but in bringing the Jewish world, the complex mish-mash of dreamers, gangsters, and professionals into the mainstream Canadian narrative, he widened the country's literary horizon. Richler remains Canada's most significant Jewish writer and among the country's literary pantheon.[30]

THE PRAIRIES

In Michael Greenstein's introduction to his anthology on the subject he writes: "Canadian-Jewish literature has traditionally been a tale of two ghettoes – Montreal's Main, or St. Lawrence, area and the north end of Winnipeg … where Jack Ludwig, Miriam Waddington and Adele Wiseman accomplished for their prairie city what Klein, Richler, Cohen and Layton had done for Montreal."[31] From Greenstein's perspective, "Montreal is the New York of the north with a Parisian twist, while Winnipeg is a northern version of Chicago with its Jewish-Ukrainian mix and Yiddish socialist background." Jack Ludwig (1922–2018) left Winnipeg for the United States. His autobiographical novel, *Above Ground* (1963), is an avant-garde work about a North-End family (Winnipeg itself is not mentioned), in which he draws on Shakespeare, Eliot, and Joyce's invocation of rivers (the Red and the Assiniboine). In Greenstein's words, "never going home again, writer and river of Jewish frontiers offer a way in and out of mindscapes."[32]

Adele Wiseman (1928–92) was born in Winnipeg to Ukrainian parents who had escaped the pogroms during the Russian Civil War (1918–22). Growing up in the socialist/yiddishist North End, she was strongly influenced by the working-class, immigrant environment. As a student at the University of Manitoba, she studied literature with her classmates, including Ludwig and the eminent Margaret Laurence, her neighbour and lifelong friend. She began working on *The Sacrifice*, her first and most successful novel, while at university. Set in Winnipeg (although, like Ludwig, the city is not named), it tells of a family from Ukraine, headed by Abraham and Sarah (no surname) and their youngest son, Isaac. The two oldest sons, Moses and Jacob, had been killed in a pogrom. Abraham, a taciturn man, works in a butcher shop. Sarah dies, Isaac marries Ruth, and then he dies trying to save a Torah from a burning synagogue. Laiah, a customer of the butcher shop, tries to seduce Abraham, and overcome by rage and loss, he murders her. His grandson, Moishele, is left. Aside from the obvious invocation of the biblical tale of the sacrifice of Isaac by Abraham that was stymied by God, the work depicts the travail of adaptation of European Jews unable to overcome their grief, and of their reduction to "greeners" even though Abraham spoke five languages. *The Sacrifice* was published in 1956, the first novel by a Canadian Jewish woman, and was awarded the Governor General's Literary Award.

Wiseman moved to Toronto, and then to Montreal where she taught at McGill until 1969. She was a mentor and muse for aspiring writers for the rest of her life. Her second novel, *Crackpot*, was conceived in 1961 and not completed until 1974. Far less well known, it tells the story of Hoda, an overweight woman, the daughter of a hunchback mother and blind father, who joyfully shares her body with men for money, and with women for affection. Wiseman wrote plays, children's stories, and essays. A memoir about her mother, *Old Women at Play* appeared in 1977.

Scholar Ruth Panofsky states that "throughout [Wiseman's] career, she wrote always as a Canadian, a woman, and as a Jew who sought to explore the human condition."[33] Quoting Wiseman, Panofsky writes: "my work, which has for me the force of vocation, to aim for other than the highest … and to miss … is only failure."[34] Adele Wiseman's place as a pioneer woman writer, for her contribution to Canadian literature and for her explication of immigrant adaptation, is a necessary corollary to this story.[35]

Music

Music is integral to Judaism. According to the Bible, David was first a musician, then the slayer of Goliath, and then king. Solomon too was a lyricist and then king of Israel. His Song of Songs, a separate book in Bible, is clearly about love between a man and a woman but came to be interpreted as God's love of Israel. Parts of the Song are recited on the eve of the Sabbath and during Passover. For centuries, a *Chazan* (cantor) leads the prayers on the Sabbath. In modern times, the Reform and Conservative movements adopted choirs, generally composed of synagogue members. Some include acoustic musicians.

Songs in Hebrew, Yiddish, and in the Sephardic and Mizrachi languages have historically bound communities together. In eastern Europe minstrels travelling from town to town performed. Their music, a mixture of Jewish, host nations', and Roma traditions, sung in Yiddish, came to be called *Klezmer*, taken from the Hebrew word for instrument. During the European Enlightenment and the Romantic eras, composers of Jewish background made significant contributions. The most well-known included Felix Mendelssohn, Georges Bizet, and Jacobo Meyerbeer. At the turn of the twentieth century, Gustav Mahler, Arnold Schoenberg, and Paul Dukas expanded the scope of modern classical music as did Eric Korngold, Ernst Bloch, Erwin Schulhoff, and George Gershwin in the interwar period.

CLASSICAL MUSIC

Classical music in the early postwar period in Canada was marked by two groups of composers and conductors of Jewish origin. The first were native Canadians, primarily students of John Weinzweig, and the second consisted of émigrés who fled Europe prior to and after World War II. Weinzweig (1913–2006) was born in Toronto, the child of Polish immigrants. His parents were Labour Zionists and it was at the Peretz School that Weinzweig played the mandolin. At Harbord Collegiate he was fortunate to be in a school that had one of the few music programs. The University of Toronto had recently created a music program from which he graduated in 1937, where he was influenced by the masters of the period – Igor Stravinsky, Bela Bartok, Arthur Schoenberg, and Alban Berg. He was the first Canadian to have incorporated the twelve-tone technique that had been inaugurated in Europe.

Weinzweig joined the Royal Conservatory in 1939, composing for radio and film. In 1952, he became a professor at the University of Toronto and developed a composition program. Among his students were Harry Somers, Harry Freedman, Murray Adaskin, Louis Applebaum, R. Murray Schafer, and Srul Irving Glick. They were instrumental (no pun intended) in founding the Canadian League of Composers, an advocacy and performance organization.

Arguably the most well-known classical music figure in Canada was the contralto Maureen Forrester (1930–2010). She was born in Montreal to a Scottish father and Irish mother. In 1957 she married Eugene Kash, a violinist and conductor, who was Jewish. Forrester converted to Judaism, and the couple raised five children. Forrester performed around the world as one of opera's leading lights. She is perhaps best known for her performance of Gustav Mahler's Symphony No. 2 ("Resurrection").

The second category of classical musicians émigré composers and conductors who arrived from central Europe during and after World War II, has been overlooked in works on Canada's Jews, despite their contribution to the nation's cultural heritage. Most prominent was the Czech conductor Oscar Morawetz (1917–2007) who came to Toronto. His compositions eschewed the avant-garde styles of serialism (adopted by Weinzweig, for example) and electronics. He stated: "Ever since I was a child, music has meant for me something terribly emotional, and I still believe there has to be some kind of melodic line."[36] His works have been performed worldwide and have featured acclaimed soloists including Maureen Forrester and pianist Anton Kuerti. Noteworthy compositions are *Carnival Overture* (1945) and *From The Diary of Anne Frank* (1970) for voice and orchestra.

The Toronto Symphony Orchestra had two Jewish émigré conductors of Czech origin. Walter Susskind (1913–80) led the orchestra from 1956 to 1965. Karel Ancerl (1908–73) was a noted conductor at a young age. During the war he was imprisoned in the Theresienstadt Concentration Camp in the Czech countryside and then sent to Auschwitz with his wife and son, who were killed. After the war, he conducted for Radio Prague and the Czech Philharmonic. He escaped during the Czech uprising against the Soviet Union in 1968, arriving in Toronto where he conducted the Toronto Symphony Orchestra until his death.

A less well known, but by no means lesser talent, Heinz Unger (1895–1965) was a German conductor who fled to the Soviet Union after the Nazi seizure of power and then to England. Arriving in Toronto in 1948, he found that there was no appreciation of Mahler by the hidebound music establishment, nor by Canadian Jews. Historian Hernan Tesler-Mabé, in uncovering Unger's life, relates his extremely mild reception in Toronto. It was largely confined to tony Forest Hill, where he conducted the community orchestra. Unger did find a more sympathetic audience in Los Angeles, home to a German Jewish community that included Max Steiner and Erich Korngold, expatriate composers who created soundtracks for memorable Hollywood movies. In fact, he received the Mahler medal there in 1959, as his work was receiving a much-delayed reception in the United States. He died of a heart attack in Toronto.

Arguably the most significant émigré musician was the violinist Jacques Israelievitch (1948–2016). He was born in France, and his talent was identified as a child. He studied in Paris under the noted teacher Nadia Boulanger, and then at the University of Indiana. His first position, at the age of twenty-two, was assistant concertmaster with the Chicago Symphony, which some experts proclaimed to be the best orchestra in the world. He became the concertmaster of the Toronto Symphony, a position that he held for his last twenty years. Israelievitch's discography features more than one hundred albums. He commissioned works by Canadian composers, was a sought-after teacher, a mentor to his associates, and a faculty member at the University of Toronto and York University. He was the recipient of awards in France and Canada. In 2016 he was diagnosed with cancer. Shortly thereafter, he was named to the Order of Canada. Unable to attend the ceremony, the lieutenant-governor of Ontario conferred the honour to him at his home.

POPULAR MUSIC

While the Jewish contribution to popular music after the war was not as extensive as was classical, it played a role in jazz, folk, and rock, reflecting the influence of American music internationally. In the 1940s, big band swing music was in its heyday. It was a mainstay in dance halls across the country. In Toronto, the main venue was Sunnyside on the Lake Ontario shore. Many of local musicians had their origins in the Jewish communities, playing at parties, weddings, bar mitzvahs, and at summer resorts in Muskoka, north of Toronto, and in the Laurentians north of Montreal.

Percy Faith (1908–76) was born and raised in Toronto. One of eight children, he played violin and piano as a child in theatres and at Massey Hall. A fire that burnt his hands led him to conducting orchestras live on CBC radio. Faith became a household name in the United States, a not uncommon story for many Jewish Canadian artists. His initial idiom, swing, evolved after the war to encompass Broadway, Hollywood, and Latin music. He arranged and conducted for Tony Bennett, Doris Day, and Johnny Mathis over a forty-year career. He recorded some one hundred albums from 1953 to 1976.

Moe (Morris) Koffman (1928–2001) was born in Toronto to immigrant parents who had a variety store. He played saxophone and flute and composed and arranged music for fifty years. A school dropout, he played in local dance bands and then in the United States. Returning to Toronto, his record, "Swinging Shepherd Blues" (1957) was a Billboard hit. Unfortunately, its popularity overshadowed his legitimate talent as a jazz and classical artist. He played multiple reed instruments simultaneously and recorded arrangements of works by Bach, Mozart, and Vivaldi. From 1956 to 1990, he fronted a band at George's Spaghetti House in Toronto.

Canadian Folk Music is incredibly varied, befitting the vastness of the country and the myriad ethnic traditions, from Indigenous nations to recent immigrants. Yet, in the 1950s, there was little knowledge and therefore appreciation of these traditions. One group, and one person, helped shed this myopia. The Travellers formed in 1953. They were campers at Naivelt (New World in Yiddish), outside Toronto, that was founded by the pro-communist UJPO. At the time, the United States was overwhelmed by the Red Scare, the paranoia that communism would engulf the country. The notorious *Black List* prevented suspected communists from employment. Indeed, there was a radical movement whose songs, about workers emphasized unity, brotherhood, and community. The most well-known exponent was the Weavers, led by folk legend Pete Seeger. Their music, some of which was in Yiddish, was emulated by the Travellers, a group of Jews and Christians, whose Canadian version of the American anthem, *This Land Is Your Land*, written by Woody Guthrie, remains a classic. The group's mainstays were Jerry Gray, Sid Dolgay, Helen Gray, Jerry Goodis, and Oscar Ross, who were raised in the radical Yiddish milieu in Toronto. They produced sixteen albums through the 1980s.

Estelle Klein (1930–2004) was born in Buffalo, NY, raised in Toronto, and attended Camp Naivelt, following the footsteps of the Travellers. In 1961, the first folk music festival in Canada took place in Orillia, Ontario. Named "The Mariposa Festival," after Steven Leacock's stories about mythical Orillia, it brought together artists from across the country, and from the United States. The Travellers were the Canadian headliners. Klein joined the festival organization and was its artistic director from 1964 until 1980. Her energy and dedication created a foundation that brought Canadian folk music to the public and to schools. Mariposa was the premier festival venue for Ian and Sylvia, Gordon Lightfoot, Joni Mitchell, Leonard Cohen, Murray McLaughlin, and Bruce Cockburn. Under Klein's tutelage, Inuit throat singers, French, Celtic, and Indigenous music and dance were among the Canadian traditions that were featured. Klein was adamant that the music be "pure" and accessible. Workshops allowed the spectators a close rapport with the performers. Mariposa remains a truly Canadian event.

Geddy Lee (b. Garry Lee Weinrib in 1953) is lead vocalist, bassist, and keyboardist for Rush, arguably Canada's the most lauded rock band. Since its formation with guitarist Alex Lifeson and drummer Neil Peart in 1968, it has been in the forefront of progressive rock around the globe. Lee was born in Toronto to Morris and Manya, survivors of the ghetto of their hometown in Poland and of the camps at Auschwitz, Bergen Belsen (Manya), and Dachau (Morris). They married at a displaced persons' camp and immigrated to Canada. Morris was a musician but died when Geddy (a nickname) was twelve. His passing inspired him to make the most of his talent. In Rush's 1984 album, *Grace Under Pressure*, Peart wrote the lyrics to "Red Sector A," dedicated to Manya.

Arthur Fogel was born in Ottawa and has promoted concert tours for forty years. He came to Toronto in late 1970s and joined Concert International Productions headed by Michael Cohl. Their first major accomplishment was securing the rights to tours by the Rolling Stones. Concert International Productions morphed into Live Nation, based in Los Angeles, the most successful global operation in this field. Fogel became the new head of the company and was dubbed "the most powerful man in music" in a 2013 biopic, "Who the F**k is Arthur Fogel."[37]

Sharon Hampson, Lois Lilienstein, and Bram Morrison were musicians and singers brought up in the radical Yiddish milieu, who performed in Toronto's folk music revival. They joined forces in 1978 using their first names to become most popular performers of music for children in Canada. Their first album, *One Elephant, Deux Éléphants*, was funded by their families at a time when they were raising young families. Its success led to the syndicated television program, *The Elephant Show*, which aired through the 1990s. Their most well-known song was "Skinnamarink." Lilienstein died of cancer in 2015.

Entertainment

The heritage of music, drama, and comedy was transported to the burgeoning Diaspora during the Great Migration. Its impact was most acute in the United States, where Jewish theatre and music incorporated American motifs. With some one million Jews in New York City by 1914, Jewish influence in Vaudeville and the "American Song Book" was the impetus for the creation of Broadway and Hollywood. Songwriter Irving Berlin, singers Al Jolson and Sophie Tucker, comedians the Marx Brothers, composer and musician/composer George Gershwin were among the prominent contributors. Hollywood was created by the likes of the Warner Brothers, Louis B. Mayer, and William Fox, all expatriate Canadians.

National popular entertainment in Canada was born with the founding of the Canadian Broadcasting Corporation in 1936 and more significantly with the advent of CBC television in 1952, when 26 per cent of Canadians had television, swelling to 60 per cent two years later. By 1957 English and French networks were broadcasting up to ten hours a day to 85 per cent of the population. A second source of national popular entertainment was the Stratford Shakespeare Festival, which opened in 1952 and was a catalyst for regional theatres across the country. Accordingly, as with the United States but on a much smaller scale, the talents of the children of Jewish immigrants were on display in the immediate postwar period.

TELEVISION

Johnny Wayne and Frank Shuster led the vanguard of Canadian performers in the heyday of CBC television. Their humour, honed first at Harbord Collegiate in Toronto, then at UC, and finally in the Canadian armed forces, led to a weekly radio show that by 1950 had three million listeners. In 1955 they moved to the small screen performing skits culled from history, literature, and their own irreverent takes on life. In 1958 they signed a contract to appear regularly on the *Ed Sullivan Show*, the most popular program on American television. For Canada, which stood deep in the shadows of the American cultural grip, their appearances were a matter of national pride.

Their skits had origins in formal Canadian education and their exposure to Jewish humour. In "Rinse the Blood off My Toga," Wayne plays a detective in Rome investigating the murder of Julius Caesar, and Shuster portrays the culprit, Brutus. Sylvia Lennick, a local actress portrayed Calpurnia, Caesar's wife, as an over-the-top Jewish woman with a thick Bronx accent. Her loud refrain, "I told him – 'Julie, don't go,'" remains a high point in Canadian comedy. In another scene, Wayne enters a bar and orders a "martinus," to which a bartender responds, "Don't you mean a martini?" Wayne retorts: "If I wanted two, I'd have asked for them." In "A Shakespearean Baseball Game," written in iambic pentameter and rhyming couplets from Hamlet and Macbeth, the duo used lines like: "O, what a rogue and bush league slob am I ... O, cursed fate, that I, who led the league, should bat .208."[38] Wayne and Shuster utilized an array of Canadian performers including ones with whom they had worked in their early days. They included Paul Kligman, Johnny Shapiro, Jacob Reinglass, and Ben Lennick (Sylvia's husband).

Three television personalities had their roots in Canada but are best known for their work in the United States. Lorne Greene (1915–87) was born to Russian immigrants in Ottawa. He was called Chaim (which means life in Hebrew) and Hyman at school. Greene acted in Jewish summer camps and at Queen's University. There, he broadcasted on campus radio before moving to the CBC. As an officer in the RCAF, he became the country's leading newsreader and a narrator of wartime documentaries. After moving to the United States he was on Broadway and television. He is best remembered as Ben "Pa" Cartwright on *Bonanza,* a popular Western, filmed in colour on CBS, from 1959 to 1973. For the next fifteen years, he was a fixture on television, including the miniseries *Roots* and *Battlestar Galactica.* He was a pseudo–father figure to a generation of viewers, combining authority and probity with his physique and sonorous voice. He was made an Officer of the Order of Canada, awarded an honorary doctor of laws at Queen's University, and a lifetime achievement award at the Canadian Gemini Awards.

William Shatner was born in Montreal in 1931. His grandparents had emigrated from eastern Europe at the turn of the century. Shatner attended schools in the inner suburb of Notre-Dame-de-Grace, and graduated with a bachelor of commerce from McGill. He then trained as a Shakespearean actor, and began performing at the Stratford Festival in 1954, and then on CBC television. His Broadway debut in 1956 was in Christopher Marlowe's play, *Tamurlaine the Great.* Through the rest of the decade and into the 1960s, he appeared in films and television, and was the equal of Steve McQueen and Paul Newman, but without their early success. He is best known for his portrayal as Captain James T. Kirk in the television series *Star Trek,* from 1966–9. Its reruns made Shatner a cultural icon. His co-star, Leonard Nimoy (Mr. Spock), also of Jewish lineage, became his lifelong friend. Among his numerous honours is the Governor General's Performing Arts Award in 2011.

Among the other prominent expatriate performers are Winnipeg's Monty Hall, who created and hosted *Let's Make a Deal*; Lorne Michaels and his then-wife Roz Shuster (Frank's daughter) from Toronto, respectively the creator and head writer of *Saturday Night Live* which included the musicians Paul Schaffer of *Late Night with David Letterman,* composers and musicians Paul Hoffert and Howard Shore, founders of the progressive rock band Lighthouse. The improvisational theatrics of *Second City*, an offshoot of the original Chicago troupe, opened in Toronto. From 1973 to 1985, two of the founders helped create and perform in *SCTV*, a scatological view of mainstream Canadian life. They were Eugene Levy from Hamilton, and Rick Moranis from Toronto. Levy spoofed Alex Trebek ("Alex Trebel") host of *Jeopardy*; Moranis was Bob McKenzie, brother of Doug, who coined the term "hosers" in the "Great White North" sketches. Levy currently acts and produces the series *Schitts Creek* with his son Daniel. An alumnus of the original Second City is David Steinberg (b. 1942), who was born in Winnipeg and moved to Chicago in 1964. For the next twenty years, he was one of the most popular comedians in the United States, frequently appearing on *The Tonight Show* with Johnny Carson.

From 1975 to 1980 Canadians were provided a glimpse of urban Jewish life on the popular television program, *King of Kensington.* Set in Kensington Market in Toronto, the hub of the immigrant community in the first half of the twentieth century, it was a situation comedy revolving around Larry King, the owner of a convenience store at a point where the market had long become a hub of intra-ethnic commerce. King, played by veteran actor Al Waxman, was the go-to person when other residents and hangers-on had problems requiring help and advice. Long-time actress of the Yiddish theatre, Helene Winston, played his mother, Gladys, and was Larry's foil, a loving critic of her son's naiveté, and disapproving of Larry's non-Jewish wife, Cathy, played by Fiona Reid. Other actors included members of *SCTV*. The show was a gentle Canadian mirror to the more vigorous social humour on American networks. It drew 1.5 to 1.8 million viewers weekly.

Waxman (1935–2001) was born to immigrants who had a lunch counter in the market. From the age of twelve, he worked on CBC radio. After *King*, he was in demand in films, television, and drama. At Stratford, he played Willy Loman in *Death of a Salesman*, directed *The Diary of Anne Frank*, and was rehearsing the role of Shylock in *The Merchant of Venice*, when he died from a heart attack. Waxman was heavily involved in the community on behalf of numerous causes related to health care as well as the United Appeal and the United Jewish Appeal. His statue stands in Bellevue Square in the market.

THEATRE

Two figures stand out in the evolution of Canadian drama. John Hirsch (1930–89) was born in Hungary. He survived the Holocaust but lost his parents and brother. He produced his first play at a refugee camp. He came to Canada on the War Orphans Project in 1948 and was adopted by Alex and Pauline Shack of Winnipeg. He recollects that the Shacks "were the most exceptional people I have ever come [across] in my life.... They mended me.... They really put me together and they did it with the only glue that can put human beings together. They did it with love and concern."[39]

In his first year in Canada, Hirsch mastered English and graduated from high school. In 1957, he co-founded the Winnipeg Little Theatre, which merged with the Manitoba Theatre Centre, where he was the principal director until 1965. Moving to the Stratford Festival as co-artistic director, he went on to be head of CBC television drama, returning as artistic director at Stratford from 1981 to 1985 where his best-known work occurred. In the United States, he won awards at New York's Lincoln Centre, and for the Yiddish language play, *The Dybbuk*, which he translated and directed in Los Angeles. Hirsch died of AIDS in Toronto in 1989.

Nathan Cohen (1923–71) was Canada's most renowned theatre critic. He was born in Sydney, Nova Scotia, moved to Toronto in 1945, became a talk show host in the early days of CBC television and was the theatre critic, briefly for the *Toronto Telegram*, and then for the *Toronto Daily Star* from 1959 until his death of heart disease. Cohen had extremely high standards and had no compunction about writing devastating reviews. He wrote a column titled "Rules for Budding Critics." He was best known as the host of CBC's *Fighting Words*. Cohen brought an intellectual rigour to the arts that ultimately elevated Canadian culture.

SOCIO-ECONOMIC MOBILITY

Chapter 4 outlined the Jewish distribution in Canada's labour force based on Louis Rosenberg's detailed analysis of the 1931 census. It showed that Jews were highly overrepresented compared to the national totals in ownership, management, manufacturing, professions, and commerce. In total 76 per cent were employed in these categories in comparison with 25 per cent for Canadians. Managers and professionals were in the middle and upper middle class; manufacturers and those in commerce were designated as lower middle and upper working class.

Thirty years later, by 1961, there were fewer Jews employed in manufacturing and commerce. Owners and managers made up 40 per cent, compared with 10 per cent of Canadians, and 14 per cent were professionals compared to 5 per cent overall – meaning that approximately half of the Jewish labour force was in the middle and upper middle class, in contrast to 17 per cent of all Canadians. The reasons for this economic mobility were due to three interrelated dynamics. First, Jews lived in cities, and cities were the heart of the postwar economic boom. Second, most Jews were no longer immigrants, but were either born or raised in Canada. Third, Jews had continually adapted to Canadian society at more rapid rate than most other ethno-cultural minorities allowing them to be better prepared to take advantage of the booming Canadian economy.

The question that arises is to what degree was this mobility was reflected in the halls of power and influence in Canada. The research of sociologist John Porter and journalist Peter C. Newman discussed social class distinctions in the 1960s. Porter's ground-breaking study, *The Vertical Mosaic: An Analysis of Social Class and Power in Canada* published in 1965, counters the proverbial image of Canada as a classless society, a perspective that was grounded in the origins of a frontier society that only receded with the onset of industrialization. The saga of Canadians as hewers of wood and drawers of water was emblazoned in the national mythology but, in fact, a rigid social class order was imposed shortly after 1760 and was perpetuated by a small coterie of families who controlled a hugely disproportionate portion of the country's wealth. Initially, it was Upper Canada's family compact and Lower Canada's river barons. They were succeeded by Montreal's barons of industry in "the Square Mile,"[40] centred on Sherbrooke Avenue between Pine and Guy streets, from 1860 to the stock market crash in 1929. Newman's *The Canadian Establishment* (1975), the first volume of a trilogy, writes that this group "looked to the late Victorian and Edwardian era for inspiration to divine their own universe – a convoluted, self-contained world,"[41] a view that permeated this establishment. Their successors across Canada capitalized in commerce (the Eaton, Bata, and Weston families [of Eaton's, Bata shoes, and Loblaws]), industry (Howard Webster), construction (E.P. Taylor), and publishing and media (the Thompson family, headed by Roy, Canada's first billionaire).

Class rigidity remained firmly in place after the war. In 1955, 1 per cent received 40 per cent of its income from dividends. While the middle class expanded in the immediate postwar era, John Porter wrote that "a high level of consumption is obtained by means which are alien to a true middle-class standard" so that "only a small proportion of Canadian families were [*sic*] able to live a middle class style of life in the middle 1950s, the high tide of post-war affluence."[42] His study exposes that a tiny elite dominated the country economically, socially, politically, and ideologically. Despite their upward mobility, Jews were excluded.

Porter, relying on Louis Rosenberg's research, indicated that Jews were overrepresented by a factor of 4.2 in the professional and financial fields in 1951 and by 7.4 in 1961. Further, he applies the seven categories of occupations as a measure of social class, formulated by Canadian sociologist Bernard R. Blishen, to Jews. They constituted 2.9 per cent of "Class One" in comparison to 0.9 per cent of all Canadians and 1.3 per cent of "British" subjects. Jews constituted 35.7 per cent of Class Two in contrast to 10.7 per cent of Canadians and 10.8 per cent of British Canadians. Forty-one per cent of Canadians were in Classes Three and Four, compared to 24 per cent of Jews. But Porter cautioned that "their high representation in the higher occupation levels should not be confused with power ... [as] Jews are scarcely represented at the higher levels of Canada's corporate institutions."[43]

The elite were determined by wealth, kinship, socialization, homogeneity in social background, outlook, and ideology, and foremost, being of British Protestant origin. In his examination of the elites, Porter reported there were no Jews in "high society," none in the political elite of 157 members, and one (Louis Rasminsky, governor of the Bank of Canada) in the federal bureaucracy composed of 202 men of whom 86 per cent were of British origin. Of the 88 listed in the ideological elite (mass media, universities, churches), there is one Jew, who is not named. Sam Steinberg, head of the Steinberg Groceries, was appointed to the Canada Council in 1962. Of the 180 dominant corporations in

1950, one had a Jewish presence – Distillers Corporation-Seagrams Ltd., of which 38.6 per cent of was owned by the Bronfman family of Montreal. In 1960, it had assets of $633 million, the third highest in the country. In discussing the federal bureaucracy, Porter stated: "Other ethnic groups in Canada, with the exception of Jews, are scarcely represented at all in the higher bureaucracy ... with freedom of entry into the bureaucracy; there may be relatively more Jewish candidates for promotion. Thus, for the Jew ethnicity may act negatively for promotion in the sense that a 'tactful balance' at the higher levels may be sought also for this ethnic group."[44] This is a polite way of saying that a lid was needed to be kept on the Jews, even though they may have been more qualified. But, as Jews are the only ethno-cultural minority mentioned in this detailed account, it speaks to their relative status at the height of the postwar boom. Porter's colleague, Wallace Clement, writing ten years later (1975) provided a different perspective. He wrote that the Jewish elite was more correctly understood "as an elite of the Jewish community, separate yet interlocking in a peripheral way with the Anglo-dominated elite."[45] By that point, Jews constituted 4.1 per cent of the Canadian elite, while only 1.4 per cent of the population.

Samuel Bronfman (1891–1971) has been considered, until recent times, as the country's most well-known Jew. His family and origins in liquor trade and production are outlined in Chapter 6. By the 1930s, from his headquarters in Montreal, he ruled over his family of three brothers, four sisters, four children (Minda, Phyllis, Edgar, Charles) with an iron fist. He was vulgar, ingratiating, a consummate businessman with an innate ability to spot opportunities and weaknesses among his competitors, fully in control of all aspects of liquor production and trade. Colloquially known as "Mr. Sam," one of his senior executives once compared him to a tiger, "If Mr. Sam smelled your fright, he'd jump you. But if you stood up to him, you'd gain his respect, and he could be totally charming and most thoughtful."[46]

In turn, Bronfman longed for respect from the Canadian social and political elite. He was a major supporter of the Liberal Party, mainly because it held the reins of power from 1935 to 1957, and because it courted most of the Jewish vote. He longed to be the first Jew to be appointed to the Senate, but that distinction was bestowed upon David Croll, much to Bronfman's anger. He also lobbied, unsuccessfully, to be the ambassador to the court of St. James. Bronfman did not become a member of the governors of McGill University until he was seventy-five. He was barely mollified by his appointment to the regulatory board of the Canada Council. Historian Michael Marrus writes in his biography of Sam that he actively sought these plaudits, feeding his hunger for acclaim as a man of honour and distinction – "to be a somebody"[47] in the words of his son Edgar.

Bronfman was much more than a tycoon. In the second half of his life, he was unquestionably the most significant Jew in Canada. He became the unpaid president of the CJC in 1939, saving it from expiration by bankrolling much of its operation. In theory the CJC was "the Parliament of Canadian Jews"; in fact, Sam was its face and voice until 1962. When the CJC opened its headquarters in Montreal in 1961, it was named the Samuel Bronfman house. During the war, he incessantly lobbied the King government to provide aid to Europe's Jews. When the nascent state of Israel needed two million dollars to buy weapons in 1950, he met with C.D. Howe, the minister in charge, to purchase surplus ammunition. Sam bargained him down to one million. Bronfman inveigled his friends, and the money was quickly raised. His philanthropy knew no bounds both to the Jewish community and to Canadian institutions, nor did his disgust with his wealthy compatriots when they did not contribute their fair share. As Marrus states: "in Montreal, the most important community of Canadian Jews, nothing important happened without Sam's blessing."[48]

His critics were legion, among them was the radical poet Irving Layton. In 1959, Layton pronounced: "The besetting sin of my people is respectability; add to this the sanctimoniousness and hypocrisy. It isn't their soulless money grubbing that makes my stomach sick; it's their stinking moralism."[49]

ASCENDANCE: 1971–2000

At the time of Bronfman's death in 1971, Jews had entered the mainstream of Canadian life. Barriers to their admission to hospitals, to law, engineering, and architectural firms had largely been eroded, as had hiring at universities. Newman's three volume encyclopedic study, *The Canadian Establishment* (1975, 1981, 1999), is an opinionated saga replete with insights into the levers, deals, partnerships, deceitful operations, and humorous anecdotes about the extraordinarily rich. As he mines the tycoons of the last quarter of the twentieth century, Jews become increasingly prominent. In the first volume, his list of the one hundred and seventy-five men in the business establishment names twelve Jews: Charles Bronfman, son of Samuel Bronfman and the head of Seagrams; H. Reuben Cohen, a corporate director from Moncton; Sol Kanee, of Winnipeg, who started his fortune in mills; Murray Koffler of Toronto, the founder of Shoppers Drug Mart; Leo Kolber of Montreal, the director of Cemp Investments (the holding and investment company for Sam Bronfman's children); Lazarus Phillips, Sam's legal advisor, who was the second Jew to be named to the Senate; and Torontonian Ray Wolfe, the CEO of the Oshawa Group (groceries).

Two sectors of the Canadian economy in which Jews were prominent were construction and merchandizing. Capitalizing on the dire need for residential, industrial, commercial and office buildings, developers took the plunge as most started with limited financial resources. They were most visible in Toronto in the 1960s. Among them were John Daniels, Eph Diamond, the Goldlist family, the Green and Latner Families (Greenwin Construction), Joseph Berman (Cadillac Fairview), and Alex Grossman (Belmont Construction). The second wave included some Holocaust survivors. It should be added that Italian Canadians, the majority being postwar immigrants, had a major impact in construction as well. Some began as labourers and tradesmen, often working for Jewish firms, before venturing on their own. Often, there was a symbiotic relationship between the two groups, born out of mutual respect and the opportunity to contribute to Canada's development. Another prominent sector of Jewish activity was in food distribution and sales. Of the ten leading merchandisers in Canada in 1974, three were grocery chains: Steinberg's Ltd. (Montreal), M. Loeb Ltd. (Ottawa), and the abovementioned Oshawa Group (Toronto).

In Newman's second volume, *The Acquisitors: The Canadian Establishment*, the Jewish presence in the establishment had grown in only six years. Of note, is the Reichmann family. In 1981, they were the world's largest property developers with assets estimated at seven billion dollars. The family was from Hungary, where Samuel and his wife Renee had established a major poultry business, and then relocated to Vienna in the 1930s. With the outbreak of the war, the family moved to Paris, and when France fell to the German onslaught, they barely escaped to neutral Spain, and then to Tangier, a French protectorate in Morocco. In the early 1950s, three brothers, Ralph, Paul, and Albert, relocated to Toronto where they opened a tile and flooring business, and quickly moved into construction. Their company, Olympia and York, went on to erect the First Canadian Place in Toronto, Canada's tallest building at the time. In 1977, they purchased eight New York skyscrapers for the bargain price of $350 million, during a period when the city was in virtual bankruptcy. As the city recovered, they acquired more property, and built Battery Park in the financial district. In 1987, they took on the development of Canary Wharf in the London docklands, but the project lapsed as it was too far from the city centre, forcing the family to declare bankruptcy in 1992. Undeterred the Reichmanns bounced back, and by the turn of the century had amassed a new real estate portfolio.

Newman's third volume, *Titans: How the New Canadian Establishment Seized Power*, released at the end of the century is a dense text. The central point is that the postwar establishment had reached its pinnacle a generation earlier and had been replaced by a new contingent (the "titans") who had risen because its predecessors had invested poorly, had not understood changes in the consumer economy, and had suffered intra-family breakdowns. Most well known was the demise of the Eaton fortune. Newman quotes Seymour Schulich, who grew up in Montreal's Plateau, and made his fortune in mining. "He said that Reputation is character, minus what you've been caught doing."[50] Lawyer Howard Beck commented that the "Family Compact has been turned upside down in the last fifteen years.... We have a new establishment."[51] And this allowed, modestly, the opportunity for other Canadians to enter into the economic elite, including, Italians, French Canadians, and Chinese.

For generations, the establishment had met in private clubs, closed to those without power and influence, to minorities, and to women. They were the preserve, a refuge from the *hoi polloi*, where deals were hatched, and bland food and premium liquor were consumed. At Ottawa's Rideau Club, for example, in Newman's words, "those with access to power ... circled one another like forest animals that smell a hunter: nose down, tail up to catch the scent."[52] Montreal's Mount Royal Club did not admit a Jew until Senator Lazarus Phillips in 1966, again much to Sam Bronfman's consternation. The Vancouver Club snubbed Walter Koerner, whose family was worth $100 million in 1975 and was a major benefactor of the city and province's institutions. Its first Jewish member, Nathan Nemetz, made the cut because he was BC's chief justice and chancellor of the University of British Columbia. The Manitoba Club reprimanded a member for having brought Sol Kanee to lunch. Aside from his fortune, Kanee was a major community figure, the president of CJC, a back room Liberal organizer and a power behind Pierre Trudeau's campaign for the party's leadership in 1968. He and other Winnipeg Jewish figures, including Chief Justice Samuel Freedman, chancellor of the University of Winnipeg, were rejected. The first Jewish member was Gerry Leibling in 1972. The first club to admit women was the Calgary Club in 1989. By that time, private clubs were in their twilight. A new generation of tycoons was ascendant. They included the aforementioned Izzy Sharp, another Izzy, Winnipeg's Asper, a media mogul and president of the provincial Liberals, and another Winnipegger, Gerald (Gerry) Schwartz, who started out with Asper, moved to Toronto, and whose Onex Corporation, with investments in numerous enterprises, was Canada's fourteenth leading company in 1997, according to the *Financial Post.* At the millennial turn, a growing coterie of Jewish businessmen had ascended into the country's financial elite.

CONCLUSION

The period from 1945 to 1971 was the second most transformative in post-Confederation history, after the Great Migration from 1896 to 1914. For Canada's Jews, it marked the emergence of a new communal sense of Canadian identity, a consequence of their contribution to the war effort, of the rapid industrialization and urbanization that rekindled the economy after the Depression, and of the move from immigrant neighbourhoods to the suburbs. This geographic mobility was mirrored by an ascendant class of professionals, managers, and businessmen, headed by captains of industry. At the millennial turn, Jews were no longer excluded from the country's economic elite.

The second half of baby boom generation, born and raised during the postwar transformation, brought about a new social consciousness that was manifested in its contribution to Canadian society in the arts, politics, and philanthropy. Canadian Jews in the second half of the century should have felt secure. But their sound sleep was disturbed by the recurrent echoes of their history, marked by concerns about the continuity of their community, the existential threats to the state of Israel, and the safety of their brethren behind the Iron Curtain. These considerations are discussed in the next chapter.

Ben Kayfetz

Source: Ontario Jewish Archives

CHAPTER NINE

Confronting History, 1945–1985

Canadian Jews entered the national mainstream and created a measure of ethnic comfort through the 1950s. As the children of immigrants, they now regarded themselves as Canadians, and in so doing, adopted a mindset that viewed their forebears' legacy of impoverishment and discrimination as a relic of the past. This was a new era, with the opportunity to merge into the Canadian mainstream. Yet global and domestic events dislodged their insularity as they brought the realities of Jewish insecurity, at home and abroad, into their living rooms. Economic mobility, in and of itself, was not powerful enough to override their confrontation with the recurrence of antisemitism, and the existential threat to Israel. These anxieties were salient in appropriating the Holocaust as a pillar of the community's collective memory.

From 1945 to 1954 a small collection of civil rights groups, including Jewish organizations, set the next stage in countering discriminatory laws and practices against racial and religious minorities. The most prominent were the CJC and B'nai Brith Canada in their JPRC; the Jewish Labour Committee (JLC), and the Association for Civil Liberties (ACL). In the words of historian James Walker, this marked "the Jewish phase in the movement for racial equality in Canada," which was also the title of an article written in *Canadian Ethnic Studies* in 2002.[1]

Canadian Jews in 1945 were uniquely prepared to take up the mantle for racial equality. The emerging middle class of the interwar period produced a coterie of professionals, mostly lawyers, who were adept in challenging discriminative practices. Although the JPRC, JLC, and ACL were Canadian organizations, the focus of their concern were discriminatory practices in Ontario.

In 1947, the CJC hired Ben Kayfetz (1916–2002) as executive director of the JPRC, a position that he was to hold for almost half a century. He possessed the innate ability to quietly, but effectively, bring together Jewish and non-Jewish organizations in combating discrimination. Eschewing stridency, Kayfetz knew how the push the right political buttons in lobbying for legislation. For his contribution to Canadian society, he was inducted as a member of the Order of Canada in 1987. In retirement, he was an advisor to community leaders, a volunteer at the Ontario Jewish Archives, and an unparalleled resource for scholars including the author.

The lay chair of the JPRC was Rabbi Abraham Feinberg of Holy Blossom Synagogue. His committee included three prominent lawyers. Bora Laskin (1912–84) was born in Fort William (now part of Thunder Bay, Ontario). After graduating from the University of Toronto, he could not find employment due to anti-Jewish discrimination. He ended up teaching in the Faculty of Law. Laskin was appointed to the Ontario Court of Appeal in 1965, to the Supreme Court in 1980, and became Canada's chief justice in 1985. Sydney Midanik was a fervent civil libertarian, a stance that put him at odds with the committee's in promulgation of criminalizing hate speech in the late 1960s. Sydney Harris (1918–2009) was one of the most prominent Jewish leaders of the postwar era. He served as chair of the Ontario Region of the CJC from 1971 to 1974 and was the national president from 1974 to 1977. The most well-known member was Joe Salsberg, an MPP from Toronto, one of two members of the LPP who is profiled in Chapter 6.

The JLC was founded in the United States in 1933 and opened a Canadian branch in 1936. Avowedly socialist, the JLC represented Jewish union members. Its first director was Moshe Loiz (1888–1950) who grew up as a Bundist in Poland. Arriving in Montreal, he changed his name to Lewis. The unpaid Lewis was succeeded by Kalmen Kaplansky (1912–97), born in Poland, and raised in Montreal, who cut his teeth at the JLC office in New York. The JLC provided the necessary link with organized labour in advocating for human rights. Kaplansky convinced the Canadian Labour Congress to set up a Standing Committee on Racial Discrimination and created local committees across the country. The ACL was born in 1949 in Toronto. James Walker cites Irving Himel, a Toronto lawyer, as the "moving spirit" for its emergence.[2] Its membership included Kayfetz, Feinberg, Laskin, Harris, and Midanik, and its chair, Vivien Mahood (not Jewish), who also worked for the JLC. Together they were a formidable collection.

The first challenge for these organizations devoted to ensuring racial equality was combating outright discrimination in Dresden, Ontario against Afro-Canadian residents. They had arrived in the 1840 via the Underground Railroad and by 1945 constituted 20 per cent of the town's population. Restricted to menial jobs and barred from services and restaurants, Mahood brought the situation to the attention of a young journalist, Pierre Berton. The ensuing publicity resulted in a referendum, which was defeated by the white majority. In response to the exposure, Leslie Frost, the Conservative premier, contacted Kayfetz for advice. Frost then asked Jacob Finkelman, a professor of law at the University of Toronto (and the first Jew to become a faculty appointee) to draft the bill. It was named the Fair Employment Practices Act (FEPA), was passed in 1951, and made discrimination on the base of race, colour, or creed illegal.

There are three main points in the Jewish phase for the campaign for racial equality. First, the "Jewish presence" was not visible to the public. The ACL undertook nominal leadership, although it was through the instigation of Himel, Kaplansky, Kayfetz, and the Jewish lay leaders that the legislation was enacted. In other words, were it to be known that Jews were the main orchestrators, public support may not have been as sympathetic. Clearly, it was much more effective if mainstream Canadians were in the forefront. Second, as historians Carmela Patrias and Ruth A. Frager have written, the coalition for racial equality, as represented in the delegation to the provincial cabinet, was diverse. It included left-wing political parties (CCF and CPC), the United Church of Canada, organized labour, women's organizations, and ethno-cultural organizations, especially those representing African, Japanese and Chinese Canadians. This assembly made a dent in the Protestant stranglehold of Ontario. Third, the JPRC, which changed the "P" to "C" (standing for community), was the central advocacy organ in the Jewish community in combating antisemitism specifically, and pressing for racial equality in general, into the next millennium.

DISCOMFORT, 1945–1967

World War II in Europe ended on May 8, 1945 and heralded four developments that were solidified in 1948: the restructuring of global alliances that created competing spheres of control, the creation of the state of Israel, the Declaration of Human Rights, and the entry of Holocaust survivors into Canada. The first three developments are central in framing postwar history globally, while the last one addresses the settlement, adaptation, and diversity of the Holocaust survivors, their relations with Canadian Jews, and their contribution to raising consciousness about the outbreak of antisemitism in the 1960s.

The Cold War

As the war in Europe ended, it was increasingly urgent that the victors, namely the United States and the Soviet Union, cooperate in the restructuring of the continent. But tensions between the allies were exacerbated with the atomic bombings of Japan in August and, under the pretense of securing its western border, the installation of Communist regimes in six central European and three Baltic states. In 1946 Winston Churchill proclaimed that an "iron curtain" had descended upon Europe. Tension was further heightened with the division of Germany between the western allies and the Soviet Union and the creation of the North American Treaty Organization (NATO). Further, 1948 marked the victory of the Communists in China, thereby extending the communist menace to Asia. The Cold War created a bi-polar world that had ramifications in conflicts between Soviet and American spheres of influence, leading to calamitous wars in Korea and Indochina.

Some three million European Jews who had survived the Holocaust were ensnared behind the Iron Curtain. Virulent antisemitic campaigns were instigated, starting in 1948, and continued over the next three decades. Denied the opportunity to emigrate, their fate became a major concern for Jews in the free world. The campaign for their release was a central factor for Jewish activism in Canada beginning in the late 1960s.

Palestine Partition

As the murder of European Jewry entered a new phase with the German invasion of the Soviet Union on June 22, 1941, Zionists worldwide increased their pressure to open the gates of Palestine that was then administered by the British. The ZO C, under its president, A.J. Freiman, established a United Zionist Council as a public relations arm, and concurrently, a parliamentary committee consisting of non-Jews was created. In December 1943, Freiman met with William Lyon Mackenzie King, who he had known in Ottawa. King dishonestly responded that the British White Paper (which restricted Jewish entry in 1936) was not aimed at limiting immigration but facilitating the creation of a Jewish national home. Nonetheless, pressure was mounted throughout the war, but to no avail. Torontonian S.J. (Sam) Zacks, the head of the United Zionist Council public relations arm in August 1944, wishfully, in the words of historian David Bercuson, "believed (that) the Canadian government could be forced to help Zionists 'force a decision' (before the war's end)."[3] These efforts were tarnished by Jewish terrorist attacks against the British administration. With the end of the war, Holocaust survivors longed to immigrate to Palestine, but the parameters of the British White Paper remained in force.

The breakthrough was the creation of the UN Special Committee on Palestine (UNSCOP) which declared that the British Mandate would expire in 1948, thereby partitioning the territory into a Jewish state and an Arab one, with Jerusalem a neutral city under international trusteeship. Consequently, when Britain announced that it would pull out of Palestine on May 15, 1948, the Arab League rejected UNSCOP's plan, and the nascent Jewish state (Israel) declared its independence on the date of the British departure. In response, seven Arab countries mounted an attack. For Jews worldwide, the exhilaration of a Jewish state after more than two millennia was offset by the fear that it would be overrun, and that its six hundred thousand Jewish inhabitants could be annihilated. Israel, however, emerged victorious. But the trepidation had barely lifted.

Universal Declaration of Human Rights

At the close of World War I, the Allied delegates to the peace conferences attempted to prevent another catastrophe. In so doing, they created the League of Nations. But due to the postwar instability in Europe, and the refusal by the American legislature to become a signatory, the League was futile in preventing aggressions by Germany, Italy, and Japan. To prevent another occurrence, the United States, Great Britain, the Soviet Union, and China met in 1944 to create a more effective global alliance. In April 1945, fifty nations drafted the UN Charter. As the atrocities committed during the war were disclosed in trials of war criminals, most notably in Nuremberg, Germany in 1947, it became apparent that the charter did not sufficiently define the violations of human rights. Hence, a commission including a Canadian, John Peter Humphrey, was established to draft a declaration. It contained thirty articles affirming individual rights, which was the backbone for subsequent treaties, national constitutions, and laws. It was passed on December 10, 1948.

Two common perceptions about the partition of Palestine that led to the state of Israel and to the UN Declaration should be put to rest. The first is that revelations about the Holocaust propelled the UN to end the British Mandate, that is, that had it not been for the destruction of European Jewry, an independent Israeli state would not have occurred. In fact, while the photographic footage of the liberations of the camps in Germany by the Allies was shocking, there was little grief over the extinction of Jewish life. The Nuremberg trials were against those who committed "crimes against humanity." Survivors of the Holocaust continued to languish in postwar Europe, many in former concentration camps. Together with those who had managed to escape the imposition of the Iron Curtain, they were denied refuge in Palestine, the United States, and Canada. UNSCOP was a tool to divide a tiny territory among two peoples with a historical claim to the land, but within a larger perspective, to end European colonization. For example, Britain's departure from Palestine was minuscule in comparison to its withdrawal from the Indian subcontinent. The Soviet Bloc voted in favour of the partition, not because of the Holocaust, but to weaken Britain, gain influence in the colonial world, and capitalize on the likely socialist orientation of the Israeli government, which might be brought into the Soviet sphere. Support for partition occurred because of politics, not sympathy for the Jews.

The second perception is that Israel was redemption for the Holocaust. This presumes that there is a divine presence that determines human action. Had Jews been asked in 1939 if they would accept the murder of half of their global population to gain an independent state, what would they have said to their children? Politics, not empathy or divine intervention, determines history.

The Arrival of Holocaust Survivors

In August 1945 the Polish and the Soviet governments agreed to allow prewar Polish citizens, who had escaped to the USSR, repatriation. Between February and June 1946 approximately 140,000 Polish Jews took this opportunity, joining some 100,000 survivors in Poland. Over the next year, most of the remainder fled largely due to attacks by local antisemites that killed approximately one thousand Jews. For most, the preferred destination was Palestine, followed by the United States, and then Canada. But, as immigration restrictions remained in place, most went to Germany, where, under the protection of the UN Relief and Rescue Administration (UNRRA), they were placed in displaced persons sites, some of which were in converted concentration camps, including the notorious one at Bergen-Belsen, which housed seven thousand refugees. The Central Jewish Committee there published a newsletter, *Unzer Sztyme* (our voice), edited by Paul Trepman, who would eventually migrate to Montreal. He wrote, using the analogy of Jews as "footballs": "We Jews have long been the 'sport' of nations and peoples, we have been kicked, murdered and gassed, pursued and buffeted … but the game is being played in a bigger arena, and the reward is life or death to us, the remnants of six million massacred European Jews."[4]

Ben Kayfetz, who had been sent to Germany as a member of the Canadian Control Commission, on meeting survivors in a displaced persons' camp, reported: "There I was in the middle of it. They were not disillusioned. The stories they told me were hair-raising."[5] Two months later, in December 1945, Kayfetz attended the World Zionist Congress, meeting with Eddie Gelber and Sam Zacks, luminaries of the Canadian Jewish community, who worked behind the scenes to loosen the Canadian restrictions. But the intransigence of the King administration was not stirred. King saw no political gain and was further convinced by a public opinion poll taken in October 1946, where, in response to the question, "If Canada allows more immigration, are there any of these nationalities which you would want to keep out,"[6] 60 per cent said Japanese, 49 per cent marked Jewish, and 34 per cent chose German. Between April 1, 1945 and March 31, 1947 Canada admitted 98,011 immigrants, of whom a mere 3 per cent were Jewish. In effect, the barriers that prevented entry during the Nazi era remained in place, despite the Holocaust.

The postwar economic recovery softened the government's obstinacy to loosen immigration restrictions, largely due to pressure from corporate Canada for massive additions to the labour force, rather than any feelings of remorse. The CJC lobbied the government to honour its wartime pledge to admit orphans, which had been approved by an order-in-council in 1945. A second initiative, dubbed the Workers' Project, was mounted by the JLC and the JIAS, in association with unions of textile workers, to allow tailors and furriers to migrate. Jewish representatives from the unions and manufacturers met with candidates in the camps, drew up lists, and presented them to immigration authorities. The arrival of approximately three thousand workers and their families and 1,100 orphans in 1948 were part of the 9,386 arrivals that year. In total, some 30–35,000 survivors, including their children born in postwar Europe, found a new home in Canada by 1956. It was the largest Jewish immigration wave since 1914. According to the 1961 census, it constituted between 13 to 15 per cent of Canada's Jewish population, the second highest proportion, after Israel, in the world. The United States, by comparison, was the destination of approximately 250,000 survivors, constituting 5 per cent of the Jewish community.

GREENER AND *GAYLE:* SETTLEMENT ADAPTATION AND DIVERSITY

The arrival of Holocaust survivors was the largest contingent of Jews since the great migration at the turn of the century. The early contingent largely came from small towns and villages in eastern and central

Europe, where they lived under the threat of antisemitic outbreaks, most in strict adherence to Jewish laws and customs, with a minority influenced by progressive political movements. Many came with some or all their families and were part of a chain migration of kinfolk and those from their home regions. Adaptation was difficult and often took at least one generation to accomplish.

The following profile reveals five significant differences between the settlement and adaptation of the two waves.

The first difference was the limited age range of the survivors. Few Jews born in the nineteenth century or between 1935 and 1945 survived. Most of the survivors were teens and young adults at the outbreak of the war. In addition were the children born in postwar Europe, whose exact number is unknown as immigration files did not differentiate them from their survivor parents.

The second difference was that the survivors had experienced a genocide, whereas their predecessors had fled from poverty, discrimination, and pogroms. Almost all the survivors had been in ghettoes, and then in camps. A miniscule number had managed to escape, were hidden, passed as non-Jews (especially women), and/or joined resistance groups. Additionally, were the Polish Jews who had fled to the Soviet Union, where most survived the German attack and the Soviet camps. They were repatriated to Poland in 1946. Of the Hungarian Jews, the last nationality to have been murdered by the Germans and their acolytes in the killing centre of Auschwitz-Birkenau, some survived deportation in hiding, by passing as gentiles, and/or due to the heroic efforts of the Swedish businessman, Raoul Wallenberg, and the Swiss diplomat, Carl Lutz. Most remained in Hungary; some arrived in the wake of the failed uprising against Soviet rule in 1956.

Third, the survivors came from a vastly different cultural and political environment than their predecessors. Interwar Europe consisted of nascent democratic states, where modernity and urbanization had transformed culture, transportation, and communication. In general, survivors were better educated and more acculturated than their predecessors had been. Fourth, they had languished in Europe for up to six years, during which many accumulated commercial and language skills that accelerated their transition to Canadian life. Finally, upon arrival, many suffered from post-traumatic stress disorder. Ultimately, it was their emotional state, rather than the traditional obstacles of language, employment, and acculturation, that proved to be the greatest impediment in adapting to life in Canada.

Most survivors arrived in Halifax from where they went by train to Ontario and Quebec, and a minority to western Canada. While we do not have exact figures for the major cities, their settlement was roughly equivalent that of Canadian Jews. For example, an estimated sixteen thousand came to Montreal, about half of the total, and a third to Toronto, mirroring the proportion of Canadian Jews in total. Their arrival put an unprecedented stress on the social services provided by local Jewish federations and organizations. Although money had been apportioned, and volunteers bolstered the overworked staff, the overwhelming task was not efficiently expedited. Communities were overburdened; organizations tended to replicate one another but were reluctant to divest power.

Integration was unlike any previous effort at immigration absorption. Few survivors had Canadian families, and those that did had been separated for at least two decades. In most cases, they had never met. While orphans were adopted, many were in their late teens and had already led independent lives. The majority were single, eager to create their own families, with other survivors or Canadian Jews. One was Donia Blumenfeld. She was born in Poland in 1927. She married a Canadian, Martin Clenman, who became a mathematics teacher. Blumenfeld Clenman employed poetry, written in her adopted language, as the vehicle for expressing her transition. One of her best-known works includes this stanza:

Sometimes
I am a stranger to my own family
For I bring Europe's ghosts
Into the well-lit living room
of Canadian internationalism …

and ends:

I was no child on arrival
And yet, so well assimilated.
Even my verses are native,
And I dream in good English too.[7]

The traditional organizations and community support systems that had made integration somewhat smoother thirty years earlier had difficulty in meeting the challenge of integration and the burden was overwhelming for the CJC and the federations. Other communal institutions, landsmanschaften, political groups (communists, socialists), and trade unions in sync with the JLC, rose to the challenge. Some survivors found work in the textile industry; others were hired by Jewish businesses, often via family and institutional connections.

While one can appreciate the difficulty for the community in responding to their arrival, it is harder to avoid criticism of the English-language Jewish press and the rigid hierarchy of the CJC in not covering the dramatic impact of the arrival. An analysis of the *Jewish Chronicle*, the most important community newspaper, is instructive as to what was **not** found – not a single article on the survivors' experiences appeared in 1948, unlike the coverage in the Yiddish press. Snippets on the workers and orphans' projects appeared, but there was little discussion as to what they endured and the adjustments that they had to make. The survivors' voices were not given an airing. The CJC, while helping to publicize memorials commemorating the Warsaw Ghetto Uprising, made no mention of the barriers to transition. At its plenary in 1949, aside from chest thumping about its role in bringing the orphans and workers projects to fruition, the arrival of the largest Jewish contingent in forty years was not worthy of a statement.

Survivors were a unique cohort in the saga of Jewish immigration. Historically, new immigrants from eastern and central Europe were dubbed, in Yiddish, as *der Greener* (roughly translated as "the greenhorns"), a somewhat pejorative term indicating that they were uncultured rubes. The earlier immigrants, in turn, became *der Gayle* (the "yellowed ones") as they eventually adjusted to living in the new world. Survivors, however, came from different milieus than their predecessors. The twenty-year gap in Jewish immigration to Canada, from the mid-1920s the late 1940s, had created a much more urbane and cosmopolitan European Jewish cohort. It was far more diverse than the cohort that settled during the Great Migration forty years earlier. Survival was the product of luck, ingenuity, and rapid adaptation. Before and after the war, some had lived in Paris, Vienna, Brussels, and arrived at Canadian cities and towns that were overwhelmingly Anglo Protestant (aside from Montreal), places devoid of European culture. The traditional obstacles to immigrant adaptation – language, customs, employment – could be overcome due to their heritage and survival. The greater challenge was dealing with trauma.

Without doubt, Canadian Jews were personally affected by the Holocaust. Many lost their European families, and valiantly appealed to the government to lessen immigration restrictions. But the experiences of the survivors were incomprehensible, even to the survivors. Nathan Leipciger, a survivor of Auschwitz, who arrived at eighteen and became an engineer remarked: "We didn't want to talk, and they didn't want to listen."[8] Canadian Jews were caught up in elevating their socioeconomic status, in celebrating the creation of a Jewish state, and in shedding the immigrant identity. The Holocaust was an unmitigated tragedy, but there was a new age beckoning. It would take the next generation of Canadian Jews to appropriate the legacy of the calamity. It took global and local events, and the voices of survivors, for Canadian Jews to eventually confront history.[9]

"THE DISEASE OF ANTISEMITISM"

On May 9, 1965 Prime Minister Lester Pearson, speaking at a memorial on Parliament Hill on the twentieth anniversary of the end of World War intoned: "Twenty years ago the guns stopped firing … It was also 20 years ago when the pitiable and few survivors stumbled out of the concentration camps.… You are commemorating the anniversary at the shrine of Canadian liberty … Your Association is on guard against these dangers while it reverently perseveres the memory their victims.… It is not enough to say 'It can't happen here.' We must be on guard to make sure it doesn't happen here – or there – or anywhere."[10] The "association" referred to the sponsors of the event – the Association of Former Concentration Camp Inmates/Survivors of Nazi Oppression, founded in Montreal in November 1960. Hereafter it will be referred to as the Association.

During the first five years of the 1960s, global and domestic events shook the calm of Canadian Jews. After the war, it appeared that systemic antisemitism was losing its luster. The rabid antisemites of the

1930s and '40s had become isolated crackpots, inasmuch because the Holocaust had given antisemitism a bad name, making it unseemly to be openly antisemitic. Provincial legislation had rendered discrimination in employment and housing to be unlawful, and slowly Jews and other European minorities were becoming more accepted in mainstream Canadian life. This comfort was shaken on Christmas Day 1959, when German synagogues were smeared with swastikas. Within days, this had turned into an epidemic in western Europe. On January 1 approximately one hundred American Jewish communities in thirty-one states were scarred. Canada was not exempt. Ontario was especially targeted. Synagogues in Toronto, Sudbury, Kingston, Kitchener, Cornwall, and Galt were defaced as were six communities in British Columbia. The onslaught ended abruptly, without explanation, on January 13.

While the fires ignited by the outbreak lessened in the spring, before the embers died, they were stoked by a shocking development. Adolf Eichmann was director of the Reich main security office of the Gestapo during the war. He was responsible for the implementation of the "Final Solution," the German code for the destruction of Europe's Jews. Eichmann was the ultimate "desk murderer," orchestrating the roundups and deportations from his Berlin office. His final act was the deportation of some half a million Hungarian Jews in the spring of 1944, the vast majority of whom were shipped directly to Auschwitz-Birkenau. In the chaos following Germany's surrender, Eichmann escaped to Argentina where he assumed a new identity. He was finally tracked down by Israeli agents on May 2, 1960 in Buenos Aires and was secretly abducted to Israel nine days later. When word spread, his capture and abduction dominated the news. The media were divided over whether these actions contravened international law. Both the *Globe and Mail* and the *Daily Star* left no doubt as to their position – Argentina's sovereignty was violated. Canadian Jews were furious that their fellow citizens would never understand that the Holocaust overrode national boundaries and international protocol.

Eichmann was charged with fifteen counts of crimes against the Jewish people, crimes against humanity and war crimes on February 21, 1961. The ensuing trial was televised worldwide. It was called "the Trial of the Century." Israel seized the opportunity to tell the world about the Holocaust. Survivors took the stand. Among the most poignant, was the testimony by Abba Kovner, the country's poet laureate, who led an escape from the ghetto in Vilna, Lithuania and created a partisan unit that disrupted German transportation and communications. The eyewitness recitations were spell binding. It can be argued that the trial was the single most important event in bringing about public awareness of the Holocaust. Eichmann was hanged, his body burnt, the ashes scattered in the sea. Nathan Leipciger recalled that the trial broke the silence. People asked him, "Did it really happen?" He added: "The trial had a profound influence on the survivors, on how to talk about it."[11]

Five months after Eichmann's capture, another shock – a Canadian Nazi party had been formed, in association with the infamous American Nazi party, led by George Lincoln Rockwell. In an interview on CBC, Rockwell, dressed in a Nazi uniform, backed by his acolytes in similar regalia, proclaimed that there were Nazi sections in Montreal and Toronto, the former led by a disciple of Adrien Arcand, the septuagenarian founder of Canadian neo-Nazis. Survivors staged a demonstration outside Rockwell's hotel in Montreal, the first public action taken by survivors. When they approached the CJC, they were told, according to survivors, that "there's nothing we can do, it's a free country."[12] This spurred the creation of The Association. It staged its first public act, a march in downtown Montreal commemorating the Holocaust and liberation, in May 1961. Lou Zablow, one of its founders, invited the CJC leaders to join. None appeared.

In February 1962 the European executive of the World Jewish Congress created a committee to examine the outbreak. In its report a year later, it concluded "that the disease of anti-Semitism [*sic*] has again become active. Like a contagious plague, it has spread across frontiers and oceans."[13] That year's CJC plenary produced the first three resolutions related to the Holocaust, stating that it "would bring amendments to the Criminal Code making it an offense to practice genocide and race hatred," and would include "lessons or race prejudice … in the curriculum."[14] It also called for the integration of "newcomers" into its structure, inviting six survivors, aka "newcomers" to the plenary of more than one thousand. The Association took credit for these measures.

But these actions did not discourage local Nazi sympathizers. From 1963 to 1965 there was a flurry of activity. Graffiti, pamphlets, and leaflets were dropped in mailboxes, and at one point from the top of buildings in downtown Toronto, stating that "Hitler Was Right" and "Communism is Jewish."[15] In 1964 there were documented incidents in six provinces. The reality was that it was disparate individuals who were responsible. Foremost was David Stanley, a young clean-cut Torontonian, and his mentor, John Ross Taylor, who had deep roots in the neo-Nazi movement. CBC interviewed Taylor and Stanley, and Rockwell again, from his lair in Virginia, eliciting another torrent of protest. In February 1964 Liberal MPs Milton Klein from Montreal and James Walker from Toronto introduced an "Act respecting Genocide," rooted in the UN Convention on Genocide in 1952. The bill was passed unanimously in July.

The CJC took advantage of the legislative momentum. Maxwell Cohen, CJC President Michael Garber, and Executive Director Saul Hayes met with Guy Favreau, minister of justice, on 17 October, 1964 to establish a committee to study legislation to "control or eliminate the publication and distribution of hate materials."[16] Cohen was to be the chair, and his appointments included a little-known law professor, Pierre Trudeau.

These developments in the early 1960s disturbed the mood of ethnic complacency. In the context of the times, this discomfort was understandable. The United States was in disarray due to the actions of white supremacists in response to the civil rights movement and was devastated by the assassination of John Kennedy on November 22, 1963. In the election the following year, the Republican candidate, Barry Goldwater, the most mainstream conservative political figure in decades, was applauded by the neo-Nazis. Dissent over the Vietnam conflict was splitting the country. In Germany, a neo-Nazi party had been formed and was set to contest elections. Survivors grew more restive. They felt that the organized community, i.e., the CJC, was not sufficiently focused on the "disease." In Toronto, a small group, including a few Canadian Jews, challenged the JPRC in Ontario for not exposing the perpetrators. It created the N3 movement (standing for Newton's Third Law of Thermodynamics – "for every action there's a complete and opposite reaction"). A tiny group that had split from Stanley, led by John Beattie, emerged because Stanley was insufficiently radical. Unbeknownst to N3, the JPRC was surveilling Beattie, and had planted two non-Jews into the group. N3 took its own action by bugging the meetings and pilfering its files of supporters.

On April 20, 1965 (the date of Hitler's birth), Beattie announced the formation of the Canadian Nazi party; ten days later, he declared that the party would hold a rally, in Nazi paraphernalia, at Allan Gardens in downtown Toronto, on May 30. The JPRC urged calm; Mayor Philip Givens, a member of the JPRC, stated that the city could not deny a permit to Beattie. N3 led the protest. Synagogues, landsmanschaften, and anti-Nazi youth organizations urged their followers to appear at the rally. On May 29 Givens told the CJC that Beattie had not applied for a permit, but that message was not circulated. On the appointed day, approximately five thousand protesters (figures vary) assembled in the park, and when Beattie showed up, alone, surrounded by a police cordon, he was attacked and hustled into a paddy wagon. He was carrying a starting pistol.

This so-called riot turned out to be the tipping point in the Jewish community's confrontation with history. The media blamed the protestors, Givens, and the CJC. The CJC designated the protestors as "vigilantes." This was the nadir of Jewish community relations. The JPRC was divided. Its chair, Sydney Harris, defended the response, while past chair, Rabbi Abraham Feinberg, decried it. The cleavage in the community, largely under the wraps for twenty years, was now in full view. The CJC, without issuing a *mea culpa*, tried to mollify the outrage by creating the Community Anti-Nazi Committee of eighty members from a broad spectrum of local Jews.[17] While not widely applauded, it allowed for more mainstream individuals to join the CJC body. Beattie, a pathetic reprobate who resurfaced twenty years later, was the catalyst for the most significant event in the postwar Toronto Jewish community.

1967

The year 1967 was a turning point for Canadians, for international developments, and for Jews worldwide. The planning for celebrations marking Canada's Centennial, one hundred years after Confederation, had begun in earnest a decade earlier. The centre piece was the World Exhibition (EXPO), awarded to Montreal in 1962, mainly due to the campaign launched by its mayor, Jean Drapeau. The site was on an artificial island in the St. Lawrence, attached to the city by a metro. Its theme, "Man and his World," was showcased in national pavilions reflecting the countries' beauty and achievements. The architecture was astounding, including a Geodesic Dome designed by Buckminster Fuller, and a housing community, Habitat, created by architect Moshe Safdie, who was born in Israel and raised in Montreal. Montreal shone in the reflected glow of the site. Canadians, many of whom had never been to Quebec, inundated the city, as did visitors worldwide. Their experience altered the prevailing perception of Canada as a reclusive backwater. It symbolized the new age, echoed in fashion, music, the mystique of Asia and Africa, and in technology – pavilions with circular and multiple screens, elevated tramways, futuristic presentations. With plans for two Christian pavilions, Montreal Jewish leaders wanted to incorporate a synagogue in the Israeli pavilion but were deterred as Israel planned to showcase its multifaith heritage. Sam Bronfman spearheaded fundraising for a synagogue in the Judaism pavilion.

In the lead up to the Centennial, Canadian Jews were no less proud of their country than other Canadians but remained disturbed about the continuing prevalence of antisemitic publications. The Cohen Committee presented its report to the House of Commons in 1966 recommending legislation to amend the Criminal Code making the promotion of genocide an indictable offense. This was not sufficient for the Association and its supporters but went too far for the civil libertarians in the CJC. Meanwhile, the legislation stalled in the House of Commons, at the end of the session in May 1967. It would not be passed for another three years. These deliberations gave oxygen to antisemites, who continued to spread their vitriol. Concern was accelerated by two developments in West Germany – invoking a statute of limitations on suspected Nazi war criminals, and the creation of the neo-Nazi Nationaldemokratische Partei Deutschlands (NPD), led by Adolph von Thadden. He had been an officer during the war, and in two state elections had received 25,000 votes. Further, he was scheduled to be interviewed in Ottawa by CBC. Due to the resulting uproar, the interview took place in Germany on January 22, 1967. Von Thadden intoned that "there is no Jewish problem in Germany because we haven't got Jews."[18] Due to international pressure, the Statute of Limitations remained in place for another decade.

Several weeks after the opening of EXPO, the celebration was rocked by events in the Middle East. On May 15 (the date of Israel's founding), during tension on the Syrian Israeli border, Egypt, supported by the Soviet Union, mobilized its forces. Its revolutionary leader, Gamal Abdul Nasser, the self-proclaimed leader of the Arab world, ordered the removal of peacekeepers from the Sinai Peninsula (including Canadians). In violation of international law, he blockaded the Straits of Tiran, closing all shipping through the Red Sea to Israel. Neighbouring Arab states and the Soviet Bloc chimed in their support. The possibility of Israel's destruction was suddenly ever more possible, fuelling the forewarning of another Holocaust. As historian Harold Troper in his seminal book, *The Defining Decade: Identity, Politics, and the Canadian Jewish Community in the 1960s,* wrote, "fearing the abyss, [Jews] rallied behind Israel. Never before or since was Canadian Jewish consciousness so simultaneously traumatized and galvanized."[19]

In the immediate aftermath of the display of strident antisemitism, the Eichmann trial, the emergence of militant Holocaust survivors, Allan Gardens, and the neo-Nazi revival, Canadian Jewry was united. Troper added that "gripped by fear that for the second time in a generation the survival of all Jews, and not just those in Israel, hung by a thread.... Many Canadian Jews seemed no longer able to distinguish where they left off as individuals and where their embrace of Israel and other Jews began."[20] There were two sets of responses. Young Jews volunteered at Zionist centres to go to Israel. Not all were accepted. Louis Greenspan, a native of Halifax, upon meeting with a Zionist official in Toronto, was asked, "What do you do?" Greenspan replied, "I'm a philosopher." The official retorted, "We already have two million philosophers."[21] Across the country, there were rallies of support and fundraising. Bronfman was hoping for $10 million; Canadian Jews donated $25 million.

On June 5, in a surprise attack, Israeli jets strafed the Egyptian air force on the ground, and invaded Egyptian-held Gaza and Sinai. Two days later, their forces reached the Suez Canal. Simultaneously they advanced against Jordan and Syria, taking the West Bank of the Jordan River and East Jerusalem from the former, and the Golan Heights from the latter.

The term "turning point" is insufficient to describe the immediate impact of the Six Day War on Jews, Arabs, and the Cold War. It united a rather fractious and diverse people. Coming less than a generation after the Holocaust, it was, and remains, the benchmark for the prospect of an even more devastating cataclysm, the eradication of the Jewish state, marking this trepidation as the bedrock of Jewish insecurity. Israel and the United States, stood alone against the Arab World and the Soviet bloc. The impact of Israel's victory remains to the present day. It led to the Israeli takeover of the conquered territories, the status of which remains contentious. This is one root of the Middle East tinderbox. Another is that the Soviet Bloc became fervently pro-Arab, and antisemitism, especially in Poland, reach its postwar height. Proportionate to its population of some two hundred thousand, Canadian Jews were in the forefront among their international brethren in rising to the challenge. Troper opines: "Israel, the Holocaust, and the historical chain of Jewish being were welded together into a seamless mass … In the heat of the crisis, Canadian Jews felt themselves inextricably bound up with a larger Jewish people and its fate."[22]

Canadian Jewish leaders interviewed by this author for *Delayed Impact: The Holocaust and the Canadian Jewish Community*, are at one in their opinion that the Six Day War was the critical factor in awakening North American Jews to the legacy of the Holocaust. Montreal businessman Stephen Cummings, a third-generation Canadian, related that "Holocaust consciousness changed … that's a post 1967 phenomenon."[23] Moe Steinberg, chair of CJC Pacific Region in the 1970s saw Holocaust remembrance and support for Israel as inseparable. Sociologist and Torontonian Cyrill Levitt, an anti-Nazi student leader in the mid-1960s felt that "it wasn't until post '67 that the established community came onside (with survivors)."[24] American scholars concurred. Historian Peter Novick, in a provocative study released concurrent with *Delayed Impact*, wrote: "It's harder to locate a single decisive moment"[25] than the Six Day War in cementing the connection between American Jews and Israel, and by extension, the Holocaust and Israel. And the American theologian, Jacob Neusner, contended that the generation that grew up in the postwar era found their Jewish identity in Israel's victory.

From 1948 to 1967, at first gradually, and then with increasing momentum, Canadian Jews were compelled to confront history. Their comfort in ascending the social-economic ladder in some respects sheltered them from the horrors of the World War II, the threat of a nuclear incident provoked by the Cold War, and Israel's insecurity. Survivors were welcomed but not easily integrated, as they were a remnant of a millennial civilization that had been extinguished, an echo from a world from which their predecessors had fled. The resurgence of active antisemitic incidents, of neo-Nazis in Germany and South America, disturbed the postwar feeling of comfort and security. The Soviet bloc's alignment with the Arab world was a further provocation, one that exploded with the isolation of Israel by Nasser's provocations. Gradually at first, and then rapidly accelerating, the history that circumscribed Jewish life and its evisceration in Europe, with the threat of a similar catastrophe to the first Jewish state in two millennia, became real in Canadian Jewish living rooms, forcing them to confront their history and ultimately their identity as Canadian Jews. The events of 1967 still resound.

In the post Centennial glow, Canadians were captivated by the contest to succeed Lester Pearson as leader of the Liberal Party. The party had had only four leaders since 1896, so many were veterans waiting their turn and being challenged by energetic newcomers. But above the fray, Pierre Elliott Trudeau, a professor of law who had no experience in politics, captured the leadership along with the hearts and minds of many Canadians. Among them were most of Canada's Jews. Harold Troper quoted Larry Zolf, the rumpled telejournalist from Winnipeg's North End who intoned that "Trudeau's love affair with Jews is probably the maddest and most passionate fling that Trudeau ever flung (observing that) Canada may be goyish but Trudeau is Jewish."[26] In the 1968 election the Liberals won a majority. Among them were seven Jews representing ridings without a significant Jewish population, and Trudeau captured the Mount Royal constituency succeeding a line of Jewish members.

Four developments unfolded over the course of the Trudeau era that pertained to the Jewish community. First, it heralded the entry of Jews from each the three national political parties into the public sphere, thereby demonstrating evidence of their place in the mainstream of Canadian life. Second, the proclamation of multiculturalism as a tenet of Canadian life stated, on paper at least, that Canada was no longer the sole preserve of descendants from the British Isles and France. Third Canadians Jews, in confronting their history, had not only the ear of politicians in the three major parties, but these politicians were also receptive to their concerns. Finally Jews were elected to all three levels of government.

COURTING THE JEWISH VOTE

The Liberal Party

Since the nineteenth century most Jews have been supporters of progressive politics for a variety of considerations: the value of charity and justice, the sympathy for disadvantaged minorities, the association of nineteenth-century liberalism with universalism and pluralism, and the targeting of antisemitism as a tool of right-wing movements. A study of federal voting preferences in Canada from 1953 to 1983 by social scientists J.A. Laponce and Laine Russ reveals the following: for Canadians – Liberals 44.4 per cent, Conservatives 34.7 per cent, CCF/NDP 14.8 per cent, Social Credit 5 per cent. For Jews, the preferences were: Liberals 62.5 per cent, Conservatives 18.5 per cent, CCF/NDP 17 per cent, Social Credit 1 per cent.

Having travelled extensively in his youth, unlike his predecessors, the cosmopolitan Trudeau was not uncomfortable associating with Canadians who were not in the Anglo elite. He selected those whom he considered to be the most qualified, including Bora Laskin as chief justice of the Supreme Court, Maxwell Cohen to the International Court at The Hague, and Alan Gotlieb as ambassador to the United States. His appointments to the civil service included deputy ministers Simon Reisman, Bernard and Sylvia Ostry, Marshall Cohen, Jack Austin, and Jerry Grafstein. During his tenure as prime minister (1968–79, 1980–4), he appointed Herb Gray from Windsor, Barney Danson and Robert Kaplan from Toronto, to the federal cabinet. Gray was the first Jewish Canadian minister at the federal level. During his forty-year tenure in Ottawa, Gray held six portfolios, including deputy prime minister under Jean Chrétien. Danson, who had served in World War II, was minister of defence, and Kaplan was solicitor-general. In 1974 long-time investigative journalist for the Vancouver Sun, Simma Holt, was elected, the first Jewish woman to hold office in Ottawa. She brought a needed fiery essence to the proceedings by objecting to be referred to "the Honourable Lady" by retorting,

"I am an Honourable Member," prompting the predictable headline, "Simma Holt says she's no lady."[27]

Jews were not as well represented at the provincial level. Two of most significant were Montrealers, Victor Goldbloom, whose contribution is discussed in the next chapter, and Sheila Finestone. In Ontario, Stuart Smith was the Liberal Party leader from 1975 to 1982, during the extended reign of the Conservatives. Monte Kwinter from Toronto was the longest tenured Jewish politician at the provincial level, having served from 1985 to 2018, during which time he held three ministerial positions. Toronto's Elinor Caplan served in the Ontario legislature (1985–90, 1995–7) during which she was minister of health, and then as an MP from 1997 to 2004, where she was minister of citizenship and immigration and then minister of national revenue.

The Progressive Conservative Party

While Jews were less inclined to the Conservative Party, inroads were made in legislatures and in the civil service. Newfoundland's Jack Marshall was an MP from 1968 to 1978 and then a senator from 1978 to 1994. Maitland Steinkopf (1912–70) of Winnipeg was an MLA from 1962 to 1966. He was appointed to the Manitoba cabinet in 1963, the first Jew to hold this position in Canadian history. His colleague, Sidney Spivak (1928–2002), was the most noteworthy Jewish figure in Manitoba. First elected MLA in 1966, Spivak was appointed to the cabinet and then became leader in 1971 until 1975 when he lost his position to whispers that he had lost the election because of antisemitism. He then served as an MP from 1988 to 2002. His wife Mira was a senator from 1986 to 2009. Quebec's Gerry Weiner served during the Mulroney era (1984–93) and was minister of immigration and multiculturalism. Toronto's Larry Grossman, who succeeded his father Alan as an MPP, lost in a close election for the party's leadership in 1987. Erminie Cohen of Saint John was appointed to the senate in 1993. Cohen advocated on behalf of women's rights, health, and anti-poverty programs.

Stanley Hartt (1937–2018) was born in Montreal. He was the most important civil servant during the Mulroney years, as deputy minister of finance (1985–8) and chief of staff (1989–90). When asked why

Hartt was chosen, Mulroney answered that "he combined both an extremely brilliant mind with a delightful sense of humour, together with a remarkable capacity to analyze complex issues and produce policy options.[28] Two important Tory figures were Torontonians Edwin (Eddy) Goodman (1918–2006) and Hugh Segal (1950–). Separated by a generation they helped frame the paths of the national and Ontario branches of the party. Goodman was a fundraiser and advisor to premiers John Robarts and Bill Davis. He became the party's national chair and vice-president. Segal was an unsuccessful candidate in the 1971 election (at the age of 21), and again in 1974. Eight years later, he was a deputy minister in the Ontario legislature and briefly served as chief of staff for Brian Mulroney. But in 1998 he lost his bid to be leader of the party.

The most significant government appointment given to a Canadian Jew, breaking the antisemitic ceiling for senior civil servants, was the selection of Louis Rasminsky (1908–98) as governor of the Bank of Canada. This occurred in 1961, during the Diefenbaker era. Rasminsky was born in Montreal and educated at the University of Toronto and the London School of Economics. At the age of 22, he was a banking specialist for the League of Nations, who joined the Bank of Canada in 1940 and was appointed its deputy governor in 1955, even though he was the most qualified candidate for the top position. Diefenbaker told Rasminsky that he had been rejected because then Prime Minister Louis St. Laurent would find it impossible to defend Rasminsky's appointment in Quebec. Diefenbaker rectified that slight. Rasminsky had now become a symbol for the Jewish community in Canada. Rasminsky and David Golden, deputy minister of defence production, opened the door for more Jewish appointments in the 1960s.

The New Democratic Party

The NDP, formed in 1961 as the successor to the CCF, is the only major national party to have had a Jewish leader – David Lewis. Lewis's early career is discussed in Chapter 6. He succeeded Tommy Douglas in 1971. In the 1972 election, Lewis dubbed the mainstream parties "corporate welfare bums."[29] This may have had a role in reducing the federal Liberals to minority status, forcing the government to rely on the NDP for support until its defeat on a vote of non-confidence. Lewis retired when he was defeated in his riding in the 1975 election. Three long serving members of Parliament in the period were David Orlikow and Saul Cherniack from Winnipeg and Max Saltsman from Kitchener. The party had more success at the provincial level, having formed governments in the period under discussion in British Columbia, Saskatchewan, Manitoba, and Ontario. The only Jew to have been elected premier[30] was Vancouverite Dave Barrett (1921–2018). Raised in the East End immigrant community, he stunned the country by upending the twenty-year reign of the Social Credit Party in 1972. Defeated in 1975 he served as an MP from 1988 to 1993. In Ontario, Stephen Lewis, the son of David, became the party leader in 1975. His lifelong friend, Gerald Kaplan, served as his right hand. The only Jewish MP that has not belonged to a national political party was Richard Marceau of the Bloc Quebecois who served from 1997 to 2006.

Mayors

While Jews have served as mayors in Canadian towns since Confederation, five have held the position in major cities. Lorry Greenberg was mayor of Ottawa from 1975 to 1978, and Steve Mandel held the position in Edmonton from 2004 to 2013, the longest tenure for a Canadian Jew. Toronto has had three prominent Jewish mayors since World War II: Nathan Phillips, Philip Givens, and Mel Lastman.

Nathan Phillips (1892–1976) was born in Brockville, Ontario and educated in nearby Cornwall. Graduating from Osgoode Hall Law School in Toronto in 1913, appointed King's Council in 1929. Phillips was first elected to Toronto City Hall as an alderman in 1924 and served in that capacity until 1955. In that year, he contested the mayoral election, defeating the incumbent Leslie Howard Sanders. Campaigning as "mayor of all the people," Phillips broke the political stranglehold of the staunchly conservative Orange Order, which had dominated Toronto's political and business establishment for more than a century. He modernized the city, tearing down old neighbourhoods, including the Ward. He was the driving force for the erection of the new city hall. The square facing the avant-garde structure is named in his honour. Phillips, a lifelong Conservative, was defeated in 1962.

In contrast to Phillips, who had a courtly demeanour, Philip Givens (1922–95) grew up in the tough Spadina neighbourhood. A graduate of Harbord Collegiate and Osgood Hall, Givens, a Liberal, sat on the city's Board of Control. When Mayor Donald Summerville suddenly died, he became acting mayor, and was then elected in 1964. Phillips was a man of the street, wise in the ways of dealing with the public, understanding of the business side of politics, and not afraid of ruffling the feathers of conservative Torontonians. He was reviled by traditionalists for leading a public campaign to purchase a sculpture, *The Archer*, by the modernist Henry Moore, to be placed in Nathan Phillips Square. Toronto got the sculpture, still much loved as a symbol of the city, but Givens lost the next election. He then served as an MP and MPP and late in life as a judge.

Mel Lastman (1933–2021), like Givens, grew up on the wrong side of the tracks, in Kensington Market. As a child, he sold produce in his family's shop. Unlike Givens, Lastman left high school for business. Adopting a larger-than-life persona, he began hawking used appliances, and started the aptly named Bad Boy Furniture store, which quickly became a chain. In television ads, he dressed in a prison uniform, where he signed off with, "Who's better than Bad Boy? … No … body!" Capitalizing on his name, he was elected to the North York Board of Control in 1969, and three years later, as mayor, a position that he held until 1997, when the Ontario government merged the municipalities into a "megacity." Lastman was elected mayor of the Greater Toronto Area, serving until 2003. Despite his flamboyance, his outrageous acts, such as bringing the army to help shovel snow during a severe storm, he employed his neighbourhood smarts to work with politicians from across the spectrum.

ACTIVISM AND APPROPRIATION, 1967–1985

In a 1970 article for the Jewish periodical, *Viewpoints*, on the predicament of Canadian Jewish identity, Saul Hayes, Sam Bronfman's successor as executive director of the CJC declared that there was a "Jewish

Emptiness in the lives of so many of the present generation" was not filled "by a return to customs and practices [of the past] … [but in] finding in Israel a real substitute for their former identification."[31]

Hayes' insight was prescient, but it provided only a part of the search for identity. The "business of Israel" was a necessary but insufficient surrogate. The postwar generation struggled to understand what their parents had tried to forget – their European heritage. Without having experienced immigrant life, this generation searched for the roots of Jewish life that had been abandoned, or not passed down, due their parents' focus on socio-economic mobility. The "little box" subdivisions were sterile, with little indication that they were predominantly Jewish, in contrast to the immigrant neighbourhoods. In the 1970s, young Jewish adults, in confronting history, began the process of adopting the legacy of the Holocaust as a marker of their ethnic identity. Had he lived longer, Saul Hayes would have witnessed that historical memory, supporting Israel, and agitating for the freedom of Jews in the Soviet Union and the Arab lands that filled the Jewish Emptiness. The activism of the 1970s culminated in the events in the early months of 1985 which ultimately marked the appropriation of Holocaust memory as a pillar of ethnic identification.

Israel's Isolation

In the aftermath of the 1967 war, altercations in the Sinai with Egypt continued for several years, as did unease with Syria in the Golan Heights (the so-called War of Attrition). On Yom Kippur, 1973, Israel was unexpectedly invaded on these two fronts, with their adversaries reaching its borders. Caught unawares, Israel's rapid mobilization of its reserves in support of its troops countered the offensive, reversing the adversaries' initial gains. The so-called Yom Kippur War called into question the state of Israel's preparedness. Meanwhile, Israel was increasingly regarded as a pariah state by the Soviet Bloc, the Arab/Muslim nations, and by most of the nonaligned countries (aka "The Third World"). In 1976 a UN resolution equating Zionism with racism was passed. Israel was regarded as an occupier in the territories captured in 1967 and was likened to South Africa in perpetrating an apartheid regime. The election of the right-wing Likud Party in 1977, breaking the hold of the Labour Party, which had led coalitions since 1948, further alienated it internationally, even though Likud reached an accord with Egypt in 1979.

Jews in Peril

The Soviet Union contained some three million Jews, the third largest community after the United States and Israel. It was largely a forgotten segment until a 1963 article in *Foreign Affairs* documented their plight. Although it stated what had been known for decades, that Judaism and Jewish identity had been repressed and Jews were prevented from assimilating or emigrating, it struck a chord in the maelstrom of the time. Protests against the death sentences of Jews for "economic crimes" were treated by Soviet leader Nikita Khrushchev as "a vicious slander."[32] Demonstrations at the Soviet Embassy in 1964 elicited Soviet consternation. The CJC organized a rabbinic conference addressed by Paul Martin, Pearson's minister of external affairs. The rabbis' appeal that a delegation be allowed to visit the Soviet Union was rejected. At the CJC Plenary in 1965, there was a call for a national conference, which was held the next year in Montreal. Students were mobilized and survivors were among the most vocal participants. A rally on the holiday *Simchat Torah* (the new cycle of Torah readings) in Toronto in 1967 became an annual event, drawing several thousand protestors. The highlight of the campaign was demonstrations in October 1971 during Soviet leader Alexei Kosygin's trip to Canada. In Ottawa the largest assembly of rabbis in Canadian history joined thousands in an overnight vigil. Marching the next day to the Soviet Embassy, a letter stating, "let the millions of Jews in our country be Jews in every sense of the word,"[33] was not be accepted by Soviet authorities. Twelve thousand protestors interrupted Kosygin's visit in Toronto, as did five thousand in Vancouver. Harold Troper writes that "the week of protest demonstrations also proved a measure of how much the decade of the 1960s had transformed the Canadian Jewish community."[34]

Jewish concern also rose in the aftermath of the Six Day War regarding the safety of Iraqi and Syrian Jews. In 1948 there were some one million Mizrachi Jews. With the establishment of Israel most had emigrated peacefully from Morocco and Tunisia. Under an agreement with Iraq,

Israeli airlifts spearheaded the departure of 90 per cent of the 140,000 Jews by 1951. Syrian Jews slowly migrated to Palestine, increasingly so as riots erupted in 1947, but left some five thousand behind. The Iraqi remnant became targets of the radical Ba'ath regime that seized power in 1963. Jews lost their jobs, investments, and were placed under surveillance and periodic house arrests. In 1967 scores were arrested, accused of spying for Israel, culminating in the public hanging of nine men, and others who died by torture. Canada joined many western countries in condemning these incidents. Mitchell Sharp, Canada's minister of external affairs met with Saul Hayes, who appealed for Canada's delegation at the UN to protest these crimes and for Canada to offer sanctuary. In February 1969 Sharp met CJC leaders off the record. Consequently, the CJC instructed that there would be no demonstrations until further notice. JIAS indicated that it would aid the immigrants, propelling cabinet to approve the proposal. Meanwhile Iraq's deteriorating economy deterred investment, and so it began issuing transit visas. All but a handful of Jews fled, most to Israel, and eventually another 1,500 to Montreal.

Syrian Jews faced a similar situation. Under the control of the Ba'ath regime headed by the dictator Hafez al-Assad, Jews were subject to extortion, not permitted to travel as family units, and only on temporary visas. Harold Troper, the author of *The Ransomed of God*, quoted a resident: "We were paying for the air we breathed."[35] After the 1967 war, the Syrian secret police tightened the noose. When Albert Elia was imprisoned in 1971, it aroused the CJC, as two of his children lived in Canada. Yet, unlike the situations in the USSR and in Iraq, the CJC could not persuade the government to intervene, for fear that it would worsen the situation for the Jewish community there. Caught between the considerations of the Canadian, American, and Israeli governments, the CJC was unable to plan a course of action. A middle-aged, upper-middle-class Toronto woman, Judy Feld Carr, stepped into the breach. She hounded the CJC, which had little truck with her aggressive tone. She organized information meetings in local synagogues and surreptitiously contacted a Syrian rabbi. Over the course of two decades, Carr prodded Canadian, American, and Israeli governments, Jewish organizations, Amnesty International, and the Red Cross. Most notably, she raised funds that were funnelled to Syrian officials and smugglers to facilitate the exodus. In 1992 the Syrian regime allowed the remaining four thousand to leave. Troper called her crusade "the remarkable story of one woman's role in the rescue of Syrian Jews."[36]

Holocaust Education

While knowledge of the Holocaust came about in the 1960s as a response initiated mostly by survivors in combatting virulent open antisemitism, public education and awareness did not come about until the next decade. The key factor for the dissemination of awareness and education about the Holocaust was the dedication and courage of the survivors across the country – as speakers, fundraisers, witnesses to history, writers/poets/ artists, storytellers in word and on screen, human rights advocates, and community leaders.

In 1972 the CJC and federations created standing Holocaust committees, led by survivors, and a year later, the CJC's National Holocaust Remembrance Committee emerged. By 1976 there were remembrance committees in twelve cities. They undertook to document the names and experiences of victims as part of the Pages of Testimony Collection, sponsored by Yad Vashem in Jerusalem, the authority responsible for commemoration and education. Further, a kit of educational materials was created for *Yom Hashoah* (the day of the Holocaust). Meanwhile as knowledge and interest grew, survivors became public speakers. The first provincial program for students took place at the University of British Columbia in 1976 and became an annual event. Survivors Robert Krell, Sophie Waldman, and Robbie Waisman were among the leading advocates. A similar annual meeting took place in Toronto for Ontario schools. The speakers included Gerda Freiberg, Nathan Leipciger, and Faye Shulman. Other provinces followed suit. Boards and ministries of education were pressured by the committees to include the Holocaust in their curricula. Three curricula were created in Toronto alone.

Holocaust survivors were subject to the viral public antisemitism of the time, and knowledge of the calamity was not widely known until it became the subject of intense academic research and represented in popular media – movies, television, and books. Publications on the Holocaust were led by historians Lucy Dawidowicz, Yehuda Bauer, and Raul Hilberg, as well as the more popular *Anne Frank – The Diary of a Young Girl*, published in 1952, and the novels of Eli Wiesel, who became the face and voice of survivors worldwide and a leading advocate for human rights. In April 1978 NBC's broadcast, *The Holocaust*, a miniseries, gripped North American audiences. Its stereotypical portrayal of perpetrators, bystanders, and most importantly, survivors, were annoying to students of this history, but its impact was widespread. It was instrumental in public education. The publication of *None Is Too Many* in 1982 shone a bright light on Canada's discriminatory immigration policy, in particular Canada's refusal to open its door to Jews trapped in German-controlled Europe. Its release amplified the call for education and commemoration by survivors and Canadian baby boomers.

In 1976 a group of young Montrealers born in Canada, headed by Stephen Cummings and a group of survivors, led by Lou Zablow, approached the Allied Jewish Community Services (AJCS), the federation for the community, to propose a project to build a Holocaust Memorial Centre. The Cummings/Zablow committee settled on a design and budget. Its mandate was for the centre to become the focus of Holocaust awareness and programming, the coordinator of educational activities, and the repository of an archive, establishing resources for scholarship. The centre opened on October 15, 1979.

The amalgam of survivors and baby boomers reverberated in Toronto, where the Holocaust Remembrance Committee was created in 1979 with public education as its primary goal. To that end, an annual symposium for high school students, featuring survivor speakers was launched in 1980. The following year, Holocaust Education Week, coincided with the anniversary Kristallnacht in Germany on November 9, 1938, was inaugurated. Keynote speakers, programs in local libraries, synagogues, churches, and community centres drew audiences across the ethno-cultural landscape. Forty years later, the scope of Holocaust Education Week is unparalleled worldwide. A group of survivors, headed by the Holocaust Remembrance Committee chairs, Nathan Leipciger and Gerda Freiberg, raised the funds for a Holocaust Memorial Centre. Overcoming the objections of the Toronto Jewish Congress (the local federation) it opened in 1985. Within a few years, several thousand high school students were visiting and meeting survivors.

Vancouver was the site of the first educational symposium in 1976. A committee, headed by survivor Dr. Robert Krell, Professor Graham Forst, and Reverend Bob Gallacher, worked with CJC's Pacific Region to create educational materials and outreach. In 1984, the Vancouver Holocaust Centre was established and opened in 1994 in the community centre. In Winnipeg, a Holocaust Memorial Committee launched Holocaust Awareness Week and an educational initiative including a three-day seminar in 1976. In 1990, a granite memorial, inscribed with the names of 3,200 victims whose families had migrated to Winnipeg, was unveiled on the grounds of the Manitoba legislature. Similar initiatives became were undertaken in Edmonton, Calgary, and Ottawa. Commemoration of Yom Hashoah on the date, according to the Hebrew Calendar, of the Warsaw Ghetto Uprising, had become a significant event across the country. Across Canada, these developments relied on volunteers across the age span, including non-Jews.

The study and teaching of the Holocaust in particular, and genocide in general, became mainstays in university curricula. Historian Michael Marrus of the University of Toronto wrote *The Holocaust in History* (1987) and established the first graduate program on the subject in Canada as the inaugural Chancellor Rose and Ray Wolfe Professor of Holocaust Studies. Concordia historian Frank Chalk and sociologist Kurt Jonassohn pioneered a course on the history and sociology of genocide in 1980, and the following year founded the Montreal Institute for Genocide and Human Rights. Their volume, *History and Sociology of Genocide,* was published in 1990. In 1996 University of Waterloo historian Robert Jan van Pelt, Canada's foremost scholar on the Holocaust, and historian Deborah Dwork, director of Clark University's Center for Holocaust and Genocide Studies, co-authored *Auschwitz from 1290 to the Present,* one of several works on the subject.

In 1988 a program launched for North American Jewish teenagers titled "March of the Living." Its purpose was threefold: education, remembrance, and continuity, and involved taking the teens on the walk from the main camp at the Auschwitz complex to the killing fields in Birkenau, a distance of a few kilometres. By bringing the students to the sites of destruction in German-occupied Poland, forty plus years after liberation, it provided them visual context and served as an act of memory. The march itself symbolized Jewish continuity. The Canadian contingent was organized by the United Israel Appeal and the Toronto Jewish Federation. The march's initial and still current director, Eli Rubenstein, a local scholar and religious leader, has refined aspects of the experience by including Canadian survivors as speakers and mentors, creating a dialogue with Polish youngsters, and incorporating knowledge of the thousand-year history of Polish Jewry. In its thirty years of operation, some nine thousand Canadian teens have participated.

By 2000 knowledge of the Holocaust was widespread in Canada. The impetus came from the dedication and commitment of the survivors. The efflorescence was due to Canadians, Jews, and gentiles, who undertook to teach, learn, and participate in education about, and in commemoration of, the Holocaust.

SPRING 1985

In 1985 hard-core antisemitism reached its nadir in proclaiming that the Holocaust was a hoax perpetrated by "international Jewry" to gain sympathy. Gaining credence in the 1960s, this calumny was seized upon worldwide. Dubbing themselves "Holocaust Revisionists," antisemites flooded the market with pseudo-scientific publications. By the 1970s the base for their global distribution was a house in downtown Toronto belonging to a German immigrant, Ernst Zundel. In response, the Jewish community, led by survivors, reacted aggressively. In Toronto, the Holocaust Remembrance Committee and B'nai Brith lobbied the postmaster general to prohibit Zundel's mailings, but Zundel's appeal was upheld. Survivors, led by militants who were angered at what they considered to be the pusillanimous approach of the Holocaust Remembrance Committee, B'nai Brith, and the CJC, created the Holocaust Remembrance Association. The association's pressure turned on the Ontario government, forcing the hands of the attorney general and the Jewish organizations. Zundel was charged with a little-known section of the criminal code – knowingly disseminating false news. This set the stage for the salient events of 1985.

The trial opened in January. Zundel was charged on two counts and was found guilty, sentenced to fifteen months in prison and freed on bail pending an appeal. The JPRC and B'nai Brith's League for Human Rights joined forces as advisers to the Crown, while the Holocaust Remembrance Association, without whom there would not have been a trial, worked behind the scenes. But, it wasn't Zundel, in fact, who was on trial, but the Holocaust itself. The judge took judicial notice that the Holocaust was open to debate. The Defence paraded Holocaust deniers and the Crown countered with historians, most importantly Raul Hilberg. Opponents of the trial, some of them Jewish, argued that it deterred freedom of speech, no matter how heinous, and were met with contempt by the Holocaust Remembrance Association. Publicity was overwhelming. The media's coverage printed the deniers' fabrications without comment. Zundel was found guilty, but it was clear that the verdict was because he was a neo-Nazi instigator, and not that he had knowingly disseminated false news.

The trial was followed three months later by a charge against James Keegstra, a history teacher in Eckville, Alberta, for promoting hate under Section 281 of the Criminal Code. Although certified only to teach auto mechanics, for years his paranoid fantasies of a world Jewish conspiracy to destroy Christianity, and the "hoax of the Holocaust," had been foisted upon history students. Again, the JPRC and the League for Human Rights worked with the Crown. Keegstra was found guilty and given one month to pay a $5000 fine or face six months in prison. The trials galvanized the Jewish community. Survivors had pushed the ball forward, and the CJC and B'nai Brith, which had been competing for supremacy in advocating for the community, put aside their differences and provided invaluable aid to the Crown attorneys.

John Crosbie, the minister of justice in the Conservative government led by Brian Mulroney, which had ended the Pierre Trudeau era in 1984, rose in the House of Commons on February 7, 1985, to proclaim that the government was establishing a commission of inquiry into allegations that Nazi war criminals were resident in Canada. The inquiry, headed by Justice Jules Deschenes, was to report to Crosbie by the end of the year. This pronouncement was completely unexpected. It appears that Mulroney made the decision without consultation of his party, advisors, or Jewish leaders. In their book, *Old Wounds: Jews, Ukrainians and the Hunt for Nazi War Criminals in Canada,* Harold Troper and Morton Weinfeld could not find a motive for Mulroney's proclamation.

From 1948 to Mulroney's action, the CJC, led by Ben Kayfetz, had been lobbying for such an investigation. The CJC had early evidence that some immigrants had participated actively and as enablers in the murder of Jews in eastern Europe. Yet the CJC was stonewalled by successive administrations, from King to Pearson, and, in time, the impetus became stalled. The cause was taken up by survivors in the advent of the explosion of antisemitic activity in the 1960s. Survivors, more intent than the CJC, brought in speakers, including the famed Nazi hunter, Simon Wiesenthal, and presented a resolution at the CJC plenary in 1977 for a hunger strike and demonstrations, one that was not passed. This author interviewed Sol Kanee and Sydney Harris, presidents of CJC from 1971 to 1977 on this divide. They responded that the CJC's focus was lobbying on behalf of Israel and pressuring the Soviet Union to relax immigration restrictions. Even so, Robert Kaplan, a Jew who was then the solicitor general, presented a private members' bill to deprive war criminals of Canadian citizenship, but it was not adopted by his party.[37] While Trudeau didn't speak publicly about the issue, his rationale being that it would enflame the eastern European communities, especially many of the one million Canadians of Ukrainian descent. Further, Trudeau was loathe to yield to nationalist pressure, whether Quebec sovereigntists, or any other ethno-cultural-religious community. The Deschenes Commission's investigations dragged on for more than a decade, as the courts were reluctant to deport those who had abetted the murder of Jews. Nevertheless, Mulroney's action was a factor in the disaffection of previous Liberal supporters in the Jewish community.

The dizzying events from February to April coalesced in three days at the end of the month. The National Holocaust Remembrance Committee, with the leadership of the CJC, held a National Gathering of Survivors and Their Children in Ottawa, to mark Yom Hashoah and the liberation of the concentration camps in Germany and Austria by Allied forces. Hoping that one thousand would attend, almost three times that number, fully 10 per cent of survivors and their offspring, participated. Madame Justice Rosalie Abella, born in a camp in Germany in 1946, was the keynote speaker. At the national cenotaph a wreath was laid at a ceremony attended by opposition leaders Ed Broadbent of the NDP and John Turner of the Liberals, and Finance Minister Michael Wilson. Speakers included Irwin Cotler, a leading human rights activist, a force in the campaign to free Soviet Jews and a past president of the CJC; Elie Wiesel; and French Nazi hunters Serge and Beate Klarsfeld.

In three heady months in 1985, the confluence of local and international events, together with the efforts of survivors and their supporters, had mobilized the Jewish community. This achievement was possible primarily because Canadian Jews had appropriated the legacy of the Holocaust as a defining pillar of their ethnic identity, even though, aside from the survivors, most had not experienced the tragedy. In response to Saul Hayes's proclamation of the "Jewish Emptiness," the Jewish community's confrontation with history created an unprecedented impetus to fill the void.

CHAPTER TEN

Consensus and Continuity, 1985–2000

In the last years of the millennium, Canadian Jews were increasingly buffeted by growing anti-Israel sentiments at home and internationally, and by the perception of increasing antisemitism. Moreover, social inequality, the stagnation of population growth (apart from immigration), a decline in synagogue attendance, barriers to women in community leadership, financing and administering Jewish education, rivalry between the CJC and local federations, and fractured leadership in the community heightened concerns regarding the continuity of Jewish life. These concerns were at the forefront at the close of the millennium.

ANTISEMITISM: PERCEPTION AND REALITY

Holocaust denial stemming from neo-Nazis/white supremacists was one of two driving forces for the hatred of Jews. Ernst Zundel appealed the guilty verdict of 1985 and won on a technicality. Charged again, in the second trial in 1988 Zundel brought forth the British pseudo-historian and Nazi apologist David Irving, while the Crown countered with historians Raul Hilberg and Christopher Browning. Found guilty once again, his conviction was overturned by the Supreme Court, which claimed that the crime of reporting false news was unconstitutional. He then started a website promoting hatred against Jews, and under investigation by the Canadian Human Rights Commission, fled to the United

States. In 2003 he was deported for violating immigration rules, and two years later, exiled from Canada to Germany because he had not been granted citizenship. There, he was charged with inciting racial hatred, and ultimately served five years in prison. He died there in 2017.

Malcolm Ross was a teacher in Moncton, New Brunswick. Outside the classroom, he was a notorious antisemite. He wrote that the Holocaust was a hoax (echoing Zundel's charge) and that abortion was part of the Jewish plot against Christianity. A human rights complaint filed by David Attis, a Jewish resident, led to his removal from the classroom and a transfer to the school library. The provincial Court of Appeal overturned the order stating that this violated his freedom of religion and expression. In 1996 the Supreme Court upheld the initial verdict, that there was a "reasonable limit" to freedom of expression. Ross' appeal to the UN Human Rights Committee was rejected in 2000.

A plethora of neo-Nazi groups paraded through the dark corners of the country in this period. Spurred by the denial movement and motivated by the actions of the KKK and other American hate groups, they held rallies and concerts, usually in isolated locations, and published hate sheets. It was a loose network spread across the country. Among the notorious groups were the Canadian Aryan Nations, the Canadian Knights of the Ku Klux Klan, the Western Guard, the Edmund Burke Society, and the Heritage Front. Monitored and exposed by the CJC and B'nai Brith, some were arrested for assault, murder, and obstruction of justice, and their hate lines were closed. Yet, as journalist and lawyer Warren Kinsella wrote in 1994: "Canada's racist leaders may face legal difficulties, but no one believes that the threat has disappeared for good.… New leaders take the place of the old. They persevere, and they learn from their mistakes."[1]

How widespread were antisemitic incidents? How did Canadians regard Jews? To the first question, B'nai Brith's *Annual Audit of Antisemitic Incidents* culled annually from police reports showed a fivefold increase since the inception of the list in 1982 to 1995, but this may be because of more effective collection procedures. To the second question, in a 1984 study, one in seven Canadians had "negative attitudes" respecting Jews, with Newfoundland, New Brunswick, and Quebec recording the highest, and Alberta the lowest.[2] In 1987 another study found that 34 per cent felt that Jews were "too pushy," while a year later 14 per cent agreed that "Jews had too much power" in national affairs.[3] Yet, in 1990, 76 per cent of those surveyed who were thirty-four and younger reported having Jewish friends, and, in 1991, 64 per cent were "very comfortable around Jews."[4] This snapshot must consider that 34 per cent of English Canadians and 68 per cent of French Canadians reported that they had little or no contact with Jews. Overall, these responses were a far cry from 1947, when half of the country opposed the admission of Holocaust survivors. Nevertheless, in a 1990 study, four-fifths of Canadian Jewish adults believed that there is "a **great** deal (emphasis added) of antisemitism in Canada," and that "it has increased in recent years" even though "outright discrimination" was experienced by a mere 3 per cent in finding a job, 1 per cent in housing, and 3 per cent in housing.[5] Sociologist Morton Weinfeld, writing in 2001, opined: "In many ways, perceptions of antisemitism today are determined by memories and received wisdoms of the past. Things were indeed much worse for Jews two generations ago, and earlier."[6]

ISRAEL

The other driving force for anti-Jewish condemnation was Israel. The basest was the cry for the elimination of the Jewish state. More complex was criticism over its policies in the disputed territories of the West Bank of the Jordan River and in the Gaza Strip. Objections came from some Israelis themselves and Jews in the Diaspora, to some left-wing movements in Europe and North America. Criticism mounted with Israel's invasion of Lebanon, during the civil war there in 1982. Entering Beirut, Israeli forces did not deter Christian Falangists from massacring Palestinians in two refugee camps. The reverberations were felt in Ottawa. For the first time, Canadian leaders expressed some dismay with Israel. Prime Minister Trudeau wrote three strongly worded letters to Prime Minister Begin and criticized Israel's determination to eradicate the Palestine Liberation Organization in Lebanon. In the House of Commons, some statements were decidedly anti-Israeli. Media coverage exacerbated this position. This was a cause for alarm by some Canadian Jews. The most strident considered the *Toronto Star* and CBC antisemitic.

During the first Mulroney mandate, from 1984 to 1988, the situation did not improve. With the outbreak of the First Intifada (the Arab word for uprising) in 1987, public sentiment veered toward the Palestinian cause. Joe Clark, minister for external affairs, in a speech hosted by the Canada Israel Committee[7] in March 1988, presented, in the words of scholars David Goldberg and David Taras, "a stinging attack on Israel's record on human rights."[8] An Environics survey found that 53 per cent of Canadians disapproved of Israel's response to the uprising. Yet, lost in the discussion, was that in comparison to polls taken in earlier decades, where only 14 per cent were sympathetic to Israel in 1958, and 30 per cent in 1974, overall public opinion had become more favourable. The percentage supporting the Arab cause never exceeded 10 per cent until the Lebanon war. Where the anti-Israel turn was most noticeable was in the Canadian Labour Congress and the Canadian Council of Churches.

The growth of condemnation of Israel's policy in Canada was a mere blip in comparison to the vitriol emanating internationally. Anti-Zionism was, by the 1980s, considered by many to be a new version of anti-semitism. At its extreme, it was a call for the physical destruction of the state, comparing Israeli policies and actions to those of Nazis. Historian Irving Abella, wrote: "The victims of the Holocaust, the people slated for destruction, must prove in court not only that they suffered, but that they have not established the successor state to Nazi Germany."[9]

"BEING JEWISH"

In the last decades of the millennium, what did it mean to "be Jewish"? Historically, one was Jewish by being the offspring, naturally or by adoption, of Jewish parents. Further, it also included converts to Judaism, and those who identified as being Jewish ethnically but practiced another religion. But the definition was unclear anyone who descended from a mixed family. Of course, one could actively, or passively, not identify as being Jewish, whether by religion, ethnicity, education, or upbringing as occurred throughout history. The National Jewish Population Survey undertaken in 1990[10] provides some insight into those Canadians who identified as being Jewish, whether via religion, ethnicity, or both. These are some of the findings:

1. Religious involvement: denomination – Orthodox, 19 per cent; Conservative, 37 per cent; Reform, 32 per cent; other, 32 per cent.

Practice – 67 per cent surveyed belonged to a synagogue, 92 per cent attended a Passover Seder, 87 per cent lit Hannukah candles, and 77 per cent fasted on Yom Kippur.

2. Communal involvement of adults: 60 per cent read a Jewish newspaper; 47 per cent volunteered for a Jewish organization; 78 per cent were friends mostly with other Jews; 25 per cent served on a Jewish board or committee.
3. Israeli connection (adults): 66 per cent had visited Israel at least once; almost all respondents noted that if Israel was destroyed, it would feel like a personal tragedy. Forty-two per cent considered themselves to be Zionist; a slight majority had favourable impressions of Israelis who were Modern Orthodox, or secular, while 35 per cent supported Israeli doves and 23 per cent Israeli hawks.
4. Regional breakdowns: Montrealers tended to be more devout and traditional, Torontonians were mainstream, and British Columbians were less connected.
5. Age breakdowns: Canadians under the age of thirty-four were less inclined to belong to synagogues yet more receptive to Orthodoxy and 35 per cent could converse in Hebrew, as compared to the national average of 24 per cent. This final category reflects the role of Jewish education and of the arrival of immigrants from Israel. Middle-aged Canadians (aged thirty-four to sixty-five) were more likely to conform to the national averages and seniors tended to be more devout.
6. In comparative terms, Canadian Jews were "more Jewish" than those in the United States (the only other country listed in the survey). Of much greater importance, Canada was the only country in the Jewish Diaspora that was growing in the final decades of the century. The driving factor for this growth was immigration from Israel and the Diaspora.

"MAINTAINING CONSENSUS"

In 1964 sociologist Raymond Breton coined the term *institutional completeness* – the extent to which the group provides its members a full range of institutions (formal organizations).[11] Comparatively speaking,

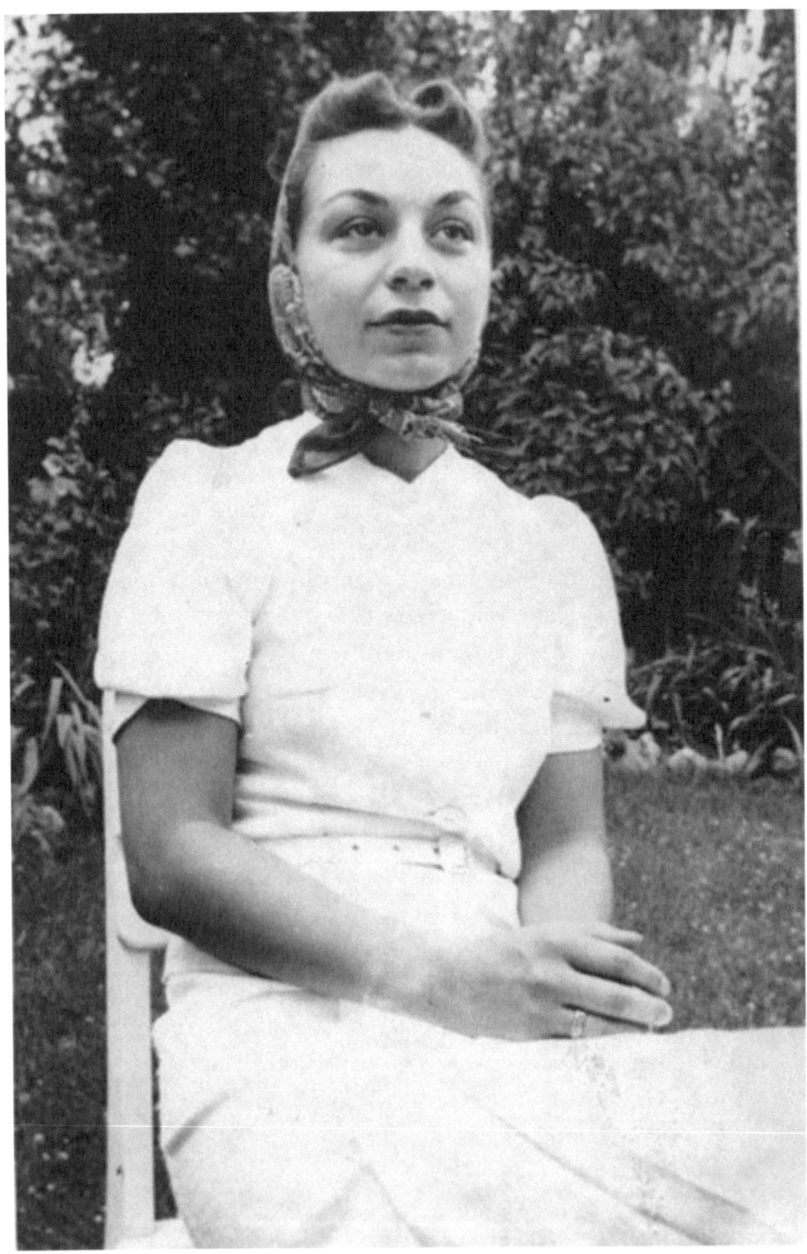

Rose Wolfe

Source: Ontario Jewish Archives

the Canadian Jewish community measures very favourably along the institutional continuum. And that has been the case since the turn of the century. Yet, it has not been a smooth process, characterized by factionalism based on socio-economic, ideological, religious, and regional divisions, and over the jurisdiction of community affairs. The oft-told joke "for every two Jews there are three organizations" speaks to the issue as a point of competition, but also reflects Jewish diversity. Hence, historically there has been an attempt at a measure of accommodation, that is, in the words of political scientists Harold Waller and Daniel Elazar, a commitment to maintaining consensus.

To a degree, the CJC had been an effective organization in smoothing over these divisions. It was self-described as the "parliament of Canadian Jewry." At its triennial national and regional plenaries, candidates for leadership positions were voted on by delegates, who represented various groups. There was a call for resolutions, and those adopted by the organizing committee of the plenary for discussion were then subject to a vote. Yet, as we have seen, the leaders of the CJC were men who had achieved prominence, whether through wealth, philanthropy, service or more likely some combination of the above, in their respective communities. This was most evident in Toronto, which became the dominant city in Canada and in the Jewish community by 1980. Quoting Waller and Elazar: "The typical key influential in the Toronto Jewish community in the 1970s was a male, over fifty years old, born (or raised – author's inclusion) in Toronto, with a university degree, residing in suburbia (particularly in Forest Hill), financially comfortable to wealthy."[12] For example, a survey taken in the early 1970s titled "Rank Order of Toronto Jewish Community Influential Individuals, by Occupation," listed twenty-one men, of whom eleven were in business, five lawyers, two rabbis, an economist, an engineer, and the director of the Jewish Federation. The executive of the Ontario Region of the JPRC was a case in point. There were no women, men under forty, academics, recent immigrants, or those of lower socio-economic status until the 1980s. Its first female chair was Rose Wolfe (her husband, Roy, headed the above list of "influential individuals"). Women were referred to as "Mrs." followed by their husband's first and family names.[13] Woe to the woman who was not married. Dorothy Reitman of Montreal in 1986 was the first female elected CJC national president.

But the CJC did not stand alone as a national organization. B'nai Brith had a longer history as an independent, international affiliation in the Diaspora, with chapters (lodges) in almost every Jewish community of more than one hundred residents. The Jewish Federation was constituted by members from across the political spectrum, from Revisionists, to Labour, Central, and Religious Zionists. As distinct organizations, the CJC, B'nai Brith, and the Federation advocated for Israel to Canadians, and especially to parliamentarians. In the aftermath of the Six Day War and the insecurity it raised in the community, it was determined that the three bodies would jointly establish the Canada Israel Committee.

The more significant competition was between the CJC and the Jewish federations, discussed in Chapter 5, that arose during the Great Depression, regarding which organization would provide social services. Although the task was undertaken by the federations, the impasse had never been fully resolved. There was a general understanding that CJC would be the advocacy arm for the community and for human rights for all Canadians, meaning that it would deal with matters of discrimination and equity. The federations would deal with immigration settlement, health, welfare, and family issues, and would be the beneficiary of the community chest. Funding for both was a national affair, through the United Jewish Appeal Campaign, which raised and distributed the funds. While the federations were central to the campaign, the CJC neither raised, nor campaigned for funds. Yet both organizations advocated to provincial and municipal governments on social issues including facilities for the aged and infirm, health, and the reduction of poverty.

One major area where responsibility was unclear was Jewish education, particularly in Ontario. Unlike Quebec, where Jewish schools were publicly funded, in Ontario there were two distinct sets of school boards, one for Catholics and one for the remainder of the population, and Jewish schools were partially funded by federations and the remainder through tuition. The issue was whether it was the federations' role to lobby the provincial government, or the Ontario Region of CJC, as per its advocacy role. A temporary solution was to merge the Federation (UJWF) and the CJC Ontario Region into a new body, the Toronto Jewish Congress. Rose Wolfe was its first chair. This merger, although temporary, was an example of following the historic pattern of consensus politics.

CONTINUITY

In the last decades of the millennium, there were clear signs that the traditional bases of Jewish life: faith; family; education; care for the aged, infirm, and poor were being subjected to the vicissitudes of settlement, adaptation, and diversity. The process of adaptation for Canadian Jews was at its apogee but remained a challenge for non-English speakers. Diversity was accelerating and the challenges to social norms – religious choice; family planning; education; where to live, work, and socialize; gender roles; and sexual preference – were rapidly increasing. The concern that had echoed for three millennia was raised again: that assimilation presaged the demise of Jewish life. Anxiety was spurred by projections that the Jewish population of the United States would decline by as much as 50 per cent by 2050 and that the Canadian community would follow suit. "Continuity" was the touchstone for community leaders.

The most troublesome considerations regarding continuity were the future of the Jewish family due to the decline in the number of Jewish births and the rising rates of divorce and intermarriage. Scholars cite the decennial censuses from 1961 to 2001 as evidence, but these numbers do not include the number of converts or mixed families that provide Jewish education, attend synagogue, and are active in Jewish community institutions and organizations.

Corresponding to the decline in the birth rate was the increase in the number of elderly Jews. In 1990 the average age was seventy-three years for men and almost eighty for women. Almost 6 per cent of Canadian Jews were aged seventy-five and over, in contrast to 4 per cent of all Canadians. Unlike the situation during the immigrant era before 1939, where the multi-generational family lived under one roof, Jewish elders, especially those who were widowed, typically lived alone, further isolating themselves from the broader community.

An underappreciated segment of the study of Jewish families was the persistence of poverty. Sociologists Jim Torczyner and Shari L. Brotman, in their study of the 1981 census,[14] found that 17 per cent of Jews were poor, in contrast to 25 per cent of Canadians. Regionally, the lowest poverty rates were in Toronto (15 per cent) and Ottawa (11 per cent), while Windsor (23 per cent) and Newfoundland and New Brunswick (29.5 per cent), albeit with small populations, were the highest. The age and gender breakdown provides a clearer perspective. Women constituted 57 per cent of the population in 1981; women over sixty-five made up 18 per cent of the Jewish population, but 38 per cent of those lived in poverty. A further consideration was the poverty of elderly persons living alone. Here, the figures were devastating. In total 47 per cent were poor; for women in this category, 65 per cent were poor; and for single-parent families (not isolating for gender), 32 per cent were poor.

CONCLUSION

History has not been kind to Jews. In periods where they lived in relative security, and even when some achieved high societal status, calamity was always a threat. In the postwar era, Canadian Jews were buffeted by national and global developments that disturbed the comfort of their relative socio-economic advances. Due to the community's postwar confrontation with history, antisemitism was perceived to be ascendant despite surveys that showed otherwise. Both 1948 and 1967 were watershed years: the former with the creation of Israel, the latter with the potential for its eradication. Due to the activism of Holocaust survivors and the baby boom generation, education created public awareness, while the events of spring 1985 solidified Holocaust memory as a pillar of ethnic identity.

At the millennial turn, aside from Israel's security, one issue dominated: Jewish continuity into the future. In the last third of the twentieth century Canadian Jews were reproducing less often, divorcing more often, and marrying or cohabiting with non-Jews far more often. One in six was poor, as were at least one in three single mothers. Women in general had barely broken the glass ceiling in traditional synagogue services, in their ability to get a religiously sanctioned divorce,[15] or in achieving leadership of communal institutions and organizations. Indeed, despite the socio-economic ascendance for many in the postwar era, the historical shadow of Jewish insecurity had not been relieved.

CHAPTER ELEVEN

The Jewish Diaspora Settles on Bathurst Street

According to demographer Louis Rosenberg, from 1760 to Confederation in 1867, approximately one thousand Jews had settled in Canada.[1] During the Great Migration from central and eastern Europe through the last decades of the century to World War I the population swelled to some one hundred and twenty thousand, mostly in Toronto, Montreal, and Winnipeg, and to smaller towns, villages, and farms across the country. Immigration restrictions, initiated in the mid-1920s and heightened through to the late 1940s, reduced the flow, so that most of the next fifty thousand were born in Canada. Holocaust survivors and their children, who arrived between 1948 and 1961, constituted the third wave of immigrants, which, combined with the baby boom, added another 60,000. Virtually all Jews in Canada up to 1961 were descendants of Ashkenazi Jews from central and eastern Europe.

Two trends were discernible in Jewish settlement from 1961 to 2001. The first was that the origins of new immigrants widened to include more of the global Jewish Diaspora. The initial wave of post-1961 immigrants were the Sephardim, so-called Spanish Jews, most of whom were of Moroccan origin, together with those from the Arab states in western Asia, the Mizrachim (eastern Jews). They primarily settled in Montreal as French was their predominant language. The second and third waves came from Israel and from the Soviet Union (until its demise in 1991) and its successor states, Russia and countries that had been Soviet Republics. The majority of these settled in Toronto. Concurrently, they were joined by Jews from South Africa, the United States, and smaller contingents from Latin America, Ethiopia, and India. Over the forty-year period ending in 2001, the Jewish population increased by 163,000 to 370,000, approximately half of whom were immigrants. This development reshaped the nature of the community – for the first time, Canadian Jews consisted of immigrants and their descendants from the entire Jewish Diaspora, creating the most ethnically diverse Jewish presence in Canada's history, and, after Israel, the United States, and France, the largest and most diverse Jewish community in the world.

The second trend was internal Jewish migration. This created two divergent results. The first was that most of the migrants moved to Toronto and most of the remainder went to Ottawa and to western Canada (Vancouver, Calgary, and Edmonton). Including immigrants, Toronto's Jewish population almost doubled from 1961 to 2001, from 88,000 to 164,000, many of whom clustered along Bathurst Street. The second result were the Jewish communities that did not grow, or were reduced, or disappeared. Most notable was Montreal, which had constituted almost one half of the population in 1961, but only one-third in 2001. Winnipeg, which historically boasted the third largest contingent, was reduced by 30 per cent, and Windsor by almost 50 per cent. Tellingly, smaller towns that had Jewish populations between one hundred and one thousand in the 1930s, other than London and Halifax, were greatly affected, and those that had had fewer than one hundred were now essentially devoid of Jewish life.

SEPHARDI AND MIZRACHI IMMIGRANTS

Following the dispersal of the Jews by the Roman Empire in 70 CE, they settled in the lands to the east (Mizrach in Hebrew), and throughout the Mediterranean littoral (Sepharad, Spain in Hebrew). With the expansion of Islam by the Arabs in the seventh century and the defeat of the Byzantine Empire in 1453, Jews lived primarily under Muslim rule until World War I. In consequence, the new nation states of Turkey, Lebanon, Syria, Transjordan, and Iraq were created under British and French mandates, and the North African states of Morocco, Tunisia, and Algeria were colonized by France, while Egypt was brought into the British sphere. World War II dismembered the mandates and led to nationalist movements in North Africa. These developments imperiled the security of the Jewish minorities.

Almost one million Jews lived in Arab lands in 1948, the majority in the French colonies of Morocco and Algeria. The Mizrachim were most prominent in Syria, Lebanon, Iraq, and Yemen. Fifty years later, there were some fifty thousand remaining, mostly in the non-Arab countries of Iran and Turkey. The compelling impetus for Jewish emigration was the establishment of Israel, which sparked violent pogroms in Iraq and Libya, and sanctions against them in the North African littoral. The exodus began immediately, followed by waves during the Arab-Israeli conflicts of 1956, 1967, and 1973. By 1958 an estimated six hundred thousand had arrived in Israel, and a smaller contingent to France. Currently, more than half of Israel's Jewish population is of Sephardic and Mizrachi descent.

Approximately half of the Sephardi immigrants who chose to come to Canada were of Moroccan origin. That community was founded during the Phoenician colonization three thousand years ago and was well integrated at the time of the Arab conquest in the seventh century BCE. It swelled following the Spanish and Portuguese expulsions of the fifteenth century. Morocco became a French colony in 1912 after which time most of the Jewish community adopted French as their main language. But there was unease due to attacks in the *mellahs* (the Jewish quarters) and the imposition of German control during World War II. Its population of 250,000 rapidly dwindled after 1948 and continued to do so after the state became independent from France in 1956. In the advent of the 1967 war, most of the remnant emigrated to Israel and France. The current Jewish population of Morocco is estimated at five thousand.

The first wave of Sephardi Jews to Canada was from 1956 to 1965, settling almost exclusively in Montreal. Further streams arrived at an accelerated rate in the following two decades, largely via Israel and France. By 2001 they numbered some thirty-six thousand, almost half of whom were born in Canada. Two-thirds still lived in Montreal and its environs, constituting 38 per cent of the city's Jewish population. About 25 per cent ended up in Toronto, 10 per cent in Vancouver, and the remainder scattered across the country.

The initial migration to Montreal was welcomed by JIAS and the Montreal Jewish Federation. As they were French speaking, they easily adapted in that regard: indeed Sephardi Jews, who increased the province's French-speaking proportion, were welcomed by the Quebec Ministry of Immigration that had been created in the early 1960s. The community, however, was relatively isolated from the native Jewish cohort. Consequently, the immigrants established l'Association sépharade francophone in 1966, and le Centre communautaire juif in 1971 and la Communauté sépharade du Quebec (CSQ) in 1976 which eventually became a constituent agency of the Association of Jewish Community Services (the Montreal Jewish Federation). Students attended L'École Maïmonide (established in 1969) and joined Le Centre Hillel at l'Université de Montréal in 1972.

Studies of the community provide an insight regarding its adaptation to Quebec and to the native Jewish community. The first was conducted in 1972 by sociologist Jean-Claude Lasry. His sample of 469 North African Jews, representing some 2,500 households, showed that there was a strong estrangement from the native Jewish community. Respondents, when asked in "which one of the following ethnic groups does one find the best friends," 68 per cent responded "North African Jews," 23 per cent "Canadian Jews" and 8 per cent "French Canadians."[2] As for neighbours, the corresponding responses were 55 per cent, 15 per cent, and 25 per cent, indicating that the majority preferred not to live in predominantly native Jewish areas. When asked about attitudes toward ten different ethnic groups, 85 per cent respondents were favourable toward "North African Jews," 70 per cent toward "Sephardim," 70 per cent toward "Israelis," 57 per cent toward "French Canadians," 35 per cent toward "English Canadians," 53 per cent toward "Canadian Jews," and 35 per cent toward "Ashkenazim." This is illuminating, that aside from overridingly positive feelings toward their fellow immigrants (including, one expects, most Israelis), there is a marked division between the "Canadian Jews" and "Ashkenazim." Effectively, the immigrants saw two native Jewish Canadian cohorts: "Ashkenazim" was a reference to foreign-born European Jews, of whom a significant portion were Holocaust survivors, whereas "Canadian Jews" indicated those born in Canada. Lasry concludes that the "hostility" between the newcomers and the dominant Jewish community is a "universal"[3] factor in every country that has experienced large-scale immigration, where each wave wanted to be accepted, but was not. Further, the newcomers were considered "Arabs," a pejorative label signalling deep cultural disparity within the community. There was also a linguistic separation, exacerbated by rising French-Canadian nationalism that was challenging the entrenched English-speaking minority's historical economic domination of Quebec, and in turn alienating a portion of the established Jewish community.

Sociologist Morton Weinfeld, writing in 2001, remarked that "these communal differences should not be overstated. All Ashkenazi and Sephardi Jews share basic religious elements … (and) both groups share a strong attachment to the goal of Jewish survival and the security and well-being of the State of Israel…."[4]

Another study, *The National Household Survey, Part 7: The Sephardic Community*, based on the Canadian census of 2011, revealed that social and economic differences between the native Jewish community and immigrants, most of whom had been in Montreal for a generation, had persisted. Sephardim tended to marry later and more readily to non-Jews, tended to divorce more frequently, had a slightly lower level of post-secondary education, and a slightly higher rate of poverty. Compared to 0.5 per cent of the rest of the Jewish community, 73 per cent of Sephardim reported that their mother tongue was French, and 62 per cent reported speaking primarily French at home, compared to 31 per cent overall. Sephardim still chose to live more exclusively in their own neighbourhoods, especially Ville St. Laurent, where they constituted approximately half of the Jewish population. But tellingly the main conclusion was that "Sephardim have adjusted well to life in Montreal, … occupy key positions of leadership and influence in the Jewish community, have developed thriving businesses, and enjoy political representation in the general community"[5] in contrast to Weinfeld's contention a decade earlier. This easing of hostility also speaks to the post-1995 generation (the date of the second referendum on sovereignty) that is far more comfortable speaking French and is less tethered to the traditional negative attitudes of cultural differentiation. Overall, after fifty years, there was a measure of adaptation.

QUEBECOIS-JEWISH LITERATURE

The obstacles to adjusting to the Canadian setting was the primary topic of French-speaking Jewish immigrant writers.

Naïm Kattan (1928–2021) was one of Canada's most decorated writers. Growing up in Baghdad, where Jews had lived for 2,500 years, he spoke Arabic, Judeo-Arabic, and French, and read Hebrew and English. In 1945 he left for Paris, at a point when the situation for Iraqi Jews had become precarious, considering a pogrom there a few years earlier that led to the airlift to Israel. After studying at the Sorbonne, he came to Montreal in 1954. He has written more than thirty books – novels, short stories, and essays. Kattan's autobiographical trilogy – translated from the French as *Farewell Babylon* (1975), *Uprooted Fruits* (1977), and *The Promised Bride* (1983), portray his journey, his "three lives." Scholar Michael Greenstein writes that Kattan, "addresses himself exhaustively to such polarities as occident and orient, north and south, Arabic and French, male and female, artist and administrator, particular and universal, reality and theatre, memory and promise"[6] – a writer of invisible borders.

Kattan is particularly eloquent in depicting the challenge of adapting to life in the Jewish community in Montreal for middle-class Iraqi Jews. In the short story, "The Dancer," he writes about the suppressed desire of Latifa, called Lena in Montreal, to express her cultural heritage, which is repressed by her husband, Selim (Solly). Fleeing Baghdad, they arrived in Tehran, where life was much safer. Having made money, they were able to gain admission to Canada. There, their children spoke English, while they continued to converse in Arabic. Solly had a successful business, but Lena, bored at home, took up belly dancing, much to Solly's chagrin. At a wedding at the Queen Elizabeth Hotel, Lena determined that she would no longer "hide her dark skin under dreary, dull-colored dresses." Two bands, one Western, the other Arab-Israeli, performed. When the latter played, Lena, "oblivious to the crowd," took centre stage. She danced alone, then was encircled, "vibrating to the movements of her thighs, her breasts, her belly … Bagdad and Montreal had disappeared in the shadow of this dance floor." Solly "never talked to her about the dancing.... [but] Lena lived in anticipation of the next wedding."[7]

Kattan's honours include Officer of the Order of Canada, Knight of the National Order of Quebec, honorary degrees from two universities, and Chevalier of the Legion d'honneur of France.

Alice Parizeau (née Poznanski) (1930–90) was born in Poland. As a teenager, she was a liaison between the Polish Home Army and the

Naïm Kattan

Source: Alex Dworkin Canadian Jewish Archives

Warsaw Ghetto. She was captured and ultimately interned in the Bergen-Belsen Concentration Camp. Following liberation, she moved to Paris, and then to Montreal in 1955 where she worked as a journalist, civil servant, and criminologist. Parizeau was also a productive author, writing nine novels including an autobiographical based trilogy: *Voyage en Pologne* (1962), *Survivre* (1965), and *Une Québécoise en Europe "rouge"* (1965). She became somewhat well known to English Canadians as the wife of Jacques Parizeau, the leader of the Parti Quebecois, who, as the provincial premier, activated the divisive second referendum on sovereignty.

Monique Bosco (1927–2007) was born in Vienna and came to Paris in 1939. Following the German invasion, she was shipped to Marseilles, where she was hidden. Arriving in Montreal in 1948, she received her doctorate from the Université de Montréal, and then served in the faculty of French Literature. She wrote eight novels, and four collections of poetry and short stories on the themes of alienation, solitude, and male domination. Some works are marked by her experience as a Jewish survivor in France, transformed into the present, as in *Sara Sage '86,* a post-biblical Sarah or in her poem, "16 Juillet 1942," which relates to the erasure of public memory of the mass deportation of Parisian Jews, who had been rounded up by French police under the command of the Germans and taken to the nearby Velodrome, from where they were deported to Auschwitz.

Régine Robin (Rivka Ajzersztein) was born in 1939 in Paris to Polish immigrants. Graduating from the Sorbonne in sociology, since 1977 she has been on the faculty of the Université du Québec à Montréal. Her writings deal with the themes of identity, culture, and dislocation. Her most well-known work, *La Québécoite* (1983), translated as "The Wanderer," is unusually expansive in expressing the cultural gap in moving from Paris to Montreal.

Chantal Ringuet was born in Quebec City to a Quebecois family. Not having known Jews in her youth, in Montreal she immersed herself in the study of the city's Jewish community and became fluent in Yiddish. Ringuet is a prolific writer of poetry, essays, and translations from Yiddish and English to French, and has published works on her own and with her husband, Pierre Anctil, who likewise is not Jewish, and is the foremost French-Canadian scholar of Canadian Jews.

RUSSIAN IMMIGRATION

Most of world Jewry in 1800 lived in the Russian Empire. The Great Migration in the three decades prior to World War I left some two million Ashkenazi Jews in Russia proper. In 1922 the consolidation of the Bolshevik revolution of 1917 created the Soviet Union (USSR), home to some three million Jews, including a significant minority in the Ukrainian Republic, with a smaller but important contingent in the Belarus, Lithuanian, and Latvian republics, and a scattered minority in the Central Asian republics, of whom the majority were not of Ashkenazi tradition. The German invasion of its former ally in June 1941, was a death knell for Jews in the western part of Russia, Ukraine, Lithuania, and Latvia, and for Polish refugees. Of a total population of 5.4 million, some 2 million civilians and 200,000 Jewish soldiers were killed by German forces and their collaborators.

Despite the imposition of Communist ideology, falsely proclaiming that all residents were citizens of the state with equal rights, antisemitism was rampant in the Soviet Union. Even though a coterie of officials, artists, professionals, and academics were of Jewish origin, Jewish heritage was almost obliterated. Communist indoctrination strangled Judaism, Jewish culture, and education. Some were executed, thousands were sent to the forced labour camps, mostly to remote Siberia, from where few returned. The iron rule of Joseph Stalin, from 1927 to 1953, largely vanquished what Jewish culture remained. Assimilation was widespread – the Jewish population of some three million in 1948 dropped to two million by 1970. Emigration, especially to Israel, was well-nigh impossible, and as discussed in Chapter 10, the campaign to free Soviet Jews in the 1970s had limited success. The gates were somewhat opened in the following decade, creating a wave of emigration that was accelerated by the collapse of the Soviet Union in 1991. From 1989 to 2011, 1.65 million Jews left, of whom approximately 1 million went to Israel, another 300,000 to the United States, and 225,000 to Germany, reducing the estimated Jewish population of the former Soviet Union to 275,000, representing 2 per cent of the world total.

In the 1970s and 1980s about 1,500 Soviet Jews were allowed entry to Canada as refugees from religious persecution. It is not accurate to refer to them as "Russian," as they did not conform to a neat definition of an ethnic community, given the transnational composition of the USSR. A much larger migration followed, but an accurate number is difficult to determine. Rabbi Joseph Zaltsman, who came in 1980 and is a spiritual leader of the community in Toronto, estimated that there were thirty thousand in Toronto and ten thousand in the rest of the country in 2011. Sociologist Jay Brodbar projected some twenty-five thousand, distinguishing between those who arrived directly and the relatively equal number who came via Israel. Demographer Charles Shahar concluded that about seven to ten thousand settled in Montreal, and about fifty thousand arrived overall. Specifically, the 2001 census records that 19,145 living in Toronto were born in the former Soviet Union. As with the Sephardi migration, these disparate figures are not conclusive. They do not distinguish between those of Sephardic, or Russian/Soviet, or Israeli origin – only their country of birth, and even this is deceiving as some children born in Israel were of Sephardic or Russian descent.

The primary reason for Russians choosing Canada was economic. Many early immigrants established small businesses that could then attract the next wave. A second factor was that Canada was "a peaceful country," likely a reason for some who first went to Israel, in deciding to move again. Further, these "secondary migrants" were also concerned about terrorist attacks and conscription. Third was that Canada was country of political freedom, without antisemitism at the highest political levels.

The concentration of Russian, Israeli, and Sephardim in Toronto was initially on the Bathurst Street corridor between Finch and Steeles Avenue. By 2001, the Jewish community in general, and immigrants specifically, had spilled northward into neighbouring Vaughan via Bathurst Street and its contiguous streets.

Sociologists Roberta Markus and Donald Schwartz in 1983 determined that settlement of the Soviet Jews in Toronto was effective largely due to JIAS, but that integration was "contentious and unresolved" creating a "large gap between the expectations of the established Toronto Jewish community and the self-identity of the émigrés." This division produced "a diffuse sense of Jewishness … proud of its achievements…. (but) suffering from a sense of alienation…. (with) likely assimilation into the broader secular community and losing whatever Jewish identity was brought with them."[8]

Consistent with the modern pattern of immigrant settlement, irrespective of national/religious/cultural origin, the Russian Jewish community of Toronto sponsored family members and friends, creating a chain migration, thereby extending the resettlement of extended families and fostering a continuation of Russian language and culture, but not necessarily Jewish tradition. JIAS offered professional services, language classes, and links to religious and communal services in eleven Canadian cities, so that adaptation, while not smooth nor rapid, had, at a minimum, a structural base.

Also consistent with immigrant patterns in general, the community read Russian language newspapers, spoke the mother tongue (95 per cent for Russian Jews but only 60 per cent for those from other republics), had their own synagogues and communal meeting points, but generally had little interest or exposure to Judaism, or to Jewish culture or education. While 90 per cent of all Jewish children had at least a modicum of Jewish schooling, only 40 per cent of Russian children participated, and those who did, did so over a shortened period. This is understandable given that some of the immigrants came from mixed marriages, and from a country that had demanded assimilation and decried religious/cultural exceptionalism. Hence, the rate of intermarriage of the immigrants was demonstrably greater than for the overall Jewish community.

The reluctance to conform was disappointing for the established community that had expected a rather seamless integration, but was not mindful of the immigrants' history, nor that every immigrant cohort that did not come from an English-speaking country and did not easily assimilate. In not divorcing themselves from their homeland, many kept their Soviet citizenship, maintained networks of relatives, business associates and friends in Russia and in the Russian Diaspora, and frequently visited their homelands. Finally, adaptation remained unfulfilled for many of these newcomers. In 2001 they had the highest rate of unemployment in the Jewish community, the highest level of poverty (35 per cent contrasted to 20 per cent of all Jewish immigrants and 8 per cent of the community as a whole), necessitating reliance on Jewish community services.

David Bezmozgis is one of Canada's most acclaimed contemporary writers and dramatists. He was born in Riga, Latvia in 1973 and came to Canada with his family during the first wave of Soviet immigration at the age of six. His career took off after graduating from the University of Toronto and the University of Southern California, where he directed, *L.A. Mohel*, the first of five films. His works portray the lives of Soviet Jewish refugees. His novels, *The Free World* (2011) and *The Betrayers* (2014), deal with refugees in Italy waiting for immigration papers to North America, and an encounter between a Soviet dissident and the man who denounced him.

Bezmozgis's first works were short stories published by *Harper's* and *The New Yorker*, eventually compiled as *Natasha and Other Stories* (2004). They are autobiographical, portraying the travails of adaptation by the Berman family in Toronto through the eyes of their son Mark. The family settled in an apartment on Goldfinch Court, at Bathurst and Finch Streets, in the tightly knit world of Soviet and Israeli immigrants. His building was home to other settlers from Latvia. This insular circle spoke Russian and struggled to learn English while Mark was already au courant with pre-adolescent jibes. One story, "Tapka," is about the Bermans' best friends' dog, a surrogate child, a link to their old world. Mark loved to play with him in a neighbouring park, but Tapka, under Mark's care, was hit by a car while chasing a toy. Severely injured, but saved through surgery, Mark was never forgiven by Rita, Tapka's owner.

"Natasha" takes place during Mark's adolescence during the late 1980s, in the heaviest phase of Soviet immigration. By then, the Bermans were living in a house in suburbia, where Mark was holed up in the basement. His uncle and second wife, Zina, had immigrated. Returning from a trip to Moscow, Zina arrived with her daughter, Natasha. In time, Mark introduced her to television, drugs, and his ne'er-do-well friends. Natasha introduced Mark to sex. Although only fourteen, she had been in the trade for two years. Upon discovery of their illicit relationship, Natasha found refuge with Mark's supplier. Mark vowed to end with subterranean life by "switching schools, changing [his] wardrobe [and] moving to another city."[9]

ISRAELI IMMIGRATION

Following the destruction of the Second Temple in Jerusalem by Rome in 70 CE, the Jewish population was greatly reduced. The subsequent dispersion left a small remnant there for more than a millennium. An estimate of the Jewish population of the province of Palestine, then under the Ottoman Empire in 1517, was five thousand, constituting less than 2 per cent of world Jewry. With the rise of Zionism, the first arrivals to Israel numbered twenty-four thousand in 1882, and at the outset of the British Mandate in 1919, it had grown to sixty thousand, but only 8 per cent of the mandate's total population. At the end of World War II, there were about 500,000, representing 30 per cent. With the arrival of Holocaust survivors, despite an embargo by the British, and a high natural growth rate, there were 700,000 at the time of the creation of the state of Israel in May 1948 constituting 82 per cent of the state. The large immigration from the Arab world, together with Ashkenazi arrivals, doubled the population to 1.6 million by 1955. Continuous immigration and a high birth rate doubled it again to three million by 1970. The arrival of approximately one million Russians was the most significant factor in raising the total to almost five million by 2000.

Immigrants to Israel are called *olim*, from the Hebrew verb "to ascend." In contrast, emigrants from Israel are *yordim*, from "to descend." There were an estimated 700,000 yordim by 2003, the vast majority in the United States, with significant numbers in England, France, Germany, and Russia. A recent survey calculates that there are seventeen thousand in Canada, about half of whom live in Toronto. The reasons for migration mirror those of the native Russian community: economic opportunity, safety, and professional development. A major difference is that most Israeli immigrants already spoke English (and some spoke French) upon arrival.

Israelis do not come from a monochromatic country. Diversity along the lines of country of origin; socio-economic status; home language (in addition to Hebrew); occupation; those raised on collective farms (plural kibbutzim), or in development towns, or in cities; adherents of traditional Orthodoxy; and atheists created a complex, vibrant nation-state. Emigrants reflect this multifaceted mosaic. The term, yordim, is somewhat pejorative. It implies that the immigrants harbour a measure of guilt for having abandoned Zionism and have an unfulfilled desire to return. Yet, long after their arrival, they continued to converse to one another in Hebrew, even in informal settings with non-Hebrew speakers. Unlike the Sephardi and Russian immigrants, their socio-economic status was comparable to the non-immigrant Jewish community.

SOUTH AFRICAN IMMIGRATION

After the United States and Israel, Canada was a favoured country for South African Jews. There are some parallels in the history of Canada and South Africa. In both cases, the first wave of immigration from eastern and central Europe was between 1880 and 1910. In the case of South Africa, in fact, the initial migration was greater, as four thousand had already arrived by 1880, about twice the number of those in Canada. By 1910 there were about sixty thousand, slightly less than in Canada at the time. Most came from Lithuania. The Jewish community's organizational structure mirrored that of the British community, with a board of deputies (akin to the CJC). The "after school" system sponsored by congregations (most of which were Orthodox) morphed into a full-day system in 1948, which was attended by 60 per cent of Jewish children by 1991. The Zionist movement was extremely active, creating the South-African Zionist Federation, with the same ideological divisions found throughout the Diaspora. A Women's Zionist Organization and a United Israel Appeal were established. The level of religious, social, and Zionist involvement was greater than elsewhere in the Diaspora.

The main distinguishing feature of South African society, in contrast to Canada, the United States, and western Europe, was its virulent racial ideology and practice (apartheid). The election of the National Party in 1948 heightened the separation, not only between races, but between the Boer and English-speaking factions. The increasing restrictions on native Africans and their liberation organizations engendered disdain for the regime and insecurity for its inhabitants. Jews were in the forefront of Europeans who supported the liberation movement. As conditions in the Black townships deteriorated, the Jewish exodus increased. From 1970 to 1991, some thirty-nine thousand Jews left, approximately one-third of the Jewish population. Their most favoured destination was the United States with almost ten thousand immigrants, followed by Israel, the United Kingdom, and Canada, with 4,100 arrivals, almost overwhelmingly to Toronto. Some returned from Israel, whereas those who favoured other destinations were much more inclined to remain.

The majority of South African Jews came from Johannesburg and Cape Town in two waves, from 1975 to 1982, and from 1986 to 1988. They were representative of the South African community with respect to Jewish education, organization membership, Zionist commitment, and synagogue affiliation. About 5 per cent arrived via Israel and a slightly higher number from the United Kingdom. A high proportion had university degrees and 80 per cent of the men and 40 per cent of women found work as managers and professionals.

The major factor in their decision to emigrate was the impact on their children's future lives in a country that practiced racial discrimination and mandatory military service. While a small group of Jewish activists were in the leadership of the anti-apartheid campaign at the outset, as the struggle intensified the community was generally supportive but fearful of an armed insurrection and violence in the townships.

The reason cited for their decision to immigrate to Toronto in particular was that Toronto was considered to have a traditional community that was more similar to South Africa than to the United States. Clearly, adaptation to life in Canada was smooth in comparison to the three major groups discussed above.

AMERICAN IMMIGRATION

Emigration from, and immigration to, the United States has been a feature of Canadian Jewish life since the late nineteenth century. For many immigrants Canada was a way station to the United States. In last years of the Great Migration, from 1908 to 1915, almost ninety thousand Jews arrived, but eighteen thousand continued on to the US.

The motivation for American immigration in the postwar years was tied to two factors. First was the political situation. From the late 1940s to the early 1950s, the Red Scare, or the apprehension regarding Communist infiltration in the government and military, particularly targeted academics and artists, a disproportionate number of whom were Jewish. In the 1960s and early 1970s opposition to American intervention in South East Asia, especially by those families affected by the draft into the armed forces, forced draft dodgers and deserters to find refuge in Canada, including young Jewish men. The second factor was career advancement. As Canada was rapidly modernizing, opportunities arose for positions in industry, commerce, and the academy. University enrolment mushroomed in the 1960s and 1970s due to the baby boom, and, as there was a dearth of Canadian academics, Americans filled the void. A telling example was the psychology department at York University in

Toronto, where a major portion of the department, which eventually became the largest in Canada, was American, including many Jews. In 2001, 6,425 Toronto Jews had been born in the United States, representing 3.6 per cent of the total.

The overriding factor for immigration to the United States has historically been, and continues to be, economic opportunity. From Louis B. Mayer from St. John and the Wonsul (Warner) Brothers from London who were among the founders of Hollywood, to current entrepreneurs and artists (music, film, drama), Canadians have flocked to the US to make it big. Some of them happen to be Jewish (as discussed in the section on entertainment). It is obvious that adaptation for immigrants to either country has not been as arduous as for other immigrants.

LATIN AMERICAN, ASIAN, AFRICAN IMMIGRATION

The 2001 census indicates that 1,100 Jews in Toronto were born in South America. It does not discriminate between those born on the continent itself and those from Mexico and Central America. Of the former, it includes 145 Chileans who escaped the crackdown on dissidents in the wake of the country's takeover by August Pinochet in 1971 including Jews who were specifically targeted. Elsewhere in Latin America, civil unrest and the lack of economic opportunities contributed to their departure. Toronto was a magnet for professionals and graduate students.

Although there is no documentation on the origins of the *Bene Israel* (sons of Israel in Hebrew) they trace their arrival to the Indian subcontinent after the Roman conquest of Palestine in 70 CE. What is known is that Portuguese explorers, among them Jews who hid their ethnic origin, established trading posts in Cochin, on the southwest coast, in the seventeenth century. The community became prominent. When India gained independence in 1947, some left for Israel because they were uneasy about their security in the wake of the British departure. A small number came to Canada in the early 1960s, mostly settling in Toronto. Further arrivals spurred the creation of the *Beth David B'nai Israel Beth Am* Congregation (BINA) in 1981.

For millennia, there has been a Jewish presence in Ethiopia. Under duress from the nationalist government after the death of Emperor

Haile Selassi and widescale famine, most were spirited to Israel. From there, a small number came to Canada, mostly to Montreal.

MIGRATION

The ascendance of Toronto as the dominant centre of Canadian Jewish life by 1980 was not only because it was the favoured destination for immigrants (aside from the Sephardim) but also because it was a magnet for internal migration. The paramount reason was that Toronto had overtaken Montreal's historic position as Canada's locale for finance, investment, media, and culture. It was one of the fastest growing metropolitan areas in North America and the desired destination for most immigrants. In the 1990s it was designated the most cosmopolitan city in the world by the UN. Further, the growth of Jewish communities in Vancouver, Edmonton, Calgary, and Ottawa, was consistent with their development as centres of trade, resource development, and government. Toronto displaced Montreal not only because of geographical proximity to North American markets but also due to the concern over Quebec's flirtation with sovereignty. Winnipeg's historical position as the city with the third-largest Jewish community and the dominant centre of western Canada was reduced due to the discovery of oil in Alberta in 1947 and the growing importance of trans-Pacific trade. Finally, across Canada, many smaller cities, most towns, and rural areas declined or failed to grow, a situation mirrored by the migration of their Jewish residents.

Montreal's Jewish population was reduced by thirteen thousand between 1981 and 2001, despite the influx of approximately twenty thousand migrants and immigrants. In Winnipeg the community was reduced by almost six thousand from its postwar high of eighteen thousand. Windsor, which had a long history of Jewish life, saw its community drop by more than half, propelled by an overall decline in the city's fortunes due to declining auto production. Of fourteen towns that had between two hundred and one thousand Jews in the 1931 census only London and Halifax kept pace. Notable declines occurred in Sydney-Glace Bay, whose population crested at 840 in 1931, but had been reduced to only a handful in 2001. St. John, which in 1911 had the seventh largest Jewish community, was reduced to 120, but nevertheless the community and its expatriates launched a new museum documenting its history and accomplishments. Regina and Saskatoon combined had 1,460 Jews in 1931, but only 700 in 2001. In contrast the Kitchener/Waterloo/Guelph region grew as it emerged as a high-tech centre.

Overall the most dramatic drop occurred in towns where between one hundred and four hundred lived in 1931. Until the 1950s one would still find a Jewish commercial presence in many of these places, such as Brantford, Ontario, Melville, Saskatchewan, and Sherbrooke, Quebec. They were displaced by the automobile, highways, mass marketing, and by the postwar generation that was more geared toward the opportunities available in metropolitan areas.

While the ascendance of Toronto made it a magnet for migrants in general, for Canadian Jews there were corresponding factors. The most compelling was that Jewish life could not maintain its vibrancy in the face of the draw of the major cities. As the postwar generation left for greener pastures, elements of the prewar community could not be sustained. Synagogue attendance dropped, some were forced to close, and others were challenged by informal congregations. Traditional homogenous Jewish residential areas were no longer present. Young adults found life partners in the larger centres, at summer camps and in youth groups, and at university. National organizations sought to maintain a presence and a voice. The CJC had a Small Communities Committee on both a national and regional level. B'nai Brith Canada maintained its long history with lodges in smaller centres. Nevertheless, as sociologist Sheva Medjuck of Halifax notes, "This lack of a critical mass means that Atlantic Jews lack collective visibility and also have become integrated into the larger society."[10]

The 401 Exodus: From Montreal to Toronto

Although we do not have definitive statistics regarding the number who left Montreal, we can discern that it was a response to two interconnected factors: the dominance of Toronto and the change in Quebec's political culture from the 1930s to the 1990s. The second factor requires a brief historical overview. The Union nationale party, which won the 1936 election, and then ruled from 1944 to 1960, was rooted in the traditional nationalist view that French-Canadian language, culture, and religion were under threat from Anglo and American domination. The

Union nationale's stranglehold relied on patronage as an instrument of blackmail, voter intimidation, and decrying unions, intellectuals and "foreign elements" (a not so subtle label for euro-ethnics in general and Jews in particular). Even so, the UN could not stop the tide of the postwar economic transformation, especially the movement from rural to urban centres. The status quo was challenged by young French-Canadian intellectuals, such as Pierre Trudeau, who advocated a new nationalism based on liberal democracy and the modernization of the economy and politics.

Following the death of the Union Nationale's leader, Maurice Duplessis, in 1959, the Liberals narrowly won the 1960 election. In the following six years, the Liberals launched the "Quiet Revolution." Among its achievements was an overhaul of education, which had been the preserve of the Catholic Church, and control over natural resources, notably the creation of Hydro Quebec. Yet, the revolution was too tepid for more radical elements. Following the return of the Union nationale to power in 1966, the more progressive wing of the Liberals broke off and created the Parti Quebecois, headed by René Lévesque, which advocated political sovereignty, creating unease within the Jewish community. That the "third solitude," the Jews, never completely integrated with either Protestants or Catholics, remained an uncomfortable fact of life.

The provincial Liberals, who regained power in the 1970 election, attempted to steer a middle course between the English Canadian domination of the civil service and private enterprise and French-Canadian nationalism. Accordingly, its passage of Bill 22, making French the language of civil administration and services, led to another victory in 1973, but it was not enough to prevent the Parti Quebecois from taking power three years later. The Quebec Separatist movement posed a serious challenge to Canadian Jewry, particularly those in Quebec. Before the 1976 election community leader Charles Bronfman called the Parti Quebecois "a bunch of bastards trying to kill us,"[11] invoking that historic fear of antisemitism generated by much Franco-Quebec hostility, even though he retracted the statement the next day.

Even so, the French struggle for cultural survival struck a responsive chord among many Jews. The postwar Jewish generation was even more likely to be bilingual than previous generations. By 1971, for example, 44 per cent of Jews were bilingual, as compared to 38 per cent of French and 32 per cent of English. Further, as historian Pierre Anctil notes, in 1968–9 the Université de Montréal, heretofore a Catholic institution, initiated the first program of Jewish studies in French.

In 1977 the Parti Quebecois enacted Bill 101 making French the official language. Among its provisions was that people moving to Quebec were required to send their children to French language schools. For some Jews, this did not appear threatening but nevertheless the majority, as Anctil contended, was unable "to understand the context [of the nationalists]."[12] Tulchinsky later concluded that "Jewish fears of Quebecois nationalism generally proved to be unfounded."[13] Unfortunately, that provided little consolation for the bulk of the English-speaking Jewish community. Although there was no overt antisemitism in the Parti Quebecois platform, and the calumny was roundly denounced by Levesque at the plenary of the CJC, more radical nationalist elements lashed out at the Jewish community.

The Parti Quebecois victory in 1976 destabilized the Canadian dollar sparking an exodus of some leading corporations. Most notable was the departure of Sun Life to Toronto in January 1978. Undaunted, Levesque was determined to test the waters for sovereignty and called for a referendum in 1980. Although it was rejected by 59 per cent of the voters, it accelerated the departure of English Canadians, particularly Jews. In the wake of the referendum, 70 per cent of Jews under the age of forty stated that they would leave if a path to independence was invoked.

Sociologist Morton Weinfeld, writing in 2013, opined that the Montreal Jewish community is "insular.... Very Jewish, arguably more than Toronto, certainly more than Vancouver or Calgary."[14] He posits that the emigration began with young university graduates in the 1960s. In addition to the fear of Quebec possibly breaking away from English Canada, the community was upset with increasing anti-Israel rhetoric emerging from prominent Francophone politicians in both the Parti Quebecois and the Liberal parties, pointing to a poll during the Lebanon conflict of 1982 where 38 per cent of Quebecers blamed Israel.

Despite the exodus of corporations along Highway 401 toward Toronto, and, pertinent to this discussion, a significant portion of Jews, the émigrés still insist that they are, at heart, Montrealers. Somewhat comically, their nostalgia is partially rooted in cuisine. Expat Montrealers, wherever they have migrated to, insist that Montreal bagels and smoked meat are supreme. More seriously, they maintain that they are more ensconced as true Canadians, given that the Jewish community is as old as is English Canada, that Jewish culture, in Yiddish, English, and French, remains vibrant, and that they are more representative of "Canadianness" because they are more likely to be bilingual. While Toronto by 2000 had emerged as one of the most important cities in North America, its Jewish population ranking eighth in the continent, the true heart of the Canadian Jewish experience continued to reside in Montreal (at least in its mythology).

Bathurst Street

As discussed in Chapter 8, the pattern of Jewish settlement in Toronto through the twentieth century had been along the north-south corridor of Bathurst Street, stretching from Lake Ontario to the northern limit of York Region, fifty-six kilometres in total. In 2001 approximately 150,000 Jews in the Metropolitan Region (comprising 85 per cent of the total), lived within four kilometres of the corridor. The concentration was in the former city of North York, where half lived, and another quarter in the contiguous city of Vaughan to the north. Within that span, the highest density was from Sheppard Avenue to Major Mackenzie Drive, some fourteen kilometres. Steeles Avenue and Bathurst Street is the hub, the epicentre of immigrant and migrant waves. This nexus represents one of the most diverse Jewish neighbourhoods in the Jewish Diaspora. In this space for forty years, the Jewish community was transformed from its Ashkenazi origins to one embracing Sephardi and Mizrachi contingents. The Bathurst corridor may be considered as an extended shtetl of Jewish commerce, prayer, education, burial, community institutions and culture, which cater to the socio-economic and religious spectra of Canadian Jewish life. The corridor encompasses estates, suburban homes, townhouses, apartments, and condominiums.

CONCLUSION

Adaptation has been multifaceted. For Jews born or raised in Canada before World War II, the process changed their identity, from immigrants to Canadians, a course that was kick started by their participation in the war effort, and accelerated via the decline of overt antisemitism, freeing them to participate in the postwar economic boom. The baby boomer generation then profited from these developments, professionally and economically, providing the opportunity for Jews to contribute in disproportionate numbers to Canadian business, academics, and culture. This was one facet of adaptation. The second facet was adaptation by immigrants, beginning with Holocaust survivors, who, in the main, made the transition in everyday life, but carried the trauma of their survival. Some channelled their energy into promoting memory via education and in combating new forms of antisemitism, specifically Holocaust denial. Subsequent immigrants from the Diaspora faced different challenges, dealing with acculturation and the tension between living in Canada and maintaining the connection with their homelands. In so doing, the face of Canadian Jewry has become diverse, not only in terms of the contributions of immigrants, but with respect to the span of socio-economic levels, religious observance, home languages, and approaches to combating antisemitism.

In the new millennium, the repercussions of these patterns augured changes within communal politics, religious expression, education, lifestyles, and responses to national and global challenges, which further stimulated diversity.

PART D

CANADA'S JEWS SINCE 2000

CHAPTER TWELVE

The Ascent of Diversity in the New Millennium

The history of the Jews of Canada is based on three interdependent and progressive themes: settlement, adaptation, and diversity. Since the turn of the century there has been little Jewish immigration into Canada in contrast to the last third of the previous century, when the Jewish Diaspora arrived on Canadian soil. As a result, immigrant adaptation has become less of a prerogative. Consequently the overriding feature of the first two decades of the new millennium has been increasing diversity. In responding to the rapid changes of the digital age that both inspire and menace the Jewish world, Canadian Jews are exploring new approaches and avenues in "being" and "living" as Jews.

The chapter opens with the demise of the CJC and proceeds to a selection of findings from the most detailed survey of an ethnic community in Canada, followed by the impact of antisemitism, voting patterns, and the wide diversity found in family structure, faith, education, and minorities. It continues with a profile of three outstanding Canadians, prominent figures in the arts and scholarship, and concludes with considerations of whether Canada has historically been an ideal home for Jews.

OUT WITH A WHIMPER: THE DEMISE OF THE CANADIAN JEWISH CONGRESS[1]

On August 30, 2011 the national press reported that the CJC had breathed its last gasp. The *National Post,* in an article titled "The Last Act of Congress" remarked "that after two years of controversy and debate the newest Jewish advocacy group (the Centre for Israel and Jewish Affairs), quietly launched that summer, consolidated the CJC (and four other national organizations) into one umbrella organization."[2] The coup de grace was the defunding of these organizations, which historically had operated from allocations by local federations that were raised from charitable contributions via the United Israel Appeal. This decision, which immediately terminated the CJC, received a surprisingly mute response from Canadian Jews. Aside from a few outcries in the national media and in *The Canadian Jewish News*, there was little reaction, nay even a realization by many that the CJC had been terminated.

The decision, in retrospect, was not surprising. It was a consequence of two developments. The first was the long-standing unease about the CJC's mandate and the high public profile of its staff and lay leaders.

Since the 1930s there had been a tacit understanding that the federations would provide services (aid, housing, health, education) and that the CJC would advocate on issues of discrimination and social justice, effectively becoming the voice of the Canadian Jews. Nevertheless, the line between the two remained blurred in the public eye. The CJC, which had a wide network of lay members across the country, was well known, not only by Canadian Jews but also by the World Jewish Congress and politicians from all three levels, as a model for other ethno-cultural and religious groups in Canada. The presidents of the CJC were considered the spokesmen (the first female president was elected in 1988) of the community. The federations had less of a public exposure, which discomfited its volunteers and donors.

The second development was a state of mind held by a coterie of the community's largest donors at the turn of the millennium based on four considerations. First, there was an overlap between the CJC and the Canada Israel Committee, established in the late 1960s,[3] as both advocated on behalf of Israel to federal bodies. Second, antisemitism in Canada was rising, and it was largely being fomented by clusters[4] from those critical of Israeli policies about the treatment of Palestinians and militants who called for the outright erasure of a national homeland for the Jews. This was fuel for the emergence anti-Israel activity on university campuses especially with the advent of Israel Anti-Apartheid Week.

Third, the CJC was historically a liberal organization with ties to the Liberal Party, which, during the Chrétien/Martin/Ignatieff era, appeared to be wavering in its unquestioned support of Israeli policy regarding relations with the Palestinians and its Arab neighbours. Fourth, there was unease that the CJC had become sidetracked from Jewish advocacy by promoting fairer treatment of Indigenous peoples, Roma refugees, and the LGBTQ+ community.

Pressure was applied by the coterie of major donors to the federations to reduce the CJC's scope by reducing its funding, leading to the creation of a new communal organization – the Canadian Centre for Israel and Jewish Advocacy (CIJA) – in 2004 to oversee the activities of the national organizations[5] funded by the community, and the creation of three new organizations, thereby reducing the CJC's autonomy. This occurred without fanfare and without consultation from the CJC. Under this arrangement, the CJC's budget, which had been reduced over the previous fifteen years, was further slashed, eroding staff and new initiatives. Not surprisingly, this top-heavy arrangement was not sustainable. By 2010 a committee constituted of major donors determined that the component organizations be folded into one uniform body that would advocate on social issues to provincial governments and for Israel at the federal level. This centralization defunded the CJC, its independent Quebec Region, and the Canada Israel Committee. This decision was also made behind closed doors, without consultation with the affected organizations. But the committee was at an impasse regarding the name of the new body. After failing to come up with an inclusive title, ("Canadian Jewish Congress" was considered, but was denied by the CJC, which had patented the name), the committee took the initials of its predecessor and changed the wording to the Centre for Israel and Jewish Affairs. Mysteriously, it omitted "Canadian" from the title.

The sum of these concerns pointed to one indisputable reality – that the CJC, which had historically been dubbed "the parliament of Canadian Jews," could no longer make that claim in the millennium. In a world rocked by the events of 9/11, linked instantaneously with a Jewish community that had assumed a secure position in mainstream society, where its diversity was rapidly transcending historical modes of worship, education, and the definition of family, the old advocacy model needed a reboot. In fact, in the new millennium, no single national organization, especially one that did not include a broad representation of lay members, could effectively speak for an increasingly diverse ethno-cultural community.

A SNAPSHOT OF CANADA'S JEWS IN 2018

In March 2019 the Environics Institute for Survey Research released the *2018 Survey of Jews in Canada*, conducted under the auspices of Keith Neuman of the institute, with research by sociologists Robert Brym of the University of Toronto and Rhonda Lenton, president and vice chancellor of York University. Brym and Lenton interviewed 2,335 individuals by phone in Toronto, Montreal, Winnipeg, and Vancouver; these individuals were selected from cohorts based on age and gender and comprised approximately 0.6 per cent of Canadian Jews. The surveys included those aged eighteen to forty-four in Montreal and immigrants from the former Soviet Union. The following summarizes the findings of seven categories of the survey.

1. Population

Of the Jewish population 20.6 per cent are foreign born, mostly in Israel and the former Soviet Union. Most of the increase in population has been the result of natural growth because immigration in the new century has declined. Overall Jews constitute about 1.2 per cent of Canadians and about 3 per cent of world Jewry. Canada has the fourth largest Jewish population in the world, after Israel, the United States, and France.

Overall, 48 per cent live in Toronto, 24 per cent in Montreal, and 16 per cent in Vancouver, Winnipeg, and Calgary combined. The highest rate of growth since 2001 has been in Vancouver, while Montreal and Winnipeg have experienced a small decline. Another 6 per cent live in the following cities: Edmonton, Hamilton, Victoria, London, Halifax, and Kitchener-Waterloo. Of these, the greatest growth has been in Victoria, which has doubled its population since 2001, with slight declines in Halifax, London, Windsor, and Hamilton.

The smaller cities that had between five hundred and one thousand Jews at mid-century[6] are not included in the study, but suffice to say, their numbers have dropped. Within the major urban areas, the bulk of the growth has been in the outer suburbs and, to a lesser degree, a return to cities' cores. Toronto's Jews, for example, have settled beyond the boundaries of the Greater Toronto Area to satellite cities such as Barrie, Oshawa, and Burlington.

2. Identity

Historically being Jewish meant practicing Judaism. With the rapid economic and technological developments of the last two centuries, identity has also been tied to ethnicity. The survey reveals that about one half of Canadian Jews identify by religion, or culture, or ancestry/descent, and the other half by a combination of those, particularly among Jews affiliated with Reform Judaism and by those not attached denominationally. Two-thirds respond that being Jewish is particularly important, but only one-third place the highest importance on connection to faith, followed by leading a moral or ethical life, remembering the Holocaust, and celebrating Jewish holidays. Four in ten identify justice and equality, Israel, intellectual curiosity, and community inclusiveness as complementary indicators. Although a majority believes in God or a universal spirit, only 20 per cent cite Jewish law, attending synagogue services, and cultural activities.

3. Life and Practice

Of those surveyed 60 per cent belong to a mainstream religious denomination and/or Jewish movements. Of the former the Conservative denomination is the largest, followed by Orthodox/Modern Orthodox, and Reform. Proportionally the largest growth has been in Orthodox and alternative movements. Thirty per cent are either not affiliated or are "just Jewish." Membership does not necessarily translate to attendance or practice. For many attendance is more focused on life cycle events: births, funerals, weddings, and bar/bat mitzvahs. More prevalent, 80 per cent, are those who donate to Jewish organizations, institutions, and causes, including those who are unaffiliated and/or under-waged. Being Jewish also entails social connections. A majority report that they have few non-Jewish friends.

4. Upbringing and Intermarriage

Jewish education is central to Jewish continuity and Jewish cohesion. Most Jewish children participate in some form of Jewish education. Forty-three per cent attend a Jewish day school and have done so for an average of nine years. Others attend a Hebrew school or Sunday school, 58 per cent go to overnight camps, and many belong to Jewish youth organizations, from Orthodox to non-religious Zionist groups. Fully 75 per cent know the Hebrew alphabet, 50 per cent read Hebrew, and 40 per cent have some conversational skill. Nine in ten males and four in ten females have had a bar/bat mitzvah. This rite of passage has become the *sine qua non*.

Intermarriage is regarded as the greatest threat to continuity, outweighing antisemitism and low fertility. This study reports that 23 per cent of Jews interviewed are intermarried. Clearly intermarriage is correlated to religious practice (negligible among Orthodox and Conservative Jews) for just over half of those who are not affiliated. But the cause for unease is that one-third of the youngest cohort, eighteen to twenty-nine, is intermarried.

5. Discrimination

Four in ten respondents reported having experienced discrimination in the past five years due to religion, ethnicity/culture, gender, and language. The range is broad, from hate crimes to being snubbed in social settings. Indigenous peoples, Muslims, and Black people are more frequent targets but are less reported. Younger Jews are less likely than older ones to report discrimination but more likely to experience it. To avoid discrimination, one third report that they downplay their Jewishness, notably in the workplace, when travelling, and when socializing with non-Jews. Thirty per cent of Montreal and of Toronto Jews feel that Jews are objects of discrimination, compared to 23 per cent of Winnipeggers and 22 per cent of Vancouverites. In 2017, 45 per cent of Quebecers held favourable opinions of Judaism relative to 36 per cent in 2009, and 59 per cent in the rest of Canada.

6. Connection to Israel

The connection to Israel among Canadian Jews is strong, arguably the strongest in the Diaspora. Most have an emotional attachment, 80 per cent have visited Israel at least once, and, on average, have done so five times. while 16 per cent have lived there for six months or more. The connection is widespread, most significant among adherents to Traditional Orthodoxy and Modern Orthodoxy, those under the age of forty-five, and those with a post-graduate degree.

Nevertheless, there is disparity in opinion regarding Israel's commitment to a viable peace settlement, the building of settlements on the West Bank, and on security. Thirty-one per cent are critical, notably among those aged eighteen to twenty-nine (49 per cent). The highest support comes from the Orthodox and those over the age of seventy-five. There is a clear divide between those who believe that Israel "was given by God to the Jews" and those who do not, revealing the rift between Orthodox and some Conservative followers, and the remainder of the community. Regarding Canada's relations with Israel, 45 per cent determined that it was "about right," 36 per cent that it was "not enough," and 6 per cent that it was "too supportive."

7. Connections to the Local Jewish Community

The interconnectedness of the community is based, primarily on denominational affiliation, and, to friendships, organizations, networks, young families with young children, interests and culture and recreation. Less associated are Jews from the former Soviet Union, those who primarily identify by ancestry/descent, and those living in Vancouver. The primary factors for not connecting are lack of interest priorities, and not identifying as Jewish. Among the recent Jews from the former Soviet Union, Sephardim, and Israelis, are more likely to connect to their fellow immigrants than the wider community.

ANTISEMITISM

In the new millennium there appears to be a relatively positive assessment as to how Canadians regard Jews. Irving Abella opined that "life [has] never been better than at the turn of the century. Today's Canada is far different – generous, open, decent, humane."[7] In 2018 a survey of Toronto Jews revealed that, while 61 per cent felt that antisemitism had increased in the previous decade, in response to "how do you feel," they unanimously responded "somewhat" or "very" safe.[8]

Nevertheless, the common perception is that antisemitism is growing quickly in Canada as found in surveys since 2000, including the one conducted by Environics. This sentiment was one factor for the creation of CIJA. Since the 1980s, B'nai Brith Canada, the oldest Jewish communal organization in Canada, has been conducting a survey culled from police records of antisemitic incidents, including incidents of hate speech and attacks and the desecration of Jewish public places, which it publicizes and responds to. The Canadian Friends of Simon Wiesenthal, named after the celebrated Nazi hunter, provide Holocaust education to school boards as an antidote to antisemitism. Smaller organizations from the political mainstream to the right-wing margin also shine a light on the scourge.

These groups point to several developments to bolster their case that antisemitism is on the rise. They include two categories: private and public. The former includes the traditional forms – vandalism, assaults, threats, and discrimination. The public one is the demonization of Israel, or more precisely, Zionism, in that, by creating a state for Jews, an indigenous people (the Palestinians) were colonized. This sentiment glides over the following facts – that Jews also had lived on these lands for millennia albeit in small numbers, that the region had never been autonomous as it was ruled by a succession of empires, and that the relationship between Jewish settlers and Arab residents was until 1948 not monochromatically hostile. Anti-Zionism has been appropriated by the extreme left in North America and Europe, and by much of the non-Western world. Since 2000 it has manifested itself on some Canadian campuses, albeit in very small numbers, by the actions and rhetoric of some Muslim organizations including the Canadian Islamic Congress, which contends that a "cabal" runs the Canadian government; the Canadian Arab Federation whose government funding was stopped over concerns that it supported terrorists and antisemitic organizations; and *Al Quds Day*, an annual march on the last day of Ramadan held in Toronto that demonizes Jews. The opposition has congealed in the Boycott/Disinvestment/Sanction movement, which seeks to isolate Israel economically, declaring it to be an *apartheid* state. Its cause has been taken up by some union locals, student unions, and academics. Much energy is spent by Jewish organizations and allies on countering these public threats, yet most of the antisemitic incidents are by private individuals, of whom many are beholden to traditional neo-Nazi white supremacists who disseminate their vile via social media.

One response to the growth of antisemitism has been public education about the Holocaust in centres and museums, survivor speakers, Yom Hashoah commemorations, and the adoption of curricula by school boards. The most well-known program is Toronto's Holocaust Education Week. Yet Naomi Azrieli, the founder of the same named organization that freely publishes and distributes survivor autobiographies, stated that the results of a 2018 survey revealed "a troubling lack of knowledge,"[9] because almost half of the respondents could not name a camp or ghetto. This is particularly disturbing given the impressive initiatives listed above, and the fact that prime ministers Chrétien, Harper, and Justin Trudeau have visited Auschwitz with survivors. A 2009 Parliamentary Coalition to Combat Antisemitism, chaired by Liberal Irwin Cotler and Conservative Jason Kenney, reported two years later that Canadian universities were hotbeds for activists with a major focus on anti-Zionism, a new kind of antisemitism. In 2019, the government announced that it was adopting the International Holocaust Remembrance Alliance (IHRA)'s definition of antisemitism.[10] The IHRA was founded in 1998, and Canada became a signatory in 2009.

The contradictory assessment of the level of antisemitism c. 2000 that opens this section is grounded in historical perspective. The opinions stated by Weinfeld et al. were based on the decline in the last decades of the twentieth century of tropes of historical discrimination as Jews ascended into the mainstream of Canadian society. It is the new antisemitism, an amalgam of the traditional hatred of Jews and rabid anti-Zionism, that propels disquiet in the new millennium. This manifestation, while not having the same quotidian impact it did historically, reinforces the apprehension that Israel faces an existential threat, an anxiety that is the product of the wars in 1967 and 1973, and coincides with the appropriation of the memory of the Holocaust as a pillar of ethnic identity. Further, the episodic desecration of Jewish institutions and of hate crimes by neo-Nazis reinforce the disquiet.

The range of responses to the Israel/Palestine imbroglio is reflective of the community's diversity. The major communal organizations, CIJA and B'nai Brith, are supportive of the Israeli government's policies without reservation, as are the host of smaller groups, notably the Canadian Friends of Simon Weisenthal. Conversely, a tiny minority, such as the Independent Jewish Voices condemn Zionism outright, and a larger cohort support Israeli organizations that work to create a more inclusive and harmonious society in Israel, such as Canadian Friends for Peace Now, J Space, and the New Israel Fund. The perception of rising antisemitism has become the most decisive factor in the Jewish vote in federal elections since 2000.

VOTING PATTERNS

Canada's Jews have been supporters of the Liberal Party since 1896. That stand was maintained for most of the next century and bolstered with the advent of multiculturalism. But cracks in Liberal support began to show in the last years of the Pierre Trudeau era. During the 1982 Israeli invasion of Lebanon he stated that "the death and destruction visited on innocent Lebanese civilians are unacceptable."[11] The *Toronto Star* was particularly critical of Israel's actions and highlighted an incident where Israeli forces stood aside as Lebanese Christians massacred Palestinian refugees, arousing consternation by many Jewish readers of the newspaper who had historically viewed the paper in a positive light. Trudeau's successors, Jean Chrétien and Paul Martin, supported Israel during the increasing anti-Israel invective at the UN, but were silent about the criticism of Israeli incursions into Lebanon and Gaza. In a public meeting that the author attended in Toronto in 2000 that lambasted Canada's support of a Security Council resolution that condemned Israel's "excessive force against Palestinians" during the Second Intifada, Keith Landy, then president of the CJC mockingly asked, "what were they thinking?"

Meanwhile, the Progressive Conservative Party, which had been in the doldrums with the departure of their prairie wing that had broken off to form the Reform Party, was revived with the re-merger to create the Conservative Party in 2003 prompting some long-time influential Jewish supporters of the Liberals to switch their allegiance, a key factor in the creation of CIJA the following year. Polls showing that an increasing number of Canadians were supportive of sanctions against Israel coupled with a comment by Michael Ignatieff, who stated in his 2006 campaign for the leadership of the Liberal Party, that the Israeli bombing in Lebanon was a war crime, only served to heighten disenchantment with the Liberals. The Conservatives, under Stephen Harper, turned the tide with minority governments in 2006 and 2008. On the surface in the 2008 election, it appeared that the Liberals remained the party of favour, because it had won eleven of the thirteen ridings with the largest Jewish cohort. Yet, its popular vote had dropped by 4 per cent.

The die was cast. The Conservatives swept the 2011 contest taking seven ridings that had never elected a Conservative. Exit polls indicated that 52 per cent of Jews supported the Conservatives. An equilibrium returned in 2015 as the Liberals took back these ridings under Justin Trudeau and Jewish support for the Conservatives dropped to 44 per cent. Eight Liberals in the 2015 election were Jewish, the highest number in Canadian history. Meanwhile, Konrad Yakabuski in the *Globe and Mail* in May 2018 wrote that "overall, Canada's voting record at the UN under the Trudeau government thus far is among the most pro-Israel in the world and is markedly different than Canada's voting record under Chrétien and Martin."[12] In the 2019 election, in which the Liberals squeaked out a minority, they won all but one of the fourteen ridings in which Jews accounted for at least 5 per cent of the populace. Nevertheless, two Jewish Liberal MPs were defeated.

THE YIDDISH REVIVAL

By 1981 Yiddish had almost disappeared as a mother tongue. Sociologist Leo Davids found that only 10.5 per cent of children under fourteen were exposed to it, in contrast to 55.2 per cent of those over the age of sixty-five. By 2000 the relative survival of Yiddish was largely due to following: the growing Traditional Orthodox denominations, where many speak colloquial Yiddish (91 per cent in Montreal claim to be fluent) but are ignorant of Yiddish secular culture; by some Holocaust survivors, especially in Montreal; by those who grew up with Yiddish in the home; by aging writers; and by a remnant of the mid-century secular left-wing anti-Zionists. But twenty years later, there were fewer survivors and, with the passing of Yehuda Elberg, Sara Rosenfeld, Simcha Simchovitch, and Chava Rosenfarb, there are almost no traditional secular Yiddish writers. There are no Yiddish periodicals, and the bulk of Canadian Yiddish literature lies in libraries. Further, the decline of Yiddish in secular Jewish schools, (aside from Montreal's Jewish People's School and the Peretz School, and Toronto's Bialik School), exacerbate the situation. The secular left's concerns, according to scholar Ester Reiter, have prioritized social justice, labour rights, and feminism over the maintenance of Yiddish.

Given this scenario, what are the reasons behind the revival of Yiddish? First is the growth of academic Yiddish at a few Canadian universities. Most notable are the University of Ottawa, where historians Rebecca Margolis,[13] Pierre Anctil, and poet Seymour Mayne hold sway; the University of Toronto where its current director of the Centre of Jewish Studies, Anna Sternshis, oversees both the undergraduate and graduate programs; York University, which provides courses in elementary and intermediate Yiddish; and McGill University, which offers a program including advanced study. While many students are Jewish, the appeal is more widespread, utilized, for example, as an entry to the study of Ashkenazi history and culture and as an accessory to German. This development has spawned academic study by the academics above and their students. One example of this interest was the 2004 conference, "New Readings of Yiddish Montreal." Since then books in Yiddish by Jewish immigrants to Canada during the Great Migration have been translated to English by Shirley Kumov, Vivian Felsen, Marcia Usiskin Basman, and Pierre Anctil who, with Chantal Ringuet, have translated works into French.

A second factor in the revival of Yiddish is the Montreal Yiddish Theatre, founded by the indefatigable Dora Wasserman (1919–2003). Born and raised in the Soviet Union, a graduate from the acclaimed Jewish Theatre of Moscow, she arrived in Montreal in 1950, conducted singing and recital workshops at the Jewish Public Library. She founded the Montreal Yiddish Theatre in 1958. It presented musical comedies, adaptations of novels by Isaac Bashevis Singer, and of Quebec dramatist

Michel Tremblay's *Les Belles-soeurs*, attracting both French and English native speakers. The home of the Montreal Yiddish Theatre has been the Saidye Bronfman Theatre, renamed the Segal Centre for the Performing Arts, while the Montreal Yiddish Theatre is now called the Dora Wasserman Theatre.

The third consideration is an upsurge of Yiddish clubs and reading circles, which hold discussions, lectures, and have choirs. They may include presentations by scholars and writers. Of note is Michael Wex, a prolific author who has incorporated Yiddishkeit into some twenty works, including *Born to Kvetch* (complain) in 2005, and Gary Barwin's rollicking novel, *Yiddish for Pirates* (2016).

The third characteristic of the revival is in popular culture, primarily the revival of Klezmer music in the last forty years. Drawing on traditional religious musical liturgy with influence of other folk idioms, such as Romany music, it was a source for vaudeville, Broadway, and jazz that erupted at the turn of the twentieth century in the United States. Klezmer's rediscovery was welcomed by a new generation, of Jews and non-Jews, who would have had little if any connection to the Yiddish language. Its popularity has spread worldwide, from Argentina to Germany and in between. In Canada, the annual festival, *Ashkenaz*, of Yiddish-inspired music, dance, and theatre in Toronto, and Klezcamp in the Laurentians, which fosters Jewish culture and history and holds creative programs for all ages, are in the forefront of preserving and advancing Yiddish culture. The leading Canadian Klezmer groups include Toronto's Flying Bulgar Klezmer Band and Montreal's Beyond the Pale.

Recently the online program *Yidlife Crisis*, a Yiddish dialogue between thirty-somethings Chaimie (pronounced "Hymie") and Leizer in Montreal, is attaining a wide following. The performers, Jamie Elman (Chaimie) and Eli Batalion (Leizer), skewer cultural norms, whether Jewish, Anglo, or French, in hilarious vignettes dealing with food, religion, politics, and culture. Its tropes are recognizable to those who grew up hearing Yiddish from their grandparents and present comic insight for those with little exposure to Jewish life.

The Yiddish revival is tinged with nostalgia for the destroyed Jewish world of eastern Europe, mixed with postmodern global culture, which celebrates traditional norms that are updated for current tastes. It brings together those of all ages and cultures. Although a small number of Canadians have become fluent, in broader terms it is an exposure to the roots of Jewish immigrant life. The spectrum of the revival encompasses Traditional Orthodox Jews to those whose Yiddishkeit is largely connected to cultural norms, revealing another instance of the growing diversity of the Canadian Jewish community.

FAITH

Until fifty years ago there were three options in choosing a synagogue membership: Orthodox, Conservative, and Reform. In all cases, the rabbis and cantors were men, and aside from the Reform movement, women were not allowed on the dais (*bima* in Hebrew), meaning that they could not touch or read from the Torah. Since then, the options have multiplied. In the new millennium, there has been an acceleration of three trends: a divide between progressive and traditional factions in the three major denominations, a decline in membership in the Conservative movement, and the growth of alternative avenues of practice.

Orthodox

For two millennia, as there was no deviation in ritual, text, or observance in the practice of Judaism, there was no need for labels. It was only with the rise of the Reform movement in Germany in the early nineteenth century that the term Orthodox arose. Gradually the challenges of the secular world, such as modernism, urbanism, and political engagement, divided the Orthodox between those who shunned these advances (the Traditionalists) and those who observed the tenets of belief while participating in secular society (the Modernists). The separation reveals a spectrum, from the most insular to the most inclusive adherents.

Traditional Orthodoxy has its roots in eastern Europe in the late eighteenth century, where rabbis assumed prominent positions in leading their followers during the revival of autocratic nationalism and fervent antisemitism. Their followers created centres of learning, Yeshivas, some of which were named for the towns in which they originated. After the Holocaust, New York became their mecca, with branches growing out into the Jewish world, including Montreal, which emerged as the second largest in North America.

Sociologist William Shaffir has devoted his research to the Tash community (named after a town in Hungary), which divorced itself from the wider traditional community in a rural setting near Montreal because of a "deteriorating moral climate."[14] The largest denomination is the Lubavitch, which reaches out to "lapsed Jews." Traditional Orthodoxy is by far the fastest growing segment of world Jewry largely due to the high birth rate of its adherents and its success in attracting young adults who are termed "returnees." While no current figure is available for Canada, the reality is that it is increasingly difficult to isolate oneself from the outside world due to the ubiquity of social media. Despite the return to traditional roots by a significant minority, adherents to Modern Orthodox still outnumber their more traditional counterparts.

Conservative

Conservative Judaism arose in the United States in the mid- to late nineteenth century as a middle road between Orthodoxy and Reform. The movement posited that belief emanated from the assent of its followers but that Jewish law (*Halakha*) is subject to historical development. The movement is decidedly American, founded in New York, the site of the JTS (Jewish Theological Seminary), from which, in 1902, Rabbi Herman Abramowitz came to Montreal's Shaar Hashomayim, the second oldest synagogue in Canada, which had moderated its Orthodox roots. By 1936, there were nine Conservative congregations in Canada led by rabbis trained at the JTS. While the Reform movement at the time rejected Zionism, the Conservative movement embraced it. In the immediate post-World War II period, rapid expansion in the suburbs corresponded with socio-economic and geographic mobility. By 1974 there were forty-nine congregations in Canada, the largest of which housed day schools and conducted summer camps, and almost half of affiliated Canadian Jews were members of the movement. Since then, the membership has dropped to 43 per cent in the 1990s, and subsequently to 37 per cent in 2017, resulting in the closure of several large congregations.

This fall in membership is the result of three developments. First was the Conservative movement's slow response to counting women in the *minyan* (the quorum of ten adults required for a service) and its rituals. Second 82 per cent of rabbis and cantors in Canada determined that the JTS had become too progressive, such that Shaar Hashomayim, for example, reverted to a mixed Orthodox-Conservative position. Other followers were attracted to either the traditional congregations or to the teachings Rabbi Mordechai Kaplan, who proclaimed that the "Jewish civilization" was continually evolving, which in turn created the Reconstructionist movement that entered Canada with the formation of Congregation *Dorshei Emet* ("Paths of Truth") in Montreal in 1967, followed by congregations in Toronto, Ottawa, Winnipeg, and Vancouver. Its congregants account for 2 per cent of Canada's Jews.

Reform

Reform in Canada has not had the same cache as in the United States. As with the other denominations, there has been division between liberal and traditional wings. The latter stems from the original attachment to the ideals of the Anglo elite vs the domination by powerful American rabbis, chief among them Maurice Eisendrath of Holy Blossom, who did not endorse Zionism, did not speak Yiddish, and infused the litany with English rather than Hebrew, all of which alienated most immigrants. In the postwar period the Reform movement eventually became inclusive of gender, and in recent times of sexual orientation. In its twenty-seven congregations, almost exclusively in the largest cities, the tension between the liberal and conservative wings still resonates over issues such as conducting interfaith marriages and ritual circumcisions for boys whose mothers are not Jewish.

Religious Alternatives

The Environics Study of 2018 reveals that about one-third of Canada's Jews do not subscribe to the three main movements. Of these the largest cohort, 28 per cent signify themselves as "just Jewish." This is an ephemeral description. It may include those who occasionally go to a synagogue, those who pray with an unaffiliated group, those who consider themselves atheists or agnostics, those who may follow holiday rituals, those whose practice of Judaism skews to alternatives reflective of post-millennial social developments, and those who have rejected all connection with the Judaic faith. Weinfeld, citing studies in Montreal and Toronto from 2005, indicates that approximately 80 per cent of this cohort observes Passover seders, half light Hanukkah candles, and 20 per cent fast on Yom Kippur. Alternative choices span the spectrum from independent groups within the three denominations to those with a loose affiliation to synagogues, secular groups that stress issues such as environmentalism, humanism, and non-theological practices, to *chavurot* (fellowships in Hebrew) that meet in members' homes but may also belong to the same mainstream or to different congregations. Some, such as the secular humanist movement, have Sunday schools, and may have a "spiritual leader," called a rabbi. Others, like the Toronto congregations, the Song Shul, led by a cantor but without a rabbi, *Shir Libenu* (song of our hearts), and Congregation *Habonim* (the builders), emphasize music and welcome congregants from all Jewish denominations. The one defining aspect of the alternative adoptions is that they are communal.

Women

A significant development in Judaism since World War II is the recognition and inclusion of women in prayer, and by extension, in lay and rabbinical leadership. Aside from the Orthodox and traditional Conservative congregations, women have assumed an almost equal place in the other branches. Girls reaching the age of twelve started to have bat mitzvahs in the 1970s. In the Reform, Reconstruction, and alternative denominations there are no gender restrictions. The largest break was the admission of women to rabbinical academies, all of which are situated in the United States. This initially occurred with the Hebrew Union College of the Reform movement. One of its graduates is Elyse Goldstein, born in the United States, and ordained in 1983. She broke the pink ceiling as an assistant rabbi at Holy Blossom Temple and then as rabbi in an American congregation. Returning to Toronto she founded the Kolel Centre for Adult Learning, and then City Shul, an alternative to mainstream Reform congregations. A prolific writer, Rabbi Goldstein has written *A Women's Torah Commentary* with contributions from fifty-four female rabbis. She was one of seven women who were the subject of a 1988 documentary, *Half the Kingdom*, by Torontonian Francine Zukerman, who attempted to pray at the Western Wall in Jerusalem, which historically has been male preserve, and was denied. Others included Norma Baumel Joseph, a major force in the women's movement within Orthodoxy, and Michele Landsberg, a Toronto-based columnist, author, and a central figure in the promotion of human rights in Canada, who self-identifies as a secular Jew.

Women now lead congregations and serve as lay presidents. They include: Yael Splansky assistant and since 2013, senior rabbi at Holy Blossom; Rabbi Tina Grimberg, who was born and raised in Ukraine, and since 2002 has been at the Reconstructionist Congregation *Darchei Noam* (Gates of Pleasantness) in Toronto; Rachel Kohl Finegold has been *Maharat* (female leader) since 2013 at Shaar Hashomayim, in Montreal; Michal Shekel is spiritual leader of *Har Tikvah* (Mount Hope) Congregation in Brampton, Ontario, and as of 2019, serves as the executive director of the Board of Rabbis; Lisa Gruschcow, at Temple Emanu-El Beth Shalom in Montreal, is an openly gay rabbi of a large synagogue as was Deborah Brin, the rabbi at Toronto's Congregation Darchei Noam in the 1980s. Esther Ghan Firestone (1925–2015) was Canada's first female cantor. A professionally trained coloratura soprano, she performed on CBC radio, and made her debut in the mid-1950s at Temple Beth El, perhaps the first alternative synagogue in Toronto. For the last thirty years of her life, she was cantor and then cantor emeritus at Congregation *Habonim*, a liberal alternative synagogue. Firestone opened the door for female cantors across the country.

Interfaith

Approximately one-quarter of Jewish families are of two different faiths. A study undertaken in 2012 by sociologist Randal Schnoor for the Toronto Jewish Federation, "Services and Resources for Interfaith families," found that 32 per cent identified as Jewish, 50 per cent had no religious affiliation, and 17 per cent identified with another faith. In cases when the mother was Jewish, 44 per cent of the families identified as Jewish and 22 per cent with another faith. Scholar Theodore Sasson in 2013 argued that those between the ages of eighteen and twenty-nine were more likely to identify as Jewish and in greater numbers than had their predecessors. Schnoor outlines the two schools of thought on reducing intermarriage. The first is an internal approach – education, Jewish friendship networks, and a proactive attitude toward conversion.

The outreach alternative is that as intermarriage is a reality, non-Jewish partners should be encouraged to integrate into the Jewish community via direct outreach and inclusion. Schnoor concludes that interfaith families are underserved. As new family structures are commonplace, access to Jewish organizations is needed for these families.

Interfaith couples cannot be married in Orthodox, Conservative, or Reform congregations. In 2017 Congregation Dorshei Emet began conducting interfaith weddings, on the conditions that the couple raises a Jewish family and that the non-Jewish partner is not a practitioner of another religion. These couples can join as full members of the congregation. Reform Rabbi Micah Streiffer of Thornhill's Temple *Kol Ami* (the voice of my people) in 2019 stated that "intermarried families are also Jewish families…. (it's) time to recognize and appreciate their significant contributions to our community."[15]

FAMILY

The traditional Jewish family – father and mother, both Jewish, with or without children, grandchildren, grandparents, etc. – had been an underpinning of Jewish continuity for millennia. In the new millennium the loosening of historic traditions, which had acted as unifying factors but also as constraints, has created a plethora of alternatives for Canadian Jewish families, due to the following developments: the acceleration of mixed marriages (by religion, sexuality, and ethnicity); divorces and separations; the decline in fertility and of multi-generational units; and the dramatic growth of the elderly portion of the population. "Being Jewish" is complicated by the range of options in faith, education, and communal life. It also demands an increasing cost in the lifestyle of middle-class families, most notably in Toronto, because of housing and Jewish education.

THE ELDERLY

In 2011, 16.9 per cent of Canadian Jews were over sixty-five compared to 13.8 per cent of the general population, from a high of 20.4 per cent in Montreal to 13.8 per cent in Vancouver. Moreover, 48 per cent of seniors were seventy-five or older, and it was more pronounced among women, of whom 40 per cent lived alone compared to 18 per cent of men. By 2020 these numbers had increased. When a spouse dies, few seniors move in with their children, as the multi-generational home became a relic of immigrant life. They are more likely to live in retirement communities, and those unable to do so because of their health and the high cost, to public senior citizens' homes that are provincially subsidized dependent on income. Of these, the Baycrest Centre in Toronto is the oldest such institution, having been founded in 1913. For those with means, they may choose to retire to the warm climes of Florida and Arizona.

BEING JEWISH IN THE NEW MILLENNIUM

It is increasingly difficult to encapsulate what it means to be Jewish. In the new millennium identities have deviated from historical norms, shaped, in the words of sociologists Alex Pomson and Randal Schnoor, by the sovereign self rather than by faith and ethnicity. This has created new approaches to Jewish education and family life. Pomson and Schnoor undertook a three-year study of the Downtown Jewish Day School in Toronto, an elementary school housed in the Miles Nadal Jewish Community Centre. Founded in 2000 as an alternative to the city's twenty or so other Jewish schools, which served 11,500 students, it was established with matching funds from a private foundation. It was differentiated in that it appealed to non-traditional families, of whom half were synagogue members compared to 85 per cent of other day school parents, reflecting a downtown state of mind, the zeitgeist of a community that had moved back from the suburbs or were English-speaking immigrants who had settled in the city centre. Further, parents were partners with the administration in shaping policy and as volunteers. The pluralistic student body reflected the diverse downtown Jewish community – intermarrieds, converts, common-law and same-sex couples, singles. For many who had received little or no Jewish education, the families were "living Judaism through their children." The authors contend that "ethnic identity is no longer fixed, but a social contract negotiated and renegotiated by the individual...."[16]

The April 10, 2018 issue of the *Canadian Jewish News* profiled the "cost of being Jewish in Canada."[17] The findings include:

i) average price to join a synagogue: $1,517 in Halifax, $1,006 in Toronto, $767 in Montreal, and $975 in Vancouver
ii) one week in an out-of-town summer camp: $1,152 in Ontario, $1,017 in Nova Scotia, $1,025 in Quebec
iii) the price of a home in a Jewish neighbourhood compared to non-Jewish neighbourhoods: Toronto $1.2 million vs. $0.75 million; Montreal $300,000 vs. $280,000; Vancouver $2.25 million vs. $1.05 million; Winnipeg $550,000 vs. $275,000
iv) a Jewish funeral: $12,000 in Toronto, $8,000 in Montreal, $6,900 in Ottawa, $15,000 in Winnipeg

Jewish Education

At Confederation, the provinces were given control of education to mollify Quebec's Roman Catholic Church as the price for entry to the union. In Quebec, Jewish schools were classified as "Protestant" and therefore subsidized. In 2019 thirteen day schools were in operation, receiving 60 per cent funding from the province. Bialik High School, the largest in the province, charges $14,000 in tuition.

In Ontario, among denominational schools, only Roman Catholic ones are funded. Consequently, under the Charter of Rights, Jewish parents with the support of the Toronto Federation and CJC launched an action against the Ontario government (Adler v. Ontario AG in 1996), and the judgment was that while there was nothing to prevent public funding of private religious schools, there was no obligation to do so. In the provincial election campaign in 2007, the Conservative leader John Tory made religious-based education funding a key plank, to benefit Evangelical Christian and Muslim voters as well as Jewish ones, but it became a significant factor in his party's defeat and impacted Toronto's Jewish schools, notably the Community Hebrew Academy, which closed its second campus in 2017 due to the drop in enrolment as tuition reached $28,000.

In the Atlantic Provinces there is no funding for religious schools, but British Columbia, Manitoba, and Alberta provide partial funding. Vancouver's King David School charged $19,650 in tuition in 2019.

Manitoba provides half the funds allocated to public schools to Winnipeg's Gray Academy for kindergarten to Grade 12, allowing tuition to be kept at $10,800.00, while the Calgary Jewish Federation, with funding from the province and the local Jewish federation charges $12,650 tuition for the Calgary Jewish Academy. Overall, approximately less than 30 per cent of Toronto's Jewish students attend day schools compared to an estimated 55 per cent in Montreal, as of 2019. This discrepancy is not entirely due to the funding issue but also due to the large cohort of traditional Jews in Montreal.

While "being Jewish" has a cost, synagogues and schools provide an allowance for those who are unable to pay the full cost of the services provided.

Jewish Minorities

Jews are a minority, but among them are visible and barely visible minorities. An insert in the *Canadian Jewish News* in 2019 titled "Being a Jew of Colour: Finding Acceptance and Inclusion," profiles several individuals, including Eliran Penkar, whose family were leaders in the Mumbai Jewish community. Arriving in Canada from Israel, he lived across the country, but it was not until he moved to Toronto at the age of thirteen that he connected with the Indian Jewish community and later in Halifax, when he joined a Jewish fraternity, that he was able to identify as an Indian Jew rather than a Jew who happened to be Indian. Diane Tobin and her late husband adopted Jonah, an African-American child, in 1998. Feeling that he was isolated, they started *Be'chol Lashon* (in every language) that runs camps and helps Jewish schools in creating curricula on Jewish diversity. Tobin maintains that "we certainly benefit from privilege, but our history is not one of being white-privileged people," contesting that white supremacists have targeted Jews because of their "race," yet darker-skinned Jews face barriers that lighter-skinned Jews don't recognize. Tema Smith is the child of a Black father and an Ashkenazic mother. She is fair, has curly hair and looks, in her own words, like a stereotypical Ashkenazi Jew. Her career as a professional in Jewish organizations and congregations has impressed upon her that, had she looked more like her father, she would have had to explain her presence in Jewish spaces. Jobim Novak was born in Guatemala and adopted by a Jewish family in Toronto. When he was scorned because he was not a "real Jew," he was more angry than sad because he had been Jewish his whole life. Moshe Modeira's mother is a north-African Jew and his father an Ethiopian rabbi, who grew up in Europe. He faced anti-Black racism when he came to Toronto at the age of eight. He came to understand this was the product of an absence of contact and experience. He feels that the only way to address racism is to connect and to learn from each other.

Strides have been made in the new millennium regarding the integration of LGBTQ+ Jews into the community. Nevertheless, having a gay child is a challenge for most Jews, even as the stigma, aside from more traditional Jews, is receding, especially among teens, where close to 90 per cent approve of same-sex marriage. As Morton Weinfeld points out, parents want grandchildren, and while this obstacle has been overcome to a degree by adoption and *in vitro* fertilization, the number of gay couples without children exceeds those pairings who are straight. The opprobrium of being gay and Jewish in the 1970s led to the creation of LGBTQ+ organizations that provided safe spaces. The first was *Naches* (from the Yiddish contentment, as in the pleasure of having grandchildren) in Montreal in 1972–3, which grew to *Yachdav* (from the Hebrew for together) in the late 1980s, and recently to *Ga'ava* (from the Hebrew for pride). In Toronto the initial group, *Ha Mishpacha* (the family in Hebrew), had difficulty being recognized in the 1980s. Twenty years later, *Kulanu* (our voice in Hebrew) was integrated into the Jewish federation and had a float in the Toronto Pride Parade with community leaders from the Federation and the CJC and rabbis on board. Congregations from the alternative ones to Reform, Reconstructionist, Conservative, and some Modern Orthodox, welcomed them. The First Narayever Synagogue, a small downtown liberal Orthodox congregation, more than a century old, performs same-sex marriages. This inclusion has not been smooth. As Rabbi Elyse Goldstein relates in "Why I'm Marching in the Pride Parade with Kulanu," is "not because its politically correct.... Because as a Jew I support pride in being who you are ... pride is a Jewish concept ... an awareness of our own dignity and worth ... a delight in who we are and what we do ... to reclaim our self-worth time and again ... because it reminds me that God's image is mysterious and diverse."[18]

Almost hidden from view are poor Jews. A 2011 survey showed that 14.6 per cent were indigent, up 1 per cent from the previous year, and virtually the same as the Canadian average of 14.8 per cent. Among major cities, Montreal was most affected at 20 per cent, and Ottawa least hard hit at 8.9 per cent. The greatest impact was on those on welfare and/or disability, children living with single mothers, Holocaust survivors, and recent immigrants. Four years later, more than 24,000 Toronto Jews, approximately 15 per cent of the total, were facing higher rents, more expensive transportation, and a dearth of housing stock. Montreal remained at 20 per cent, in part because one-fifth of the Jewish population consisted of seniors, while Vancouver, where rents were consuming the lion's share of the expense, had a poverty rate among Jews of 16 per cent. Increasingly, the Traditional Orthodox community is bearing the brunt. A study in 1997 revealed that 41 per cent were in poverty pointing out that many married men chose to study rather than work, and that those who did work lacked the education and skills for better paying jobs. Finally, even those who did earn a modest income, their large families kept them under the line. Morton Weinfeld writes that this "'most Jewish' of sub-communities,' is (in) the greatest danger of deep-seated structural poverty that can persist over many generations."[19] Historically, Jewish communities have provided for the poor and destitute. This commandment has not eroded. Charity, from federations, Jewish institutions, synagogues, philanthropists from across the economic spectrum, and a bevy of communal organizations respond to this call. At best, they can hardly alleviate the travails of the invisible poor.

The overriding trend since 2000 is that Canada's Jews are more diverse in every measure than in any previous era as determined by numerous measure, including socio-economic status, religious adherence, home language, ethnicity, visibility, politics, sexuality, and geography.

Defining the Jewish Artist

Aubrey Drake Graham may be considered one of the world's most well-known artists since the release of his first disc, *So Far Gone*, in 2009. He was born in 1986 in Toronto to Dennis Graham, an African American from Memphis and Sandra (Sandi) Graham, née Sher, an Ashkenazi Jew and a dual Canadian-American citizen. They divorced when Drake was five, and he was brought up by his mother, as his father returned to Memphis, where Drake spent the summers. He and Sandi first lived in a working-class neighbourhood and moved to the more affluent Forest Hill in 2000, albeit in a shared house. He had a bar mitzvah but did not easily fit into the predominantly upper-middle-class student body. Displaying artistic talent, he became a regular on the television series *De Grassi Street* and dropped out of school.

His career in the context of this study raises the question – can Drake be considered a Canadian-Jewish artist? According to Jewish law, he is Jewish via matrilineal descent. He had a bar mitzvah requiring him to learn to read and chant in Hebrew. An outrageous video recreates the bar mitzvah party. We do not know if he was exposed to Jewish life beyond this.

The question of "Jewish authenticity" has been posed for centuries. Both Felix Mendelssohn and Karl Marx for example, are considered Jewish, even though their fathers converted to Christianity. As such, the delineation between "Jewish art" and "Jewish artists" cannot be precise. At best, one may determine that although an artist is Jewish, the artist's work may not reflect the artist's lineage. In the new millennium, when the question of "who is Jewish" is complicated by the variations of religious observance, family ritual, and descent, Drake is Jewish. Michael Fraiman in *The Canadian Jewish News* quotes Amara Pope, a doctoral candidate at the University of Western Ontario: "Drake's Judaism is just one facet of a carefully constructed identity that balances his blackness, Canadianness and Jewishness all at once."[20]

LITERATURE

The first two decades of the new millennium have produced an unprecedented flow of literary output, primarily by women. A major theme is Holocaust and memory, drawing on the heritage of A.M. Klein, Irving Layton, Adele Wiseman, and two acclaimed authors of the 1990s, Matt Cohen, and Anne Michaels. Cohen (1942–99) is best known for his novels in small-town eastern Ontario. His foray into Jewish themes appear in three works: *The Spanish Doctor* (1984), which deals with the heritage of Sephardi Jews; *Nadine* (1987) who is hidden in Paris during the war and comes to Toronto as an orphan; and *Sentimental Education* (1990), about three people trapped in Paris during the deportations, one of whom ends up in eastern Ontario and is visited by the others several decades later. Michaels (1958–), a poet, wrote her first novel *Fugitive Pieces* (1998) about a little boy, Jakob Beer, who is rescued during a slaughter of Polish Jews, including his family, by Athos, a Greek archeologist, who raises him on a Greek island, followed by a move to Toronto. The novel reads like an expanded poem, blending loss, memory, rescue, and immigrant adaptation in compelling fashion. It was awarded the Orange Prize for fiction. Michaels wrote *Correspondences* (2013), with portraits by Bernice Eisenstein (1948–), linking European Jewish writers, scientists, artists, and thinkers who are connected to the destruction of European Jewry. Eisenstein is the author and illustrator of *I Was a Child of Holocaust Survivors* (2006) dealing with her family's adaptation to postwar life in Toronto.

Less well known and thus underappreciated is J.J. Steinfeld, who was born in a displaced person's camp in Germany in 1946. A resident of Charlottetown, in his words, "he is patiently waiting for Godot's arrival and a phone call from Kafka." He has written eighteen collections of poems and short stories, including *Would You Hide Me?* (2003) and *Dancing at the Club Holocaust: Stories New and Selected* (1993).

Among current Jewish male writers, Michael Redhill and Ken Sherman are noteworthy. Redhill (1966–) is a Toronto-based poet, dramatist, and novelist. His novels, *Martin Sloane* (2001) and *Belleville Square* (2017), were recipients of the Canada First Novel Award, and the Scotia Bank Giller Prize (Canada's most prestigious literary award), respectively. The former is set in Ireland and Canada, where the protagonist, Joseph Cornell, has a dual identity: an American and an Irishman with Jewish roots. The latter work is situated in Toronto's Kensington Market, about a woman who may have a doppelganger taking her, and the reader, through a maze of encounters. From its setting in the old immigrant Jewish neighbourhood, with reference to the woman's Jewish mother-in-law, it is tangentially a Jewish work. Redhill also writes mystery novels under the pen name Inger Asher Wolfe. Scholar Michael Greenstein maintains that "crossing," geographically and ethnically, is a major theme of contemporary Canadian Jewish writers.[21]

Ken Sherman (1950–) was born in Toronto. He studied with Irving Layton and Eli Mandel at York University. He has published ten collections of poetry and his work has appeared in some twenty anthologies since 1972. Most recently, *Wait Time: A Memoir of Cancer* (2015), is based on a notebook of his illness and treatment for kidney cancer.

Jason Sherman and Hannah Moscovitch are celebrated playwrights. Sherman (1962–) was born in Montreal and graduated from York University's program in creative writing and literature. From 1992 to 1999 he was playwright-in-residence in Toronto's Tarragon Theatre, at SoulPepper Theatre in Toronto from 2002 to 2003, and adapted plays by Chekhov and Brecht for the National Arts Centre and Theatre Calgary. His play *Three in the Back and Two in the Head* (1994) won the Governor-General's Award for Drama. Sherman writes with wit and vigour. Among his themes are his Jewish heritage and his connection to Judaism and Israel. His play, *Reading Hebron* for Toronto's Factory Theatre (1996) revealed his opposition to radical Zionism.

Hannah Moscovitch (1978–), born in Ottawa to a Jewish father and a Christian mother, was raised in her words, "as an atheist." In short time, she has established herself as one of Canada's most prominent playwrights, with fifteen works to her credit between 2005 and 2017. They range on themes related to the Holocaust (*East of Berlin*) to Canadian troops in Afghanistan (*This Is War*) to her most recent work, *Old Stock: A Refugee Love Story*, a hybrid production punctuated with Klezmer music, and inspired by true depictions of two Rumanian refugees. She is the recipient of numerous awards, including the Windham-Campbell Literature Prize (2016), the first Canadian woman to have been so chosen.

MUSIC

Since the 1990s, the contribution by Canadian Jews to popular music has been notable. The majority are female singers whose family histories shine through their art. Amanda Martinez is the daughter of a South African Jewish woman and a Mexican man. She blends these traditions in her jazz/world music compositions in four albums: *Sola* (2006), *Amor* (2009), *Mañana* (2013), and *Libre* (2019). She has performed in numerous clubs and concert halls in Canada and United

States, has been a radio host where she launched Canada-Latino jazz, and as an actress on television. Martinez is the recipient of numerous awards in Canada including Latin Jazz Artist of the Year and Best World Music Artist. She is a musical ambassador for SOS Children's Villages Canada, which provides homes for children without families. Her song, "African Skies," from her most recent album, is influenced by rhythms of Madagascar and Costa Rica.

Nikki Yanovsky (1992–) is a Montreal-based jazz-pop singer who gained national prominence in singing the theme song, "I Believe," at the 2010 Winter Olympic Games in Vancouver. She was raised in a musical family where jazz, especially female vocalists, were revered. Her first album, *Ella ... Of Thee I Sing* in 2008 at the age of fourteen, a tribute to Ella Fitzgerald, earned two Juno nominations. Her voice and interpretation of her idol belied her age. Since then, she has released four albums, the most recent being *Big Mouth*, and has collaborated with Herbie Hancock, Elton John, and Quincy Jones. Yanovsky has helped raise over $10 million for charities, including the Montreal Children's Hospital and the Children's Wish Foundation, and has created a scholarship at McGill University.

Sophie Millman (1983–) was born in the former Soviet Union. Despite restrictions on western music, her father collected jazz records sparking Millman's love for the genre which effloresced in Israel, where the family moved. In Toronto she quickly established herself as a virtuoso interpreter of jazz standards, and of songs in Spanish, Yiddish, Russian, and French. Her first album, self-titled, in 2006 drew wide acclaim. She is a fixture in concerts and music festivals, and is a recipient of Juno Vocal Jazz Album of the year.

Jewish male singers have taken a back seat to their female counterparts in the new millennium. Two of note, are Steven Page and Josh Dolgin. Page (1970–) is a founder of Barenaked Ladies, one of Canada's most popular bands in the 1990s. Raised in Toronto by a Jewish mother and a Protestant father who had converted to Judaism, he took piano and vocal lessons. Page was the band's main song writer, lead singer, and played acoustic and electric guitar. The band disassembled in 2009 but reunited for its induction into the Canadian Music Hall of Fame in 2018. Since his departure, he has made four albums, beginning with *Page One*, in 2010. He performed Leonard Cohen's "Hallelujah" at the state funeral of NDP leader Jack Layton in 2011.

Josh Dolgin, aka "Socalled," is a Montreal singer and song writer whose blend of hip hop, klezmer, jazz, and folk music falls into the rap idiom. His family's background is Ukrainian, Romanian, and Russian. He plays piano and accordion. He has performed with clarinetist David Krakauer's band Klezmer Madness. He is the subject of Montreal documentarian Gary Beitel's 2010 film, *The "Socalled" Movie*. From 2003 to 2013 Dolgin released six albums including *The Socalled Seder: A Hip Hop Hagadah* (2005) and *Consensus: Live in Concert* (2005) with the klezmer band Beyond the Pale.

Leo Szpilman (1913–2012) was born in Ostrowiec, Poland where he became a pianist. When the war broke out, he and his wife Mary were taken to the town ghetto where he formed an orchestra. With the aid of a sympathetic German guard, they fled to the forest where they were sheltered by a Pole. After the war, the Szpilmans went to a displaced persons camp in Germany where Szpilman composed a rhapsody in three parts, ending in a joyful movement to exclaim liberation. Arriving in Toronto in 1948, he anglicized his name to Spellman. The rhapsody was packed in a suitcase and put away in a garage. Starting a new life, he formed a popular orchestra that played at weddings and parties for three decades. In the late 1990s the Holocaust Museum in Washington asked Leo's cousin Wladyslaw Szpilman, whose life was memorialized the movie *The Pianist*, for his Jewish compositions. He replied that he had not written such but that his cousin had. Consequently, Spellman's work, renamed *Rhapsody 1939–1945* was performed in the United States. Finally, with the support of Paul Hoffert, the cofounder of the Canadian fusion band Lighthouse, the rhapsody was recorded with musicians following Spellman's precise instructions and was released at Toronto's Ashkenaz Festival. Hoffert and his wife Brenda then made a documentary about Spellman's life. A few months before his death, the rhapsody was performed to a sold-out audience in Toronto.

SCHOLARS

A recurrent characteristic of the postwar period is the over representation of Jews as leaders in business, the arts, and politics. One of the predominant reasons for this development is education. Beginning in the interwar period, and accelerating through the postwar era, Jews have chosen post-secondary education at higher levels than the national average. This is traced to three interrelated factors. The most significant is that faith and historical conditions determined that scholarship was instilled in childhood and carried through life. Second was the gradual diminution of restrictions, in the way of quotas, for Jewish acceptance into university programs, and then into their chosen professions. Third was that postwar socio-economic mobility provided the financial resources necessary for the costs of post-secondary education. These factors have produced a broad spectrum of men and women who have made a significant impact on scholarship.

The most prestigious global award for scholarship is the Nobel Prize. By 2018 twenty-five Canadians have had this distinction, of whom fourteen have been recipients since 1986. Of this group, four are Jewish.[22] Myron Scholes (1941–) was born in Timmins, Ontario and grew up in Hamilton. After graduating from McMaster University in 1997 he did his graduate work at the University of Chicago under the supervision of George Stigler and Milton Friedman, future Nobel recipients. His research created the option pricing model for asset allocation. He moved to the Massachusetts Institute of Technology and then to Stanford University, from where he retired in 1996. He shared the Nobel Prize in Economics with Robert Merton.

Sidney Altman was born in 1939 in Montreal to eastern European immigrants. As his family's financial situation became secure, he studied physics at the Massachusetts Institute of Technology and the University of Colorado, from where he received his doctorate in 1968, and was hired at Yale University, becoming the chair, and then the dean of the college. Returning to research, his team investigated the catalytic properties of an RNA (ribonucleic acid) earning him the Nobel Prize in Chemistry in 1989.

Rudolph A. Marcus was born in Montreal in 1923, where he attended Baron Byng High School and then McGill University, earning his doctorate in chemistry in 1946. His research showed that electron transfer is a basic form of chemical reaction that is central to all respiratory functions, including photosynthesis. He is the recipient of numerous honours and awards, culminating in the Nobel Prize for Chemistry in 1992.

Joseph Steinman was born in Montreal in 1943 and raised in Sherbrooke, Quebec. He received his bachelor and medical degrees at McGill University and had a distinguished career in medical research in immunology. The Nobel committee announced in 2011 that he was the co-recipient with two others, unaware that Steinman had died three days earlier. Since the award cannot be made posthumously, the committee decided that the prize "was made in good faith."

The highest civilian honour in Canada is the Order of Canada. It was instituted on the centenary of Confederation in 1967. There are three levels, of which the highest is Companion, given to approximately five hundred people to date, from all fields and walks of life including approximately forty of Jewish origin. Among them are poet-songwriter Leonard Cohen, film maker David Cronenberg, architects Jack Diamond, Moshe Safdie, and Frank Gehry, jurists Morris Fish and Bora Laskin, politicians Victor Goldbloom, David Lewis and Stephen Lewis, television producer Lorne Michaels, journalist Peter C. Newman, philanthropists Peter Munk, H. Reuben Cohen and Charles Bronfman, composers R. Murray Schafer, Harry Somers, and Louis Applebaum, and psychologist Ellen Bialystok.

THREE CANADIANS

Stephen Lewis, Irwin Cotler, and Rosalie Abella are among the most notable Canadians of the last forty years for their dedication to upholding and promoting human rights in Canada and globally through justice, diplomacy, and activism.

Lewis (1937–) was born "Sholem," a Yiddish derivation of the Hebrew word "Shalom" which means peace, to David and Sophie Lewis who were long-life products of the Jewish socialist movement, the Bund. Stephen was raised in a highly politicized family, the son and grandson of David and Moshe. At the University of Toronto, he was a skilled debater who took on the then Senator John Kennedy (Lewis lost). Dropping out of law school, Lewis worked in newly independent Ghana and travelled across Africa. Upon his return he was elected as an MPP in Ontario in 1963, became the party leader in 1971, and leader of the Official Opposition in 1975.

Lewis turned his sights to labour mediator, columnist, broadcaster, and panelist on CBC radio, but felt unfulfilled until Prime Minister

Stephen Lewis – Wikimedia
Source: Alexis MacDonald

Irwin Cotler

Source: Ontario Jewish Archives

Rosalie Abella
The image of Rosalie Abella is by photographer Paul J. Lawrence of Toronto.
Source: Alex Dworkin Canadian Jewish Archives

Mulroney appointed him Canada's "Permanent Representative to the United Nations" in 1984 from where he ascended to become the deputy director of UNICEF. This turned him into a fierce advocate for stemming the HIV/AIDS crisis in Africa as he condemned the gap between promises and action in stemming the pandemic. Following his departure from the diplomatic world the Stephen Lewis Foundation and AIDS-Free World were created in 2003 in partnership with grass roots community organizations to stem the plague is sub-Saharan Africa. As of 2018 the foundation had partnered with over three hundred local groups and disbursed some $115,000,000. Its executive director is Lewis' daughter, Ilana, and Graca Machel, the widow of Nelson Mandela, is the chair of the Africa board.

Irwin Cotler (1940–) is a lawyer, politician, academic, and a trail blazer in promoting human rights across the globe. Born in Montreal, he received his BA from McGill and his master's degree in law from Yale University. As a professor of law at McGill, he directed the university's human rights program from 1973 to his election as an M P for the Liberal Party in the 1999. During this period, he represented prisoners of conscience across the globe, including Andrei Shakharov and Natan Sharansky from the former Soviet Union, Nelson Mandela, and Jacobo Timmerman of Argentina. Cotler was also the first president of the CJC (1980–3) who was an academic. As minister of justice and attorney general from 2003 to 2006, he reformed the composition of the Supreme Court and the Ontario Court of Appeal by appointing representatives of gender, Indigenous, and visible minorities. He initiated laws on human trafficking, equality for gays and lesbians, quashing wrongful convictions, and introduced the National Justice Initiative against Racism and Hate. From 2007 until his retirement in 2015 he was parliamentary critic and special counsel for human rights.

Cotler has been recognized for his contribution to Canada and internationally as the recipient of fourteen honorary doctorates, inducted as an Officer of the Order of Canada, chosen Parliamentarian of the Year by his colleagues in 2014, and in 2015 by the Law Society of Upper Canada's Inaugural Human Rights Award for transforming "the lives of many" as a professor, legal scholar, human rights lawyer, counsel to prisoners of justice, and public intellectual. In 2015 he established the Raoul Wallenberg Centre for Human Rights in

Montreal. It is named after the Swedish diplomat who rescued Hungarian Jews by finding safe houses for them in Budapest. Wallenberg had been arrested by the Red Army, imprisoned, and "disappeared." The centre is dedicated to protecting liberal democracy from authoritarianism and populism by joining with local and international committees committed to these principals, advocating on behalf of political prisoners and women's rights, establishing an international tribunal responding the Rwandan and Bosnian genocides, and countering antisemitism, including the demonization of Israel by maintaining that world bodies, including the UN, apply a double standard towards Israel.

Rosalie Silberman Abella was born in a displaced persons camp in Stuttgart, Germany in 1946 to Jacob and Fanny who had married in 1939. Their two-year-old daughter was murdered during the Holocaust. They individually survived the concentration camps and were reunited in a displaced person's camp in Germany. Jacob, who had received a law degree in Poland before the war but wasn't allowed to practice, oversaw legal services for the residents of the camp.

The Silbermans, including younger daughter Toni, arrived in Canada in 1950, but Jacob could not resume his profession because he was not a citizen. This stung his pride and was a major consideration in Rosie's choice of a career. Consequently, she graduated from the University of Toronto law faculty in 1970, opened a practice in civil and criminal litigation, and six years later was appointed to the Ontario Family Court, the youngest person to have done so and the first female Jewish judge. In the interim she was a member of commissions and tribunals advocating for human rights and fairer employment practices, culminating in the lessening of obstacles to women, Indigenous peoples, and the disabled in the workplace. These provisions were enshrined in the Charter of Rights and Freedoms in the Constitution in 1982.

In 1992 she was elevated to the Ontario Court of Appeal and then to the Supreme Court in 2004, the first Jewish woman to have gained this position. As a legal scholar, she has written four books and almost one hundred articles, spoken in some dozen countries, received approximately twenty honorary degrees, and was the first woman to have received the Distinguished Alumnus Award from the University of Toronto law faculty. The president of the Canadian section of the International Commission, in presenting her with the Award for Human Rights by the Canadian Bar Association and the International Commission of Jurists in 2004, remarked that Abella's "entire life has revolved around the cause of human rights … has had a profound impact on human rights law and policy outside Canada. Her contributions to society as a lawyer, teacher, commissioner, and judge have always been shaped by her profound humanity."[23]

In an address in honour of the 70th anniversary of the Supreme Court in November 2018, Judge Abella, in relation to Canada's judicial independence, stated, as independent courts were under siege by oligarchs, "I learned that democracy is strengthened in direct proportion to the strengths of rights and an independent judiciary.… In a polarized society, it is especially crucial to have an institution whose only mandate is to protect the rule of law."[24]

Stephen Lewis, Irwin Cotler, and Rosalie Abella are the products of the Jewish heritage of law and charity, of commandments from holy and human declarations, and of their upbringing. Lewis was the grandson of European Jews who in the dark decades of Russian rule created a political movement that included non-Jews striving to create a more equitable life through socialism. Cotler, growing up during World War II, took his father Nathan's proscription to heart that the struggle for justice was more important than the Ten Commandments, and from his mother, who believed that to fight for justice, one had to seek out injustice. Abella carries the imprint of the so-called "second generation," whose parents' survival occurred by chance alone, and that humans who do not live in a fair and equitable society are in danger of becoming perpetrators, or bystanders, or much less likely, survivors.

"NO BETTER HOME"

In the fall of 2017 York University hosted a celebration of Canada's one hundred and fiftieth anniversary. Among the programs was a symposium titled: "Has There Ever Been a Better Home for the Jews than Canada"? It was convened by professor David S. Koffman, the J. Richard Shiff Chair of Canadian Jewish Studies, and it featured nine speakers. The symposium papers are being published by the

University of Toronto Press. In Koffman's introductory paper, he writes: "The question is seldom asked. This is curious, because Canada may very well be the safest, most socially welcoming, economically secure, and possibly most religiously tolerant home for the Jews than any other diaspora country, past or present." He continues that Canada "is home to the fourth largest Jewish population, behind Israel, the United States and France, and may well overtake France for third place within decades."[25] But, to put this into perspective, Canada's three hundred thousand Jews constitute but 2 per cent of the global Jewish population of 14.8 million as of September 2018. Nevertheless, the question is intriguing and deserves consideration for four reasons.

First, the word "ever" is problematic. Given the Jewish nation's four-thousand-year time span, it is difficult to compare the Canadian story to the early history of the Jewish nation that terminated in the destruction of the First Temple in 586 BCE by the Babylonians or to the subsequent dispersal of the survivors across the Mediterranean littoral and the Middle East, or to the return of a fragment of a country seventy years later. How do we assess Jewish life under Hellenistic and Roman occupation, which ended tragically with the murder of much of the populace and the expulsion of most of survivors? The "golden age" in Iberia and in the Arab world in the Middle Ages was punctuated by attacks by Muslim invaders and collapsed with their expulsion under the Christian reconquest, following a pattern that already had been set in Britain, France, and in parts of Germany. Did the "Jewish Paradise" in the Kingdom of Poland in the sixteenth century produce a better home, a *Paradise Judeorum*, even though this period was short lived? Or did the promise of freedom in western Europe during the Enlightenment and Emancipation that presaged the Holocaust? To the present, how does one counter the argument that the Jewish state, Israel, is not a better home because Jews have self-determination for the first time in more than two thousand years, while facing a persistent existential threat to its survival?

Second, as it is well-nigh impossible to compare the brief history of Canadian Jews to that of the periods and locations alluded to above, it is also impossible to compare this history to that of the Jews of the United States. Given that their origins predate those of Canadian Jews by one hundred and fifty years, that the American Jewish population is fifteenfold that of Canada (constituting 1.7 per cent of the total, in contrast to 1.1 per cent of Canada), and that American Jews are greatly overrepresented in the academy, the arts, business, and culture, most observers would conclude that they have a "better home" than do Canadian Jews. Yet, historically the United States has not provided a more secure environment for its residents than has Canada. The hostilities on its soil, from the Civil War, the most deadly encounter in the world in the nineteenth century, to the Spanish and Native American conflicts, to the three hundred years of slavery and denial of equal rights to African Americans, to the current epidemic of violence and political instability, has not made it a safer home for its citizens than has Canada. The shootings at synagogues in Pittsburgh and in Southern California in 2018–19, and the efflorescence of its unchecked white supremacy faction is further evidence that the Jewish-American "home" is not unscathed.

Third, until the 1950s, Canada had not been a welcome home for immigrants. Jews were not embraced during the Great Migration at the turn of the twentieth century. Twenty years later, Jewish immigration was restricted, and from 1933 to 1948, curtailed. Canada became a "better home" because of the Jewish community's achievements in the face of discrimination and government restrictions. Yet their travail paled next to indentured Chinese workers and the internment of Japanese Canadians during World War II, not to mention the cultural genocide of Canada's First Nations.

Fourth, the story of Canada's Jews is an immigrant saga. The process of settlement, adaptation and diversity is one common to all immigrants, but the Jewish story is unique because of several factors. The original Jewish settlers were Canada's first non-Anglo-Celtic contingent and its first non-Christian immigrants. This tiny cohort did not have to struggle in its adaptation, as it spoke English, was entrepreneurial, and had commercial contacts in the Thirteen Colonies and England. As Jews did not arrive from a "Jewish" homeland, historically they were constantly adapting to their situation. To this end, they had certain advantages due to their religion and culture, foremost among them was literacy, allowing them to establish themselves in secondary and tertiary enterprises. By extension, adaptation produced diversity, consistent with the experience of ethnic minorities in general.

The relationship between Jews and their adopted homeland, Canada, has been largely symbiotic, especially since World War II. Jewish contributions have been matched by the security that Canada has afforded, and the lifting of barriers to their freedom to choose their paths within society. But history has determined that there are no guarantees for the security of ethnic minorities. Whether Canada proves to be the "best" home for Jews is for future generations to determine.

Leonard Cohen in 1988

Source: Wikimedia – Gorupdebesanez – Cohen in 1988

Epilogue: "Hallelujah"

Leonard Cohen (1934–2016) is Canada's most well-known Canadian Jew worldwide due to his art and his totemic presence that has inspired three generations, primarily through his songs, or more correctly, poems put to music. What is less well known is that his heritage encapsulates the narrative of Canadian Jews. His story is part of this story.

The Cohen line is traced to his great-grandfather, Lazarus (1844–1914), born in the small town of Budwitch, Poland in a traditional Jewish home. He was sent to the Eitz Chaim Yeshiva in Lithuania, and lived his life as a pious Jew, wearing traditional dress and was marked by a long beard. He immigrated to Canada in 1869, at a point where there were approximately one thousand Jews, the majority of whom were in Montreal. Cohen (the name means priest in Hebrew), settled in the small town of Malbery in Eastern Ontario. He rapidly moved from being a lumber salesman to the owner of a coal company. While little else is known about these first years, his move to Montreal in 1883 marked him as a community builder. He quickly became part of the Jewish elite, which included descendants of some of the original families that had arrived in 1760. He increased his fortune with investments in metals and dredging. He visited Palestine in 1894 where he purchased land. He joined and eventually became president of Congregation Shaar Hashomayim, was an officer of the philanthropic Baron de Hirsch Institute which, among other endeavours, helped create the Jewish agricultural colonies in the Prairies. He was survived by his sons

Lyon and A.Z. Although their arrival occurred a century after the first Jewish settlers, Lazarus' exploits prior to the Great Migration were as much of the fabric of Jewish life as were those of the pioneers.

Lyon Cohen (1868–1937) arrived with his father, Lazarus, in Canada at the age of two. He became the most significant and well-known Canadian Jew in the first third of the twentieth century. His contributions are discussed in Chapter 5. Unlike Lazarus, he was a thoroughly modern individual, establishing his home in tony Lower Westmount, as homes in Upper Westmount would not be sold to Jews. He was survived by four children, including Nathan, Leonard's father, who did not inherit his father or grandfather's drive and personality. Returning home from his service as a lieutenant in World War I Nathan never regained full health. He married Masha Klonitsky-Kline, the daughter of Solomon, an esteemed rabbi and author who was a mythical figure in Leonard's life, who had come to the United States in 1927, from where Masha settled in Montreal. Lyon and Masha's eldest child, Esther, was born in 1929.

Leonard was brought up close to the rest of the Cohen family. As his father was a quiet man who worked long hours in the family clothing industry, Leonard was closer to Masha. She was the consummate eastern European, a flamboyant woman, who sang for her children in Yiddish and Russian. Leonard absorbed this rare dual heritage as the product of the wealthy, prominent Jewish upper-middle-class family that had its origins at the birth of British North America, and of immigrants who carried Old World customs and traditions, thereby inheriting the saga of Canada's Jews.

Nathan's sudden death when Leonard was nine was deeply felt. Like his father, Leonard was small in stature. Like Masha, he was a book hound, a lover of music, a loner who scoured Westmount to the top of Mount Royal, where the giant cross dominates the city. After his bar mitzvah, with minimal parental oversight, he would wander downtown late into the night, imbibing the heady mixture of wealth and destitution, the bars and brothels that he longed to enter into of the second most open town in North America. The contrast between the sacred, Shaar Hashomayim and the suffocating Catholic presence on the one hand, and the profane, far removed from the insularity of Westmount, was to dominate his sense of self, and to profoundly influence his art. Before other regional connections were established, Cohen was foremost a Montrealer, albeit as a Jew, always as an outsider caught between the two solitudes.

While at Westmount High School he bought a book of poetry by Frederico Garcia Lorca, a fabled poet, playwright, and a devotee of flamenco music who was murdered by fascists during the Spanish Civil War. Inspired, Cohen started writing poetry, bought a Spanish guitar, and discovered that this made him popular, especially among girls. He was also influenced by the American group The Weavers, who sang in English and Yiddish of the travails of workers and of Black people.

In 1951 he entered McGill University, where he was an underwhelming student, preferring to play, write, and drink. He discovered debating and despite his shyness, loved the limelight and acclaim. Louis Dudek, an English professor, poet, essayist, and publisher, was of great influence in his intellectual maturation. Dudek taught the great European modernists, including Goethe, Schiller, Tolstoy, and Joyce. Dudek was also one the Canadian modernists, including F.R. Scott and Hugh MacLennan, who had their initiation during the Depression. Less well known at the time was the irrepressible Irving Layton, who had the most formative influence on Cohen, and whose work is discussed in Chapter 8. A generation older, born in Europe to a poor family, Layton wanted to change the world through his art and his presence. He detested the puritanism of Canadians. Another source of inspiration was the abstract expressionist art movement exemplified by Montreal artists Jean-Paul Riopelle and Paul Emile Borduas.

Cohen's first published poems appeared in 1954 and he won McGill's literary prize the following year. In 1956, *Let Us Compare Mythologies*, a collection of forty-four poems edited by Dudek, was published to some acclaim. He was now one of the "Montreal Group," who produced a record and appeared on the CBC. That year he enrolled as a graduate student at Columbia University.

New York in the mid-1950s was the hub of experimental music, art, and drama that radiated from Greenwich Village. Though miles from Columbia, Cohen made rare appearances there because he was captivated by the Beat Movement led by the poet Allen Ginsberg, who shredded the norms of language. Further uptown on Fifty-second Street the bebop artists Charlie Parker, Thelonious Monk, and Dizzy Gillespie, expressed freedom, improvisation, and experimentation in sound. But Cohen's poetry was more traditional and was derided by the Beats. Yet, the energy, the cultural relevance, and the foreignness of the period had a profound impact on Cohen. Returning to Montreal, he began writing a novel and worked in the family business. Frustrated with his situation, he applied and received a grant from the Canadian Council for the Arts to work in London in 1959.

But Cohen was restless. Infatuated with Greece, he left London and settled on the island of Hydra, initiating the next phase of Cohen's life as a citizen of the world. He bought a small house there, met his muse Marianne Ihlen, and from 1961 to 1966 produced two collections of poetry and two novels, *The Favourite Game* (1963) and *Beautiful Losers* (1966). As Cohen emerged as a song writer and singer in the late 1960s, his popularity soared, and the myth of Cohen as a renegade associated with the revival of folk music grew, his novels faded from popular appreciation. Yet, while the first novel was a straight-ahead pseudo-autobiography of his adolescence and early adulthood, and the second, the first post-modernist work by a Canadian, was propelled by the staccato of the Beats, Gershwin's "Strike up the Band," and Ray Charles' voice, both provided a window on the postwar established Montreal Jewish community.

In *The Favourite Game*, Cohen's alter ego, Lawrence Breavman, states: "The Breavmans founded and presided over most of the institutions which make the Montreal Jewish community one of the most powerful in the world today. The joke around the city is: The Jews are the conscience of the world and the Breavmans are the conscience of the Jews.... Ten years ago Breavman compiled the Code of Breavman: 'We are Victorian gentlemen of Hebraic persuasion. We wish to be regarded as peers, united by class, education, power, differentiated by home rituals.'"[1]

Beautiful Losers is essentially a book without a plot set in Montreal during the violent interlude of rabid French-Canadian nationalism. The anonymous narrator is a Montreal Jew, who is in a love triangle with a French-Canadian nationalist (F) and an Amerindian woman (Edith), and is smitten by the story of Catherine Tekakwitha, an Indigenous woman in the seventeenth century who converted to Christianity and became a saint. As the narrator and F walk along Sherbrooke Street, they encounter a nationalist demonstration. As the narrator becomes aroused, the crowd turns on him. "He looks English! He looks Jewish!"[2] He's rescued by F.

Cohen in these works expressed the essential Jewish dilemma – that irrespective of their ascent in modern, liberal society, Jews could never really be comfortable under the spectre of rabid antisemitism.

Ever the peripatetic artist, Cohen lived in Greece, Montreal (where he bought a home in 1970 off the Blvd St. Laurent [the Main] proximate to Schwartz' Deli, which he never sold), New York, Nashville, and California. Even though he was in isolation for long periods, particularly between 1984 and 1990, practicing yoga and Buddhism as a disciple of his guru, Roshi Joshu Sasaki, on Mount Baldy in Southern California, from 1960 to 2018 he produced fourteen collections of poetry and fifteen music albums. Because of the fraudulent actions of his business manager, now broke, he undertook world tours, the first from 2008 to 2010, in the process becoming a global cultural icon. His DVD, *Live in London* (2009), was one of two hundred and forty-six concerts, usually three hours long, in that span of time. Audiences were multigenerational and multilingual. The concerts were marked not only by the lyrics, but by the musical arrangements featuring backup female singers and accomplished instrumentalists. His last tour was in 2012–13.

Cohen's artistic output was broad. It had many themes, among them Montreal, relationships, the Holocaust, religion, love, lust, aging, nature, art, and Layton. Scholar and author Norman Ravvin, writes in the introduction to George A. Walker's, *Songbook*, a collection of illustrations of woodcuts of Cohen's life: "Radios. Oldsmobiles. Window Blinds. Coffee cups of the kind once found in coffee shops. Airport waiting rooms. Small children reading. These are the nearly secret, neglected accoutrement of the poet's, the novelist's, the songwriter's most average afternoon. Some of these things spring to life in Cohen's own work."[3]

Cohen's words and songs interplay with each other. One example is his poem "The Genius," from his second collection, *The Spice-Box of Earth*. Each stanza begins with "For You I will be" followed by "a ghetto Jew," "an apostate Jew," "a banker Jew," "a Broadway Jew," "a doctor Jew," "a Dachau Jew,"[4] as the poem navigates through historical stereotypes from the Middle Ages to the Holocaust. This sober recitation takes on a more comedic tone in his song, "I'm Your Man" (1988), also the title of a documentary film. It begins, "If you want a lover, I'll do anything for you" continuing to "if you want a partner," "if you want a boxer," "if you want a father for your child."

One of Cohen's themes was prophecy. His rabbi grandfather, Solomon Klonitsky-Kline, was an expert on Isaiah, the prophet who was in a constant state of despair about the transgressions of the Jews against God's words, justice, and charity for those in need. In the Yom Kippur service, on the holiest day of the Jewish calendar, where Jews are commanded to fast, they read from Isaiah in which he rails: "Behold, while you are fasting, you engage in business, and your worker you continue to oppress.... Is this the kind of fast that I delight in?"[5] Cohen in "Isaiah" asks, during the one period when Israel was thriving (c. 700 BCE), "Why did Isaiah rage and cry, Jerusalem is ruined, your cities are burned with fire?"[6] a premonition of the destruction of the Temple and the expulsion of the Jews by the Babylonians in 586 BCE.

His final album, *You Want It Darker*, was recorded at his home in Los Angeles and launched on October 21, 2016. The album's title song is accompanied by the male chorus of his Westmount synagogue, Shaar Hashomayim. It's a soaring cry to God, evoking Abraham's response, *hineni* (literally "I'm here" but in Cohen's words "I'm ready, my Lord") to God's order on Mount Moriah to smite Isaac, his only child, and thereby halt the existence of the Jewish people.

Nineteen days later, Cohen died of cancer, one day before the election of Donald Trump. He was buried in a simple grave, the funeral attended by his children and a few friends, after which his death was made public. Perhaps his final words were prophetic. The dark side of humanity was a trope in his art, for example, in the brooding tone and lyrics in his "Everybody Knows" song.

Had Cohen lived to see that *You Want It Darker* received the Grammy Award for "Best Rock Performance" of 2018, with Gideon Zelemyer, the cantor of Shaar Hashomayim accepting the trophy, he would have relished the irony of the situation.

"Hallelujah," on the album *Various Positions*, was released in 1984. There are over three hundred versions. Two of note were Steven Page's rendition at the funeral of NDP leader Jack Layton, and that of Kate McKinnon, portraying Hillary Clinton on the opening of *Saturday Night Live*, on November 12, 2016, four days after the election of Donald Trump.

Leonard Cohen personifies the story of Canadian Jews. He was the grandson of immigrants, of Lyon Cohen who not only adapted to his new life but who became the paragon of the rapidly developing Canadian

Jewish community, and of Solomon Klonitsky-Klein, a rabbi and author, who inspired Cohen's quest for knowledge and attracted him to faith and mysticism, from Judaism to Zen Buddhism. While Cohen was foremost a Montrealer, the city could not fulfill his wanderlust. Emerging from that cocoon he became a citizen of the world, a man of unceasing curiosity, incorporating diverse experiences into his artistic output. Leonard Cohen is not only the most well-known Canadian Jew in the world but also the planet's most revered Canadian artist.

Notes

1. Creating a Community: The Jews of Quebec

1 Ira Robinson, *A History of AntiSemitism in Canada* (Waterloo: Wilfred Laurier Press, 2015), 29–30.
2 Gerald Tulchinsky, *Taking Root: The Origins of the Canadian Jewish Community* (Waltham, MA: Brandeis University Press, 1993), 26.
3 Joe King, *From the Ghetto to the Main: The Story of the Jews of Montreal* (Montreal: Montreal Jewish Publication Society, 2003), 58.
4 Robinson, *A History of AntiSemitism in Canada*, 32.
5 Robinson, *A History of AntiSemitism in Canada*, 31.

2. The Jews of the Atlantic, Pacific, Ontario, and the Prairies

1 Robin McGrath, *Salt Fish and Shmattes: A History of the Jewish in Newfoundland and Labrador from 1770* (St. John's, NL: Creative Book Publishing, 2006), 3.
2 Cyril Leonoff, *Pioneers, Pedlars, and Prayer Shawls: The Jewish Communities of British Columbia and the Yukon* (Vancouver: Sono Nis Press, 1978), 41.
3 Leonoff, *Pioneers, Pedlars, and Prayer Shawls*, 58–9.
4 Leonoff, *Pioneers, Pedlars, and Prayer Shawls*, 149.
5 Leonoff, *Pioneers, Pedlars, and Prayer Shawls*, 91.
6 Anna Brownell Jameson, *Sketches in Canada, and Rambles among the Red Men* (London: Longman, Brown, Green, and Longmans, 1852), 9.
7 Special thanks to Dr. Paula Draper for providing the documentation of the Frankel family.
8 Irving Abella, *A Coat of Many Colours: Two Centuries of Jewish Life in Canada* (Toronto: Lester Orpen Dennys, 1990), 78.

9 Erna Paris, *Jews: An Account and Their Experience in Canada* (Toronto: MacMillan, 1980), 213.
10 Michael Usiskin, *Uncle Mike's Edenbridge: Memoirs of a Jewish Pioneer Farmer.* Translated by Marcia Usiskin Basman (Winnipeg: Peguis, 1983), 2.
11 Usiskin, *Uncle Mike's Edenbridge*, 63.

3. The Great Migration

1 David J. Hall, "Sifton, Clifford (1861–1929)," in *Encyclopedia of the Great Plains*, edited by David J. Wishart (Lincoln, NE: University of Nebraska-Lincoln, 2011).
2 Joseph Kage, *With Faith and Thanksgiving: The Story of Two Hundred Years of Jewish Immigration and Immigrant Aid Effort in Canada (1760–1960)* (Montreal: Eagle Publishing Co, 1962), 52.

4. Yiddish Canada

1 Israel Medres, *Montreal of Yesterday: Jewish Life in Montreal 1900–1920* (Montreal: Véhicule Press, 2000), 21–3.
2 Mordechai Richler, "Their Canada and Mine: A Memoir," *Commentary*, August 1961, https://www.commentary.org/articles/mordecai-richler/their-canada-and-mine/.
3 Pierre Anctil, *Saint-Laurent: Montreal's Main* (Montreal: Septentrion: 2002), 87.
4 John Lorinc et al., *The Ward: The Life and Loss of Toronto's First Immigrant Neighbourhood* (Toronto: Coach House Books, 2015), 16.
5 Rosemary Donegan, *Spadina Avenue* (Toronto: Douglas and McIntyre, 1985), 8.
6 Donegan, *Spadina Avenue*, 8.
7 Allan Levine, *Coming of Age: The History of the Jewish People of Manitoba* (Winnipeg: The Jewish Heritage Centre of Western Canada, 2009), 34.
8 Dedicated with appreciation to the memory of Eiran Harris, archivist emeritus at the JPL in Montreal, who wrote this story.
9 Morley Torgov, *A Good Place to Come From* (Toronto: Bev Editions, 2011), 11.
10 Gerald Tulchinsky, *Shtetl on the Grand* (Victoria, BC: Friesen Press, 2015), 2.
11 Tulchinsky, *Shtetl on the Grand*, 29.
12 Ruth Frager, *Sweatshop Strife: Class, Ethnicity, and Gender in the Jewish Labour Movement of Toronto, 1900–1939* (Toronto: University of Toronto Press, 1992), 20.
13 Frager, *Sweatshop Strife*, 18–19.
14 Canada Privy Council Office, *Royal Commission on Price Spreads* (Ottawa: J.A. Patenaude Printer to the King, 1935), 111, https://publications.gc.ca/site/eng/9.828272/publication.html?wbdisable=true.

15 *Shul* is a somewhat confusing term, in that it is the colloquial term in Yiddish for synagogue and for school. The context determines the meaning.
16 Rebecca Margolis, *Jewish Roots, Canadian Soil: Yiddish Cultural Life in Montreal, 1905–1945* (Montreal and Kingston: McGill-Queen's: 2011), xiii–xxi.
17 Stephen A. Speisman, *The Jews of Toronto: A History to 1937* (Toronto: McClelland & Stewart, 1987), 61.
18 Abella, *A Coat of Many Colours*, 124.
19 Gerald Tulchinsky, *Canada's Jews: A People's Journey* (Toronto: University of Toronto Press, 2008), 292.
20 Ben Kayfetz, "Recollections and Experiences with the Jewish Press in Toronto," *Polyphony: Bulletin of the Multicultural History Society of Ontario: Toronto's People* 6, no. 1 (Spring/Summer 1984), 228.
21 David Roskies, "Yiddish in Montreal: The Utopian Experiment," in *An Everyday Miracle: Yiddish Culture in Montreal*, ed. Ira Robinson, Pierre Anctil, and Mervin Butovsky (Toronto: Véhicule Press, 1990), 22–38.
22 Reprinted with permission. Ida Maze, *A Mame* (Montreal: Idische Kultur Gezelshaft, 1931).
23 Reprinted with permission. Ida Maze, *Lider far kinder* (Warsaw: Farlag H. Bzshoza, 1936).
24 Written and translated by Chava Rosenfarb. Chava Rosenfarb, *Exile at Last: Selected Poems*, ed. Goldie Morgentaler (Toronto: Guernica Editions, 2013).
25 David G. Roskies, "Yiddish in Montreal," 22–38.

5. Organizations

1 Ira Robinson, "Kabbalist and Communal Leader: Rabbi Yudel Rosenberg and the Canadian Jewish Community," *Canadian Jewish Studies/Études juives canadiennes* 1 (1993): 53.
2 Ben Kayfetz and Stephen Speisman, *Only Yesterday: Collected Pieces on the Jews of Toronto* (Toronto: Now and Then Books, 2013), 127.
3 Levine, *Coming of Age*, 317–19.
4 Lesley Marrus Barsky, *From Generation to Generation: A History of Toronto's Mount Sinai Hospital* (McClelland & Stewart, 1998).
5 Levine, *Coming of Age*, 194.
6 Paris, *Jews: An Account of their Experience*, 122.
7 Gerald J. Tulchinsky, "De Sola, Clarence Isaac," in *Dictionary of Canadian Biography*, vol. 14 (University of Toronto/Université Laval, 2003), http://www.biographi.ca/en/bio/de_sola_clarence_isaac_14E.html.
8 Tulchinsky, *Taking Root*, 128.
9 Tulchinsky, *Taking Root*, 128.

10 "The Balfour Declaration," Israel Ministry of Foreign Affairs, accessed September 2021, https://mfa.gov.il/MFA/AboutIsrael/Maps/Pages/The-Balfour-Declaration.aspx.
11 Britain was provided a mandate over Palestine following the defeat of the Ottoman Empire in World War I.
12 Jack Lipinksy, *Imposing Their Will: An Organizational History of Jewish Toronto, 1933–1948* (Montreal: McGill-Queen's University, 2011), 77.
13 Lipinksy, *Imposing Their Will*, xxi.

6. The Socio-Political Landscape: Workers, Liberals, Reformers, Radicals, Rogues

1 Frager, *Sweatshop Strife*, 188.
2 Lorinc et al., *The Ward*, 157.
3 Tulchinsky, *Canada's Jews*, 149.
4 Levine, *Coming of Age*, 164.
5 Levine, *Coming of Age*, 166.
6 Frager, *Sweatshop Strife*, 213.
7 Frager, *Sweatshop Strife*, 217.
8 Irving Abella, "Portrait of a Jewish Professional Revolutionary: The Recollections of Joshua Gershman," *Labour/Le Travail* 2 (January 1977), 188.
9 "David Croll – Biography," *JewAge*, accessed September 2021, https://www.jewage.org/wiki/he/Article:David_Croll_-_Biography.
10 Nelson Wiseman, "Jewish Politics and the Jewish Vote in Comparative Perspective," in *Jewish Radicalism in Winnipeg, 1905–1960*, ed. Daniel Stone (Winnipeg: Jewish Heritage Centre of Western Canada, 2003), 156–71.
11 Abella, "Portrait of a Jewish Professional Revolutionary," 1–28.
12 Abella, "Portrait of a Jewish Professional Revolutionary," 1–28.
13 Abella, "Portrait of a Jewish Professional Revolutionary," 190, 212–13.
14 See Chapter 2 of Tulchinsky, *Joe Salsberg: A Life of Commitment* (Toronto: University of Toronto Press, 2013).
15 Tulchinsky, *Joe Salsberg*, 187.
16 Louis Rosenberg, *Canada's Jews: A Social and Economic History of Jews in Canada in the 1930s*, ed. Morton Weinfeld (Montreal and Kingston: McGill-Queen's University Press, 1993), 288–90.
17 Stephen Schneider, *Iced: The Story of Organized Crime in Canada* (Wiley, 2009), 162.
18 Schneider, *Iced*, 180.
19 Schneider, *Iced*, 302.
20 Howard Moscoe, "My Mother, the Bootlegger," in Lorinc et al., *The Ward*, 31.

7. "The Line Must Be Drawn Somewhere": Shades of Antisemitism in Canada, 1760–1945

1 The word is correctly spelled antisemitism, although commonly it's either Anti-semitism, or anti-semitism. These are incorrect, because they mean that it's a condemnation of people who speak a Semitic language. Clearly that was not Marr's intent, nor is it the view of his followers.
2 Ira Robinson, *A History of Antisemitism in Canada*, 30.
3 Tulchinsky, *Taking Root*, 72.
4 Alan Mendelson, *Exiles from Nowhere: The Jews and Canadian Elite* (Montreal: R. Brass Studio, 2008), 11–54.
5 Tulchinsky, *Taking Root*, 237.
6 Michael Brown, *Jew or Juif? Jews, French Canadians and Anglo Canadians, 1759–1914* (Philadelphia: The Jewish Publication Society, 1986), 245–6.
7 Robinson, *A History of Antisemitism in Canada*, 47.
8 Michael Brown, "From Stereotype to Scapegoat: Anti-Jewish Sentiment in French Canada from Confederation to World War I," in *Antisemitism in Canada: History and Interpretation*, ed. Alan Davies (Waterloo, ON: Wilfrid Laurier University Press: 2006), 46.
9 Robinson, *A History of Antisemitism in Canada*, 78.
10 Esther Delisle, *The Traitor and the Jew: Anti-Semitism and the Delirium of Extremist Right-Wing Nationalism in French Canada from 1929–1939* (Montreal: Robert Davies, 1993), 26.
11 Robinson, *A History of Antisemitism in Canada*, 60.
12 Robinson, *A History of Antisemitism in Canada*, 77.
13 Leonard Dinnerstein, *Uneasy at Home: Antisemitism and the American Jewish Experience* (New York: Columbia University Press: 1987), 260.
14 Howard Palmer, "Politics, Religion and Antisemitism in Alberta, 1880–1950," in Davies, *Antisemitism in Canada*, 170.
15 Janine Stingel, *Social Discredit: Anti-Semitism, Social Credit, and the Jewish Response* (Montreal-Kingston: McGill-Queen's University Press: 2000), 9.
16 Stingel, *Social Discredit*, 19.
17 Stingel, *Social Discredit*, 23.
18 Stingel, *Social Discredit*, 23.
19 Palmer, "Politics, Religion and Antisemitism," 181.
20 Stingel, *Social Discredit*, 188.
21 Lita-Rose Betcherman, *The Swastika and the Maple Leaf: Fascist Movements in Canada in the Thirties* (Toronto: Fitzhenry and Whiteside, 1978), 93.
22 Robinson, *A History of Antisemitism in Canada*, 93.
23 Cyril Levitt and William Shaffir, *The Riot at Christie Pits* (Toronto: University of Toronto Press, 1987), conclusion.
24 Personal correspondence.
25 Rosenberg, *Canada's Jews*, quoted in Robinson, *A History of Antisemitism in Canada*, 67.

26 Robinson, *A History of Antisemitism in Canada*, 77.
27 James H. Gray, *The Winter Years* (Calgary: Fifth House Publishers, 2003), 126–7.
28 Paul Axelrod, *Making a Middle Class: Student Life in English Canada during the Thirties* (Montreal-Kingston: McGill-Queen's University Press, 1990), 7.
29 Axelrod, *Making a Middle Class*, 32.
30 Axelrod, *Making a Middle Class*, 32.
31 Axelrod, *Making a Middle Class*, 5.
32 Irving Abella and Harold Troper, *None Is Too Many: Canada and the Jews of Europe, 1933–1948* (Toronto: Lester Publishing Ltd., 1983), xii–xiii.
33 In 1935 Germany passed two laws that stripped Jews of citizenship and outlawed the marriage of Jews and non-Jews.
34 Harold Troper, "New Horizons in a Jew Land: Jewish Immigration to Canada," in *From Immigration to Integration: The Canadian Jewish Experience*, ed. Ruth Klein and Frank Dimant (Toronto: Institute for International Relations, 2001), 11–14.
35 Abella and Troper, *None Is Too Many*, 8.
36 Abella and Troper, *None Is Too Many*, 64.
37 Abella and Troper, *None Is Too Many*, 38.
38 Abella and Troper, *None Is Too Many*, 37.
39 A recent study by Justin Cromartin puts the figure at 8,787. Justin Comartin, "Opening Closed Doors: Revisiting the Canadian Immigration Record (1933–1945)," *Canadian Jewish Studies/Études juives canadiennes* 24 (2016), https://doi.org/10.25071/1916-0925.39961.

8. "Into the Mainstream": From Immigrants to Canadians

1 Derek J. Penslar, *Jews and the Military: A History* (Princeton University Press, 2013), 3.
2 J.L. Granatstein, "Ethnic and Religious Enlistment in Canada during the Second World War," *Canadian Jewish Studies* 21 (2013/2014): 178.
3 John Ward, "Barney Danson, former politician, minister and soldier dead at 90," *Toronto Star*, Tuesday, October 18, 2011.
4 Richard Menkis, "'There Were Cries of Joy, Some of Sorrow': Canadian Jewish Soldiers and Early Encounters with Survivors," *Canadian Jewish Studies* 27 (2019): 125–38, https://doi.org/10.25071/1916-0925.40108.
5 Menkis, "'There Were Cries of Joy,'" 128.
6 Menkis, "'There Were Cries of Joy,'" 129.
7 Menkis, "'There Were Cries of Joy,'" 129.
8 Mark Celinscak, *Distance from the Belsen Heap* (Toronto: University of Toronto Press, 2015), 50.
9 Celinscak, *Distance from the Belsen Heap*, 194.

10 Royal Canadian Mounted Police, "War Series, No. 39, December 23, 1940," in *RCMP Security Bulletins*, ed. Gregory S. Kealey and Reg Whitaker (St. John's, NL: Committee on Canadian Labour History, 1989), 311, https://journals.lib.unb.ca/index.php/RCMP/issue/view/821.
11 Royal Canadian Mounted Police, "War Series, No. 45, July 19, 1941," in Kealey and Whitaker, *RCMP Security Bulletins*, 382, https://journals.lib.unb.ca/index.php/RCMP/issue/view/821.
12 The data employed in this section are taken from detailed analyses of Census Tracts, undertaken every decade in the year ending in 1, by Statistics Canada. The analyses were made by demographers employed by Jewish Federations of Canada.
13 The Montreal data are courtesy of the office files of demographer Charles Shahar of Federation CJA.
14 Leonoff, *Pioneers, Pedlars, and Prayer Shawls*, 87.
15 Doug Owram, *Born at the Right Time: A History of the Baby Boom Generation* (Toronto: University of Toronto Press, 1996), 108.
16 He wrote a memoir of this ordeal in 1944. It was translated and published in 2016 as *The Vale of Tears.*
17 Sugihara issued some two thousand transit visas, many to students, unbeknownst to Japanese authorities. On his return, he lived in repute. He is hailed as one among "The Righteous Among The Nations," a designation for those who saved Jews during the Holocaust.
18 "David Hartman, the Iconic Jewish Educator Celebrated for his Pursuit of Pluralism, Had His Start in Canada," *National Post*, February 13, 2013, https://nationalpost.com/news/world/israel-middle-east/david-hartman-the-iconic-jewish-educator-celebrated-for-his-pursuit-of-pluralism-had-his-start-in-canada.
19 Emil L. Fackenheim, "The 614th Commandment," in "Jewish Values in the Post-Holocaust Future: A Symposium," *Judaism* 16 (Summer 1967), 295.
20 W. Gunther Plaut, *Unfinished Business* (Toronto: Lester, Orpen, Dennys, 1981), 128.
21 Owram, *Born at the Right Time*, chap. 1.
22 Erna Paris, "Growing Up a Jewish Princess in Forest Hill," in *The Spice Box: An Anthology of Jewish Canadian Writing*, ed. Gerri Sinclair and Morris Wolfe (Toronto: New Jewish Press, 1981).
23 Paris, "Growing Up a Jewish Princess."
24 Paris, "Growing Up a Jewish Princess."
25 Sharon Abron Drache, "Ruhama Fishbein and Me," in *Barbara Klein-Muskrat: Then and Now* (Toronto: Inanna Publications, 2012), 73–88.
26 Rosalie Sharp, *Growing Up Jewish: Canadians Tell Their Own Stories* (Toronto: McClelland & Stewart, 1997), 184.
27 Julia Koschitsky, "From Cardiff to Canada," in Sharp, *Growing Up Jewish*, 193.

28 Interview with the late Alan Borovoy.
29 Mordechai Richler, in George Woodcock, *Mordechai Richler* (Toronto: McClelland & Stewart, 1971), 58.
30 The acclaimed poet, Irving Layton, is discussed in the epilogue.
31 Michael Greenstein, *Contemporary Jewish Writing in Canada: An Anthology* (Lincoln, NE: University of Nebraska Press, 2004), xxxi–xxxii.
32 Greenstein, *Contemporary Jewish Writing in Canada*, xxxiii.
33 Ruth Panofsky, *Force of Vocation: The Literary Career of Adele Wiseman* (Winnipeg: The University of Manitoba Press, 2006), 5.
34 Panofsky, *Force of Vocation*, 5.
35 In addition to Ludwig and Wiseman, there were also the poets Miriam Waddington from Winnipeg and Eli Mandel from Saskatchewan.
36 Veronica Sedivy and Evan Ware, “Oskar Morawetz,” *The Canadian Encyclopedia*, published online November 22, 2007, https://www.thecanadianencyclopedia.ca/en/article/oskar-morawetz-emc.
37 “Who the F**k is Arthur Fogel,” directed by Ron Chapman (Toronto: Chapman Productions, 2013).
38 Johnny Wayne and Frank Shuster, “A Shakespearean Baseball Game,” *The Wayne and Shuster Hour* (Toronto: CBC Television, May 22, 1958).
39 Franklin Bialystok, *Delayed Impact: The Holocaust and the Canadian Jewish Community* (Montreal and Kingston: McGill-Queen’s University Press, 2000), 85.
40 The term was coined by author Hugh MacLennan.
41 Peter C. Newman, *The Canadian Establishment* (Toronto: Penguin Canada, 1999), 219.
42 John Porter, *The Vertical Mosaic: An Analysis of Social Class and Power in Canada, 50th Anniversary Edition* (Toronto: University of Toronto Press, 2015), 5.
43 Porter, *The Vertical Mosaic*, 88.
44 Porter, *The Vertical Mosaic*, 442.
45 Wallace Clement, *Canadian Corporate Elite* (Ottawa: Carleton University Press, 1975), 204.
46 Nicholas Faith, *The Bronfmans: The Rise and Fall of the House of Seagram* (New York: Thomas Dunne Books, St. Martin’s Griffin, 2006), 14.
47 Michael R. Marrus, *Mr. Sam: The Life and Times of Samuel Bronfman* (Toronto: Viking Press, 1991), 346.
48 Michael R. Marrus, *Samuel Bronfman: The Life and Times of Seagram’s Mr. Sam* (Waltham, MA: Brandeis University Press, 1991), 418.
49 Marrus, *Samuel Bronfman*, 417–18.
50 Peter C. Newman, *Titans: How the New Canadian Establishment Seized Power* (Toronto: Viking Canada, 1998), 131.
51 Newman, *Titans*, 17.
52 Newman, *Titans*, 79.

9. Confronting History, 1945–1985

1 James W.St.G. Walker, "The 'Jewish Phase' in the Movement for Racial Equality in Canada," *Canadian Ethnic Studies Journal* 34, no. 1 (Spring 2002): 1–30.
2 Walker, "The 'Jewish Phase.'"
3 David J. Bercuson, *Canada and the Birth of Israel: A Study in Canadian Foreign Policy* (Toronto: University of Toronto Press, 2014), 26.
4 Bialystok, *Delayed Impact*, 38.
5 Bialystok, *Delayed Impact*, 38.
6 Bialystok, *Delayed Impact*, 39.
7 Donia Blumenfeld Clenman, *I Dream in Good English Too* (self-pub., Flowerfield and Littleman, 1988).
8 Bialystok, *Delayed Impact*, 82.
9 For an excellent study of survivor adaptation, see Adara Goldberg, *Holocaust Survivors in Canada: Exclusion, Inclusion, Transformation, 1947–1955* (Winnipeg: University of Manitoba Press, 2015).
10 Bialystok, *Delayed Impact*, 116–18.
11 Bialystok, *Delayed Impact*, 109.
12 Bialystok, *Delayed Impact*, 104–5.
13 Bialystok, *Delayed Impact*, 109.
14 Bialystok, *Delayed Impact*, 108.
15 Bialystok, *Delayed Impact*, 111.
16 Bialystok, *Delayed Impact*, 117.
17 There is no roster of the members, but it is likely that it did not include women.
18 Bialystok, *Delayed Impact*, 157.
19 Harold Troper, *The Defining Decade – Identity, Politics, and the Canadian Jewish Community in the 1960s* (Toronto: University of Toronto Press, 2010), 126. Troper devotes approximately one-third of the text to impact of the Six Day War.
20 Troper, *The Defining Decade*, 130.
21 Conversation with author.
22 Troper, *The Defining Decade*, 161.
23 Bialystok, *Delayed Impact*, 161.
24 Bialystok, *Delayed Impact*, 161.
25 Bialystok, *Delayed Impact*, 161.
26 Troper, *The Defining Decade*, 205.
27 Rob Mickleburgh, "From News to Politics, Simma Holt Leaves Behind an Empowering Legacy," *Globe and Mail*, February 19, 2015.
28 Ron Csillag, "Remembering Stanley Hartt, Brian Mulroney's Former Chief of Staff, *Canadian Jewish News*, January 10, 2018.
29 David Lewis, *Louder Voices: The Corporate Welfare Bums* (Toronto: James Lewis & Samuel, Publishers, 1972).

30 Tom Marshall of the Conservatives was interim premier of Newfoundland for ten months in 2014.
31 Saul Hayes, "The Changing Nature of the Jewish Community," *Viewpoints* 5, no. 3 (1970): 24–8, quoted in Bialystok, *Delayed Impact*, 164.
32 Troper, *The Defining Decade*, 264.
33 Troper, *The Defining Decade*, 275.
34 Troper, *The Defining Decade*, 283.
35 Harold Troper, *The Ransomed of God: The Remarkable Story of One Woman's Role in the Rescue of Syrian Jews* (Malcolm Lester Books, 1999), 28.
36 Troper, *The Ransomed of God.*
37 For more on Robert Kaplan, see Bernie M. Farber, "Robert Kaplan Fought to Uncover Nazis in Canada," *Toronto Star*, November 6, 2012.

10. Consensus and Continuity, 1985–2000

1 Warren Kinsella, *Web of Hate* (Toronto: HarperCollins, 1995), 426.
2 B'nai Brith Canada and League for Human Rights, *Annual Audit of Antisemitic Incidents 1984* (Toronto: B'nai Brith Canada, 1984).
3 B'nai Brith Canada and League for Human Rights, *Annual Audit of Antisemitic Incidents 1987* (Toronto: B'nai Brith Canada, 1987).
4 B'nai Brith Canada and League for Human Rights, *Annual Audit of Antisemitic Incidents 1990* (Toronto: B'nai Brith Canada, 1990) and B'nai Brith Canada and League for Human Rights, *Annual Audit of Antisemitic Incidents 1991* (Toronto: B'nai Brith Canada, 1991).
5 B'nai Brith Canada, *Annual Audit of Antisemitic Incidents 1990.*
6 Morton Weinfeld, *Like Everyone Else But Different*, 2nd ed. (Montreal-Kingston: McGill-Queen's University Press, 2018), 310.
7 The Canada Israel Committee was created in the late 1960s to represent the community on Parliament Hill. It had representatives from CJC, B'nai Brith, and the Federation with offices in Montreal, Toronto, and Vancouver.
8 David Taras and David H. Goldberg, *The Domestic Battleground: Canada and the Arab-Israeli Conflict* (Montreal-Kingston: McGill-Queen's University Press, 1989), 212.
9 Robinson, *A History of Antisemitism in Canada*, 165.
10 Sidney Goldstein et al., *The National Jewish Population Survey* (New York: Council of Jewish Federations, 1990).
11 Raymond Breton, "Institutional Completeness of Ethnic Communities and the Personal Relations of Immigrants," *American Journal of Sociology* 70, no. 2 (September 1964), 193–205.
12 David J. Elazar and Harold M. Waller, *Maintaining Consensus: The Canadian Jewish Polity in the Postwar World* (Lanham, MD, New York, and London: University Press of America and the Jerusalem Center for Public Affairs, 1990), 189.

13 Elazar and Waller, *Maintaining Consensus*, 199.
14 Jim Torczyner and Shari L. Brotman, *The Jews of Canada: A Profile from the Census* (New York: American Jewish Committee), 1995.
15 According to Jewish law, to effectuate a divorce, the husband must sign a document prepared by a religious court to be given to his wife. The document is called a *get* from the Hebrew. There is no English translation. When the husband refuses to do so, it means that his wife cannot remarry.

11. The Jewish Diaspora Settles on Bathurst Street

1 Rosenberg, *Canada's Jews*, 10.
2 Jean-Claude Lasry, "Sephardim and Ashkenazim in Montreal," *Contemporary Jewry* 6, no. 2 (Fall/Winter 1983), 26–33.
3 Lasry, "Sephardim and Ashkenazim in Montreal," 26–33.
4 Weinfeld, *Like Everyone Else But Different*, 17–20.
5 Weinfeld, *Like Everyone Else But Different*, 77.
6 Michael Greenstein, *Third Solitudes: Tradition and Discontinuity in Jewish-Canadian Literature* (Montreal-Kingston: McGill-Queen's University, 1980), 173.
7 Michael Greenstein, "Naïm Kattan: 'The Dancer,'" in *Contemporary Jewish Writing in Canada: An Anthology* (Lincoln Nebraska: University of Nebraska Press, 2004), 68.
8 Roberta Markus and Donald Schwartz, "Soviet Jewish Emigres in Toronto: Ethnic Self-Identity and Issues of Integration," *Canadian Ethnic Studies* 16, no. 2 (January 1, 1984).
9 David Bezmozgis, *Natasha and Other Stories* (New York: Harper Collins, 2011), 81–110.
10 Sheva Medjuck, "Atlantic Canada," *Encyclopedia.com* (September 24, 2021), https://www.encyclopedia.com/religion/encyclopedias-almanacs-transcripts-and-maps/atlantic-canada.
11 Quoted in Peter Brimelow, "Separatism May Scare Businessmen, But It's the Socialism that Terrifies," *Macleans*, November 29, 1976.
12 Jean Francois Lisee, "Interview with Pierre Anctil," in *Boundaries of Identity: A Quebec Reader*, ed. William Dodge (Toronto: Turnerbooks, 1992), 151–6.
13 Tulchinsky, *Canada's Jews*, 445.
14 Weinfeld, *Like Everyone Else But Different* (2013), 85–6.

12. The Ascent of Diversity in the New Millennium

1 Disclosure: the author was a lay member of the CJC from 1978 until 2011. The sources for this section include the author's notes and documents during that period.
2 Kathryn Blaze Carlson, "'Bad Blood' As Change Comes to Jewish Advocacy Groups," *National Post*, August 30, 2011.

3 The Canada Israel Committee was created in the wake of the Six Day War. Initially it had representatives from the CJC, B'nai Brith Canada, and the Federation but by the late 1970s it had become an independent body.
4 These included a segment of the United Church of Canada, some trade unions, some Islamic organizations, some human rights groups such as Kairos (Canadian Ecumenical Justice Initiatives), student activists, and radical Jewish factions.
5 Aside from the CJC, they included the Canada Israel Committee, the Quebec Region of the CJC, Hillel (the Jewish organization on campuses), and two new groups, National Jewish Campus Life, and the University Outreach Committee.
6 Regina, Saskatoon, Saint John, Quebec, Sydney-Glace Bay are the among the most notable.
7 Irving Abella, "Canada Still Has Much to Learn from None Is Too Many," *Globe and Mail*, February 26, 2013.
8 Robert Brym, Keith Neuman, and Rhonda Lenton, *2018 Survey of Jews in Canada*, Environics Institute for Survey Research, March 11, 2019.
9 Brym, Neuman, and Lenton, *2018 Survey of Jews in Canada*.
10 For the definition, see https://www.holocaustremembrance.com/resources/working-definitions-charters/working-definition-antisemitism.
11 Mira Sucherov, "A Brief History of Canada-Israel Relations," *Canadian Jewish News*, July 11, 2017.
12 Konrad Yakabuski, "On Israel, Trudeau Is Harper's Pupil," *Globe and Mail*, May 11, 2018.
13 Margolis is now a professor at the University of Melbourne in Australia.
14 William Shaffir, "Separation from the Mainstream in Canada: The Hasidic Community of Tash," in *The Jews of Canada*, ed. Robert Brym, William Shaffir, and Morton Weinfeld (Toronto: Oxford University Press, 2010), 120.
15 Rabbi Micah Streiffer, "Intermarried Families Are Also Jewish Families," *Canadian Jewish News*, January 30, 2019.
16 Alex Pomson and Randal F. Schnoor, *Back to School: Jewish Day School in the Lives of Adult Jews* (Detroit: Wayne State University Press, 2009), 152–3.
17 Michael Fraiman, "The Cost of Being Jewish in Canada," *Canadian Jewish News*, October 3, 2018.
18 Rabbi Elyse Goldstein, "Why I'm Marching in the Pride Parade," *Canadian Jewish News*, June 24, 2012.
19 Weinfeld, *Like Everyone Else But Different*, 104.
20 Michael Fraiman, "Jew from the 6IX: Dissecting Drake's Complicated Relationship with Judaism," *Canadian Jewish News*, March 16, 2017.
21 Greenstein, *Contemporary Jewish Writing in Canada*, 219.
22 In addition, author Saul Bellow (1914–2005) was accorded the Prize in Literature in 1976. He grew up in Montreal, but the family moved to Chicago when he was a child and the city has remained his home.

23 Ankita Gupta, "Judicial Biography: Rosalie Silberman Abella," *theCourt.ca*, August 29, 2019.

24 Rosalie Abella, "An Attack on the Independence of a Court Anywhere Is an Attack on All Courts," *Globe and Mail*, October 26, 2018.

25 David S. Koffman, "What Does It Mean to Ask the Question, 'Has There Ever Been a Better Home for the Jews than Canada?'" in *No Better Home? Jews, Canada, and the Sense of Belonging*, ed. David S. Koffman (Toronto: University of Toronto Press, 2020), 3.

Epilogue: "Hallelujah"

1 Leonard Cohen, *The Favourite Game* (New York: Avon, 1963), 11.

2 Leonard Cohen, *Beautiful Losers* (New York: Bantam, 1966), 155.

3 George A. Walker, *The Wordless Leonard Cohen: Songbook* (Erin, ON: The Porcupine's Quill, 2014), 13.

4 Leonard Cohen, *The Spice-Box of Earth* (Penguin, 1961).

5 Isaiah 57:14–58:14.

6 From Cohen, *The Spice-Box of Earth.*

Select Bibliography

Abella, Irving. *A Coat of Many Colours: Two Centuries of Jewish Life in Canada.* Toronto: Lester and Orpen Dennys, 1990.

– "Portrait of a Jewish Professional Revolutionary: The Recollections of Joshua Gershman." *Labour/Le Travail* 2 (January 1977): 185–213.

Abella, Irving, and Harold Troper. *None Is Too Many: Canada and the Jews of Europe, 1933–1948.* Toronto: University of Toronto Press, 2012.

Abron Drache, Sharon. *Barbara Klein-Muskrat Then and Now.* Toronto: Inanna, 2012.

Adelman, Howard, and John H. Simpson, eds. *Multiculturalism, Jews, and Identities in Canada.* Jerusalem: Magnes Press, 1998.

Anctil, Pierre. *Histoire des Juifs du Québec.* Montréal: Boréal, 2017.

– "Interlude of Hostility: Judeo-Christian Relations in Quebec in the Interwar Period, 1919–1939." In *Antisemitism in Canada: History and Interpretation,* edited by Alan Davies, 135–65. Waterloo, ON: Wilfrid Laurier University Press, 1992.

– *Jacob Isaac Segal: A Montreal Yiddish Poet and His Milieu.* Translated by Vivian Felsen. Ottawa: University of Ottawa Press, 2017.

– *Jacob-Isaac Segal (1896–1954) : Un poète yiddish de Montréal et son milieu.* Québec, QC: Presses de l'Université Laval, 2012.

– *Les Juifs de Québec: Quatre cents ans d'histoire.* Québec, QC: Presses de l'Université du Québec, 2015.

– *A Reluctant Welcome for Jewish People: Voices in Le Devoir's Editorials, 1910–1947.* Translated by Tõnu Onu. Ottawa: University of Ottawa Press, 2019.

– *Saint-Laurent: La Main de Montréal.* Montreal: Septentrion, 2002.

Axelrod, Paul. *Making a Middle Class: Student Life in English Canada during the Thirties.* Montreal and Kingston: McGill-Queen's University Press, 1990.

Barsky, Lesley Marrus. *From Generation to Generation: A History of Toronto's Mount Sinai Hospital.* Toronto: McClelland and Stewart, 1998.

Bauer, Yehuda. *A History of the Holocaust.* London: Franklin Watts, 1982.

Belkin, Simon. *Through Narrow Gates: A Review of Jewish Immigration, Colonization and Immigrant Aid Work in Canada.* Montreal: Canadian Jewish Congress, 1966.

Bercuson, David J. *Canada and the Birth of Israel: A Study in Canadian Foreign Policy.* Toronto: University of Toronto Press, 1985.

Bercuson, David J., and Douglas Wertheimer. *A Trust Betrayed: The Keegstra Affair.* Toronto: University of Toronto Press, 1995.

Bessner, Ellin. *Double Threat: Canadian Jews, the Military, and World War II.* Toronto: New Jewish Press, 2018.

Betcherman, Lita-Rose. *The Swastika and the Maple Leaf: Fascist Movements in Canada in the Thirties.* Toronto: Fitzhenry and Whiteside, 1978.

Bialystok, Franklin. *Delayed Impact: The Holocaust and the Canadian Jewish Community.* Montreal and Kingston: McGill-Queen's University Press, 2000.

Bilsky, Anna. *A Common Thread: A History of the Jews of Ottawa.* Ottawa: Ottawa Jewish Historical Society, 2009.

Bossin, Bob. *Davy the Punk: A Story of Bookies, Toronto the Good, the Mob and My Dad.* Erin, ON: The Porcupine's Quill, 2015.

Brown, Michael. "From Stereotype to Scapegoat: Anti-Jewish Sentiment in French Canada from Confederation to World War I." In *Antisemitism in Canada: History and Interpretation,* edited by Alan Davies, 39–66. Waterloo, ON: Wilfrid Laurier University Press, 1992.

– *Jew or Juif? Jews, French Canadians, and Anglo Canadians, 1759–1914.* Philadelphia: Jewish Publication Society, 1987.

– "On Campus in the Thirties: Antipathy, Support, and Indifference." In *Nazi Germany, Canadian Responses: Confronting Antisemitism in the Shadow of War,* edited by L. Ruth Klein, 144–83. Montreal and Kingston: McGill-Queen's University Press, 2012.

Brym, Robert, Keith Neuman, and Rhonda Lenton, eds. *2018 Survey of Jews in Canada: Final Report.* Environics Institute for Survey Research. www.environicsinstitute.org.

Brym, Robert J., William Shaffir, and Morton Weinfeld, eds. *The Jews in Canada: A Comprehensive Study of the Canadian Jewish Community.* Toronto: Oxford University Press, 2010.

Clement, Wallace. *The Canadian Corporate Elite.* Toronto: McClelland and Stewart, 1975.

Cobden, Michael. *Simon Spatz: From Holocaust to Halifax – A Story of Survival and Success.* Halifax: Nimbus, 2016.

Cochrane, Jean. *Kensington.* Toronto: Stoddardt, 2000.

Cohen, Leonard. *Beautiful Losers.* New York: Bantam, 1966.

– *Book of Longing.* Toronto: McClelland and Stewart, 2006.

– *Favourite Game.* New York: Avon, 1963.

– *The Flame: Poems and Selections from Notebooks*. Edited by Robert Faggen and Alexandra Pleshoyano. Toronto: McClelland and Stewart, 2018.

– *Selected Poems, 1956–1968*. Toronto: McClelland and Stewart, 1968.

Dawidowicz, Lucy. *The War against the Jews: 1933–1945*. New York: Holt, Rinehart and Winston, 1975.

Delisle, Esther. *The Traitor and the Jew: Anti-Semitism and the Delirium of Extremist Right-Wing Nationalism in French Canada from 1929–1939*. Montreal: Robert Davies, 1993.

Donegal, Rosemarie. *Spadina*. Toronto: Douglas and MacIntyre, 1985.

Eisenstein, Bernice. *I Was a Child of Holocaust Survivors*. New York: Penguin, 2006.

Elazar, Daniel J., and Harold M. Waller. *Maintaining Consensus: The Canadian Jewish Polity in the Postwar World*. Boston: The University Press of America, 1990.

Elazar, Daniel J., and Morton Weinfeld, eds. *Still Moving: Recent Jewish Migration in Comparative Perspective*. New Brunswick, NJ: Transaction Press, 2000.

Frager, Ruth A. *Sweatshop Strife: Class, Ethnicity, and Gender in the Jewish Labour Movement of Toronto, 1900–1939*. Toronto: University of Toronto Press, 1992.

Geddes, Gary, ed. *15 Canadian Poets x 3*. 4th ed. Toronto: Oxford University Press, 2001.

Gladstone, Bill. *A History of the Jewish Community of London Ontario: From the 1850s to the Present Day*. Toronto: Now and Then Books, 2011.

Godfrey, Sheldon J., and Judith C. Godfrey. *Search Out the Land: The Jews and the Growth of Equality in British Colonial America, 1740–1867*. Montreal and Kingston: McGill-Queen's University Press, 1995.

Goldberg, Adara. *Holocaust Survivors in Canada: Exclusion, Inclusion, Transformation, 1947–1955*. Winnipeg: University of Manitoba Press, 2015.

Goldberg, David H., and David Taras, eds. *The Domestic Battleground: Canada and the Arab-Israeli Conflict*. Montreal and Kingston: McGill-Queen's University Press, 1989.

Goldbloom, Victor C. *Building Bridges*. Montreal and Kingston: McGill-Queen's University Press, 2015.

Granatstein, J.L., and Dean E. Oliver. *The Oxford Companion to Canadian Military History*. Toronto: Oxford University Press, 2011.

Greenstein, Michael, ed. *Contemporary Jewish Writing in Canada: An Anthology*. Lincoln: University of Nebraska Press, 2004.

– *Third Solitudes: Traditional Discontinuity in Jewish-Canadian Literature*. Montreal and Kingston: McGill-Queen's University Press, 1989.

Gutkin, Harry. *The Worst of Times, the Best of Times: Growing Up in Winnipeg's North End*. Toronto: Fitzhenry and Whiteside, 1987.

Halpern, Monda. *Alice in Shandehland: Scandal and Scorn in the Edelson/Horowitz Murder Case*. Montreal and Kingston: McGill-Queen's University Press, 2015.

Hart, Arthur D., ed. *The Jew in Canada.* Facsimile edition of the 1926 publication. Toronto: Now and Then Books, 2010.

Helmer, Paul. *Growing With Canada: The Émigré Tradition in Canadian Music.* Montreal and Kingston: McGill-Queen's University Press, 2009.

Hilberg, Raul. *The Destruction of the European Jews.* New Haven: Yale University Press, 1961.

Hirschprung, Pinchas. *The Vale of Tears.* Translated by Vivian Felsen. Toronto: The Azrieli Foundation, 2016.

Jacobs, Jane. *Dark Age Ahead.* New York: Random House, 2004.

James, R. Warren. *People's Senator: The Life and Times of David A. Croll.* Vancouver and Toronto: Douglas & McIntyre, 1990.

Kage, Joseph. *With Faith and Thanksgiving: The Story of Two Hundred Years of Jewish Immigration and Immigrant Aid Effort in Canada, 1760–1960.* Montreal: Eagle Press, 1962.

Kayfetz, Benjamin, and Stephen Speisman. *Only Yesterday: Collected Pieces on the Jews of Toronto.* Toronto: Now and Then Books, 2013.

Keillor, Elaine. *Music in Canada: Capturing Landscape and Diversity.* Montreal and Kingston: McGill-Queen's University Press. 2006.

Kelly, Ninette, and Michael Trebilcock. *The Making of the Mosaic: A History of Canadian Immigration Policy.* 2nd ed. Toronto: University of Toronto Press, 2010.

King, Joe. *From the Ghetto to the Main: The Story of the Jews of Montreal.* Montreal: Jewish Publication Society, 2003.

Kinsella, Warren. *Web of Hate: Inside Canada's Far Right Network.* Toronto: Harper Collins, 1996.

Knight, Andrea, Paula Draper, and Nicole Bryck. *The Tailor Project: How 2,500 Holocaust Survivors Found a New Life in Canada.* Toronto: Second Story Press, 2020.

Koffman, David S., ed. *No Better Home? Jews, Canada, and the Sense of Belonging.* Toronto: University of Toronto Press, 2021.

Koven, Marcia. *Weaving the Past into the Present: A Glimpse into the 150 Year History of the Saint John Jewish Community.* Saint John: Saint John Jewish Historical Museum, 2008.

Leonoff, Cyril Edel. *Centennial of Vancouver Jewish Life: 1886–1986.* Vancouver: The Jewish Western Bulletin, 1986.

– *Pioneer Jewish Merchants of Vancouver Island and British North America.* Vancouver: The Jewish Historical Society of British Columbia and The Jewish Western Bulletin, 1984.

– *Pioneers, Pedlars and Prayer Shawls: The Jewish Communities in British Columbia and the Yukon.* Victoria: Sono Nis Press, 1978.

Levine, Allan. *Coming of Age: A History of the Jewish People of Manitoba.* Winnipeg: Heartland, 2009.

– *Toronto: Biography of a City.* Madeira Park, BC: Douglas & McIntyre, 2014.

Levitt, Cyril, and William Shaffir. *The Riot at Christie Pits.* Toronto: Lester and Orpen Dennys, 1987.

Lewis, David. *The Good Fight: Political Memoirs 1909–1958.* Toronto: Macmillan, 1981.

Lipinsky, Jack. *Imposing Their Will: An Organizational History of Jewish Toronto, 1933–1948.* Montreal and Kingston: McGill-Queen's University Press, 2011.

Lorinc, John, Michael McClelland, Ellen Scheinberg, and Tatum Taylor, eds. *The Ward: The Life and Loss of Toronto's First Immigrant Neighbourhood.* Toronto: Coach House Books, 2015.

Luftspring, Sammy. *Call Me Sammy.* With Brian Swarbrick. Toronto: Prentice-Hall, 1975.

Magocsi, Paul Robert. *Historical Atlas of Central Europe.* Toronto: University of Toronto Press, 2002.

Margolis, Rebecca. *Jewish Roots, Canadian Soil: Yiddish Cultural Life in Montreal, 1905–1945.* Montreal and Kingston: McGill-Queen's University Press, 2011.

Marrus, Michael R. *Mr. Sam: The Life and Times of Samuel Bronfman.* Toronto: Penguin, 1991.

McGrath, Robin. *Salt Fish and Shmattes: A History of the Jews in Newfoundland and Labrador from 1770.* St. John's: Creative Book Publishing, 2006.

McKay, Ian. "Joe Salsberg, Depression-Era Communism, and the Limits of Moscow's Rule." *Canadian Jewish Studies: Oyfn Veg, Essays in Honour of Gerald Tulchinsky* 21 (2013–14): 130–42.

Medjuck, Sheva. *The Jews of Atlantic Canada.* St. John's: Breakwater, 1986.

Medres, Israel. *Montreal of Yesterday: Jewish Life in Montreal 1900–1920.* Translated by Vivian Felsen. Montreal: Véhicule Press, 2000.

Mendelson, Alan. *Exiles from Nowhere: The Jews and the Canadian Elite.* Montreal: Robin Brass Studio, 2008.

Menkis, Richard. "Antisemitism and Anti-Judaism in Pre-Confederation Canada." In *Antisemitism in Canada: History and Interpretation,* edited by Alan Davies, 11–38. Waterloo, ON: Wilfrid Laurier University Press, 1992.

– "Historiography, Myth and Group Relations: Jewish and Non-Jewish Quebecois on Jews and New France." In *The Canadian Jewish Studies Reader,* edited by Richard Menkis and Norman Ravvin. Markham, ON: Red Deer Press, 2004.

Michaels, Anne. *Fugitive Pieces.* Toronto: McClelland and Stewart, 1996.

Moore, Christopher. "Colonization and Conflict: New France and Its Rivals (1600–1760)." In *The Illustrated History of Canada,* edited by Craig Brown, 95–180. Toronto: Key Porter, 2002.

Morgan, Michael. *A Holocaust Reader: Responses to the Nazi Extermination.* New York: Oxford University Press, 2001.

Newman, Peter C. *Bronfman Dynasty: The Rothschilds of the New World.* Toronto: McClelland and Stewart, 1978.

– *The Canadian Establishment.* Vol. 1. Toronto: McClelland and Stewart Bantam, 1975.

– *The Canadian Establishment*. Vol. 2, *The Acquisitors*. Toronto: McClelland and Stewart, 1981.

– *The Canadian Establishment*. Vol. 3, *Titans: How The New Canadian Establishment Seized Power*. Toronto: Penguin, 1999.

Norrie, Kenneth, and Doug Owram. *A History of the Canadian Economy*. 4th ed. Toronto: Harcourt, Brace, Jovanovich, 2007.

Ouellet, Fernand. *Lower Canada 1791–1840*. Toronto: McClelland and Stewart, 1980.

Owram, Doug. *Born at the Right Time: A History of the Baby Boom Generation*. Toronto: University of Toronto Press, 1996.

Palmer, Bryan D. *Working Class Experience: Rethinking the History of Canadian Labour, 1800–1991*. Toronto: McClelland and Stewart, 1991.

Palmer, Howard. "Politics, Religion and Antisemitism in Alberta, 1880–1950." In *Antisemitism in Canada: History and Interpretation*, edited by Alan Davies, 167–96. Waterloo, ON: Wilfrid Laurier University Press, 1992.

Panofsky, Ruth. *The Force of Vocation: The Literary Career of Adele Wiseman*. Winnipeg: University of Manitoba Press, 2006.

Paris, Erna. *Jews: An Account of Their Experience in Canada*. Toronto: MacMillan, 1980.

Penslar, Derek J. *Jews and the Military: A History*. Princeton, NJ: Princeton University Press, 2013.

Plaut, Gunther. *Unfinished Business: An Autobiography*. Toronto: Lester and Orpen Dennys, 1981.

Polonsky, Antony. *The Jews in Poland and Russia*. 2 vols. Oxford: Littman Library of Jewish Civilization, 2010.

Pomson, Alex, and Randal F. Schnoor. *Back to School: Jewish Day School in the Lives of Adult Jews*. Detroit: Wayne State University Press, 2008.

– *Jewish Family: Identity and Self-Formation at Home*. Bloomington: Indiana University Press, 2018.

Porter, John. *The Vertical Mosaic: An Analysis of Social Class and Power in Canada*. Toronto: University of Toronto Press, 1965.

Ravvin, Norman. *Hidden Canada: An Intimate Travelogue*. Markham, ON: Red Deer Press, 2001.

Ravvin, Norman, and Sherry Simon, eds. *Failure's Opposite: Listening to A.M. Klein*. Montreal and Kingston : McGill-Queen's University Press, 2011.

Redhill, Michael. *Belleville Square*. Toronto: Doubleday, 2017.

Richler, Mordecai. *The Apprenticeship of Duddy Kravitz*. Toronto: McClelland and Stewart, 1959.

Richler, Nancy. *The Imposter Bride*. Toronto: Harper Collins, 2012.

Ringuet, Chantal. "There's a Crack in Everything," translated by Jonathan Kaplansky, in *Biographical Wall in Ten Key Moments*. Montreal: Montreal Museum of Modern Art, 2017. Exhibition catalogue.

Robin, Martin. *Shades of Right: Nativist and Fascist Politics in Canada, 1920–1940*. Toronto: University of Toronto Press, 1992.

Robinson, Ira, ed. *Canada's Jews: In Time, Space and Spirit.* Brookline, MA: Academic Studies Press, 2013.

– *A History of Antisemitism In Canada.* Waterloo, ON: Wilfrid Laurier University Press, 2015.

– "Kabbalist and Communal Leader: Rabbi Yudel Rosenberg and the Canadian Jewish Community." *Canadian Jewish Studies/Études juives canadiennes* 1 (1993): 41–58.

Robinson, Ira, Pierre Anctil, and Mervin Butovsky, eds. *An Everyday Miracle: Yiddish Culture in Montreal.* Montreal: Véhicule Press, 1990.

Rome, David. *The First Two Years: A Record of the Jewish Pioneers on Canada's Pacific Coast, 1858–1860.* Montreal: Caiserman, 1942.

Rome, David, and Bernard Figler. *Hannaniah Meir Caiserman – A Biography.* Montreal: Northern Print, 1962.

Rosenberg, Louis. *Canada's Jews: A Social and Economic History of Jews in Canada in the 1930s.* Edited by Morton Weinfeld. Montreal and Kingston: McGill-Queen's University Press, 1993.

Rosenberg, Stuart. *The Jewish Community in Canada.* Vol. 1. Toronto: McClelland and Stewart, 1970.

Rosenfarb, Chava. *Exile at Last: Selected Poems.* Edited by Goldie Morgentaler. Toronto: Guernica Press, 2013.

Sachar, Howard M. *The Course of Modern Jewish History: The Classic History of the Jewish People from the Eighteenth Century to the Present Day.* New York: Virgin, 1990.

Sack, Benjamin G. *History of the Jews in Canada: From the Earliest Beginnings to the Present Day.* Vol. 1. Montreal: Canadian Jewish Congress, 1945.

Schild, Erwin. *The Very Narrow Bridge: A Memoir of an Uncertain Passage.* Toronto: Adath Israel Synagogue, 2001.

Schneider, Stephen. *Iced: The Story of Organized Crime in Canada.* Toronto: Wiley, 2009.

Shapiro, Shmuel Mayer. *The Rise of the Toronto Jewish Community.* Toronto: Now and Then Books, 2010.

Sharp, Rosalie Wise. *Rifke: An Improbable Life.* Toronto: Penguin, 2007.

Sharp, Rosalie, Irving Abella, Edwin Goodman, eds. *Growing Up Jewish: Canadians Tell Their Own Stories.* Toronto: McClelland and Stewart, 1997.

Sherman, Kenneth. *Wait Time: A Memoir of Cancer.* Waterloo: Wilfrid Laurier University Press, 2015.

Simmons, Sylvie. *I'm Your Man: The Life of Leonard Cohen.* New York: Harper Collins, 2012.

Speisman, Stephen A. *The Jews of Toronto: A History to 1937.* Toronto: McClelland and Stuart, 1977.

Srebrnik, Henry Felix. *Creating the Chupah: The Zionist Movement and the Drive for Jewish Communal Unity in Canada, 1898–1921.* Boston: Academic Studies Press, 2011.

Stingel, Janine. *Social Discredit: Anti-Semitism, Social Credit, and the Jewish Response.* Montreal and Kingston: McGill-Queen's University Press, 2000.

Stone, Daniel, ed. *Jewish Radicalism in Winnipeg: 1905–1960.* Winnipeg: Jewish Heritage Centre of Western Canada, 2003.

Tesler-Mabé, Hernan. "Performing Jewish? Heinz Unger, Gustav Mahler, and the Musical Strains of German-Jewish Identity in Canada and the United States." In *Neither in Dark Speeches Nor in Similitudes: Reflections and Refractions between Canadian and American Jews,* edited by Barry L. Stiefel and Hernan Tesler-Mabé, 153–73. Waterloo, ON: Wilfrid Laurier University Press, 2016.

Torgov, Morley. *A Good Place to Come from.* Toronto: Bev Editions, 2011.

Troper, Harold. *The Defining Decade: Identity, Politics, and the Canadian Jewish Community in the 1960s.* Toronto: University of Toronto Press, 2010.

– "New Horizons in a New Land: Jewish Immigration to Canada." In *From Immigration to Integration: The Canadian Jewish Experience: A Millennium Edition,* edited by Ruth Klein and Frank Dimant. Toronto: Institute for International Affairs, 2001.

– *The Ransomed of God: The Remarkable Story of One Woman's Role in the Rescue of Syrian Jews.* Toronto: Malcolm Lester, 1999

Troper, Harold, and Morton Weinfeld. *Old Wounds: Jews, Ukrainians, and the Hunt for Nazi War Criminals in Canada.* Toronto: Viking, 1988.

Tulchinsky, Gerald. *Branching Out: The Transformation of the Canadian Jewish Community.* Toronto: Stoddart, 1998.

– *Canada's Jews: A People's Journey.* Toronto: University of Toronto Press, 2008.

– "Goldwin Smith: Victorian Canadian Antisemite." In *Antisemitism in Canada: History and Interpretation,* edited by Alan Davies, 67–92. Waterloo, ON: Wilfrid Laurier University Press, 1992.

– *Joe Salsberg: A Life of Commitment.* Toronto: University of Toronto Press, 2013.

– *Shtetl on the Grand.* Victoria: Friesen Press, 2015.

– *Taking Root: The Origins of the Canadian Jewish Community.* Toronto: Lester, 1992.

Tulchinsky, Karen X. *The Five Books of Moses Lipinsky.* Vancouver: Raincoast Books, 2003.

Usher, Peter J. *Joey Jacobson's War: A Jewish Canadian Airman in the Second World War.* Waterloo, ON: Wilfrid Laurier University Press, 2018.

Usiskin, Michael. *Uncle Mike's Edenbridge: Memoirs of a Jewish Pioneer Farmer.* Translated by Marcia Usiskin Basman. Winnipeg: Penguin, 1983.

Vaugeois, Denis. *Les Juifs et la Nouvelle-France.* Trois-Rivières: Les Éditions Boréal Express, 1968.

Vipond, Robert C. *Making a Global City: How One Toronto School Embraced Diversity.* Toronto: University of Toronto Press, 2017.

Waite, Peter. "Between Three Oceans: Challenges of a Continental Destiny, 1840–1900." In *The Illustrated History of Canada,* edited by Craig Brown, 277–376. Toronto: Key Porter, 2002.

Walker, George A. *The Wordless Leonard Cohen – Songbook: A Biography in Eighty Wood Carvings.* Erin, ON: Porcupine's Quill, 2014.

Walker, James. "Claiming Equality for Canadian Jewry: The Struggle for Inclusion, 1930–1945." In *Nazi Germany, Canadian Responses: Confronting Antisemitism in the Shadow of War*, edited by L. Ruth Klein, 218–62. Montreal and Kingston: McGill-Queen's University Press, 2012.

Weinfeld, Morton. *Like Everyone Else But Different: The Paradoxical Success of Canadian Jews.* 2nd ed. Montreal and Kingston: McGill-Queen's University Press, 2018.

Weinfeld, M., William Shaffir, and Irwin Cotler, eds. *The Canadian Jewish Mosaic.* Toronto: John Wiley & Sons, 1981.

Weintraub, William. *City Unique: Montreal Days and Nights in the 1940s and '50s.* Toronto: McClelland and Stewart, 1997.

Wynn, Graeme. "On the Margins of Empire (1760–1840)." In *The Illustrated History of Canada*, edited by Craig Brown, 181–276. Toronto: Key Porter, 2002.

Index